Quick Recipes
on Symbian OS

Mastering C++ Smartphone Development

Quick Recipes on Symbian OS

Mastering C++ Smartphone Development

Michael Aubert

With
**Alexey Gusev, Tanzim Husain, Jenny Mulholland,
Antony Pranata, Jukka Silvennoinen, Jo Stichbury**

Reviewed by
**Sandip Ahluwalia, Ashlee Godwin, Douglas Feather,
Maximiliano R. Firtman, Matthew O'Donnell, Tong Ren,
Attila Vamos, Jacek Wojciechowski, Colin Ward,
Hamish Willee**

Head of Symbian Press
Freddie Gjertsen

Managing Editor
Satu McNabb

John Wiley & Sons, Ltd

Other Wiley Editorial Offices

John Wiley & Sons Inc., 111 River Street, Hoboken, NJ 07030, USA

Jossey-Bass, 989 Market Street, San Francisco, CA 94103-1741, USA

Wiley-VCH Verlag GmbH, Boschstr. 12, D-69469 Weinheim, Germany

John Wiley & Sons Australia Ltd, 42 McDougall Street, Milton, Queensland 4064, Australia

John Wiley & Sons (Asia) Pte Ltd, 2 Clementi Loop #02-01, Jin Xing Distripark, Singapore 129809

John Wiley & Sons Canada Ltd, 6045 Freemont Blvd, Mississauga, Ontario, L5R 4J3, Canada

Wiley also publishes its books in a variety of electronic formats. Some content that appears
in print may not be available in electronic books.

Library of Congress Cataloging-in-Publication Data

Aubert, Michael.
  Quick recipes on Symbian OS : mastering C++ smartphone development /
Michael Aubert, with Alexey Gusev . . . [et al.]
      p. cm.
  Includes bibliographical references and index.
  ISBN 978-0-470-99783-3 (pbk. : alk. paper)
  1. Smartphones – Programming. 2. Symbian OS (Computer file) 3. C++
(Computer program language) I. Gusev, Alexey. II. Title.
   TK6570.M6A92 2008
   005.26'8 – dc22

                                                    2008013156

British Library Cataloguing in Publication Data

A catalogue record for this book is available from the British Library

ISBN: 978-0-470-99783-3

Typeset in 10/12pt Optima by Laserwords Private Limited, Chennai, India
Printed and bound in Great Britain by Bell & Bain, Glasgow
This book is printed on acid-free paper responsibly manufactured from sustainable forestry
in which at least two trees are planted for each one used for paper production.

Pour Marcel et Paulette

Contents

List of Recipes

Foreword

David Wood, Executive Vice President Research, Symbian

This book has been designed for people who are in a hurry.

Perhaps you are a developer who has been asked to port some software, initially written for another operating system (such as may run on a desktop computer), to Symbian OS. Or perhaps you have to investigate whether Symbian OS could be suited to an idea from a designer friend of yours. But the trouble is, you don't have much time, and you have heard that Symbian OS is a sophisticated and rich software system with a not insignificant learning curve.

If you are like the majority of software engineers, you would like to take some time to investigate this kind of task. You might prefer to attend a training course, or work your way through some of the comprehensive reference material that already exists for Symbian OS. However, I guess that you don't have the luxury of doing that – because you are facing tight schedule pressures. There isn't sufficient slack in your schedule to research options as widely as you'd like. Your manager is expecting your report by the end of the week. So you need answers in a hurry.

That's why Symbian Press commissioned the book you are now holding in your hands. We are assuming that you are a bright, savvy, experienced software developer, who is already familiar with C++ and with modern software programming methods and idioms. You are willing to work hard and can learn fast. You are ready to take things on trust for a while, provided you can quickly find out how to perform various tasks within Symbian OS. Over time, you would like to learn more about the background and deeper principles behind Symbian OS, but that will have to wait – since at the moment, you're looking for quick recipes.

Congratulations, you have found them!

In the pages ahead, you will find recipes covering topics such as Bluetooth, networking, location-based services, multimedia, telephony, file handling, personal information management – and much more. In most recipes we provide working code fragments that you should be able to copy and paste directly into your own programs, and we provide a full set of sample code for download from the book's website (***developer.symbian.com/quickrecipesbook***). We have also listed some common gotchas, so you can steer clear of these potential pitfalls.

Since you are in a hurry, I will stop writing now (even though there is lots more I would like to discuss with you), so that you can proceed at full pace into the material in the following pages. Good speed!

David Wood, Symbian, March 2008

About this Book

This book sets out to accomplish two goals:

- For readers who don't know Symbian OS C++ development, this book is a two-week crash-course in developing applications for mobile phones.

- For readers who know Symbian OS C++ development, this book explains how to use 10 different technologies in a condensed form. It can be used as a desk reference or to learn a new technology in a familiar environment.

The focus of the book is on the reader being able to manage the time it takes to understand and implement the new concepts in Symbian OS.

Chapter 1 will explain how to set up a development environment. It also contains useful information for you to read while you wait for your software development kit to download and install.

Chapter 2 is about your first HelloWorld application and basic use of the new toolchain.

Chapter 3 explains the essentials of the common Symbian C++ APIs and idioms. Without understanding these, you cannot make much progress.

Chapter 4 is the main course of this book. It consists of recipes for ten self-contained technologies, each explained as a time-bound development learning task. For each technology, the recipes are listed in order of increasing complexity.

Chapter 5 will help you reach the next level of Symbian OS development expertise.

Chapter 6 is dedicated to commercial-grade application development.

This book is by no means an introduction to software development in general or even to the C++ language. The authors expect the readers to be familiar with both.

We have included some links to help you find additional information, but to avoid repetition, we don't always refer you to the Symbian Developer Library API reference documentation whenever we introduce a new API. It's worth mentioning it here though. You'll find a huge amount of reference material in the Symbian Developer Library, which is available in every SDK, and can also be browsed online on the Symbian Developer Network (*developer.symbian.com/ main/oslibrary/osdocs*). Chapter 6, Section 6.3 contains other links and suggestions for how to get more information.

About the Authors

Michael Aubert

Michael has worked on Symbian OS for 7 years, in the Java team at Symbian itself and the R&D team at iAnywhere. During that time, he has received in-depth exposure to a wide range of technologies including telephony, messaging, 3D graphics, networking, multimedia, PIM, cryptography, platform security and software deployment.

He holds an MSc in Software Engineering from E.S.I.A.L. and is probably the only person to have ever explained the crazy Java Team Event Server Framework to a French audience.

Alexey Gusev

Alexey started to play with mainframes at the end of the 1980s, using Pascal and REXX, but soon switched to C/C++ and Java on different platforms before moving into mobile technologies. After working for almost a decade as a team leader and architect on Windows Mobile, he decided to join the Symbian Core Development team, originally working on Security and later on USB.

He holds an MSc in Applied Mathematics and Physics from the Moscow Institute of Physics and Technology. He is also an Accredited Symbian Developer and regular author at *www.developer.com*.

Tanzim Husain

Tanzim joined Symbian in 2004 as a member of the networking technology team and has worked there ever since, surviving two architectural changes and three team re-organizations. Before joining Symbian, he worked extensively on Windows Mobile, delivering pioneering applications in the areas of mapping and GIS.

Tanzim holds a B.S. in Computer Science from NSU. Outside work, he likes to fiddle around with photography and enjoys escaping to the countryside. He tries to maintain an infrequently updated website/blog at **www.tanzim.co.uk**.

Jenny Mulholland

Since graduating with an MSc in Physics from the University of Cambridge in 2006, Jenny has worked in Symbian's Licensee Product Development team, as a member of the Comms Porting Group. Jenny recently renewed her Accredited Symbian Developer status.

Outside of work, when she is not in the pub with her colleagues, she enjoys performing concerts with the Chandos Chamber Choir and has recently taken up the flute.

Antony Pranata

Antony holds an MSc in Information Technology from the University of Stuttgart, Germany.

He has been involved in a number of Symbian OS projects in different technology areas, including security, tools, multimedia and location-based services. He currently works for Nokia in Canada.

Antony is a Forum Nokia Champion, Accredited Symbian Developer and Accredited S60 Developer. He has a personal website and blog at **www.antonypranata.com**. He now lives in Vancouver with his wife, Emi.

Jukka Silvennoinen

Jukka holds a PhD in Computer Information Systems.

Before joining Forum Nokia recently, he spent several years developing many Symbian OS applications, mainly for the Asian markets. As a certified Nokia Trainer he was also a visiting lecturer in one of the best universities in Thailand.

Jukka can often be found haunting the Forum Nokia developer discussion boards and wiki. He recently renewed his Accredited Symbian Developer and Accredited S60 Developer status.

Jo Stichbury

Jo is Senior Technical Editor with Symbian Press. She has worked within the Symbian ecosystem since 1997; in the Base, Connectivity and Security teams of Symbian, as well as for Advansys, Sony Ericsson and Nokia.

Jo is the author of *Symbian OS Explained: Effective C++ Programming for Smartphones*, published by Symbian Press in 2004; she also co-authored *The Accredited Symbian Developer Primer: Fundamentals of Symbian OS* with Mark Jacobs, in 2006. Her most recent publication is *Games on Symbian OS: A Handbook for Mobile Development*, published in early 2008.

Jo became an Accredited Symbian Developer in 2005 and a Forum Nokia Champion in 2006 and 2007.

Acknowledgments

The authors would like to thank the Symbian Press team for allowing us this opportunity, for their patience and for making the process as smooth as possible.

The authors would also like to thank all the technical reviewers for their invaluable comments and for stopping us from making fools of ourselves.

Michael would like to thank: my fellow authors on this book for making me look cleverer than I am, the kind people at Symbian Press for entrusting this project to a new author, David Wood for initiating the project, my family and my current or former colleagues for their help and inspiration.

Tanzim would like to thank: my great colleagues, particularly Nadeem, Tom and Petr, for their insightful knowledge of the Symbian OS networking architecture, and my fellow authors for their helpful suggestions.

Jenny would like to thank: Aaron for all the weekends when his living room became my study, and the Quick Recipes team for all their help.

Antony would like to thank: Emi for her support and understanding during this project and my uncle, William Suryawijaya, for introducing me to the wonderful world of programming back in the 1990s.

Symbian Press would like to thank: each of the authors, who gave up so much of their time to contribute to this book, and our technical reviewers, for their generous feedback. In particular, we'd also like to thank Tanzim for dropping everything to work with us on the copy edits. We'd also like to thank Daniel Mattioli, for letting us 'borrow' Tanzim, and Emmanouil Papathanassiou and Neil Taylor, for help with our example code.

Symbian OS Code Conventions and Notations Used in the Book

For you to get the most out of this book, let's quickly run through the notation we use. The text is straightforward, and where we quote example code, resource files, or project definition files, they will be highlighted as follows:

```
This is example code;
```

Symbian C++ uses established naming conventions. We encourage you to follow them too, in order for your own code to be understood most easily by other Symbian OS developers, and because the conventions have been chosen carefully to reflect object cleanup and ownership, and make code more comprehensible. An additional benefit to using the conventions is that your code can then be tested with automatic code analysis tools, which can flag potential bugs or areas to review.

The best way to get used to the conventions is to look at code snippets in this book, and those provided with your chosen SDK.

1.1 Capitalization

The first letter of class names is capitalized:

```
Class TColor;
```

The words making up variable, class, or function names are adjoining, with the first letter of each word capitalized. Classes and functions have their initial letter capitalized while, in contrast, function parameters, local, global, and member variables have a lower case first letter.

Apart from the first letter of each word, the rest of each word is given in lower case, including acronyms. For example:

```
void CalculateScore(TInt aCorrectAnswers, TInt aQuestionsAnswered);
class CActiveScheduler;
TInt localVariable;
CShape* iShape;
class CBbc;//Acronyms are not usually written in upper case
```

1.2   Prefixes

Member variables are prefixed with a lower case 'i', which stands for 'instance':

```
TInt iCount;
CBackground* iBitmap;
```

Parameters are prefixed with a lower case 'a', which stands for 'argument'. We do not use 'an' for arguments that start with a vowel.

```
void ExampleFunction(TBool aExampleBool, const TDesC& aName);
```

(*Note*: TBool aExampleBool rather than TBool anExampleBool).
Local variables have no prefix:

```
TInt localVariable;
CMyClass* ptr = NULL;
```

Class names should be prefixed with the letter appropriate to their Symbian OS type (usually 'C', 'R', 'T', or 'M'), as will be described further in Chapter 3:

```
class CActive;
class TParse;
class RFs;
class MCallback;
```

Constants are prefixed with 'K':

```
const TInt KMaxFilenameLength = 256;
#define KMaxFilenameLength 256
```

Enumerations are simple types, and so are prefixed with 'T'. Enumeration members are prefixed with 'E':

```
enum TWeekdays {EMonday, ETuesday, ...};
```

1.3 Suffixes

A trailing 'L' on a function name indicates that the function may leave:

```
void AllocL();
```

A trailing 'C' on a function name indicates that the function returns a pointer that has been pushed onto the cleanup stack:

```
Ccylon* NewLC();
```

A trailing 'D' on a function name means that it will result in the deletion of the object referred to by the function:

```
TInt ExecuteLD(TInt aResourceId);
```

1

Introduction and Setup

The first part of this chapter will help you set up your development environment using free tools.

While your computer is busy downloading and installing software, you should read the second part of this chapter. It contains a host of critical information you need before you start using the development tools.

When all the tools are installed, there are a few more minor configuration steps to go through in the last part of this chapter.

1.1 Tools: What You Need and Where to Find It

1.1.1 System Requirements

System requirements for C++ development on Symbian OS v9.x are as follows:

- Microsoft Windows 2000 Professional with Service Pack 3 or MS Windows XP Professional with Service Pack 2, running on a laptop or desktop computer. At the time of writing this book, most Symbian OS SDKs do not support Windows Vista.

- At least 512 MB of RAM (1.5 GB recommended).

- 1-GHz or faster Pentium-class processor (2-GHz Pentium-class processor recommended).

- At least 1 GB of free disk space (5 GB recommended).

- 16-bit color display capable of a 1,024 × 768 pixels resolution.

- Java™ Runtime Environment (JRE) 1.4.1_02 or later (available from *java.sun.com*).

- ActivePerl 5.6.1 build 568 or later (available from *activestate.com*).

- Microsoft Core XML Services (MSXML) 4.0.

- ZIP decompression software to open the installation package.

- Local-administrator rights for installation and removal of software.

- The PC Suite software for your handset. You should find the latest version of this software on the website of the manufacturer of the handset.

ActivePerl may be bundled in some of the Software Development Kit packages you will be installing.

1.1.2 IDE

The recommended Integrated Development Environment for Symbian OS C++ development is called Carbide.c++. You can download the free Express Edition from: *forum.nokia.com/carbide*. Section 1.2.1 describes Carbide.c++ in more detail.

1.1.3 SDKs

Symbian OS is split into two platforms: S60 3rd Edition and UIQ 3. (There is a third one, called MOAP, available only in Japan, which this book doesn't cover.)

Each platform is replaced as different versions (or Feature Pack numbers for S60).

Once you know which handsets you want your applications to run on, you can identify all your target platforms and their version using the following websites: *www.s60.com/life/s60phone* (for S60) and *www.uiq.com/uiqphones* (for UIQ).

You need to download all the SDKs for all your target platforms. At the time of writing, this could mean up to five different SDKs for development on Symbian OS v9.x: S60 3rd Edition Maintenance Release, Feature Pack 1 and Feature Pack 2 Beta, along with UIQ 3.0 and UIQ 3.1.

The SDKs can be downloaded from: *developer.symbian.com/main/ tools*.

1.1.4 Compilers

There are two free compilers used for Symbian OS C++ development.

The Nokia x86 compiler targets the Symbian OS emulator for Microsoft Windows included in the SDK. You will see this referenced as WINSCW.

The open source GCC-E compiler targets the actual handsets, where Symbian OS runs on an ARM processor.

Both compilers should be bundled in the SDK installation package, but GCC-E must be installed to a folder whose path contains no 'space' characters or your builds will fail with 'missing separator' errors.

1.2   While You are Waiting

1.2.1   Carbide.c++

There are four different editions of Carbide.c++:

- Express Edition
- Developer Edition
- Professional Edition
- OEM Edition.

The free Express Edition is the only one that doesn't allow debugging an application running on the actual phone (on-target debugging). All versions allow emulator debugging.

Carbide.c++ is based on Eclipse and is highly customizable. You can even create your own plug-ins to extend its functionality.

When you first launch Carbide.c++ it allows you to define a 'workspace'. We suggest you create a different workspace for each SDK.

There is a very nice Flash tutorial to introduce Carbide.c++ at **developer.symbian.com/main/learning/flash**, and a booklet about getting started with Carbide.c++ available from **developer.symbian.com/carbide_booklet_wikipage**.

1.2.2   Development Communities

In order to get more information, meet your fellow developers, ask questions and find out the solutions for common problems, you should visit the following links:

- Symbian Developer Network: **developer.symbian.com**.
- Forum Nokia: **forum.nokia.com**.
- UIQ Developer Community: **developer.uiq.com**.
- Sony Ericsson Developer Forum: **developer.sonyericsson.com**.
- MOTODEV Developer Forum: **developer.motorola.com**.

While you are waiting, you should register on, at the very least, the following website:

- Symbian Signed: **www.symbiansigned.com**.

There are also many independent sites, which contain a lot of helpful and educational information; for instance, **www.newlc.com**.

1.2.3   Concepts of Mobile Development

On an open operating system such as Symbian OS, third-party developers like you can install their own applications.

Programming for smartphones puts you in a position where you have quite limited resources, such as CPU capabilities, battery power, input methods, available memory amount and so on. Software developers targeting such a challenging environment need to focus on code efficiency and robustness more than they may be used to for desktop platforms.

We are working in an environment where any heap memory allocation can fail and where the cost of forcing the CPU to switch between processes (or even between threads) is non-negligible.

Several Symbian OS development efforts are worth being aware of:

- Open Source projects at **www.symbianos.org**.

- P.I.P.S. and Open C are there to help you port applications using the Posix libraries to Symbian OS (see **www.forum.nokia.com/openc**).

- The Standard Template Library is being ported to Symbian OS.

- The Net60 framework from Red Five Labs allows you to use Microsoft .NET Compact Framework (see **www.redfivelabs.com**).

- There are runtime environments for Java, Ruby and Python available for Symbian OS (see **developer.symbian.com/main/getstarted/hub/runtimes_hub.jsp**).

1.2.4   ARM Hardware

When targeting the actual handset, Symbian OS binaries are based on the Application Binary Interface (ABI) for the ARM Architecture. ABI is a standard for the interfaces of binary code running in ARM environments. The specification is published by ARM at: **www.arm.com/products/DevTools/ABI.html**.

We will not go into the details of various ARM instruction sets and ABI versions in this book.

1.2.5   Emulator

In addition to debugging using a stack trace, breakpoints and variable monitoring, the emulator allows you to test your deployment packages to ensure your application will be installed properly on the real smartphone.

The S60 emulator preferences allow you to set up several useful parameters, like Bluetooth and IrDA (Infrared) ports and platform security

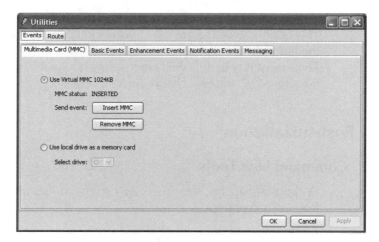

Figure 1.1   S60 Utilities

settings. In addition, the emulator has a powerful utilities application which helps you test your software by triggering various events, like memory card insertion (Figure 1.1).

The UIQ emulator also offers some configuration capabilities via a separate utility – *SDKConfig* (Figure 1.2) – a graphical configuration tool located in the ...\epoc32\tools\distrib folder of your SDK.

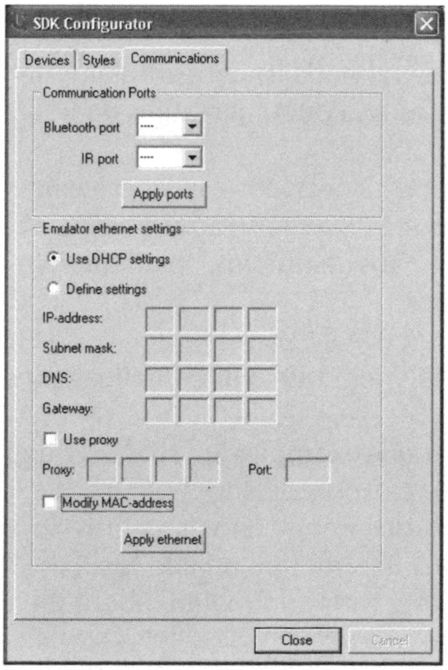

Figure 1.2   UIQ SDK Configurator

SDKConfig launches a number of scripts from `...\epoc32\tools`. This utility can be used to select the default device, change the UI style of the emulator and set up communication ports and Ethernet connection. The easiest way to define Ethernet setting is to use DHCP and uncheck the 'Modify MAC-address' checkbox.

1.3   Post-Installation

1.3.1   Command Line Tools

Without arguments, the `devices` command lists all the installed SDKs from a DOS prompt:

```
S60_3rd:com.nokia.s60
S60_3rd_FP2_Beta:com.nokia.s60 - default
S60_3rd_FP1:com.nokia.s60
UIQ3.1:com.symbian.UIQ
```

It also allows you to switch between SDKs as follows:

```
devices -setdefault @S60_3rd_FP1:com.nokia.s60
```

1.3.2   SDK Directories Structure

Each SDK installs its own emulator binaries, handset libraries, tools code examples and documentation on your hard drive.

`...\epoc32\winscw\` is where you will find the emulator drives.
`...\epoc32\release\winscw\udeb\` is where you will find the binaries for the emulator, particularly `epoc.exe` which launches the emulator.
`...\epoc32\release\gcce\urel` is where you will find the ARM libraries your code will compile against.

The code examples are split between the generic Symbian OS examples and the examples using APIs specific to the S60 or UIQ platform.
SDK documentation is mainly in the form of CHM or PDF files. It contains information related to all the APIs publicly available in Symbian OS, along with information about the tools included in the SDK.

1.3.3 Emulators

The DOS command line to start the emulator is always:

```
...\epoc32\release\winscw\udeb\epoc.exe
```

On a UIQ 3.1 emulator, it is recommended to lower the color depth by replacing `WINDOWMODE COLOR16MU` by `WINDOWMODE COLOR64K` in the file

```
...\epoc32\release\winscw\udeb\z\system\data\wsini.ini
```

In the Symbian OS file system, the Z: drive represents the phone's ROM.

2

Quick Start

This chapter explains how to create a Hello World application for Symbian OS and deploy it to a smartphone. You will also learn how to make a small modification to the Hello World application.

2.1 Hello World Project Template

Carbide.c++ includes several project templates, that you can use to develop a Hello World application. There are project templates to create S60 GUI applications and UIQ GUI applications.

This book provides an additional template of the Hello World application for Carbide.c++. Our template creates a Hello World project that can be compiled for both S60 3rd Edition and UIQ 3 platforms. The template can be downloaded from the web page for this book (*developer.symbian.com/quickrecipesbook*).

To install the Hello World template from this book, extract the ZIP file to the plug-ins folder of Carbide.c++. For example, the default plug-in folder for Carbide.c++ v1.3 is c:\apps\carbide.c++v1.3\plugins. You may have a different folder name depending on where you installed Carbide.c++. Note that the Carbide.c++ IDE has to be restarted after the new template is copied.

2.2 Running Carbide.c++ IDE

Carbide.c++ can be run from the Start menu or Windows Desktop. When first launched, it will ask for the workspace (see Figure 2.1). A workspace is a folder where your projects are stored. Note that a workspace path should not contain spaces, because of limitations of the tool chain (you

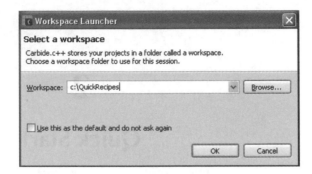

Figure 2.1 Selecting a Workspace in Carbide.c++

will get a compilation error when using a workspace with a path that contains spaces).

After selecting a workspace, you will see the main window of Carbide.c++ (Figure 2.2), which is also known as a 'perspective'. This book does not explain the user interface of Carbide.c++. Please refer to Carbide.c++ Help to learn about it, or refer to the Symbian Press booklet at **developer.symbian.com/carbide_booklet_wikipage**.

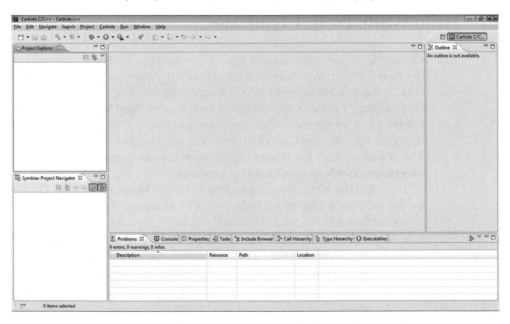

Figure 2.2 Main Window of Carbide.c++

2.3 Generating the Hello World Project

Follow the instructions below to create a new Hello World project.

1. From the Carbide.c++ main window, select the *File | New | Symbian OS C++ Project* menu.

2. On the *New Symbian OS C++ Project* dialog, select *Quick Recipes on Symbian OS > Hello World* (see Figure 2.3).

Figure 2.3   Create a New Project Using the Hello World Project Template

3. Click *Next* and enter the project name (see Figure 2.4). Note that the project name should not contain any spaces. For this example, let's use 'HelloWorld' as the project name.

Figure 2.4   Enter a New Project Name

4. Click *Next* and select the SDK where you want to build the project (see Figure 2.5). Note that this template is compatible with S60 3rd Edition (all Feature Packs) and UIQ 3 (UIQ 3.0 and 3.1). You can choose S60 3rd Edition or UIQ 3.x or both of them.

Figure 2.5   Select SDK

5. Click *Next* to enter the basic properties of the project (see Figure 2.6). The most important field on this dialog is the Application UID. It is a unique identifier for your application.

Figure 2.6   Entering Basic Properties of the Project

You can apply for UIDs for your applications on the Symbian Signed website (***www.symbiansigned.com***). For now, for development and testing purposes, you can use UIDs in the range of 0xE0000000-0xEFFFFFFF. By default, Carbide.c++ assigns a random UID in this range for your project.

6. Click *Finish* button to create the project.

If successful, Carbide.c++ will have created a Hello World project that contains several folders (see Figure 2.7):

*   `group` contains the project files used to build the application.

*   `src` contains the source code files (`.cpp` files).

*   `inc` contains the header files (`.h` files).

*   `data` contains the resource definition files (`.rss` files) used to create menus and some other UI-related components.

*   `gfx` contains the graphic files used to create icons.

*   `sis` contains the package files (`.pkg` files) used to create an installation file.

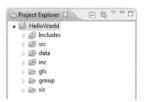

Figure 2.7   The Folders Created for a Standard Symbian C++ Project

2.4   Building the Hello World Project

A Symbian OS project can be built for the emulator or for a smartphone (sometimes known as a device or target hardware). Separate builds are required for the emulator and the smartphone; that is, an executable file for the emulator cannot be run on the smartphone, and vice versa. To allow you to switch easily between these builds, Carbide.c++ creates a 'configuration' for each.

Building a project from Carbide.c++ IDE can be done by selecting the *Project | Build* project menu. Alternatively, you can also right click the project name and select the *Build* project menu.

Before building a project, you can set the active configuration, to build for the emulator or device target. Setting the active configuration can be done by right clicking the project name and selecting the *Build configurations | Set Active configuration* menu (see Figure 2.8).

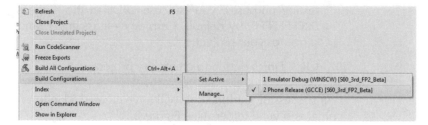

Figure 2.8   Selecting the Active Build Configuration on Carbide.c++ IDE

There are normally two build configurations:

- Emulator Debug (WINSCW). This requires a compiler, called *Nokia Codewarrior C/C++ Compiler for Windows/x86*. This compiler is installed with Carbide.c++.

- Phone Release (GCCE). This requires the GCC-E (*GNU Compiler Collection for Embedded*) compiler. The SDKs provide this free compiler as part of their installation packages.

(If you have the RVCT compiler installed, you may have additional build configurations available for smartphone builds. For the discussion in this chapter, we will be concentrating on WINSCW and GCCE build configurations only, but more information about the differences between the GCC-E and RVCT compilers can be found in Chapter 6, Section 6.1.3.)

> **Tip:** At the time of writing this book, most SDKs do not support Windows Vista. There is a workaround available from the Forum Nokia wiki (see links section at the end of this chapter) to make an SDK work on Windows Vista.

2.5   Running the Hello World Application on the Emulator

Select the *Run | Run* menu from the Carbide.c++ IDE to run Hello World on the emulator. You can select the *Run | Debug* menu to debug the project. Alternatively, you can also right click the project name to select the same menus.

Figure 2.9 shows the Hello World application running from the emulator. The S60 3rd Edition emulator is shown on the left, and the UIQ 3 emulator on the right.

This Hello World application simply displays the text 'HelloWorld', which is the project name, on the screen, as can be seen in Figure 2.9.

(a) S60 3rd Edition emulator   (b) UIQ 3 emulator

Figure 2.9   Hello World Application Running on the Emulators

The application also contains a single menu item that can be selected either via the *Option* softkey on S60 or by a mouse click on the 'HelloWorld' title on UIQ (that area is called the title bar). Selecting the *Command1* menu item displays a notification dialog.

2.5.1   Configuring the Emulator

The S60 emulator is configurable to represent different screen resolutions and orientations (portrait or landscape). To do this, click the button at the top left of the emulator's window. Figure 2.10 shows the same Hello World application running in the landscape mode. Notice that the Options menu is on the bottom right of the screen and the Exit menu on the top right of the screen.

Figure 2.10   Hello World Application Running on the S60 3rd Edition Emulator in Landscape Mode

The UIQ emulator can be configured to represent different input modes, softkey or pen mode, as well as screen orientation. This can be done using the `uiqenv` command. The following command changes the input mode to pen mode and the screen orientation to landscape:

```
uiqenv -ui penlandscape
```

The following command changes the input mode to softkey mode:

```
uiqenv -ui softkey
```

Figure 2.11 shows the same Hello World application running on the UIQ 3 emulator in softkey mode. Notice that now the application has a 'More' softkey label at the bottom right of the screen. Pressing the right softkey on the emulator will bring up the menu.

Figure 2.11   Hello World Application Running on the UIQ Emulator in Softkey Mode

Please refer to the SDK documentation for more information about various UI configurations.

2.6   Running the Hello World Application on the Device

Running the Hello World application on the device requires a SIS installation file (`.sis` file). The installation file is created from the PKG package file (`.pkg` file), located in the `\sis` folder of the project. More information about the syntax to use in a PKG file can be found in the Symbian Developer Library CHM documentation, found in each SDK.

During the build process, the SIS file will be created automatically from the `HelloWorld.pkg` file. The result is `HelloWorld.sis` and `HelloWorld.sisx`. The `.sis` file is an unsigned installation file and the `.sisx` a signed installation file. Nothing enforces that difference in

filename extensions. Although it is unlikely you will ever see an unsigned
.sisx file, signed .sis files are common.

You can use a number of ways to transfer the SIS file from your
PC to the smartphone. For example, the phone manufacturers normally
provide a PC application to install the SIS file to the smartphone (Nokia
releases *Nokia PC Suite* for S60 devices; Sony Ericsson releases *PC Suite
for Smartphones* for their UIQ 3 devices). So you could use the PC
application that comes with the phone to install the SIS file or you could
send an SMS that can be used to point the web browser of the phone to
the SIS file, so that you can download and install it. Alternatively, you can
simply use a Bluetooth connection between a PC and the smartphone to
send it to the phone.

Figure 2.12 shows the Hello World application running on S60 3rd
Edition and UIQ 3 devices.

(a) S60 3rd Edition device   (b) UIQ 3 device

Figure 2.12   Hello World Application Running on the Device

What may go wrong when you install the SIS file:

You may get an error message when you come to install the SIS file,
which reads something like "Certificate error. Contact the application
supplier."

This is because some devices, such as most S60 3rd Edition devices,
do not allow installation of unsigned SIS files. You must self-sign the
SIS file, using your own certificate (or you could get it signed by a
certificate/key pair from Symbian Signed).

There are also some smartphones, such as Nokia ESeries phones,
that do not allow the installation of self-signed applications by default.
You have to make a change in the Settings menu to enable installation
of self-signed applications.

On the other hand, there are some other devices, such as UIQ 3
devices from Sony Ericsson, which allow installation of unsigned SIS
files.

The bottom line is that each device manufacturer may have a
different policy about installing unsigned and self-signed applications.
The developer community for your platform can help you sort it all out.

2.7   Modifying the Hello World Project

This section shows how to add a new menu item to display a notification dialog. The modification will include source code changes on both platforms, S60 and UIQ.

2.7.1   Adding a New Menu Item

1. Open \data\s60_3rd\HelloWorld.rss, which is the resource definition that contains the menu definition for S60. Add the lines written in bold below to the menu definition r_helloworld_ menupane.

```
RESOURCE MENU_PANE r_helloworld_menupane
  {
  items =
    {
    MENU_ITEM
      {
      command = EHelloWorldSelectMe;
      txt = string_r_helloworld_selectme;
      },
    MENU_ITEM
      {
      command = EHelloWorldCommand1;
      txt = string_r_helloworld_command1;
      },
    MENU_ITEM
      {
      command = EEikCmdExit;
      txt = string_r_helloworld_exit;
      }
    };
  }
```

These additional lines add a new menu item with the command identifier EHelloWorldSelectMe and the text string_r_ helloworld_selectme. We will be defining the identifier and the string later.

2. Open \data\uiq3\HelloWorld.rss and do the same thing for the resource definition for UIQ.

```
RESOURCE QIK_COMMAND_LIST r_helloworld_commands
  {
  items =
    {
    QIK_COMMAND
      {
      id = EEikCmdExit;
      type = EQikCommandTypeScreen;
```

```
    stateFlags = EQikCmdFlagDebugOnly;
    text = string_r_helloworld_close_debug;
    },
QIK_COMMAND
    {
    id = EHelloWorldSelectMe;
    type = EQikCommandTypeScreen;
    text = string_r_helloworld_selectme;
    },
QIK_COMMAND
    {
    id = EHelloWorldCommand1;
    type = EQikCommandTypeScreen;
    text = string_r_helloworld_command1;
    }
    };
}
```

3. Open \inc\HelloWorld.hrh. It is the header file for the resource file. Add a new command identifier, EHelloWorldSelectMe.

```
enum THelloWorldCommand
    {
    EHelloWorldCommand1 = 0x1000,
    EHelloWorldSelectMe
    };
```

4. Open \data\HelloWorld_01.rls, which contains the definition of localized strings. The suffix _01 in the filename indicates that it is the localization file for UK English language. Add a new line below to HelloWorld_01.rls.

```
rls_string string_r_helloworld_selectme "Select me"
```

At this point, if you build and run the application, you should see a new item (see Figure 2.13). This menu item does not do anything yet. The next section discusses how to handle the menu event from this new item.

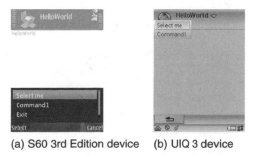

(a) S60 3rd Edition device   (b) UIQ 3 device

Figure 2.13   Hello World Application With a New Menu Item

2.7.2 Handling a Menu Event

1. Open \data\HelloWorld_01.rls to add the string that is going to be displayed when the menu item is selected.

```
rls_string string_r_helloworld_title        "Title"

rls_string string_r_helloworld_description "Congratulations on your
                                   first Symbian OS application."
```

The two lines above added two strings to the localization file for UK English language. The first string is used as the title for the notification dialog and the second one is used as the content.

2. Open \data\HelloWorld_string.rss to add resources that point to the two strings above.

```
RESOURCE TBUF256 r_helloworld_title
  { buf = string_r_helloworld_title; }

RESOURCE TBUF256 r_helloworld_description
  { buf = string_r_helloworld_description; }
```

The lines above added two string resources with the maximum length of 256 characters.

3. Open \src\HelloWorldAppUi.cpp. This file contains the definition of CHelloWorldAppUi class, which handles various aspects of the application's user interface, including the menu bar.
   Every GUI application should have its own AppUi class derived from CEikAppUi or one of its derivative classes. For example, S60 applications usually use CAknAppUi and UIQ applications usually use CQikAppUi.
   One of the main roles of the AppUi class is to handle commands from the UI in its HandleCommandL() method. Add the code written in bold below in CHelloWorldAppUi::HandleCommandL() to handle the menu event from our new menu item.

```
void CHelloWorldAppUi::HandleCommandL(TInt aCommand)
  {
  switch (aCommand)
    {
#ifdef __SERIES60_3X__
    // For S60, we need to handle this event, which is normally
    // an event from the right soft key.
    case EAknSoftkeyExit:
#endif
    case EEikCmdExit:
```

```
    {
    Exit();
    break;
    }

case EHelloWorldCommand1:
    {
    iEikonEnv->InfoWinL(R_HELLOWORLD_CAPTION,
        R_HELLOWORLD_CAPTION);
    break;
    }

case EHelloWorldSelectMe:
    {
    iEikonEnv->InfoWinL(R_HELLOWORLD_TITLE,
        R_HELLOWORLD_DESCRIPTION);
    break;
    }

default:
    // Do nothing
    break;
    }
}
```

Figure 2.14 shows the notification dialog that is shown when the user selects our new item on S60 and UIQ devices.

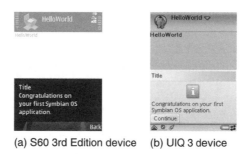

(a) S60 3rd Edition device   (b) UIQ 3 device

Figure 2.14   Displaying the Notification Dialog on the Hello World Application

---

Tip: This example uses a generic dialog, `CEikonEnv::InfoWinL()`, to make it compatible with S60 and UIQ. Each platform also has more types of dialog that can be used for different purposes. For example, S60 has `CAknInformationNote` to display information and `CAknErrorNote` to display error messages.

2.8   Advanced Topics on Carbide.c++

This section describes some more advanced topics when using Carbide.c++:

- Modifying the project files.

- Importing project files.

- Changing the certificate/key pair.

You may prefer not to read this section now, but to continue to the next chapter and come back later as needed.

2.8.1 Modifying the Project Files

A Symbian OS project is represented by a build configuration file (known as a `bld.inf` file) and one (or several) project (MMP) files. Most examples in this book have only one MMP file.

Both `bld.inf` and MMP files are ASCII text files. Carbide.c++ provides a user interface to edit them visually (see Figure 2.15a). They can also be edited using the standard text editor (see Figure 2.15b).

(a) An MMP file in the GUI editor   (b) An MMP file in the text editor

Figure 2.15   Editing an MMP File using Carbide.c++

A `bld.inf` file is made up of a number of sections, such as a list of MMP files to build and a list of files to be exported. The following code shows the content of `bld.inf` for our Hello World project:

```
PRJ_MMPFILES
HelloWorld.mmp

#ifndef UIQ_UMTS_AVAILABLE
gnumakefile icons_scalable_dc.mk
#endif
```

As you can see, the `bld.inf` above contains one MMP file, which is `HelloWorld.mmp`. It also includes a GNU makefile, `icons_scalable _dc.mk`, which is invoked if the macro `UIQ_UMTS_AVAILABLE` is not defined. This macro is defined on the UIQ SDK only. In other words, the

GNU makefile will be used if the project is compiled using S60 SDK. This particular makefile will build a scalable icon to be used to represent the application in the main menu of the smartphone.

An MMP file specifies the properties of a project in a platform- and compiler-independent way. During the build process, Symbian OS build tools convert the MMP file into makefiles for particular platforms.

The following code shows the first couple of lines of `HelloWorld.mmp`:

```
TARGET          HelloWorld.exe
TARGETTYPE      EXE
UID             0x100039CE 0xEF1D5F42

CAPABILITY      None

LANG            SC

...
```

When do you need to modify the project files? One case that you will find very often in the following chapters is adding libraries. The Hello World project includes some general libraries (see Figure 2.16). In order to use some specific APIs, such as multimedia or telephony, you would need to add additional libraries. To add libraries, click *Add* and select the libraries you want to add.

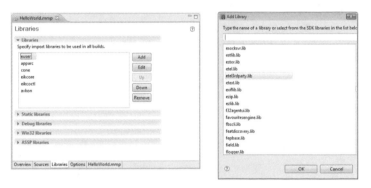

Figure 2.16 Adding Libraries to the Project File

Another case that you will also find quite often is adding platform security capabilities (they are described in Chapter 3). The Hello World project does not include any capabilities, as you can see in Figure 2.17. Many APIs discussed in this book require additional capabilities. For example, the telephony API requires `NetworkServices`. Click *Choose* to add more capabilities to the project file, as shown in Figure 2.17.

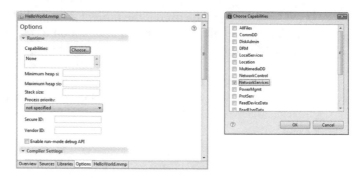

Figure 2.17 Adding Capabilities to the Project Files

2.8.2 Importing Project Files

All sample codes from this book are available for download from ***developer.symbian.com/quickrecipesbook***. In order to compile them in Carbide.c++, you need to import their project files (`bld.inf` files). Follow the steps below to import a project file:

1. Select *File | Import* menu from Carbide.c++ IDE.

2. In the *Import* dialog, select *Symbian OS | Symbian OS Bld.inf file* (see Figure 2.18).

3. Click *Next* and select the `bld.inf` file you want to import (see Figure 2.19).

Figure 2.18 Import a Project File into Carbide.c++

Figure 2.19 Browse to the `bld.inf` of the Project to be Imported

4. Click *Next* and select the SDK. The dialog is similar to the one when creating a new project (shown in Figure 2.5).

5. Click *Next* to select the MMP files to be imported (see Figure 2.20). Since most examples contain only one MMP file, you can just press *Next* again.

6. The next dialog asks for project name and location (see Figure 2.21). You can usually just use the default values and click *Finish*.

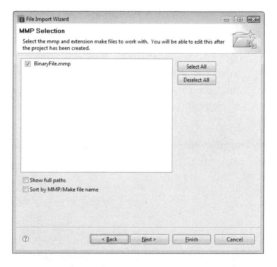

Figure 2.20 Select the MMP Files to be Imported

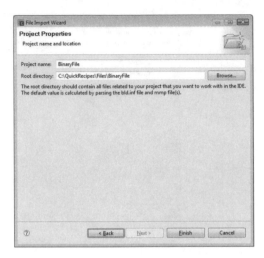

Figure 2.21   Enter the Project Name and Location

2.8.3   Changing the Certificate/Key Pair

By default, Carbide.c++ creates a self-signed certificate/key pair when creating a SIS file. A self-signed certificate is sufficient for many applications. However, there are cases when you need to apply for a developer cerificate at Symbian Signed (*www.symbiansigned.com*), for example when using the Location API (see Section 4.10). The developer certificate allows your application to use restricted APIs that cannot be accessed using a self-signed certificate.

Follow the instructions below to change the certificate/key pair of your project:

1. Right click the project name and select *Properties*.

2. In the *Properties* dialog, select *Carbide.c++ | Carbide Build Configuration*. On the SIS Builder box, select the name of the SIS file and click *Edit* (see Figure 2.22).

3. In the SIS *Properties* dialog, enter the certificate/key pair files (see Figure 2.23). If your key requires a password, you can enter it here as well.

2.9   Links

- Code samples for Symbian Press books, including this one: *developer.symbian.com/quickrecipesbook*.

- Forum Nokia wiki – Moving to Windows Vista: *wiki.forum.nokia. com/index.php/Moving_to_Windows_Vista*.

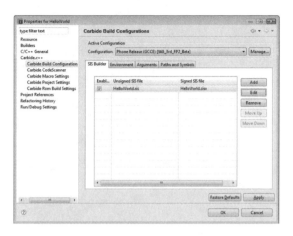

Figure 2.22   SIS Builder in Carbide.c++ IDE

Figure 2.23   Change the Certificate/Key Pair in the SIS Builder

- Information about errors that occur when installing self-signed, or unsigned, SIS files: ***www.antonypranata.com/articles/ interpreting-signing-error-messages-s60-3rd-edition***.

3

Symbian OS Development Basics

This chapter explains some of the essential topics needed to write C++ on Symbian OS. To discuss every Symbian C++ concept would take an entire book, so we only discuss the concepts that you need to understand the examples and discussion in the following chapters of this book.

3.1 Fundamental Data Types on Symbian OS

Symbian OS defines a set of fundamental types which, for compiler independence, are used instead of the native built-in C++ types. These are provided as a set of `typedefs` as shown in Table 3.1, and can be found in the Symbian header file `e32def.h`.

The fundamental Symbian OS types should always be used instead of the native types (that is, use `TInt` instead of `int` and so on). However, there is one exception, which is that you should always use `void` when a function or method has no return type, instead of `TAny`.

The following example defines an 8-bit signed integer `x` and assigns the value 123:

```
TInt8 x = 123;
```

The following example defines a 64-bit signed integer `y` and assigns a value to it:

```
TInt64 y = MAKE_TINT64(0x1234567, 0x89ABCDEF);
```

The following example defines two 32-bit unsigned integers, `a` and `b`, and assigns them with the low word and high word of `y` respectively:

```
TUint32 a = I64LOW(y);
TUint32 b = I64HIGH(y);
```

Table 3.1 Fundamental Data Types on Symbian OS

Data types	Description	C++ built-in types
`TInt`	Signed integer. It is guaranteed to be at least 32 bits in all implementations	`signed int`
`TUint`	Unsigned integer. It is guaranteed to be at least 32 bits in all implementations	`unsigned int`
`TInt32, TInt16,` `TInt8`	32-bit, 16-bit and 8-bit signed integer	`long int, short int,` `signed char`

`TUint32, TUint16,`
`TUint8`
	32-bit, 16-bit and 8-bit unsigned integer	`unsigned long int,`
		`unsigned short int,`
		`unsigned char`

`TInt64`	64-bit integer	`long long`
`TUint64`	64-bit unsigned integer	`unsigned long long`
`TText`	Build-independent text character. It is mapped to `TText16`	`unsigned short int`
`TText8, TText16`	8-bit and 16-bit unsigned character	`unsigned short int,` `unsigned char`
`TReal32`	32-bit floating point number	`float`
`TReal, TReal64`	64-bit floating point number	`double`
`TBool`	Boolean type	`int`
`TAny`	Pointer type	`void`

3.2 Symbian OS Class Conventions

By convention, there are several class types on Symbian OS, each of which has different characteristics, such as where objects may be created (on the heap, on the stack, or on either) and how those objects should later be cleaned up. The classes are named with a prefix according to type, and this convention makes the creation, use and destruction of objects more straightforward. When writing code, the required behavior of a class should be matched to the Symbian OS class characteristics. Later, a user of an unfamiliar class can be confident in how to instantiate an object, use it and then destroy it without leaking memory.

3.2.1 T Classes

Class names prefixed with T are used for classes that behave like the fundamental built-in data types (it is for this reason that they are prefixed with the same letter as the `typedefs` described above – the 'T' is for 'Type').

Just like the built-in types, T classes do not have an explicit destructor. In consequence, T classes must not contain any member data which itself has a destructor. T classes contain all their data internally and have no pointers, references or handles to data, unless that data is owned by another object responsible for its cleanup.

T-class objects are usually stack-based but they can also be created on the heap – indeed, some T classes should only ever be heap-based because the resulting object would otherwise occupy too much stack space. A good rule of thumb is that any object larger than 512 bytes should always be heap-based rather than created on the stack, since stack space is limited for applications running on Symbian OS. One way to prevent the object from being instantiated on the stack is to rename the class, and make it a C class, since C-class objects are always created on the heap, as the next subsection describes.

Tip: T classes can be created on the heap as well as on the stack.

3.2.2 C Classes

C-class objects must always be created on the heap. Unlike T classes, C classes may contain and own pointers.

For Symbian OS memory management to work correctly, every C class must ultimately derive from class CBase (defined in the Symbian OS header file e32base.h). This class has three characteristics, which are inherited by every C class:

- Safe destruction. CBase has a virtual destructor, so a CBase-derived object is destroyed properly by deletion through a base-class pointer.

- Zero initialization. CBase overloads operator new to zero-initialize an object when it is first allocated on the heap. This means that all member data in a CBase-derived object will be zero-filled when it is first created, so this does not need to be done explicitly in the constructor.

- CBase also declares a private copy constructor and assignment operator. Their declaration prevents calling code from accidentally performing invalid copy operations on C classes.

On instantiation, the member data contained within a C class typically needs to perform operations that may fail. A good example is instantiation of an object that performs a memory allocation, which fails if there is insufficient memory available. This kind of failure is called a leave on Symbian OS, and is discussed in more detail shortly. A constructor should never be able to leave, because this can cause memory leaks, as we will discuss in Section 3.6 on two-phase construction. To avoid the potential for memory leaks upon construction, C classes are characterized by an idiom called two-phase construction, which also prevents accidental creation of objects of a C class on the stack.

C classes will be discussed more when we deal with two-phase construction and the cleanup stack.

3.2.3   R Classes

R classes own an external resource handle, for example a handle to a server session. R classes are diverse, and vary from holding a file server session handle (e.g., class RFs) to memory allocated on the heap (e.g., class RBuf). R classes are often small, and usually contain no other member data besides the resource handle. R-class objects may exist as class members, as local stack-based variables or, occasionally, on the heap.

Initializing R classes usually requires calling a special method, such as Open(), Create() or Connect(). Similarly, destroying R classes usually involves calling a special cleanup method, which is usually named Close() although it may sometimes be named something else, such as Reset(). It is rare for an R class to have a destructor too – it generally does not need one because cleanup is performed in the cleanup method.

Although you will probably use a number of Symbian R classes, there are only a few cases where you may need to write your own R class, for example when you are creating a client-server application.

3.2.4   M Classes

On Symbian OS, M classes are often used in callback or observer classes. An M class is an abstract interface class which declares pure virtual functions and has no member data. A concrete class deriving from such a class typically inherits from CBase (or a CBase-derived class) as its first base class and from one or more M-class 'mixin' interfaces, and implements the interface functions.

An M class should usually have only pure virtual functions, but may occasionally have non-pure virtual functions.

Tip: The only form of multiple inheritance encouraged on Symbian C++ is that which uses one CBase-derived class and mixes in one or more M classes. The correct class-derivation order is always to put the CBase-derived class first, to emphasize the primary inheritance tree and ensure proper cleanup through the cleanup stack.

3.2.5 Static Classes

Some Symbian OS utility classes, such as `User`, `Math` and `Mem`, take no prefix letter and contain only static member functions. The classes themselves cannot be instantiated; their functions must instead be called using the scope-resolution operator – for example, `User::After()` which suspends the currently running thread for the number of microseconds specified as a parameter of the function. A static class is sometimes implemented to act as a factory class.

3.3 Leaves and Exception Handling

Leaves can be thought of as the equivalent of exception handling on Symbian OS. Think of them as using just one exception class, and simply including an integer (known as a 'leave code') inside the exception to identify its cause.

> **Tip:** Symbian OS v9 also supports C++ standard exceptions. This makes it easier to port existing C++ code to Symbian OS. However, even if your code only uses standard C++ exceptions, leaves are a fundamental part of Symbian error handling and are used throughout the system, so it pays to understand them thoroughly.

How do you know whether a function may leave? This is where we see another Symbian C++ naming convention, which is to terminate the name with a trailing 'L'. In fact, of all Symbian OS naming conventions, this one is probably the most important rule: if a leaving function is not named correctly, callers of that function cannot know about it and may leak memory in the event a leave occurs. We'll see how this could happen shortly.

> **Tip:** It is standard practice when defining leaving functions to avoid returning an error code as well. That is, since leaving functions already highlight a failure (through the leave code), they should not also return error values. Any error that occurs in a leaving function should be passed out as a leave; if the function does not leave it is deemed to have succeeded and will return normally. Except under exception circumstances, leaving functions should return void unless they return a pointer or reference to a resource that they have allocated.

Since it is not part of the C++ standard, the trailing L cannot be checked during compilation, and can sometimes be forgotten. Symbian OS provides a helpful tool, LeaveScan, to check code for incorrectly named leaving functions. Some other static code-analysis tools are discussed in Chapter 6.

3.3.1 The Difference between Panics and Leaves

Before any further discussion of leaves, it is important to make the distinction between leaves (which are Symbian exceptions) and panics.

Leaves are used to propagate errors to where they can be handled. A leave does not terminate the flow of execution on Symbian OS. In contrast, panics are used to stop code running. They are intended to ensure robust code logic by flagging up programming errors in a way that cannot be ignored. Unlike a leave, a panic cannot be trapped, because it terminates the thread in which it occurs.

On phone hardware, a panic is seen as an 'Application closed' message box. When debugging on the emulator builds, the panic breaks the code into the debugger by default, so you can look at the call stack and diagnose the problem.

To cause a panic in the current thread, the `Panic()` method of the static `User` class can be used. It is not possible to panic other threads in the system, except those running in the same process. To panic another thread in the running process, your code should open an `RThread` handle and call `RThread::Panic()`. We'll discuss how to work with Symbian OS threads later in this chapter.

Symbian OS has a set of well-documented panic categories (for example, `KERN-EXEC`, `E32USER-CBASE`, `ALLOC`, `USER`), the details of which can be found in the reference section of the Symbian Developer Library in the SDK.

3.3.2 TRAP and TRAPD Macros

The `TRAP` and `TRAPD` macros can be used to 'catch' a leave and to extract the leave code integer. If a leave occurs in a function called within a `TRAP`, control will return immediately to the `TRAP` harness macro. The `TRAP` macro requires that the integer variable has been defined beforehand, while `TRAPD` defines the variable for you. The following code shows how to trap a leaving method:

```
TInt leaveCode;
TRAP(leaveCode, LeavingMethodL());
if (KErrNone == leaveCode)
  {
  // If no error, do something.
  }
```

```
else
  {
  // If an error happened, handle it here.
  }
```

Alternatively, using TRAPD, the code is expressed as follows:

```
TRAPD(leaveCode, LeavingMethodL());
if (KErrNone == leaveCode)
  {
  // If no error, do something.
  }
else
  {
  // If an error happened, handle it here.
  }
```

You can find the list of Symbian OS system-wide error codes which, apart from KErrNone (which is 0), are negative numbers – in \epoc32\ include\e32err.h and in the Symbian Developer Library of each SDK.

TRAP macros can also be nested to catch and handle leaves at different levels of code, where they can best be dealt with. However, each TRAP has an impact on executable size and execution speed, and the number of TRAPs should be minimized where possible.

3.3.3   What Causes a Leave?

If you are writing a function which must not leave, the TRAP macro must be used to prevent a potential leave from propagating. For example:

```
TInt NonLeavingMethod()
  {
  TRAPD(err, LeavingMethodL());
  ... // Handle the error
  }
```

Since NonLeavingMethod() cannot leave, it must call Leaving-MethodL() within a TRAP and handle the error internally, or return it. But what can cause a leave?

A leave may occur in a function if it:

- Explicitly calls one of the system functions in class User that cause a leave, such as User::Leave() or User::LeaveIfError().

- Uses the Symbian OS-overloaded form of operator new, which takes ELeave as a parameter.

- Calls code that may leave (for either of the reasons above) without using a `TRAP` harness.

> **Warning:** `User::Leave()` doesn't have a trailing 'L', yet it can leave. This is one of a few exceptions to the naming convention, and we will indicate others in this book as we come to them.

3.3.4 `new(ELeave)`

Symbian OS overloads the global operator `new` to leave if there is insufficient heap memory for successful allocation. Use of this overload allows the pointer returned from the allocation to be used without a further test that the allocation was successful, because the allocation would have left if it were not (in this respect, it is similar to the standard C++ `new` operator which throws an exception when allocation fails). For example:

```
CBook* InitializeBookL()
  {
  CBook* book = new(ELeave) CBook();
  book->Initialize(); // No need to test book against NULL
  return (book);
  }
```

3.4 The Cleanup Stack

If memory is allocated on the heap and referenced only by a stack-based local variable, what happens if a leave occurs? For example, consider the following:

```
void UnsafeFunctionL()
  {
  CAnotherClass* theObject = new (ELeave) CAnotherClass();
  theObject->InitializeL(); // Leave happens here...
  // theObject will be orphaned on the heap!
  delete theObject ; // This will never be called
  }
```

The memory allocated on the heap to store `theObject` will become inaccessible if the call to `InitializeL()` leaves. If that happens, `theObject` can never be deallocated (it is said to be 'orphaned'), resulting in a memory leak. It is not 'leave-safe'. One way to make the `theObject` pointer leave-safe is to place a `TRAP` (or `TRAPD`) macro around every potential leaving call that follows its creation. However, the use of TRAPs should be limited for reasons of efficiency, and to avoid clumsy code which constantly traps leaves and checks leave codes.

As a more sophisticated alternative, the Symbian OS cleanup stack can be used to prevent this, by storing pointers to heap-based objects upon it before calling any method that may leave. The example above can be rewritten using the cleanup stack as shown below:

```
void SafeFunctionL()
  {
  CAnotherClass* theObject = new (ELeave) CAnotherClass();

  // Push to the cleanup stack before calling
  // any methods that may leave.
  CleanupStack::PushL(theObject);

  // If leave happens here, theObject will still be
  // deleted.
  theObject->InitializeL();

  // Pop the object from the cleanup stack.
  CleanupStack::Pop(theObject);

  // And finally delete the object.
  delete theObject;

  // Alternatively, the last 2 lines of code can
  // be expressed in one line, as follows:
  // CleanupStack::PopAndDestroy(theObject);
  }
```

In the event of a leave, the cleanup stack takes responsibility for releasing the memory referenced by the pointers stored upon it.

While heap variables referenced only by local variables are orphaned if a leave occurs, member variables do not suffer a similar fate (unless the destructor neglects to delete them when it is called at some later point). The following code is safe:

```
void CTestClass::SafeFunctionL()
  {
  // Heap allocation of a member variable
  iTheObject = new(ELeave) CAnotherClass();
  iTheObject ->InitializeL(); // Safe for iTheObject
  }
```

The heap-based iTheObject member is stored safely, and deleted at a later stage with the rest of the CTestClass object, through the class destructor.

The cleanup stack can also be used to make instances of heap-based T classes leave-safe too. You can also use it for R classes to make them leave-safe, but R-class objects need to be pushed onto the cleanup stack differently, because their cleanup method (e.g., Close())

must be called to release the resources they own. Instead of using
`CleanupStack::PushL()`, R-class objects are pushed using special global methods: `CleanupClosePushL()` or `CleanupRelease-
PushL()`, depending on how the object should be destroyed. For
example:

```
RFs fileServer;
User::LeaveIfError(fileServer.Connect());

// Push file server handle to the cleanup stack.
CleanupClosePushL(fileServer);

// Call methods that may leave here.
// ...

// This will close the file server as well.
CleanupStack::PopAndDestroy(fileServer);
```

3.5   The Cleanup Stack FAQ: Advanced Information

This section contains some advanced information that may answer some
of the questions you have had while using the cleanup stack. It's a useful
reference, but if this is the first time that you've encountered the cleanup
stack, you may prefer to skip ahead to the next section, and return here
when you've had a chance to experiment with some code that uses it.

3.5.1   Why Does `PushL()` Leave?

In the examples above, you may have noticed that `PushL()` is a leaving
function, which at first sight appears to be self-defeating. If the cleanup
stack is supposed to make pointers leave-safe, how can it cause a leave
when you call it and yet still be helpful?

The reason `PushL()` may leave is that it may need to allocate memory
to store the pointers passed to it (and in low-memory conditions this could
fail). However, the object passed to `PushL()` will not be orphaned if
it leaves. This is because, when the cleanup stack is created, it has at
least one spare slot. When `PushL()` is called, the pointer is added to
a vacant slot, and then, if there are no remaining slots available, the
cleanup stack attempts to allocate some for future calls to `PushL()`. It is
if that attempted allocation fails, that a leave occurs. The pointer passed
in was stored safely before any leave could occur, so the object it refers
to is safe, and is cleaned up as usual.

3.5.2   Why Do I Get a Panic When I Try To Use the Cleanup Stack?

The cleanup stack is only available to code executed inside a TRAP
macro. Don't worry, most of the code you can modify is in that situation,

unless you are writing a console application or creating your own server. Trying to use `CleanupStack::PushL()` outside of any TRAP macro will result in an `E32User-CBase66` panic.

3.5.3   Why Do I Get a Panic When My Code Leaves a **TRAP**?

The cleanup stack must be emptied by the correct number of `Cleanup-Stack::Pop()` calls before it is destroyed at the end of the TRAP macro that created it or your application will panic.

3.5.4   Why Do I Get a Panic When I Call **CleanupStack::Pop()**?

There are several possible reasons for a panic when you call the `Pop()` method. For example, calling `CleanupStack::Pop()` when the cleanup stack is empty will result in yet another panic.

Another reason could be that you are calling `Pop()` and passing in the pointer you expect to be taken off the cleanup stack, but another is actually being popped instead. The cleanup stack is implemented as a stack, so for any series of pushes, the corresponding pops must occur in reverse order.

It is a good idea to name the pointer as it is popped, so debug builds can check that it is the correct pointer and flag up any programming errors. For example:

```
void TestUIQPhonesL()
  {
  // Each object is pushed onto the cleanup stack immediately
  // it is allocated, in case the next allocation leaves
  CUiq3Phone* phoneP1i = CUiqPhone::NewL(EP1i);
  CleanupStack::PushL(phoneP1i);
  CUiq3Phone* phoneM600i = CUiqPhone::NewL(EM600i);
  CleanupStack::PushL(phoneM600i);
  CUiq3Phone* phoneP990i = CUiqPhone::NewL(EP990i);
  CleanupStack::PushL(phoneP990i);

  ... // Leaving functions called here

  // Various ways to remove the objects from the stack and delete them:
  // (1) All with one anonymous call -  OK
  // CleanupStack::PopAndDestroy(3);

  // (2) Each object individually to verify the code logic
  // Note the reverse order of Pop() to PushL()
  // This is long-winded

  // CleanupStack::PopAndDestroy(phoneP990i);
  // CleanupStack::PopAndDestroy(phoneM600i);
  // CleanupStack::PopAndDestroy(phoneP1i);

  // (3) All at once, naming the last object - best solution
  CleanupStack::PopAndDestroy(3, phoneP1i);
  }
```

3.5.5   How Do I Mix Leaves, Exceptions and the Cleanup Stack?

Symbian OS TRAPs and leaves are implemented internally in terms of C++ exceptions (a leave is a XLeaveException), and a TRAP will panic if it catches any other kind of exception. This means that, if you are mixing C++ exceptions in with traditional Symbian OS leaves and TRAPs, you must not throw an exception within a leaving function unless you also catch and handle it internally in that function.

A standard catch block will not manage the Symbian OS cleanup stack correctly either, so code that throws exceptions should not use the cleanup stack directly or indirectly. If you are calling leaving functions from exception-style code, do not use the cleanup stack, but make the calls as required and catch and handle any exceptions that arise. For more information about mixing leaves, exceptions and the cleanup stack, please refer to a paper on the Symbian Developer Network called 'Leaves and Exceptions' to located at ***developer.symbian.com/main/downloads/papers/Leaves%20and%20Exceptions.pdf***.

3.6   Two-Phase Construction

Consider the following code, which allocates an object of type CExample on the heap and sets the value of foo accordingly:

```
CExample* foo = new(ELeave) CExample();
```

The code calls the new operator, which allocates a CExample object on the heap if there is sufficient memory available. Having done so, it calls the constructor of class CExample to initialize the object. But if the CExample constructor leaves, the memory already allocated for foo and any additional memory the constructor may have allocated will be orphaned.

This leads to a fundamental rule of memory management on Symbian OS: **A C++ constructor should never leave.**

However, it may often be necessary to write initialization code that leaves, say to allocate memory to store another object, or to read from a configuration file, which may be missing or corrupt. There are many reasons why initialization may fail, and the way to accommodate this on Symbian OS is to use two-phase construction.

Two-phase construction breaks object construction into two parts, or phases:

1. **A C++ constructor that cannot leave.**
   This is the constructor that is called by the new operator. It implicitly calls base-class constructors and may also invoke functions that

cannot leave, and/or initialize member variables with default values or those supplied as arguments to the constructor.

2. **A separate initialization method (typically called `ConstructL()`).** This method may be called separately once the object, allocated and constructed by the `new` operator, has been pushed onto the cleanup stack; it will complete construction of the object and may safely perform operations that may leave. If a leave does occur, the cleanup stack calls the destructor to free any resources which have already been successfully allocated and destroys the memory allocated for the object itself.

A class typically provides a public static function which wraps both phases of construction, providing a simple and easily identifiable means to instantiate it (the two construction methods can then be made private or protected to avoid accidental usage). The factory function is typically called `NewL()` and is static so that it can be called without first having an existing instance of the class. For example:

```
class CExample : public CBase
  {
public:
  static CExample* NewL();
  static CExample* NewLC();
  ~CExample(); // Must cope with partially constructed objects
  ... // Other public methods, e.g. Foo(), Bar()
private:
  CExample();        // Guaranteed not to leave
  void ConstructL(); // Second-phase construction code, may leave
  CPointer* iPointer;
  };
```

Note that there is also a `NewLC()` function in class `CExample`. This method is also a factory function, but its implementation leaves a pointer on the cleanup stack when it returns.

Tip: If a pointer to an object is pushed onto the cleanup stack and remains on it when that function returns, the Symbian OS convention is to append a C to the function name. This indicates to the caller that, if the function returns successfully, the cleanup stack has additional pointers on it.

Let's see the code for typical implementations of `NewL()` and `NewLC()`:

```
CExample* CExample::NewLC()
  {
```

```
CExample* me = new (ELeave) CExample(); // First-phase construction
CleanupStack::PushL(me);
me->ConstructL(); // Second-phase construction
return (me);
}
CExample* CExample::NewL()
{
CExample* me = CExample::NewLC();
CleanupStack::Pop(me);
return (me);
}
```

The NewL() factory function is implemented in terms of the NewLC() function rather than the other way around (which would be slightly less efficient since this would require an extra PushL() call to put a pointer back onto the cleanup stack).

Each factory function returns a fully constructed object, or leaves, either if there is insufficient memory to allocate the object (that is, if operator new(ELeave) leaves) or if the second-phase ConstructL() function leaves for any reason. This means that, if an object is initialized entirely by two-phase construction, the class can be implemented without the need to test each member variable to see if it is valid before using it. That is, if an object exists, it has been fully constructed. The result is an efficient class implementation without a test against each member pointer before it is de-referenced.

3.7 Thin Templates

Symbian OS uses the thin template pattern in all its container classes, collections and buffers, to get the benefits of type-safety, while reducing the amount of duplicated object code at compile time.

The thin template idiom implements the container using a generic base class with TAny* pointers. A templated class is then defined that uses private inheritance of the generic implementation. (If your C++ is a bit rusty, private inheritance allows implementation to be inherited, but the methods of the base class become private members. The deriving class does not inherit the interface of the base class so the generic implementation can only be used internally and not externally, which avoids accidental use of the non-type-safe methods.) Instead of a generic interface, the derived class presents a templated interface to its clients and implements it inline by calling the private base-class methods. The use of templates means that the class can be used with any type required and that it is type-safe at compile time.

Let's look at an example to make it clearer. A snippet of the Symbian OS `RArrayBase` class and its deriving class `RArray` are shown below (the `RArray` class will be discussed later in Section 3.9.2). `RArrayBase` is the generic base class that implements the code logic for the array, but the code cannot be used directly because all its methods are protected.

```
class RArrayBase
  {
protected:
  IMPORT_C RArrayBase(TInt aEntrySize);
  IMPORT_C RArrayBase(TInt aEntrySize,TAny* aEntries, TInt aCount);
  IMPORT_C TAny* At(TInt aIndex) const;
  IMPORT_C TInt Append(const TAny* aEntry);
  IMPORT_C TInt Insert(const TAny* aEntry, TInt aPos);
  ...
  };
```

The derived `RArray` class is templated, defining a clear, usable API for clients. The API is defined inline and uses the base-class implementation which it privately inherits from the base class. Elements of the array are instances of the template class.

```
template <class T>
  class RArray : private RArrayBase
  {
public:
  ...
  inline RArray();
  inline const T& operator[](TInt aIndex) const;
  inline T& operator[](TInt aIndex);
  inline TInt Append(const T& aEntry);
  inline TInt Insert(const T& aEntry, TInt aPos);
  ...
  };

template <class T>
inline RArray<T>::RArray()
  : RArrayBase(sizeof(T))
  {}

template <class T>
inline const T& RArray<T>::operator[](TInt aIndex) const
  {return *(const T*)At(aIndex); }

template <class T>
inline T& RArray<T>::operator[](TInt aIndex)
  {return *(T*)At(aIndex); }

template <class T>
inline TInt RArray<T>::Append(const T& aEntry)
  {return RArrayBase::Append(&aEntry);}
```

```
template <class T>
inline TInt RArray<T>::Insert(const T& aEntry, TInt aPos)
  {return RArrayBase::Insert(&aEntry,aPos);}
```

3.8   Descriptors – Symbian OS Strings

Descriptors are the string classes used on Symbian OS. They are so called because they are self-describing strings. That is, a descriptor holds the length of the string of data it represents as well as type information to identify the underlying memory layout of the descriptor data. Descriptors protect against buffer overrun and don't rely on NULL terminators to determine the length of the string.

Descriptors are used throughout the operating system, from the very lowest level upwards, and are designed to be very efficient, using the minimum amount of memory necessary to store data, while describing it fully in terms of its length and location. Descriptors are strings and can contain text data. However, they can also be used to manipulate binary data, because they don't rely on a NULL-terminating character to determine their length.

There are probably as many string classes as there are programming platforms, and everyone has their favorite. Many developers find Symbian OS descriptors hard to get used to at first, because there are many different classes to become familiar with. They can also be confusing because they aren't a direct analog to standard C++ strings, Java strings or the MFC CString (to take just three examples), since their underlying memory allocation and cleanup must be managed by the programmer. Before calling a modifiable descriptor method that may expand the descriptor, it is necessary to ensure that there is sufficient memory available for it to succeed.

3.8.1   Character Size

Symbian OS supports 8-bit and 16-bit character sizes. The character size of a descriptor class can be identified from its name. If the class name ends in 8 (for example, TPtr8) it has narrow (8-bit) characters, while a descriptor class name ending with 16 (for example, TPtr16) manipulates 16-bit character strings.

There is also a set of neutral classes which have no number in their name (for example, TPtr). The neutral classes are 16 bit, and it is good practice to use the neutral descriptor classes where the character width does not need to be stated explicitly. However, to work with binary data, the 8-bit descriptor classes should be used explicitly, and some Symbian OS APIs (e.g., those to read from and write to a file) all take an 8-bit descriptor.

3.8.2 `TDesC`

All Symbian OS descriptor classes derive from the base class `TDesC`, apart from the literal descriptors which we will discuss later in Section 3.8.9. In naming this class, the T prefix indicates a simple type class, while the C suffix reflects that the class defines a *non-modifiable* type of descriptor – that is, one whose contents are constant.

`TDesC` provides methods for determining the length of the descriptor (`Length()`) and accessing its data (`Ptr()`). Using these methods, it also implements all the standard operations required on a constant string object, such as data access, matching and searching. The derived classes all inherit these methods, and all constant descriptor manipulation is implemented by `TDesC`, regardless of the derived type of the descriptor used.

3.8.3 `TDes`

The modifiable descriptor types all derive from the base class `TDes`, which is itself a subclass of `TDesC`. `TDes` stores the maximum length of data allowed for the current memory allocated to the descriptor. The `MaxLength()` method of `TDes` returns this value. Like the `Length()` method of `TDesC`, it is not overridden by derived classes. The contents of the descriptor can shrink and expand up to this value.

`TDes` defines a range of methods to manipulate modifiable string data, including those to append, fill and format the descriptor. All the manipulation code for descriptor modification is implemented by `TDes` and inherited by its derived classes. The descriptor API methods for both modifiable and non-modifiable descriptor base classes are fully documented in the Symbian Developer Library.

3.8.4 The Derived Descriptor Classes

The descriptor base classes `TDesC` and `TDes` implement all the generic descriptor manipulation code, but cannot be instantiated. Derived des-triptor classes, which add their own construction and assignment code, are the classes that are actually used to manipulate strings on Symbian OS.

The derived descriptor types come in two basic memory layouts: pointer descriptors, in which the descriptor points to data stored else-where; and buffer descriptors, where the data forms part of the descriptor. Figure 3.1 shows the inheritance hierarchy of the descriptor classes.

3.8.5 Pointer Descriptors: `TPtrC` and `TPtr`

The string data of a pointer descriptor is separate from the descriptor object itself and is stored elsewhere, for example, in ROM, on the heap or on the stack. The memory that holds the data is not 'owned' by

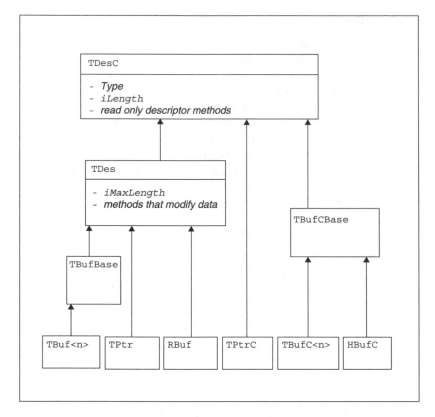

Figure 3.1 Descriptor Class Inheritance

the pointer descriptor, which is agnostic about where the memory is located. The class defines a range of constructors to allow `TPtrC` objects to be constructed from other descriptors, a pointer into memory, or a zero-terminated C string.

`TPtrC` is the equivalent of using `const char*` when handling strings in C. The data can be accessed but not modified; that is, the data in the descriptor is constant. All the non-modifying operations defined in the `TDesC` base class are accessible to objects of type `TPtrC`, but none of the modification methods of `TDes`.

In comparison, the `TPtr` class can be used for access to, and modification of, a character string or binary data. All the modifiable and non-modifiable base-class operations of `TDes` and `TDesC`, respectively, are accessible to a `TPtr`.

3.8.6 Stack-Based Buffer Descriptors `TBufC` and `TBuf`

The stack-based buffer descriptors may be modifiable or non-modifiable. Unlike the pointer descriptors, the string data forms part of the descriptor object.

TBufC<n> is the non-modifiable buffer class, used to hold constant string or binary data. The class derives from TBufCBase (which derives from TDesC, and exists only as an inheritance convenience). TBufC<n> is a thin template class which uses an integer value to fix the size of the data area for the buffer descriptor object at compile time.

TBuf<n> is used when a modifiable buffer is required. It derives from TBufBase, which itself derives from TDes, and inherits the full range of descriptor operations in TDes and TDesC. The class defines a number of constructors and assignment operators, similar to those offered by its non-modifiable counterpart, TBufC<n>. The buffer descriptors are useful for fixed-size strings, but should be used conservatively since they are stack-based except when used as members of a class whose objects are instantiated on the heap.

3.8.7 Dynamic Descriptors: HBufC and RBuf

The HBufC and RBuf descriptor classes are used for dynamic string data whose size is not known at compile time, and for data that cannot be stack-based because it is too big. These classes are used where malloc'd data would be used in C.

HBufC

The HBufC8 and HBufC16 classes (and the neutral version HBufC, which is typedef'd to HBufC16) provide a number of static NewL() functions to create the descriptor on the heap. These methods may leave if there is insufficient memory available. All heap buffers must be constructed using one of these methods or from one of the Alloc() or AllocL() methods of the TDesC class, which spawn an HBufC copy of any existing descriptor. Once the descriptor has been created to the size required, it is not automatically resized if more space is required. Additional memory must be reallocated using the ReAlloc() or ReAllocL() methods.

As the C suffix of the class name, and the inheritance hierarchy shown in Figure 3.1, indicates, HBufC descriptors are not directly modifiable, although the class provides assignment operators to allow the entire contents of the buffer to be replaced. To modify an HBufC object at runtime, a modifiable pointer descriptor, TPtr, must first be created using the HBufC::Des() method.

```
_LIT(KTestBuffer, "Heap Based");
// create a heap-based descriptor and place it on cleanup stack
HBufC* pHeap = HBufC::NewLC(32);
// create a pointer descriptor around pHeap
TPtr ptr(pHeap->Des());
// modify pHeap indirectly via ptr
ptr = KTestBuffer;
...
```

```
// clean up
CleanupStack::PopAndDestroy(pHeap);
```

RBuf

Class `RBuf` is derived from `TDes`, so an `RBuf` object can be modified without the need to create a `TPtr` around the data first, which often makes it preferable to `HBufC`. On instantiation, an `RBuf` object can allocate its own buffer or take ownership of pre-allocated memory or a pre-existing heap descriptor. To comply with the Symbian OS class-name conventions discussed at the beginning of this chapter, the `RBuf` class is not named `HBuf` because, unlike `HBufC`, it is not directly created on the heap. `RBuf` descriptors are typically created on the stack, and hold a pointer to a resource on the heap for which it is responsible at cleanup time.

Internally, `RBuf` behaves in one of two ways:

- Like a `TPtr`, which points directly to the descriptor data stored in memory, which the `RBuf` object allocates or takes ownership of.

- As a pointer to an existing heap descriptor, `HBufC*`. The `RBuf` object takes ownership of the `HBufC`, and holds a pointer to memory that contains a complete descriptor object (compared to a pointer to a simple block of data as in the former case).

However, this is all transparent, and there is no need to know how a specific `RBuf` object is represented internally. Using this descriptor class is straightforward too, through the methods inherited from `TDes` and `TDesC`, just as for the other descriptor classes.

`RBuf` is a relatively recent addition to Symbian OS, first documented in Symbian OS v8.1 and used most extensively in software designed for phones based on Symbian OS v9 and later. A lot of original example code won't use it, but it is a simpler class to use than `HBufC` if you need a dynamically allocated buffer to hold data that changes frequently. The next subsection will examine how to instantiate and use `RBuf` in more detail.

`HBufC` is still ideal when a dynamically allocated descriptor is needed to hold data that doesn't change; that is, if no modifiable access to the data is required.

3.8.8 Using **RBuf**

`RBuf` objects can be instantiated using the `Create()`, `CreateMax()` or `CreateL()` methods to specify the maximum length of descriptor data that can be stored. It is also possible to instantiate an `RBuf` and copy the contents of another descriptor into it, as follows:

```
RBuf myRBuf;
LIT(KHelloRBuf, "Hello RBuf!"); // Literal descriptor
myRBuf.CreateL(KHelloRBuf());
```

CreateL() allocates a buffer for the RBuf to reference. If that RBuf previously owned a buffer, CreateL() will not clean it up before assigning the new buffer reference, so this must be done first by calling Close() to free any pre-existing owned memory.

Alternatively, an RBuf can be instantiated and take ownership of a pre-existing section of memory using the Assign() method.

```
// Taking ownership of HBufC
HBufC* myHBufC = HBufC::NewL(20);
RBuf myRBuf;
myRBuf.Assign(myHBufC);
```

Assign() will also orphan any data already owned by the RBuf, so Close() should be called before reassignment, to avoid memory leaks.

The RBuf class doesn't manage the size of the buffer or reallocate it if more memory is required for a particular operation. If a modification method, such as Append(), is called on an RBuf object for which there is insufficient memory available, a panic will occur. As a programmer, you are responsible for making sure that the RBuf object has sufficient space in its internal buffer, by using the ReAllocL() method if necessary:

```
// myRBuf is the buffer to be resized e.g. for an Append() operation
myRBuf.CleanupClosePushL(); // push onto cleanup stack for leave-safety
myRBuf.ReAllocL(newLength); // extend to newLength
CleanupStack::Pop();        // remove from cleanup stack
```

Note that the previous example uses the CleanupClosePushL() method of the RBuf class to push it onto the cleanup stack. As is usual for other R classes, cleanup is performed by calling Close() (or CleanupStack::PopAndDestroy() if the RBuf was pushed onto the cleanup stack by a call to RBuf::CleanupClosePushL()).

3.8.9 Literal Descriptors

Literal descriptors are somewhat different from the other descriptor types. They are equivalent to static const char[] in C and because they are constant, they can be built into ROM to save memory at runtime. A set of macros, found in e32def.h, can be used to define Symbian OS literals of two different types, _LIT and _L.

The _LIT macro is preferred for Symbian OS literals, since it is more efficient. It is typically used as follows:

```
_LIT(KSymbianOS, "Symbian OS");
```

The _LIT macro builds a named object (KSymbianOS) of type TLitC16 into the program binary, storing the appropriate string (in this case, "Symbian OS"). The explicit macros _LIT8 and _LIT16 behave similarly, except that _LIT8 builds a narrow string of type TLitC8.

TLitC8 and TLitC16 do not derive from TDesC8 or TDesC16, but they have the same binary layouts as TBufC8 or TBufC16. This allows objects of these types to be passed wherever TDesC is used.

Symbian OS also defines literals to represent a blank string. There are three variants of the *null descriptor*, defined as follows:

```
// Build independent:
_LIT(KNULLDesC,"");
// 8-bit for narrow strings:
_LIT8(KNULLDesC8,"");
// 16-bit for Unicode strings:
_LIT16(KNULLDesC16,"");
```

Use of the _L macro is now deprecated in production code, though it may still be used in test code (where memory use is less critical). It can be defined and used in a single line of code, as follows:

```
TBuf<10> KSymbianBuf(_L("Symbian OS"));
```

3.8.10   Descriptor Class Types: Summary

The previous subsections discussed the characteristics of each of the various descriptor types and classes. Table 3.2 summarizes them for reference.

Figure 3.2 summarizes how the knowledge in Table 3.2 can be applied when deciding what type of descriptor class to use.

3.8.11   Using the Descriptor APIs

Length() and Size()

TDesC::Size() returns the size of the descriptor in bytes, while TDesC::Length() returns the number of characters it contains.

For 8-bit descriptors, the length and size of a descriptor are equivalent because the size of a character is a byte. In native 16-bit strings, each character occupies two bytes. Thus Size() always returns a value double that of Length() for neutral and explicitly wide descriptors.

Table 3.2 Descriptor Classes in Summary

Name	Modifiable	Approximate C equivalent	Type	Notes
TDesC	No	n/a	Not instantiable	Base class for all descriptors (except literals)
TDes	Yes	n/a	Not instantiable	Base class for all modifiable descriptors
TPtrC	No	const char* (doesn't own the data)	Pointer	The data is stored separately from the descriptor object, which is agnostic to its location
TPtr	Yes	char* (doesn't own the data)	Pointer	The data is stored separately from the descriptor object, which is agnostic to its location
TBufC	Indirectly	const char []	Stack buffer	Thin template – size is fixed at compile time
TBuf	Yes	char []	Stack buffer	Thin template – size is fixed at compile time
HBufC	Indirectly	const char* (owns the data)	Heap buffer	Used for dynamic data storage where modification is infrequent
RBuf	Yes	char* (owns the data)	Heap buffer	Used for modifiable dynamic data storage
TLitC	No	Static const char []	Literal	Built into ROM

`MaxLength()` and length modification methods

`TDes::MaxLength()` returns the maximum length of the modifiable descriptor on which it is invoked.

`TDes::SetLength()` can be used to adjust the descriptor length to any value between zero and its maximum length.

`TDes::Zero()` sets the length of the descriptor object on which it is invoked to zero.

`TPtr(C)::Set()` and `TDes::operator =()`

`TPtr` and `TPtrC` both provide `Set()` methods. These can be used to set the pointer to reference different string data. The length and maximum length members of the descriptor object are updated accordingly.

`TDes` provides an assignment operator to copy data into the memory already referenced by a modifiable descriptor. The length of the descriptor is updated to that of the new contents, but the maximum length is unchanged. So it is important that the length of new data assigned to the descriptor is no longer than the maximum length, because

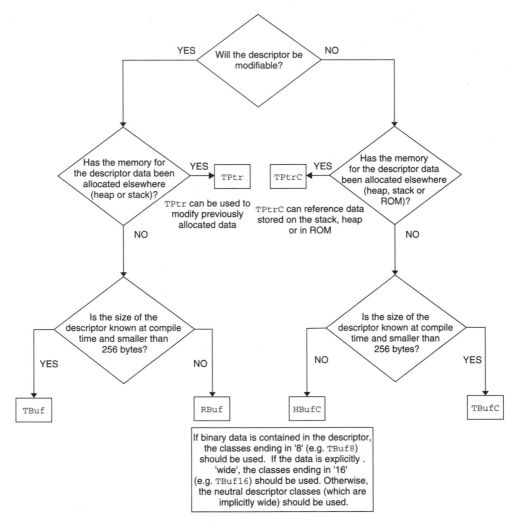

Figure 3.2   Flow Chart to Guide the Choice of Descriptor Type

otherwise the copy will cause a panic. It is easy to confuse `Set()` with `TDes::operator =()`.

TBufC::Des() and HBufC::Des()

`TBufC` and `HBufC` both provide a `Des()` method which returns a modifiable pointer descriptor to the data held in the buffer. While the content of a non-modifiable buffer descriptor cannot be altered directly, calling `Des()` makes it possible to change the data. The method updates the length members of both the modifiable pointer descriptor and the

constant buffer descriptor it points to, if necessary. For example, for
`HBufC`:

```
HBufC* heapBuf = HBufC::NewLC(20);
TPtr ptr(heapBuf->Des()); // Use ptr to modify heapBuf
```

A common inefficiency when using `HBufC` is to use `Des()` to return
a modifiable pointer descriptor object (`TPtr`), when a non-modifiable
descriptor (`TDesC`) is required. It is not incorrect, but since `HBufC` itself
derives from `TDesC`, it can simply be de-referenced, which is clearer and
more efficient.

```
const TDesC& CExample::Inefficient()
  {
  return (iHeapBuffer->Des());
  // could be replaced more efficiently with
  return (*iHeapBuffer);
  }
```

Some of the other most commonly used APIs are:

- `TDesC::Find()`, `TDesC::Locate()`, `TDesC::Match()`.

- Substring extraction using `TDesC::Left()`, `TDesC::Right()` and
  `TDesC::Mid()`.

- Adding data with the different variants of `TDes::Append()`.

- Data transfer between descriptors, by calling the various overloads of
  `TDes::Copy()`.

You can find out more about each of the descriptor APIs in the Symbian
Developer Library.

3.8.12 Descriptors as Function Parameters and Return Types

As Sections 3.8.2 and 3.8.3 described, the `TDesC` and `TDes` descriptor
base classes provide and implement the APIs for all descriptor operations.
This means that the base classes can be used as function arguments
and return types, allowing descriptors to be passed around in code
transparently without forcing a dependency on a particular type.

A function will simply declare whether a descriptor parameter should
be modifiable or non-modifiable, and whether it should be 8 or 16 bits
in width. It doesn't have to know the type of descriptor passed into
it. Unless a function takes or returns ownership, it doesn't even need to
specify whether a descriptor is stack-based or heap-based. When defining
functions, the abstract base classes should always be used as parameters

or return values. All descriptor parameters should be passed and returned by reference, either as `const TDesC&` for constant descriptors or `TDes&` when modifiable. The only exception comes when transferring ownership of a heap-based descriptor as a return value. This should be specified explicitly so that the caller can clean it up appropriately and avoid a memory leak.

```
// Read only parameter (16 bit)
void SomeFunctionL(const TDesC& aReadOnlyDescriptor);

// Read only return value (8 bit)
const TDesC8& SomeFunction();

// Read/Write parameter (16 bit)
void SomeFunctionL(TDes& aReadWriteDescriptor);

// Return ownership of HBufC*
HBufC* SomeFunctionL();
```

For additional information about descriptors, you should consult the Symbian Developer Library or one of the Symbian Press books, listed at the end of Chapter 6.

3.9   Arrays on Symbian OS

Symbian OS does not include an implementation of the collections found in the Standard Template Library. Instead, it offers various templatized classes for static and dynamic arrays. This section will help you make it clearer which array class does what and how.

The most basic class is `TFixedArray`, which is a static array class, to be used when you know at build time how many data items the array will contain.

3.9.1   Static Arrays

`TFixedArray` wraps a standard fixed-length C++ `[]` array to add range checking, and prevent out-of-bounds access by panicking to flag the programming error. The range-checking assertions are called in debug builds only, or in both debug and release builds if you require it, by calling different methods on the class to access the elements. The class also provides some additional functions to navigate to the beginning and end, return the number of elements in the array, and clean up the elements it contains. Further information can be found in the Symbian Developer Library that accompanies each SDK.

3.9.2 Dynamic Arrays

On Symbian OS, the implementation of a dynamic array may either use:

- A single heap cell as a 'flat' buffer to hold the array elements, which is resized as necessary. This memory layout is preferred when the speed of element lookup is an important factor or if the array is not expected to be frequently resized.

- A number of segments, using a doubly linked list to manage them. This layout is best for large arrays which are expected to be resized frequently, or when elements are regularly inserted into or deleted, since repeated reallocations in a single flat buffer may result in heap thrashing as elements are shuffled around.

The original dynamic array classes provided in early versions of Symbian OS were C classes, of which there are a number of different types, all of which have names prefixed by "CArray". We refer to them here generically as "CArrayX" classes. The different types of array exist to store various types of array element:

- Fixed elements – all items have the same fixed size (e.g., TInt, TRect).

- Variable elements – the items may have different size, so they are pointers to objects of variable lengths contained elsewhere on the heap (e.g., HBufC* or TAny*).

- Pointer elements – the items are the pointers to CBase-derived objects.

- Packaged elements – the items are 'packed' T-class objects of variable length; that is, each element is preceded by its length.

Table 3.3 summarizes the combinations defined in the SDK.

As Symbian OS evolved, a second set of dynamic array classes (RArray and RPointerArray) was added later (the CArrayX classes were retained). The newer array classes are R classes, and may thus be instantiated on the heap or the stack, but are usually stack-based. As R classes, they hold a handle to a block of memory used to store the array buffer, which in both cases is a resizable flat buffer rather than a doubly linked list of segments.

For performance reasons, when CArrayFixFlat is the type of array needed, we recommend that you actually use RArray, and when CArrayPtrFlat is a good choice, we recommend that you use RPointerArray instead.

Table 3.3 Array Combinations Defined in the SDK

Class name	Elements and memory layout	Element cleanup
CArrayFixFlat	Fixed size elements contained in the array. Occupies a single memory buffer that is resized as necessary.	Destroyed automatically by the array.
CArrayFixSeg	Fixed size elements contained in the array. Occupies segments of memory.	Destroyed automatically by the array.
CArrayVarFlat	Elements are pointers to variable size objects contained outside the array. Occupies a single memory buffer that is resized as necessary.	Destroyed automatically by the array.
CArrayVarSeg	Elements are pointers to variable size objects contained outside the array. Occupies segments of memory.	Destroyed automatically by the array.
CArrayPtrFlat	Elements are pointers to CBase-derived objects stored outside the array. Occupies a single memory buffer that is resized as necessary.	CArrayPtrFlat::ResetAndDestroy().
CArrayPtrSeg	Elements are pointers to CBase-derived objects stored outside the array. Occupies segments of memory.	CArrayPtrFlat::ResetAndDestroy().
CArrayPakFlat	Variable size elements occupy the array, each preceded by its length. Occupies a single memory buffer that is resized as necessary.	Destroyed automatically by the array.

3.9.3 Cleanup of the RArray Classes

RArray<class T> is an array of elements of the same size which are stored within the array buffer. The Close() or Reset() functions must be called to clean up the array by freeing the memory allocated for the elements.

- RArray::Close() frees the memory used to store the array and closes the array object.

- RArray::Reset() frees the memory used to store the array but simply resets its state so it can be reused.

RPointerArray<class T> is an array of pointer elements address-ing objects stored elsewhere. The ownership of these objects must be addressed separately when the array is destroyed. If pointers to the objects are held elsewhere (by other components), then calling Close() or Reset() to clean up the memory for the array of pointers is sufficient.

However, if the array has ownership of the objects its elements point to, it must take responsibility for cleanup. `ResetAndDestroy()` must be called to delete the object associated with each pointer element in the array, and then destroy the array itself.

3.9.4   When Should You Use `CArrayX` Arrays?

The `CArrayX` classes have been retained for legacy code, and because they provide a segmented-memory implementation which may be more appropriate for arrays that are frequently resized. Thus, `CArrayFixSeg` and `CArrayPtrSeg` are useful alternatives to `RArray` and `RPointer-Array`, respectively, when segmented memory is required, but `RArray` should always be preferred over `CArrayFixFlat`, and `RPointer-Array` always preferred over `CArrayPtrFlat`.

The only drawback of the `RArray` classes is the requirement for all elements to be 4-byte-aligned in memory. Check the classes you develop for this or you risk unhandled exceptions when running your applications on phones.

3.9.5   Sorting and Searching

Sorting is based on `TKeyArrayXXX` classes for `CArrayX` arrays and the `TLinearOrder` class for `RArrays`. The same is true for insert and find methods, which perform 'in order' operations.

The `_FOFF` macro is used to find the offset of a member variable in the binary representation of an object in memory. For example:

```
class TElementSort
  {
public :
  TElementSort(){}
public :
  TBuf<4> iData;
  };
...
CArrayFixFlat<TElement>* fixflat =
    new (ELeave) CArrayFixFlat<TElement>(3);

// populate fixflat here
TKeyArrayFix key(_FOFF(TElementSort, iData), ECmpNormal);
TInt res = fixflat->Sort(key);

// the elements inside fixflat have been ordered
...
delete fixflat;
```

To insert elements in the array so that it remains ordered throughout, use the `InsertIsqL()` method with such a sort key.

`TLinearOrder` is used differently and requires the class of the element objects to define its own ordering:

```
class CPerson : public CBase
  {
public:
  static CPerson* NewLC(const TDesC& aFirstName,
                        const TDesC& aLastName);

  static TInt CompareByLastName(const CPerson& person1,
                               const CPerson& person2);
protected:
  CPerson(const TDesC& aFirstName, const TDesC& aLastName);
private:
  TBuf<64> iFirstName;
  TBuf<64> iLastName;
  };

TInt CPerson::CompareByLastName(const CPerson& person1,
                                const CPerson& person2)
  {
  return person1.iLastName().CompareC(person2.LastName());
  }

RPointerArray<CPerson> people;
CleanupClosePushL(people);

CPerson* tyler = CPerson::NewLC(_L("Sam"), _L("Tyler"));
CPerson* hunt = CPerson::NewLC(_L("Gene"), _L("Hunt"));

people.AppendL(hunt);
CleanupStack::Pop(hunt);  // Now owned by people array
people.AppendL(tyler);
CleanupStack::Pop(tyler); // Now owned by people array

TLinearOrder<CPerson> byLastName(CPerson::CompareByLastName);
people.Sort(byLastName);

CleanupStack::Pop(people);
people.ResetAndDestroy();
people.Close();
```

After the elements in the array are sorted, the `FindInOrder()` functions can perform a binary search using the same ordering.

3.10 Executable Files

There are two common executable files on Symbian OS: EXE and DLL.

You have already seen an example of a Carbide.c++ project, which creates HelloWorld.exe, in Chapter 2. You can also use Carbide.c++ to create a Symbian OS DLL file. If you do so, it is worth examining the differences between the MMP file for an EXE and a DLL file. In particular, you will notice a difference between the `TARGETTYPE` and `UID` values specified in the MMP file.

TARGETTYPE indicates the type of file to be built, for example an EXE, in the case of an executable application, or a DLL. The most commonly used Symbian OS target types are DLL, EXE and PLUGIN (ECOM plug-in). Other supported types include PDD and LDD (physical device driver and logical device driver, respectively), LIB (a static library whose binary code is included directly in any component that links against it – as compared to a shared library, which is released as a separate binary), and EXEXP (an executable which exports functions, so they can be used by other applications or DLLs).

UID specifies the final two of the target's three unique identifiers (UIDs) that are used to uniquely identify the binary. On Symbian OS, each UID is a 32-bit value. The three UIDs are as follows.

3.10.1 UID1

This is the system-level identifier that distinguishes between EXEs and DLLs. For example, the TARGETTYPE specified for a shared library is DLL. This means that UID1 is set by the build tools to be KDynamic-LibraryUid (0x10000079). An application has UID1 set to be KExecutableImageUid (0x1000007a) by specifying a TARGETTYPE EXE.

The value of UID1 is built into the binary by the build tools depending on the keyword used with the TARGETTYPE identifier in the MMP file, and the value of UID1 does not need to be specified in an MMP file because it is automatically applied.

3.10.2 UID2

For DLLs, this UID is used to differentiate between shared library and polymorphic interface DLLs. For shared libraries, UID2 is KShared-LibraryUid (0x1000008d) but the value for polymorphic DLLs varies depending on their plug-in type (for example, the socket server protocol module UID2 value is 0x1000004A). You can find out more about the difference between the DLL types in the Symbian Developer Library documentation in your SDK.

UID2 is not relevant for TARGETTYPE EXE and can simply be set to 0 or not specified at all in the MMP file.

3.10.3 UID3

The third UID value identifies a file uniquely. No two executables may have the same UID3 value, and values must be requested from Symbian, which allocates them from a central database to ensure that each binary has a different value. You must register with Symbian Signed (*www.symbiansigned.com*) to request values for use as UID3 values in production code, but you can assign yourself a value from the development range ($0xE1000000-0xEFFFFFFF$) for test code.

3.11 Platform Security: Capabilities

Platform security on Symbian OS v9 prevents applications from having unauthorized access to hardware, software and system or user data. The intention is to prevent malware, or even just badly written code, from compromising the operation of the phone, corrupting or stealing confidential user data, or adversely affecting the phone network.

Every Symbian OS process is assigned a level of privilege through a set of capabilities which are like tokens. A capability grants a process the trust that it will not abuse the services associated with the associated privilege. The Symbian OS kernel holds a list of capabilities for every running process and checks it before allowing a process to access a protected service.

The Symbian OS software installer verifies the digital signature of software at install time to ensure that it is authorized to use the capabilities it was built with, and the digital signature can only come from a trusted authority. This prevents applications from arbitrarily assigning themselves the capabilities they want prior to installation.

There are 20 capabilities in Symbian OS (see Table 3.4). You can check the capabilities needed for a certain API from the SDK Help. An application must define the capabilities it is going to use by including them in its MMP file. For example:

```
CAPABILITY UserEnvironment NetworkServices
```

This statement means that the application uses two capabilities, `UserEnvironment` and `NetworkServices`.

There are four different types of platform security capability, when digital signing is considered. The differences arise because of the sensitivity of the data or system resources the capabilities protect, and the requirements that are placed on the developer before they are given permission to use them. Please refer to Chapter 6 for more information about Symbian Signed, the scheme that performs digital signing on commercial software, to grant platform security capabilities to developers.

The capabilities of a process cannot be changed at runtime. The Symbian OS loader starts a process by reading the executable and checking the capabilities it has been assigned. Once the process starts running, it cannot change its capabilities, nor can the loader or any other process or DLL that loads into it affect the capability set of the process.

Table 3.4 Platform Security Capabilities on Symbian OS

Capability type	Capability name	Description	Signing options
User capabilities	LocalServices Location NetworkServices ReadUserData UserEnvironment WriteUserData	Symbian signing is not essential if these capabilities are used – the user is instead able to grant permissions to applications that use the capabilities, although they will be warned that the software is untrusted. (*Warning*: Different device manufacturers may have different policies.)	Self-signing. All signing options from Symbian Signed.
System capabilities	PowerMgmt ProtServ ReadDeviceData SurroundingsDD SwEvent TrustedUI WriteDeviceData	System capabilities that protect system services, device settings and some hardware features.	All signing options from Symbian Signed. No self-signing is allowed.
Restricted system capabilities	CommDD DiskAdmin NetworkControl MultimediaDD	System capabilities that protect file system, communications and multimedia device services.	Open Signing with Publisher ID and Certified Signed only.
Device manufacturer capabilities	AllFiles DRM TCB	Capabilities that require device manufacturers' approval.	Requires approval from device manufacturers.

For Symbian OS DLLs, capabilities are also declared in the MMP file, but they have a different meaning: they represent to a loading process the amount of trust that can be placed in a DLL. An EXE cannot load a DLL if it possesses more capabilities than the DLL, because then the DLL may not be trustworthy to run securely within the process. A process can only load a DLL if that DLL is trusted with at least the same capabilities as that process.

However, a process can load a DLL which has been assigned more capabilities than itself, but that DLL will only be allowed to use the capabilities of the process in which it runs – it doesn't add trust to the process. This means that DLL code cannot assume it will always be running with the capabilities it needs, since these are dependent on the process it has been loaded into. If a DLL requires a particular capability, this should be clearly specified in its documentation.

3.12   Platform Security: Data Caging

The Symbian OS file system is partitioned to protect system files (critical to the operation of the phone), application data (to prevent other applications from stealing copyrighted content or accidentally corrupting data) and data files personal to the user (which should remain confidential). This partitioning is called data caging. It is not used on the entire file system; there are some public areas for which no capabilities are required. However, some directories in the file system can only be accessed using certain capabilities.

Table 3.5 shows how data caging is related to capabilities.

Table 3.5 Data Caging and Capabilities

Directory		Capabilities			
		None	**AllFiles**	**TCB**	**AllFiles+TCB**
\resource	Read	✓	✓	✓	✓
	Write	×	×	✓	✓
\sys	Read	×	✓	×	✓
	Write	×	×	✓	✓
\private\<ownSID>	Read	✓	✓	✓	✓
	Write	✓	✓	✓	✓
\private\<otherSID>	Read	×	✓	×	✓
	Write	×	✓	×	✓
\<anyOther>	Read	✓	✓	✓	✓
	Write	✓	✓	✓	✓

Each Symbian OS process has its own private folder, which can be created on internal memory or removable media. The folder name is based on the Secure Identifier (SID) of the process. A SID is required to identify each EXE on the phone and is used to create its private directory. The SID is similar to the UID3 identifier described in Section 3.10.3, and the default value of the SID is the UID3 value if a SID is not explicitly specified by use of the SECUREID keyword in the MMP file. It is usually recommended not to specify a SID, but simply allow it to default to the UID3 value as assigned by Symbian Signed.

3.13   Stack Size and Heap Size

On Symbian OS, by default, the default stack size for an application is 8 KB. However, it can be adjusted by using the EPOCSTACKSIZE keyword in the project's MMP file. For example:

```
EPOCSTACKSIZE 0x5000
```

The statement above changes the stack size of the executable to 20 KB (0 × 5000 bytes in hexadecimal or 20,480 byes in decimal). The maximum stack size is 80 KB.

The default minimum heap size for an application is 4 KB. The default maximum heap size is 1 MB. Both can be adjusted, again in the project's MMP file, using the macro EPOCHEAPSIZE. For example:

```
EPOCHEAPSIZE 0x5000 0x100000
```

The statement above changes the default minimum heap size to 20 KB (0 × 5000 bytes) and the maximum heap size to 1 MB (0 × 10000 bytes). What does it mean?

- The process cannot be started if the available memory is less than 20 KB.

- The process cannot consume heap memory more than 1 MB.

3.14 Streams

A stream in Symbian OS is the object's external representation. The process of storing the object's data into the stream is called *externalization*, and the opposite mechanism – *internalization* – reads the data from a stream and reconstructs an object as appropriate. Streams are quite useful for storing simple data structures, and a stream may contain the data of one or more objects.

There are two base classes, which implement the concept of the streaming functionality: RReadStream and RWriteStream. These classes provide a set of methods to read and write operations for built-in integer and real types as well as for descriptors. They also have operators >> and <<, respectively, for internalizing and externalizing data. Please note that after creating the stream, you should call the stream's PushL() method rather than CleanupStack::PushL(), if you need to push it to the cleanup stack in order to make it leave-safe.

Symbian OS has several concrete implementations of those stream base classes – each of them works with specific media; for instance, files, descriptors or memory buffers. They always exist in pairs: one for reading and one for writing. The following list gives you an idea of some of the available stream classes:

- RFileReadStream

- RFileWriteStream

- RDesReadStream

- RDesWriteStream

- RBufReadStream

- RBufWriteStream

- RMemReadStream

- RMemWriteStream.

You should consult the API documentation for each class in the Symbian Developer Library.

3.14.1 Externalize and Internalize

For an object to be written to a stream, its class must implement an ExternalizeL() method, while for an object to be read from a stream, its class must implement an InternalizeL() method.

Here is an example of a class which supports both internalization and externalization:

```
#include <s32mem.h>

class CSampleClass : public CBase
  {
public:
  ...
  void ExternalizeL(RWriteStream& aStream) const;
  void InternalizeL(RReadStream& aStream);
  ...
private:
  TInt iIntVal;
  TBuf<64> iBuffer;
  };
```

```
// Assume we have the code for the rest of the class
void CSampleClass::ExternalizeL(RWriteStream& aStream) const
  {
  aStream.WriteInt32L(iIntVal);
  aStream << iBuffer;
  }

void CSampleClass::InternalizeL(RReadStream& aStream)
  {
  iIntVal = aStream.ReadInt32L();
  aStream >> iBuffer;
  }
...
void SampleFuncL(TAny* aMemPtr, TInt aMaxLen)
  {
  RBuf buf;
  buf.CreateL(64);
  buf.CleanupClosePushL();
```

```
buf.Append(KSampleBuffer1);

CSampleClass* objVar = CSampleClass::NewLC(1,buf);

RMemWriteStream writer;
writer.PushL();
writer.Open(aMemPtr, aMaxLen);
writer << *objVar;
writer.CommitL();
CleanupStack::PopAndDestroy(&writer);

...

// Later on, read it into new object
buf = KSampleBuffer2;
CSampleClass* objVar2 = CSampleClass::NewLC(2,buf);
RMemReadStream reader;
reader.PushL();
reader.Open(aMemPtr,aMaxLen);
reader >> *objVar2;

CleanupStack::PopAndDestroy(4);
}
```

> **Tip:** Please note that a stream's operators << and >> leave, so you have to handle this fact in your code.

It could be very inefficient to externalize a modifiable descriptor when its current length is well below its maximum length. However, `HBufC::NewL()` has an overload that takes a `RReadStream` and is recommended.

3.15 Active Objects

Active objects are used for lightweight event-driven multitasking on Symbian OS, and are fundamental for responsive and efficient event handling. They are used in preference to threads to minimize the number of thread context switches that occur, and make efficient use of system resources. This section describes what active objects are, how to use them, and how to avoid the most common programming errors that can occur.

Symbian OS uses event-driven code extensively for user interaction (which has a non-deterministic completion time) and in system code, for example for asynchronous communications. An event-driven system is important on a battery-powered device. The alternative to responding to events is for the submitter of an asynchronous event to keep polling to check if a request has completed. On a mobile operating system this can lead to significant power drain because a tight polling loop prevents the OS from powering down all but the most essential resources.

The 'active object framework' is used on Symbian OS to simplify asynchronous programming. It is used to handle multiple asynchronous tasks in the same thread and provides a consistent way to write code to submit asynchronous requests and handle completion events.

A Symbian OS application or server will usually consist of a single main event-handling thread with an associated active scheduler that runs a loop waiting on completion events. The events are generated by asynchronous services encapsulated in active objects, each with an event-handling function that the active scheduler calls if the request associated with the active object completes.[1] So, when the asynchronous service associated with an active object completes, it generates an event, which is detected by the active scheduler. The active scheduler determines which active object is associated with the event, and calls the appropriate active object to handle the event.

> **Tip:** An active object encapsulates a task; it requests an asynchronous service from a service provider and handles the completion event later when the active scheduler calls it.

Within a single application thread, active objects run independently of each other, similar to the way that threads are independent of each other in a process. A switch between active objects in a single thread incurs a lower overhead than a thread context switch, described shortly, which is ideal for lightweight event-driven multitasking on Symbian OS.

3.15.1 Preemption

Within a single thread, the active object framework uses non-preemptive multitasking. Once invoked, an event handler must run to completion before any other active object's event handler can run – it cannot be preempted.

Some events strictly require a response within a guaranteed time, regardless of any other activity in the system (e.g., low-level telephony). This is called 'real-time' event handling. Active objects are not suitable for real-time tasks and on Symbian OS real-time tasks should be implemented using high-priority threads. Symbian OS threads are scheduled *preemptively* by the kernel, which runs the highest-priority thread eligible. The

---

[1] Windows programmers may recognize the pattern of message loop and message dispatch which drives a Win32 application. The active scheduler takes the place of the Windows message loop and the event-handling function of an active object acts as the message handler.

kernel controls thread scheduling, allowing the threads to share system resources by time-slice division, preempting the running of a thread if another, higher-priority thread becomes eligible to run.

A *context switch* occurs when the current thread is suspended (for example, if it becomes blocked, has reached the end of its time-slice, or a higher-priority thread becomes ready to run) and another thread is made current by the kernel scheduler. The context switch incurs a runtime overhead in terms of the kernel scheduler and, if the original and replacing threads are executing in different processes, the memory management unit and hardware caches.

3.15.2   Class `CActive`

An active object class must derive directly or indirectly from class `CActive`, defined in `e32base.h`. `CActive` is an abstract class with two pure virtual functions, `RunL()` and `DoCancel()`.

Construction

On construction, classes deriving from `CActive` must call the protected constructor of the base class, passing in a parameter to set the priority of the active object. Like threads, all active objects have a priority value to determine how they are scheduled. As the previous subsection described, once an active object is handling an event, it cannot be preempted until the event-handler function has returned back to the active scheduler. During this time, a number of completion events may occur. When the active scheduler next gets to run, it must resolve which active object gets to run next. It would not be desirable for a low-priority active object to handle its event if a higher-priority active object was also waiting, so events are handled sequentially in order of the highest priority rather than in order of completion.

In its constructor, the active object should also add itself to the active scheduler by calling `CActiveScheduler::Add()`.

Making a request and handling its completion in `RunL()`

Figure 3.3 illustrates the basic sequence of actions performed when an active object submits a request to an asynchronous service provider. An active object class supplies public methods that submit such a request, for which the standard behavior is as follows.

1.   Check for outstanding requests.
     An active object must never have more than one outstanding request, so before attempting to submit a request, the active object must check to see if it is already waiting on completion.

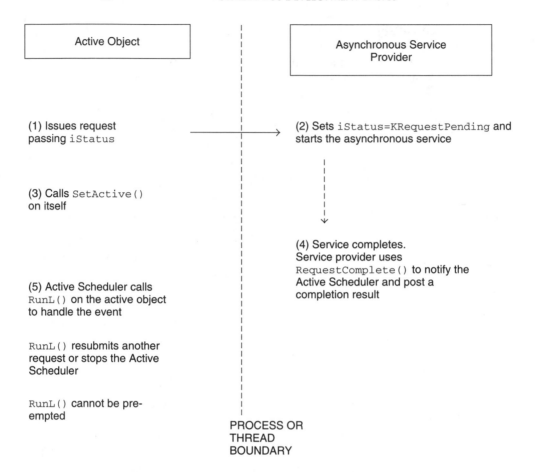

Figure 3.3   A Request to an Asynchronous Service Provider, which Generates an Event on Completion

2. Submit the request.
    The active object submits a request to the service provider, passing
    in the TRequestStatus member variable (iStatus). The service
    provider must set this value to KRequestPending before initiating
    the asynchronous request.

3. Call SetActive() to mark the object as 'waiting'.
    A call to CActive::SetActive() indicates that a request has
    been submitted and is currently outstanding. This call should not be
    made until after the request has been submitted.

Each active object class must implement the pure virtual RunL()
method inherited from the CActive base class. This is the event handler method called by the active scheduler when a completion event
occurs.

RunL() should check whether the asynchronous request succeeded by inspecting its completion code, which is the 32-bit integer value store in the TRequestStatus object (iStatus) of the active object. The complexity of RunL() code can vary considerably, but since RunL() cannot be preempted by other active objects' event handlers while it is running, it should complete as quickly as possible so that other events can be handled without delay.

DoCancel()

An active object must be able to cancel an outstanding asynchronous request. An active object class must implement the pure virtual Do-Cancel() method of the base class to terminate a request by calling the appropriate cancellation method on the asynchronous service provider. DoCancel() must not leave or allocate resources and should not carry out any lengthy operations, but simply cancel the request and perform any associated cleanup.

CActive::Cancel() calls DoCancel() and waits for notification that the request has terminated. Cancel() must be called whenever a request is to be terminated, not DoCancel(), since the base class method checks whether a request is outstanding and performs the necessary wait until it has terminated.

RunError()

The CActive base class provides a virtual RunError() method which the active scheduler calls if RunL() leaves. If the leave can be handled, this should be done by overriding the default implementation of CActive::RunError() to handle the exception.

Destruction

The destructor of a CActive-derived class should always call Cancel() to cancel any outstanding requests. The CActive base-class destructor checks that the active object is not currently active. It panics with E32USER-CBASE 40 if any request is outstanding; that is, if Cancel() has not been called. This catches any programming errors where a call to Cancel() has been forgotten. Having verified that the active object has no issued requests outstanding, the CActive destructor removes the active object from the active scheduler.

The reason it is so important to cancel requests before destroying an active object is that otherwise the request would complete after the active object had been destroyed. This would cause a 'stray signal' because the active scheduler is unable to find a handler for the event. This results in a panic (E32USER-CBASE 46).

3.15.3 Class `TRequestStatus`

One of the most ubiquitous classes of Symbian OS is `TRequestStatus`. It is used for all kinds of purposes: synchronization, multithreading, multiprocessing, system interaction and asynchronous calls.

A `TRequestStatus` object is basically a thread-specific rendezvous object. One Symbian OS thread can wait for another using `User::WaitForRequest()`, passing in a `TRequestStatus` object. Likewise, one thread can notify another using `User::RequestComplete()`.

Each thread can only wait on one `TRequestStatus` at any time. The exception to this rule is `User::WaitForAnyRequest()`, which makes the thread wait for any completion event.

Each Symbian OS thread keeps track of how many of its requests were completed, so that if it waits on one request (A) while another request (B) is completed, the completion information is retained and the next call to `User::WaitForRequest(B)` will return immediately.

Each `TRequestStatus` also contains an integer instance variable, which is set to `KRequestPending` just before calling `User::WaitForRequest()`, either directly or through a call to an API that calls an asynchronous method, such as those provided by Symbian OS.

When a request is completed, the instance variable allows some inter-thread information transfer, usually an error code or `KErrNone`.

3.15.4 The Active Scheduler

Most threads running on Symbian OS have an active scheduler, which is usually created and started implicitly by a framework (for example, CONE for the GUI framework). There is only one active scheduler created per thread, although it can be nested in advanced cases.

Console-based test code must create an active scheduler in its main thread if it depends on components which use active objects. The code to do this is as follows:

```
CActiveScheduler* scheduler = new(ELeave) CActiveScheduler;
CleanupStack::PushL(scheduler);
CActiveScheduler::Install(scheduler);
```

Once the active scheduler has been created and installed, its event-processing wait loop must be started by calling `CActiveScheduler::Start()`. The event-processing loop starts and does not return until a call is made to `CActiveScheduler::Stop()`. For implementation reasons, there must be at least one asynchronous request issued before the loop starts, otherwise the thread simply enters the wait loop indefinitely. Let's look at why this happens in more detail by examining the active scheduler wait loop:

1. When it is not handling other completion events, the active scheduler suspends a thread by calling `User::WaitForAnyRequest()`, which waits for a signal to the thread's request semaphore.

2. If no events are outstanding in the system entirely, it is at this point that the OS can power down to sleep.

3. When an asynchronous server has finished with a request, it indicates completion by calling `User::RequestComplete()` (if the service provider and requestor are in the same thread) or `RThread::RequestComplete()` otherwise. The `TRequestStatus` associated with the request is passed into the `RequestComplete()` method along with a completion result, typically one of the standard error codes.

4. The `RequestComplete()` method sets the value of `TRequestStatus` to the given error code and generates a completion event in the requesting thread by signaling a semaphore.

5. When a signal is received and the thread is next scheduled, the active scheduler determines which active object should handle it. It checks the priority-ordered list of active objects for those with outstanding requests (these have their `iActive` Boolean set to `ETrue` as a result of calling `CActive::SetActive()`).

6. If an object has an outstanding request, the active scheduler checks its `iStatus` member variable to see if it is set to a value other than `KRequestPending`. If so, this indicates that the active object is associated with the completion event and that the event handler code should be called.

7. The active scheduler clears the active object's `iActive` Boolean and calls its `RunL()` event handler.

8. Once the `RunL()` call has finished, the active scheduler re-enters the event processing wait loop by issuing another `User::WaitForAnyRequest()` call. This checks the thread's request semaphore and either suspends it (if no other events need handling) or returns immediately to lookup and event handling.

The following pseudo-code illustrates the event-processing loop:

```
EventProcessingLoop()
  {
  // Suspend the thread until an event occurs
  User::WaitForAnyRequest();
  // Thread wakes when the request semaphore is signaled
  // Inspect each active object added to the scheduler,
  // in order of decreasing priority
  // Call the event handler of the first which is active & completed
```

```
FOREVER
  {
  // Get the next active object in the priority queue
  if (activeObject->IsActive())&&
     (activeObject->iStatus!=KRequestPending)
    {// Found an active object ready to handle an event
    // Reset the iActive status to indicate it is not active
    activeObject->iActive = EFalse;
    // Call the active object's event handler in a TRAP
    TRAPD(r, activeObject->RunL());
    if (KErrNone!=r)
      {// event handler left, call RunError() on active object
      r = activeObject->RunError();
      if (KErrNone!=r) // RunError() didn't handle the error,
        Error(r);      // call CActiveScheduler::Error()
      }
    break; // Event handled, break out of lookup loop and resume
    }
  } // End of FOREVER loop
}
```

3.15.5   Common Problems with Active Objects

Stray signal panics

The most common problem when writing active objects is when you encounter a stray signal panic (E32USER-CBASE 46). These occur when an active scheduler receives a completion event but cannot find an active object to handle it. Stray signal panics are notoriously extremely difficult to debug. Stray signals can occur because:

- CActiveScheduler::Add() was not called when the active object was constructed.

- SetActive() was not called after submitting a request to an asynchronous service provider. You usually only need to add the active object to the active scheduler once, however, it is common to reuse an active object several times to make several asynchronous requests and it needs to be reactivated every single time.

- The asynchronous service provider completed the request more than once, which is unlikely when using a Symbian OS system server, but conceivable when using a third-party server.

If you receive a stray signal panic, the first thing to do is work out which active object is responsible for submitting the request that later generates the stray event. One of the best ways to do this is to use file logging in every active object and, if necessary, eliminate them from your code one by one until the culprit is tracked down.

Unresponsive UI

In an application thread, in particular, event-handler methods must be kept short to allow the UI to remain responsive to the user. No single active object should have a monopoly on the active scheduler since that prevents other active objects from handling events. Active objects must cooperate and should not:

- Have lengthy `RunL()` or `DoCancel()` methods.

- Repeatedly resubmit requests that complete rapidly, particularly if the active object has a high priority, because the event handler will be invoked at the expense of lower-priority active objects waiting to be handled.

- Have a higher priority than is necessary.

Other causes of an unresponsive UI are temporary or permanent thread blocks that result because of:

- A call to `User::After()`, which stops the thread executing for the length of time specified.

- Incorrect use of the active scheduler. There must be at least one asynchronous request issued, via an active object, before the active scheduler starts. If no request is outstanding, the thread simply enters the wait loop and sleeps indefinitely.

- Incorrect use of `User::WaitForRequest()` to wait on an asynchronous request, rather than correct use of the active object framework.

3.16   Threads

In many cases on Symbian OS, it is preferable to use active objects rather than threads, since these are optimized for event-driven multitasking on the platform. However, when you are porting code written for other platforms, or writing code with real-time requirements, it is often necessary to write multithreaded code. The Symbian OS class used to manipulate threads is `RThread`, which represents a handle to a thread; the thread itself is a kernel object.

The `RThread` class defines several functions for thread creation, each of which takes a descriptor for the thread's name, a pointer to a function in which thread execution starts, a pointer to data to be passed to that function (if any), and the stack size of the thread. `RThread::Create()` is overloaded to allow for different heap behavior, such as definition of the thread's maximum and minimum heap size or whether it shares the creating thread's heap or uses a separate heap.

A thread is created in the suspended state and its execution initiated by calling `RThread::Resume()`. On Symbian OS, threads are preemptively scheduled and the currently running thread is the highest-priority thread ready to run. If there are two or more threads with equal priority, they are time-sliced on a round-robin basis. A running thread can be removed from the scheduler's ready-to-run queue by a call to `RThread::Suspend()`. It can be restarted by calling `Resume()`. To terminate a thread permanently, you should call `Kill()` or `Terminate()` – to stop it normally – and `Panic()` to highlight a programming error.

Please see the Symbian Developer Library for more information about working with Symbian OS threads. Example code is also provided in the SDK to show the use of `RThread` and other Symbian OS system classes.

3.17 Timers and Callbacks

The `RTimer` class provides a very useful service and one of the simplest ways of making an asynchronous request is to use an active object: `RTimer::After()` is the asynchronous request and `RTimer::Cancel()` is used to cancel the request if, for example, the application is closed before the kernel completes the request.

`RTimer::AtUTC()` is a good way to implement alarms on your phone and `RTimer::Inactivity()` can be used both to save battery life and to prevent the phone's keyboard and screen from locking.

Another useful class is `TCallback`, which is really just a fancy way of saying 'method pointer'. Actually, `TCallback` can only represent a static non-leaving method that must return an integer and have exactly one pointer parameter, which can be cast to a known type in order to access its methods.

`TCallback` is used by two different specialized active objects that regenerate their own asynchronous requests: `CPeriodic` and `CIdle`. Both of them will be reactivated by the time their `RunL()` method returns. In both cases, `RunL()` is already overwritten and calls the `TCallback` you define.

`CPeriodic::Start()` uses a kernel timer to decide when its request will be completed.

`CIdle` is a fairly strange exception amongst active objects: its request is not really asynchronous as it is already completed by the time `CIdle::Start()` returns. There would still be a delay before `CIdle::RunL()` is called, though, since it has to be called from the active scheduler's main loop.

One thing to notice about `CIdle` is that it will not regenerate its request if the `TCallback` method returns 0.

3.18   Summary

Now you've seen the essentials of Symbian C++, you should be confident with the fundamental idioms and concepts. So it's time to move on to the good stuff. The next chapter will list some 'recipes' for common tasks when working on Symbian OS. If you need further information about anything you've read in this chapter, or want to find out more, please visit this book's wiki page (***developer.symbian.com/quickrecipesbook***) for links to additional documentation.

4

Symbian C++ Recipes

This chapter forms the major part of the book. It contains ten sections, each of which contain recipes to guide your development, step by step. The following subjects are described in the numbered sections below:

4.1   File Handling

4.2   Contacts and Calendar

4.3   Networking

4.4   Messaging

4.5   Graphics and Drawing

4.6   3D Graphics Using OpenGL ES

4.7   Multimedia

4.8   Telephony

4.9   Connectivity

4.10 Location-Based Services

Each recipe lists some preliminary information, as follows:

Amount of time required:
The amount of time to read the recipe, reflect on the major points in the snippets of example code shown in the book, and examine the full code sample (which can be downloaded from ***developer. symbian.com/quickrecipesbook***).
Location of example code: (e.g., \Files)
This is the location in the set of example codes in which you can find the example code associated with the recipe.

Required library(s): (e.g., `efsrv.lib`)
A code project must link to this Symbian library in order for the code shown in the recipe to be successfully linked. You can either add the library to the MMP file, using the `LIBRARY` keyword, or add it using the MMP editor in the Carbide.c++ IDE. We always assume that your code project links to the Symbian OS user library (`euser.lib`) – since every recipe requires it – and do not list it below.

Required header file(s): (e.g., `f32file.h`)
The Symbian OS system header file required to access the APIs discussed in the recipe. Unless otherwise stated, the header file will be in the `\epoc32\include` directory of your SDK installation.

Required platform security capability(s): (e.g., `ReadUserData`)
Please see Chapter 3, Section 3.11, for more information about platform security capabilities.

Each recipe then presents the problem you are trying to solve, and provides a solution and further discussion. We have also highlighted some potential issues and gotchas, and given you some advanced tips where appropriate.

4.1 File Handling

Almost all applications require access to the smartphone's file system. Many applications need to store a user's settings; for example, a game may need to store high-score data; a customizable dictionary application needs to store word entries. This section contains file system-related recipes, such as reading from and writing to the file.

Symbian OS has a file server to handle all file-related aspects, such as creating, renaming, deleting and accessing files, creating and removing directories, and receiving change notifications when the file system is modified. An application uses the client-side file server API to send requests to the file server. The recipes in this section discuss the file server API in detail.

Symbian OS uses a VFAT (Virtual File Allocation Table) file system. VFAT supports long filenames, up to 255 characters in length. The filenames are not case-sensitive, which means 'c:\data\test.dat' is the same as 'C:\DATA\test.DAT'.

Like many other VFAT operating systems, a filename in Symbian OS consists of:

- a drive letter
- a path
- a filename
- an extension (optional).

On Symbian OS, a filename and its extension are separated by a period character (.). The drive letter and the path are separated by a backslash character (\), and the path and the filename are also separated by a backslash character (\). However, when quoting path specifiers in a Symbian OS descriptor that describes a file path, you must use double backslashes (\\).

A drive letter can be labeled from A: to Z:, where C: is always the phone's internal memory and Z: is always the ROM drive. Other drives may be used differently by manufacturers. For example, most S60 devices use the E: drive for the external memory card or hard drive. Most UIQ devices use the D: drive for the external media.

4.1.1 Easy Recipes

4.1.1.1 Get a File Server Session

Amount of time required: 10 minutes
Location of example code: \Files
Required library(s): efsrv.lib
Required header file(s): f32file.h
Required platform security capability(s): None

Problem: You want to get a handle to a file server session.

Solution: The file server handles all aspects related to files. It runs in its own process, EFILE.EXE. To call any API relating to file operations, you need a handle to a file server session, and must use class RFs, which is declared in f32file.h. The library name is efsrv.lib.

There are two common ways of getting a file server session:

- Connect to the file server by calling RFs::Connect().

```
RFs fileServer;
User::LeaveIfError(fileServer.Connect());

// Use the file server session here
// ...

fileServer.Close();
```

- A GUI application can use a file server session owned by the CCoeEnv class. The following code shows how to get a file server session from CCoeEnv:

```
RFs& fileServer = iCoeEnv->FsSession();
```

Note that the code has to be written in any class that defines iCoeEnv as its member variables. Examples of such classes are CEik-Application, CCoeAppUi and CCoeControl.

If you are writing code that runs inside the application framework, within a class that does not have the iCoeEnv variable, you can use CCoeEnv::Static() to access CCoeEnv. For example:

```
RFs& fileServer = CCoeEnv::Static()->FsSession();
```

4.1.1.2   Write Binary Data to a File

Amount of time required: 15 minutes
Location of example code: \Files\BinaryFile
Required library(s): efsrv.lib
Required header file(s): f32file.h
Required platform security capability(s): None

Problem: You want to write binary data to a file.

Solution: The basic operation to write binary data to a file uses the RFile class, which is a class that handles low-level file operations. The method of RFile that is used to write binary data is RFile::Write(). There are several variants of Write() methods, which can be divided into two categories:

- Synchronous requests (i.e., blocking).
- Asynchronous requests (i.e., complete some time later).

For each category, there are variants that allow us to write binary data with a specific length and/or from a specific position.

The binary data in Symbian OS is normally stored in an 8-bit descriptor. Specifically, it is stored in one of the TDesC8-derived classes, that is, TBufC8, HBufC8 or RBuf8. Please refer to Chapter 3 for an introduction to descriptors.

The following example shows how to write binary data in a descriptor to a file:

```
void CBinaryFileAppUi::WriteDesCToFileL(RFs& aFs,
    const TDesC& aFileName, const TDesC8& aBuffer)
{
RFile file;
User::LeaveIfError(file.Replace(aFs, aFileName, EFileWrite));
CleanupClosePushL(file);

User::LeaveIfError(file.Write(aBuffer, aBuffer.Length()));

CleanupStack::PopAndDestroy(&file);
}
```

Discussion: The `aFileName` parameter is the filename where we want to write the descriptor. The filename is in the format 'x:\directory\filename.extension'.

What may go wrong when you do this: Some directories in Symbian OS require special capabilities for read/write access. For example, you need TCB capability to write to the \resource directory. Please refer to Chapter 3 for more information about data caging.

The `RFile::Replace()` method overwrites an eventual existing file. If you don't want to overwrite an existing file, use the `RFile::Create()` method instead. It returns an error code, `KErrAlreadyExists` (-11), if the file already exists, in which case you should use `RFile::Open()` to open the existing file and write into it.

Notice that the file is pushed to the cleanup stack using `Cleanup ClosePushL()`. It means `PopAndDestroy()` will also close the file. It will not destroy the file or its contents, as the name could imply!

What may go wrong when you do this: Remember to always check the return value of any `RFile` methods, such as `Replace()` and `Write()`. If you don't check, your application may panic later. The complete list of Symbian OS error codes can be found at \epoc32\include\e32err.h.

You can check the error using a standard `if` statement and then display a dialog when an error happens.

```
TInt err = file.Replace(aFs, aFileName, EFileWrite);
if (KErrPathNotFound == err)
  {
  // Do something when path is not found,
  // for example display dialog to the user.
  }
```

Alternatively, you can use `User::LeaveIfError()`, as in the previous snippet.

The following code shows how to call the `WriteDesCToFileL()` function:

```
// CONSTANTS
const TInt KMaxBuffer = 512;
_LIT(KNewFileName,     "c:\\data\\newfile.dat");

...
```

```
RFs& fileServer = iCoeEnv->FsSession();

// Create a buffer to be written to the file.
RBuf8 buffer;
User::LeaveIfError(buffer.CreateMax(KMaxBuffer));
CleanupClosePushL(buffer);

// Fill the buffer with your data.
// ...

// Write buffer to the file.
WriteDesCToFileL(fileServer, KNewFileName, buffer);

// Delete the buffer.
CleanupStack::PopAndDestroy(&buffer);
```

The example above uses a public folder, c:\data, to store the data. Note that this folder is not protected using data caging (see Chapter 3). It means any other application can access it. If you want to protect your data, use the \private\<SID> folder, where SID is the secure identifier for your application (see Chapter 3, Section 3.12 for more information).

Tip: The default file manager from S60 or UIQ phones cannot browse through all folders on the phone. The default S60 file manager can only browse the c:\data folder. The default UIQ file manager can only browser the c:\Media files folder.

If you want to browse all folders on the phone, you will need a third-party file manager. The following are available for S60 and UIQ:

- Active File – see *developer.symbian.com/wiki/display/pub/File+Browsers*.

- SwissManager – a free file manager for UIQ, *www.cellphonesoft.com*.

- SysExplorer – a free file manager that supports S60 and UIQ, *www.newlc.com*.

- Y-Browser – a free file manager for S60, *www.drjukka.com*.

4.1.1.3   Read Binary Data from a File

Amount of time required: 15 minutes
Location of example code: \Files\BinaryFile
Required library(s): efsrv.lib
Required header file(s): f32file.h
Required platform security capability(s): None

Problem: You want to read binary data from a file.

> **What may go wrong when you do this:** The drive letter for the memory card can differ between devices. For example, most S60 devices use E: as the drive letter for the memory card, while many UIQ devices use D:. There are some devices that have a hard disk.
>
> You can check the drive type using the `RFs::Drive()` method. For example:
>
> ```
> TDriveInfo driveInfo;
> User::LeaveIfError(iCoeEnv->FsSession().Drive(driveInfo, EDriveE));
> ```
>
> On return, `driveInfo.iType` will have the type of drive E:. It will have the value of `EMediaHardDisk` if drive E: is the memory card or hard disk. If drive E: is not available, it will have the value of `EMediaNotPresent`.

Solution: You can use the `RFile` class to read binary data. There are several variants of the `RFile::Read()` method for different purposes. In general, there are two types: synchronous and asynchronous. For each type, there are variants to write the entire descriptor or with specific length and/or from a specific index.

The following example shows how to read the binary data from the file:

```
void CBinaryFileAppUi::ReadDesCFromFileL(RFs& aFs,
      const TDesC& aFileName, TDes8& aBuffer)
  {
  RFile file;
  User::LeaveIfError(file.Open(aFs, aFileName, EFileRead));
  CleanupClosePushL(file);

  // Get the file size.
  TInt fileSize;
  User::LeaveIfError(file.Size(fileSize));

  // If the maximum length of the buffer is less than the file size,
  // it means we don't have enough space.
  if (aBuffer.MaxLength() < fileSize)
    {
    User::Leave(KErrOverflow);
    }
  User::LeaveIfError(file.Read(aBuffer, fileSize));

  CleanupStack::PopAndDestroy(&file); // file
  }
```

Discussion: The `ReadDesCFromFileL()` method reads the contents of a file, `aFileName`, into a buffer, `aBuffer`. Note that `aBuffer` must have enough space to hold the entire contents of the file.

The `RFile::Open()` method can return error codes such as `KErr-NotFound` (-1) when the file cannot be found or `KErrPathNotFound` (-12) when the path cannot be found. For a complete list of error codes, please check `\epoc32\include\e32err.h`.

The file size information is needed to read the file to the buffer. It is also used to check whether the buffer has enough space to hold the data.

Note that this function reads the whole contents of the file at once. It is not recommended to do it this way if the file is large. The application will block at the `RFile::Read()` method. The user interface will not be responsive during that period.

Besides, this method creates a buffer that has the same size as the file size. For a large file, you may end up in an out-of-memory situation.

A better way of handling a large file is by creating an active object and using the asynchronous overload of `RFile::Read()`.

Using the `ReadDesCFromFileL()` function and the `WriteDesCTo-FileL()` from the previous recipe, we can write a simple copying program. Here is an example:

```
RFs& fileServer = iCoeEnv->FsSession();

// Create a new buffer
RBuf8 buffer;
User::LeaveIfError(buffer.CreateMax(KMaxBuffer));
CleanupClosePushL(buffer);

// Read from the file.
// We have to make sure that the buffer has enough space,
// otherwise it will panic.
ReadDesCFromFileL(fileServer, KSourceFileName, buffer);

// Write the buffer to a file.
WriteDesCToFileL(fileServer, KDestFileName, buffer);

// Delete the buffer.
CleanupStack::PopAndDestroy(&buffer);
```

You can do many interesting things by modifying the buffer after reading but before writing. For example:

- Replace characters with some other characters, such as replace '<' with '<'.

- Insert or delete some characters.

- Encrypt or compress the buffer.

> **Tip:** You can copy a file using a method called `CFileMan::Copy()`.
> For example:
>
> ```
> CFileMan* fileMan = CFileMan::NewL(fileServer);
> CleanupStack::PushL(fileMan);
> fileMan->Copy(KOrgFileName, KNewFileName, CFileMan::EOverWrite);
> CleanupStack::PopAndDestroy(fileMan);
> ```

4.1.1.4   Read Text from a File

Amount of time required: 15 minutes
Location of example code: `\Files\TextFile`
Required library(s): `efsrv.lib`
Required header file(s): `f32file.h`
Required platform security capability(s): None

Problem: You want to read a text file.

Solution: A text file is basically a file that has an EOL (End-Of-Line) delimiter that separates one line from another. The delimiter that is commonly used in Symbian OS is the LF (`0x0A`) character, which is the same as on a UNIX platform. Note that it is different from Windows, which uses CR LF (`0x0D 0x0A`). On Symbian OS, a text file is usually stored in Unicode format.

The class to read/write a text file is `TFileText`. It is declared in the `f32file.h` header file and the library name is `efsrv.lib`.

Before using `TFileText`, you have to open a file using `RFile` because the `TFileText` class does not have an `Open()` method.

There are two basic methods in `TTextFile`; that is, `Read()` and `Write()`. Both of them require a 16-bit descriptor parameter because Symbian OS stores text files in Unicode format.

The following code shows how to read a text file:

```
void CTextFileAppUi::ReadFromTextFileL(RFs& aFs,
    const TDesC& aFileName)
{
// Open the file for reading.
RFile file;
User::LeaveIfError(file.Open(aFs, aFileName,
            EFileRead | EFileStreamText));
CleanupClosePushL(file);

// Create a new instance of TFileText that
```

```
// points to file.
TFileText fileText;
fileText.Set(file);

// Create a buffer to read the text file.
TBuf<KMaxBuffer> buffer;

// Loop to read the buffer.
// It reads the buffer until err is KErrEof,
// which means it reached the end of the file.
TInt err = KErrNone;
while (err != KErrEof)
  {
  err = fileText.Read(buffer);

  // If the error code is other than KErrNone
  // or KErrEof, leave this function.
  if ((err != KErrNone) && (err != KErrEof))
    {
    User::Leave(err);
    }

  if (KErrNone == err)
    {
    // Do something with the buffer.
    }
  }

CleanupStack::PopAndDestroy(&file);
}
```

Discussion:

> **Tip:** You can use `TFileText` to read a Unicode file that has CR LF or LF as delimiter. It is able to handle a file that contains BOM (*Byte-Order Mark*) as well.

Note the `EFileStreamText` flag, which indicates the opened file will be used as a text file. The end of file is indicated by the return value of `TFileText::Read()`, which is `KErrEof`.

> **What may go wrong when you do this:** Do not use `TFileText` to open a file other than Unicode. You will get garbage characters if trying to access non-Unicode files, such as ASCII files.

4.1.2 Intermediate Recipes

4.1.2.1 Get the Path of a Private Folder

Amount of time required: 15 minutes
Location of example code: `\Files\FileSharingCreator`

Required library(s): `efsrv.lib`
Required header file(s): `f32file.h`
Required platform security capability(s): None

Problem: Data caging provides protection to some special folders. One of them is the application's private folder. It is located at `\private\<SID>`, where `<SID>` is the secure identifier of the application. This folder is normally used by the application to store its own data, which cannot be accessed by other processes. Since `<SID>` depends on the secure identifier of the application, how do we get the path of the private folder at runtime?

Solution: The `RFs::PrivatePath()` method returns the private path in the format of '`\private\<SID>`'. For example, if the application has a secure identifier which is `0xA1234567`, then the private path will be '`\private\`
`A1234567`' (without '`0x`').

Discussion: How do we add a filename to the path? For example, we want to add '`myfile.dat`' at the end of the private path.

Furthermore, how do we add a drive letter that is the same as the application's drive letter? For example, if the application is installed on the E: drive, we want to access the private folder located at `e:\private\<SID>`.

Constructing a full filename can be done manually using descriptor methods, such as `TDes::Insert()` and `TDes::Append()`.

There is another way of constructing the filename, which is using the `TParse` class. This class is usually used to construct a filename based on its components. The construction is done with the method `TParse::Set()`:

```
IMPORT_C TInt Set(const TDesC& aName, const TDesC* aRelated,
                               const TDesC* aDefault);
```

The first parameter, `aName`, is the file specification to be parsed.

The second parameter, `aRelated`, is the related specification of `aName`. Any missing component, such as a path or filename, in the first parameter will be set to those in the second parameter. For example, if the first parameter contains the path only, you can set a drive letter using the second parameter. If there is no related specification, then set this parameter to `NULL`.

The third parameter is the default file specification. Like the second parameter, if a component has no value in the first and second parameters, it will be assigned the value in the third parameter.

Let's take a look at a real example to see how it works:

```
// Get the private path of the application.
RBuf privatePath;
privatePath.CreateL(KMaxFileName);
CleanupClosePushL(privatePath);
User::LeaveIfError(fs.PrivatePath(privatePath));

// Add name and extension to the path.
_LIT(KNameAndExt, "example.txt");
TParse parse;
// "\private<SID>\example.txt"
User::LeaveIfError(parse.Set(privatePath, 0, &KNameAndExt));
```

The filename after `Set()` will be '`\private\<SID>\example.txt`'. Notice that the first parameter, `privatePath`, contains no filename. Since there are no name and extension in this path, after calling `Set()`, they are assigned according to `KNameExt`.

The following code adds a drive letter to the private path:

```
// Get the private path of the application.
RBuf privatePath;
privatePath.CreateL(KMaxFileName);
CleanupClosePushL(privatePath);
User::LeaveIfError(fileServer.PrivatePath(privatePath));

// Add name and extension to the path.
_LIT(KNameAndExt, "c:example.txt");
TParse parse;
User::LeaveIfError(parse.Set(privatePath, 0, &KNameAndExt));
```

Tip: When creating a package file for software installation, you can specify '`!:`' as the drive letter in the PKG file. For example:

```
"myfile.dat"-"!:\private\A1234567\myfile.dat"
```

This means that the file will be installed to the drive selected by the user. It can be C: if the user selects the phone memory. It can be D: or E: if the user selects the memory card or hard drive.

That is why it is not recommended to use a hard-coded drive letter in the source code.

How do we add a drive letter that is the same as the application's drive letter? Firstly, we need to get the full path of the application and extract the drive letter from it:

```
// Get the private path of the application.
RBuf privatePath;
privatePath.CreateL(KMaxFileName);
CleanupClosePushL(privatePath);
User::LeaveIfError(fileServer.PrivatePath(privatePath));
```

```
// Get the application's full name.
TParsePtrC parseAppPath(Application()->AppFullName());

_LIT(KNameAndExt, "hello.txt");
TParse parse;
User::LeaveIfError(parse.Set(parseAppPath.Drive(), &privatePath,
                                                   NameAndExt));
```

Suppose that the application is installed on the E: drive and the SID of the application is 0xA1234567; parse will have the value of 'e:\private\A1234567\example.txt'.

The first two lines get the private path of the application. There is nothing special here. They are the same as the previous examples.

The next line gets the full application name using `CEikApplication::AppFullName()`. The return value of `AppFullName()` is in the form of 'c:\sys\bin\myapp.exe'.

Note that this example uses `CEikAppUi::Application()` to get a pointer to the instance of `CEikApplication`. It also means that you can only write the code above in one of the `AppUi` methods. If you want to write it in another class, you need to find a way to get the instance of `AppUi`. For example:

```
CEikAppUi* appUi = static_cast<CEikAppUi*>
              (CCoeEnv::Static()->AppUi());
TParsePtrC parseAppPath(appUi->Application()->AppFullName());
```

It is also possible to get the application filename using the `RProcess::FileName()` method. The result is the same as `CEikApplication::AppFullName()`.

> **Tip:** Any classes derived from `TParseBase` can be used to extract filename components, such as drive letter, path, name and extension. There are three classes that are commonly used to do extraction; that is, `TParse`, `TParsePtr` and `TParsePtrC`.
>
> The `TParse` class stores the full filename in the type of `TFileName`. It means this class requires 512 bytes in the stack memory to store the filename. The `TParsePtr` and `TParsePtrC` classes use less space in the stack memory because they store a reference to the filename. We recommend using `TParsePtr` or `TParsePtrC` if you only want to parse a filename. Use `TParse` only when you need to construct a filename from its components.
>
> The following code shows how to use `TParsePtrC`:
>
> ```
> _LIT(KFileName, "c:\\folder\\subfolder\\myfile.dat");
> TParsePtrC parse(KFileName);
> ```

```
TPtrC drive(parse.Drive());              // "c:"
TPtrC drivePath(parse.DriveAndPath());   // "c:\folder\subfolder\"
TPtrC name(parse.Name());                // "myfile"
TPtrC nameExt(parse.NameAndExt());       // "myfile.dat"
TPtrC ext(parse.Ext());                  // ".dat"
TPtrC path(parse.Path());                // "\folder\subfolder\"
```

4.1.2.2   Read from and Write to a File Stream

Amount of time required: 30 minutes
Location of example code: \Files\FileStream
Required library(s): efsrv.lib, estor.lib
Required header file(s): f32file.h, s32file.h
Required platform security capability(s): None

Problem: You want to read/write variables such as integers or descriptors from/to a file using a file stream rather than the RFile API.

Solution: RFile provides some methods to read and write binary data. You can use it to write a variable, such as an integer or a floating point number, but you need to convert them to descriptors. There is an easier way to write variables by using a stream. RFileReadStream and RFileWriteStream are the two classes for reading and writing the stream, respectively (they were discussed briefly in Chapter 3, Section 3.14).

Writing to a File Stream

The following example shows how to write an integer to a file:

```
void CFileStreamAppUi::WriteInt32ToStreamL(RFs& aFs,
             const TDesC& aFileName, TInt32 aValue)
  {
  // Open the file stream.
  RFileWriteStream writeStream;
  User::LeaveIfError(writeStream.Replace(aFs, aFileName, EFileWrite));
  writeStream.PushL();

  // Write a TInt32 to the stream.
  writeStream.WriteInt32L(aValue);

  // Commit the change and close the stream.
  writeStream.CommitL();
  CleanupStack::PopAndDestroy(&writeStream);
  }
```

The first three lines create a new instance of a stream and then push it to the cleanup stack.

```
RFileWriteStream writeStream;
User::LeaveIfError(writeStream.Replace(fileServer, aFileName,
                                                EFileWrite));
writeStream.PushL();
```

If you don't want to overwrite an existing file, use `RFileWrite-Stream::Create()`. It will return an error code when the file already exists.

Tip: You can use `BaflUtils::EnsurePathExistsL()` to create one or more folders if they do not already exist, for example:

```
BaflUtils::EnsurePathExistsL(iCoeEnv->FsSession(), KFileName);
```

The method is declared in the `bautils.h` header file and the corresponding library is `bafl.lib`.

The sample code above uses `RWriteStream::PushL()` to push itself on to the cleanup stack. An alternative way to push the stream to the cleanup stack is by calling `CleanupClosePushL()`. For example:

```
CleanupClosePushL(writeStream);
```

The next line of `WriteInt32ToStreamL()` writes an integer value, aValue, to the file:

```
writeStream.WriteInt32L(aValue);
```

The writing statement above can be replaced by the << operator:

```
writeStream << aValue;
```

Note that the << operator can also leave. It means you have to push any objects created before this statement on to the cleanup stack.

What may go wrong when you do this: The << operator does not support the `TInt` type. If you do something like the following code:

```
TInt x = 10;
writeStream << x;
```

you will get an error message during compilation saying that there is something wrong in \epoc32\include\s32strm.inl. If you get an error message from this header file, check the usage of the << operator. You may have used it to write unsupported types, such as TInt.

Also note that the << operator may leave, and must be treated as a leaving function call.

What may go wrong when you do this: If you forget to call RWrite-Stream::Release(), there will be a memory leak. Always make sure that you release the stream when you are not using it anymore.

You can usually detect a memory leak by exiting your application from the emulator. The emulator should panic with an ALLOC message.

Reading from a File Stream

The following code reads the integer written with the example above:

```
TInt32 CFileStreamAppUi::ReadInt32FromStreamL(RFs& aFs,
      const TDesC& aFileName)
 {
 // Open the file stream.
 RFileReadStream readStream;
 User::LeaveIfError(readStream.Open(aFs, aFileName, EFileRead));
 CleanupClosePushL(readStream);

 // Read a TInt32 from the stream.
 TInt32 value;
 readStream >> value;

 // Close the stream and return the read TInt32.
 CleanupStack::PopAndDestroy(&readStream);
 return value;
 }
```

Reading and writing descriptors can be done in the same way. For example:

```
TBuf<KMaxBuffer> buffer;
readStream >> buffer;
```

Note that you don't need to store the length of the descriptor to the buffer. The << operator will store the length for you.

Appending to a File Stream

When you open a file using `RFileWriteStream::Open()`, the file pointer is set to the beginning of the file. It means if you write something to the stream, the current data will be overwritten.

To avoid this problem, the file pointer has to be moved to the end of file. It can be done by calling the `MStreamBuf::SeekL()` method.

How can we get an instance of `MStreamBuf`? `RFileWriteStream` has a method called `Sink()` that returns `MStreamBuf*`. Similarly, `RFileReadStream` has a method called `Source()` that returns `MStreamBuf*`.

The following code shows how to append a new integer to a file stream:

```
void CFileStreamAppUi::AppendInt32ToStreamL(RFs& aFs,
               const TDesC& aFileName, TInt32 aValue)
  {
// Open the file stream.
  RFileWriteStream writeStream;
  TInt err = KErrNone;
  if (BaflUtils::FileExists(iCoeEnv->FsSession(), aFileName))
    {
    err = writeStream.Open(aFs, aFileName, EFileWrite);
    }
  else
    {
    err = writeStream.Create(aFs, aFileName, EFileWrite);
    }
  User::LeaveIfError(err);
  writeStream.PushL();

  // Move the file pointer to the end of file.
  writeStream.Sink()->SeekL(MStreamBuf::EWrite, EStreamEnd, 0);

  // Write a TInt32 at the end of file.
  writeStream.WriteInt32L(aValue);

  // Commit the change and close the file.
  writeStream.CommitL();
  CleanupStack::Pop(&writeStream);
  writeStream.Release();
  }
```

There are two major differences between this function and the previous writing function, `WriteInt32ToStreamL()`:

- The method that is used to open the file. It uses `RFileWriteStream ::Open()` if the file already exists; or `RFileWriteStream:: Create()` if the file does not exist yet.

- There is a call to `MStreamBuf::SeekL()` to move the file pointer to the end of the file.

There are several different versions of `SeekL()`. The one that is used by the method above is the following:

```
TStreamPos SeekL(TMark aMark, TStreamLocation aLocation, TInt aOffset=0);
```

The `aMark` parameter indicates the type of mark, whether read or write. The file stream maintains independent read and write pointers. They can be manipulated differently.

The `aLocation` parameter is the location in the stream on which the calculation of the new position is based. There are three different possible values for `aLocation`, that is:

- `EStreamBeginning`. The seek position is calculated relative to the beginning of the stream.

- `EStreamEnd`. The new position is calculated relative to the end of the stream. It is the one used in the example above.

- `EStreamMark`. The new position is calculated relative to the existing mark in the stream.

The `aOffset` parameter is the offset value.

Detecting End of File

The previous reading example reads one integer only. How do we read more integers until EOF (End of File)? Unfortunately, `RFileReadStream` and `RFileWriteStream` do not provide a method to check EOF. There are two ways of reading more integers:

- Store the number of integers in the beginning of the file. It will give information on how many times you have to read the stream. You can use a simple `for` statement to read the entire file.

- Call `MStreamBuf::SizeL()` to get the file size and then call `MStreamBuf::TellL()` to check whether the file pointer has reached EOF or not.

The following code shows how to read integers from the stream until EOF. All the integers are stored in an array.

```
void CFileStreamAppUi::ReadAllTInt32FromStreamL(RFs& aFs,
        const TDesC& aFileName, RArray<TInt>& aArray)
    {
```

```
// Open the file stream.
RFileReadStream readStream;
User::LeaveIfError(readStream.Open(aFs, aFileName, EFileRead));
CleanupClosePushL(readStream);

// Get the EOF position.
TStreamPos eofPos(readStream.Source()->SizeL());

// Get the current position of file pointer.
TStreamPos currentPos(0);

// Read all TInt2's until EOF.
while (currentPos < eofPos)
  {
  TInt32 value;
  readStream >> value;
  aArray.Append(value);

  currentPos = readStream.Source()->TellL(MStreamBuf::ERead);
  }

CleanupStack::PopAndDestroy(&readStream);
}
```

Discussion: The `RFileWriteStream` provides several variants of the writing methods for different data types, that is:

- **Integer:** `WriteInt8L()`, `WriteInt16L()`, `WriteInt32L()`, `WriteUint8L()`, `WriteUint16L()`, `WriteUint32L()`.

- **Floating point:** `WriteReal32L()`, `WriteReal64L()`.

- **Descriptor:** `WriteL()`. There are several variants of `WriteL()` for different purposes. Please check the SDK documentation for detailed information.

- **Other stream:** `WriteL()`.

Similarly, the `RFileReadStream` also provides several variants of the reading methods:

- **Integer:** `ReadInt8L()`, `ReadInt16L()`, `ReadInt32L()`, `ReadUint8L()`, `ReadUint16L()`, `ReadUint32L()`.

- **Floating point:** `ReadReal32L()`, `ReadReal64L()`.

- **Descriptor:** `ReadL()`. There are several variants of `ReadL()` for different purposes. Please check the SDK documentation for detailed information.

- **Other stream:** `ReadL()`.

It is also possible to read from or write to a file stream using the `>>` and `<<` operators. Remember that these operators can also leave.

Besides `RFileWriteStream` and `RFileReadStream`, there are some other classes to read/write different types of streams. For example: `RDesWriteStream` and `RDesReadStream` for descriptor streams; `RDictionaryWriteStream` and `RDictionaryReadStream` for dictionary streams; and some more. All of them are derived either from `RWriteStream` or `RReadStream`.

4.1.2.3   Read and Write Class Members from and to a File Stream

Amount of time required: 15 minutes
Location of example code: \Files\FileStream
Required library(s): efsrv.lib, estor.lib
Required header file(s): f32file.h, s32file.h
Required platform security capability(s): None

Problem: You want to read/write member variables of a class from/to a file; for example, you have a class that contains employee information.

Solution: This problem can be solved by the serialization features of file streams. Suppose that we have a class that contains employee information. For simplicity, let's assume that there are three member variables only: identifier, name and phone number. The identifier here means a unique number, such as employee number. I am using it only to show you the difference between integer and descriptor handling.

```
const TInt KMaxEmployeeName   = 40;
const TInt KMaxEmployeeNumber = 20;

...

class CEmployee: public CBase
  {
public: // New methods
  CEmployee();

  inline void SetIdentifier(TUint32 aIdentifier)
  { iIdentifier = aIdentifier; }

  inline TUint32 Identifier() const
  { return iIdentifier; }

  inline void SetName(const TDesC& aName)
  { iName.Copy(aName); }

  inline const TPtrC Name() const
  { return iName; }

  inline void SetPhoneNumber(const TDesC& aPhoneNumber)
  { iPhoneNumber.Copy(aPhoneNumber); }

  inline const TPtrC PhoneNumber() const
  { return iPhoneNumber; }
```

```
private:
  TUint32 iIdentifier;
  TBuf<KMaxEmployeeName> iName;
  TBuf<KMaxEmployeeNumber> iPhoneNumber;
  };
```

Externalizing means writing an instance of this class to a file. In practice, you can write the following code to write to a file:

```
writeStream << *employee;
```

Internalizing is the opposite; that is, reading a file and storing the result into this object. For example:

```
readStream >> *employee;
```

In order to support internalize/externalize, add the following two methods to the CEmployee class:

```
void InternalizeL(RReadStream& aStream);
void ExternalizeL(RWriteStream& aStream) const;
```

The following code shows the implementation of InternalizeL():

```
void CEmployee::InternalizeL(RReadStream& aStream)
  {
  aStream >> iIdentifier;
  aStream >> iName;
  aStream >> iPhoneNumber;
  }
```

You can see here how easy it is to write each member variable to the file. You can use the operator << to write the integer and descriptor.

The following code shows the implementation of ExternalizeL():

```
void CEmployee::ExternalizeL(RWriteStream& aStream) const
  {
  aStream << iIdentifier;
  aStream << iName;
  aStréam << iPhoneNumber;
  }
```

What may go wrong when you do this: When reading a descriptor, make sure that the descriptor has enough space. If the maximum length of the descriptor is not enough, the application will leave with KErrOverflow (-9).

Discussion: After defining `ExternalizeL()`, we can write an employee to the stream easily using the operator <<. For example:

```
void CFileStreamAppUi::WriteEmployeeToStreamL(RFs& aFs,
   const TDesC& aFileName, const CEmployee& aEmployee)
{
// Open the file stream.
RFileWriteStream writeStream;
User::LeaveIfError(writeStream.Replace(aFs, aFileName, EFileWrite));
CleanupClosePushL(writeStream);

// Write employee to the stream.
writeStream << aEmployee;

// Commit the change and close the file.
writeStream.CommitL();
CleanupStack::PopAndDestroy(&writeStream);
}
```

Similarly, after defining `InternalizeL()`, we can read an employee from the stream using the operator >>. For example:

```
void CFileStreamAppUi::ReadEmployeeFromStreamL(RFs& aFs,
         const TDesC& aFileName, CEmployee& aEmployee)
{
// Open the file stream.
RFileReadStream readStream;
User::LeaveIfError(readStream.Open(aFs, aFileName, EFileRead));
CleanupClosePushL(readStream);

// Read a employee from the stream.
readStream >> aEmployee;

// Close the stream.
CleanupStack::PopAndDestroy(&readStream);
}
```

4.1.3   Advanced Recipes

4.1.3.1   Read from and Write to a File Store

Amount of time required: 30 minutes
Location of example code: \Files\FileStore
Required library(s): efsrv.lib, estor.lib
Required header file(s): f32file.h, s32file.h
Required platform security capability(s): None

Problem: You want to read from and write to a file using a file store. For example, you want to store multiple streams in a single file.

Solution: A store is a collection of streams (see Figure 4.1.1). It can be in the form of a file store or in-memory store. Furthermore, a store can also

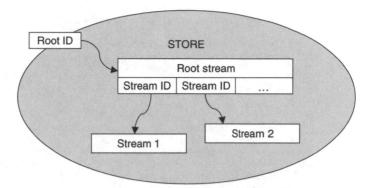

Figure 4.1.1 An Example of a File Store

embed other stores. This recipe discusses file store only. Please check the SDK documentation for more information about in-memory store.

There are two types of file store:

- Direct file store.
- Permanent file store.

A direct file store implements a file store that cannot be changed once it has been committed and closed. It is normally used by an application where in-memory data is the primary copy. The class for direct file store is `CDirectFileStore`.

A permanent file store implements a file store in which the existing stream can be changed. It is normally used by an application where data in the store is the primary copy. The class for permanent file store is `CDictionaryFileStore`.

All the file store classes are declared in the `s32file.h` header file. The library name is `estor.lib`.

Writing to a File Store

In order to see the difference between file streams and file stores, I am going to use the same data structure as the previous example, `CEmployee` (see Recipe 4.1.3.1).

The following code shows how to write an employee to the direct file store. Note that this example only has one stream, which is the root stream.

```
void CFileStoreAppUi::WriteEmployeeToStoreL(RFs& aFs,
      const TDesC& aFileName, const CEmployee& aEmployee)
 {
 // Create a new file store.
 CFileStore* store = CDirectFileStore::ReplaceLC(aFs,
                            aFileName, EFileWrite);
```

```
store->SetTypeL(KDirectFileStoreLayoutUid);

// Create a new stream on the store.
RStoreWriteStream writeStream;
TStreamId rootId = writeStream.CreateLC(*store);

// Write Employee to the stream.
writeStream << aEmployee;

// Commit the changes to the stream and close the stream.
writeStream.CommitL();
CleanupStack::PopAndDestroy(&writeStream);

// Set the root identifier of the store to this stream.
store->SetRootL(rootId);

// Commit the change to the store and close the store.
store->Commit();
CleanupStack::PopAndDestroy(store);
}
```

Like with file streams, the CFileStore::ReplaceLC() method overwrites an eventual existing file. As an alternative, you can use CreateLC() so that you get an error code when the file already exists.

The SetTypeL() method sets the type of this store. There are two possible types:

- KPermanentFileStoreLayoutUid

- KDirectFileStoreLayoutUid.

Alternatively, you can also call the CDirectFileStore::Layout() method, which returns KDirectFileStoreLayoutUid:

```
store->SetTypeL(store->Layout());
```

Similarly, you can call CPermanentFileStore::Layout() to set the type of permanent file store.

What may go wrong when you do this: You need to call CFileStore::SetTypeL() when creating a file store. You don't need to call it when opening an existing store for reading.

If you call SetTypeL() when opening a store, you will get an error code, KErrAccessDenied (-21). On the other hand, if you forget to call SetTypeL() when creating a store, you will get an error code, KErrNotReady (-18) in further operations.

As explained above, a file store is a collection of streams. There is a root stream in a file store, which can be thought of as the 'main' stream. Since our example above has only one stream, this stream will become the root stream. We will take a look at how to store multiple streams later. Setting the root stream is done by calling the `CPersistentstore::SetRootL()` method:

```
store->SetRootL(rootId);
```

Note that `rootId` is the stream identifier that is returned from `RStoreWriteStream::CreateLC()`.

What may go wrong when you do this: If you forget to commit the stream before committing the stores, you will get a `KERN-EXEC 3`panic.

Reading from a File Store

The following shows how to read an employee from the file store:

```
void CFileStoreAppUi::ReadEmployeeFromStoreL(RFs& aFs,
        const TDesC& aFileName, CEmployee& aEmployee)
  {
  // Open the store.
  CFileStore* store = CDirectFileStore::OpenLC(aFs,
                        aFileName, EFileRead);

  // Get the root stream. In this case, we have only one stream.
  RStoreReadStream readStream;
  readStream.OpenLC(*store, store->Root());

  // Read the Employee.
  readStream >> aEmployee;

  CleanupStack::PopAndDestroy(2, store); // readStream and store
  }
```

Discussion: The previous example contains only one stream. Let's make the example more interesting by introducing more streams. We will add a new stream that acts like a header file. It contains the following information:

- *Signature.* A unique signature that identifies this file store. It is always a good idea to make sure that the file we are reading is not some random file.

- *Version.* The version number might be needed in the future when we update the application.

- *Number of employees.* The number of employees stored in this file.

Since there are two streams, we need to maintain a dictionary that stores the identifier of both streams. The dictionary itself is another new stream. So, we will have three streams:

- root stream, which is a streams dictionary;

- header information stream;

- employee information stream.

The root identifier points to the stream dictionary, which contains a list of identifiers of two other streams. If needed, you can add more streams. For example, you may want to split the employee stream into several different streams – one stream for marketing employees, one stream for development employees and one stream for finance employees.

```cpp
void CFileStoreAppUi::WriteEmployeesWithMultiStreamsL(RFs& aFs,
                                   const TDesC& aFileName,
                       const RPointerArray<CEmployee>& aArray)
  {
// Create a new file store.
CFileStore* store = CDirectFileStore::ReplaceLC(aFs,
                          aFileName, EFileWrite);
store->SetTypeL(store->Layout());

// Write header information.
RStoreWriteStream headerStream;
TStreamId headerId = headerStream.CreateLC(*store);

headerStream << KSignature;
headerStream << KVersion;
headerStream << (TUint32) aArray.Count();

headerStream.CommitL();
CleanupStack::PopAndDestroy(&headerStream);

// Create a new employee to the store.
RStoreWriteStream employeeStream;
TStreamId employeesId = employeeStream.CreateLC(*store);

// Write Employees to the stream.
for (TInt i = 0; i < aArray.Count(); i++)
  {
  employeeStream << *aArray[i];
  }

employeeStream.CommitL();
CleanupStack::PopAndDestroy(&employeeStream);

// Create a stream dictionary.
CStreamDictionary* dictionary = CStreamDictionary::NewLC();
dictionary->AssignL(KHeaderUid, headerId);
dictionary->AssignL(KEmployeesUid, employeesId);

// Write stream dictionary in the root stream.
RStoreWriteStream dictionaryStream;
```

```
TStreamId rootId = dictionaryStream.CreateLC(*store);
dictionaryStream << *dictionary;
dictionaryStream.CommitL();

CleanupStack::PopAndDestroy(2, dictionary);

// Set the root identifier of the store to this stream.
store->SetRootL(rootId);

// Commit the change to the store and close the store.
store->Commit();
CleanupStack::PopAndDestroy(store);
}
```

Note that we need to store the stream identifier of the employees in the root stream.

> **Tip:** A permanent file store allows you to modify the data, for example deleting a stream by calling `CPermanentFileStore::DeleteL()`. If you do this several times, your files may get fragmented. It also means that your file will be getting bigger. It is recommended that from time to time you compact the store file by calling `CPermanent-FileStore::CompactL()`. This method will defragment your file store.

The following code shows the method to read all the employees to an array:

```
void CFileStoreAppUi::ReadEmployeesWithMultiStreamsL(RFs& aFs,
                                  const TDesC& aFileName,
                           RPointerArray<CEmployee>& aArray)
{
// Open the new file store.
CFileStore* store = CDirectFileStore::OpenLC(aFs,
                          aFileName, EFileWrite);

// Read stream dictionary
CStreamDictionary* dictionary = CStreamDictionary::NewLC();
RStoreReadStream dictionaryStream;
dictionaryStream.OpenLC(*store, store->Root());
dictionaryStream >> *dictionary;
CleanupStack::PopAndDestroy(&dictionaryStream);

// Get the identifier of each stream in this store.
TStreamId headerId = dictionary->At(KHeaderUid);
TStreamId employeesId = dictionary->At(KEmployeesUid);
CleanupStack::PopAndDestroy(dictionary);

// Read header information.
RStoreReadStream headerStream;
headerStream.OpenLC(*store, headerId);
```

```
HBufC* signature = HBufC::NewLC(headerStream, KMaxBuffer);
// If needed, check the signature here.
CleanupStack::PopAndDestroy(signature);
TUint32 version;
headerStream >> version;
TUint32 numberOfEmployees;
headerStream >> numberOfEmployees;

CleanupStack::PopAndDestroy(&headerStream);

// Read the employees streams.
RStoreReadStream employeeStream;
employeeStream.OpenLC(*store, employeesId);

for (TUint32 i = 0; i < numberOfEmployees; i++)
  {
  CEmployee* employee = new(ELeave) CEmployee();
  CleanupStack::PushL(employee);
  employeeStream >> *employee;
  aArray.Append(employee); // ownership is transferred
  CleanupStack::Pop(employee);
  }

CleanupStack::PopAndDestroy(&employeeStream);

// Commit the change to the store and close the store.
CleanupStack::PopAndDestroy(store);
}
```

4.1.3.2   Share Files between Processes

Amount of time required: 20 minutes
Location of example code: \Files\FileSharingCreator and
\Files\FileSharingClient
Required library(s): efsrv.lib
Required header file(s): f32file.h
Required platform security capability(s): None

Problem: You want to share files with another process without giving that process `AllFiles` capability. For example, you have a file stored in the private folder that needs to be read by another process.

Solution: As explained in Chapter 3, a data-caging mechanism prevents a process from accessing files stored in the private folder of another process. There is actually a way of sharing files between processes. A file handle can be passed from one process to another process. Furthermore, a file handle can be passed from a client to a server or vice versa.

The following `RFile` member methods support file handles sharing between processes:

- `RFile::TransferToClient()`,

- `RFile::AdoptFromClient()`,

- RFile::TransferToServer(),

- RFile::AdoptFromServer(),

- RFile::TransferToProcess(),

- RFile::AdoptFromCreator().

The TranferToXyz() methods are used to transfer the file handle to another process, which includes another server or client. The Adopt-FromXyz() methods are used to read the file handle that is shared by another process.

The following example shows how to transfer a file handle, file-sharing.txt, from a process to another process:

```
// CONSTANTS
_LIT(KDataFileName,   "filesharing.txt");
_LIT(KClientFileName, "FileSharingClient.exe");

const TInt KFileServerSlot = 1;
const TInt KFileHandleSlot = 2;

void CFileSharingCreatorAppUi::DoTransferFileL()
  {
  // Connect to the file server session and share it.
  RFs fs;
  User::LeaveIfError(fs.Connect());
  CleanupClosePushL(fs);
  User::LeaveIfError(fs.ShareProtected());

  // Get the file name that is located in the private folder.
  TFileName privatePath;
  User::LeaveIfError(fs.PrivatePath(privatePath));
  TParsePtrC parseAppPath(Application()->AppFullName());
  TParse parse;
  User::LeaveIfError(parse.Set(parseAppPath.Drive(), &privatePath,
                                               &KDataFileName));

  // Open the file to be shared.
  RFile file;
  User::LeaveIfError(file.Open(fs, parse.FullName(), EFileRead));
  CleanupClosePushL(file);

  // Create the process that will use the file.
  RProcess process;
  User::LeaveIfError(process.Create(KClientFileName, KNullDesC));
  CleanupClosePushL(process);

  // Transfer to process storing the RFs handle into
  // environment slot KFileServerSlot and
  // the RFile handle into slot KFileHandleSlot.
  User::LeaveIfError(file.TransferToProcess(
      process, KFileServerSlot, KFileHandleSlot));

  // Resume the process, which means start it.
  process.Resume();
```

```
// Cleanup the resources.
CleanupStack::PopAndDestroy(3, &fs); // close p, file, and fs
}
```

Discussion: The second and third parameters of `TransferToProcess` are indexes in the `TIpcArgs`/`RMessage2` couple used for Inter-Process Communication. See Chapter 5 for more information on the subject. Note that you cannot use slot 0, since this is reserved.

The following code shows how we can adopt the shared file handle in the `FileSharingClient.exe` process:

```
GLDEF_C TInt E32Main()
    {
    // Adopt the file using the RFs handle into
    // environment slot KFileServerSlot
    // and the RFile handle into slot KFileHandleSlot
    RFile file;
    TInt err = file.AdoptFromCreator(KFileServerSlot, KFileHandleSlot);

    // If there is no error, read the file.
    if (KErrNone == err)
        {
        TBuf8<KMaxBuffer> buffer;
        file.Read(buffer);

        // Use the buffer here.
        }

    return EikStart::RunApplication(NewApplication);
    }
```

The code above adopts the file handle from the creator. It will then read the entire contents of the file to a buffer.

4.1.4   Resources

- Symbian Developer Library:
  - *Symbian OS Guide > Base > File Services (F32) > File server client side.*
  - *Symbian OS Guide > System Libraries > Using Store.*
- Harrison and Shackman, *Symbian C++ for Mobile Phones*, Volume 3, Symbian Press, 2007. See chapter 7 for additional information about how to use the file system on Symbian OS.

4.2   Contacts and Calendar

These recipes will teach you how to use the Contact and Calendar engines. These are part of the personal information management (PIM) services, and are accessed through APIs delivered by the Application Engines subsystem. More information can be found in the Symbian Developer Library documentation in your SDK or online on the Symbian Developer Network. The Application Engines section of the Symbian OS Guide is a good place to start, with information about specific APIs available in the Symbian OS Reference.

There is a split across three distinct modules:

- The data itself is stored using the Symbian OS database management system to allow for atomic updates (see the System Libraries section of the Symbian Developer Library for more information about databases on Symbian OS).

- A Symbian OS application engine contains the code that configures the database, supports standard data formats and links to other parts of the system.

- Each UI platform (UIQ and S60) defines an application that uses the appropriate application engine. The application is split into a platform-specific reusable module that exports graphical components and the application executable that uses it.

We are going to spend some time discussing both the Contacts and Calendar application engines, and the most useful basic operations that each makes available to you. The UI applications that use the engines lie outside the scope of this book (although Chapter 5 gives you a head-start on the useful graphical components you may want to reuse).

The usual Symbian platform security model needs to be considered when using the Contacts and Calendar APIs since the data needs to be protected from unauthorized use. Most applications using any PIM functionality will require the `ReadUserData` and `WriteUserData` capabilities.

4.2.1 Before You Start with Contacts

Unsurprisingly, the Contacts database contains contact items. They are either cards or groups. Each item has an identifier during its lifetime in the database, and each item contains fields. The fields each contain:

- A content type, which identifies the meaning of the information contained in the field (such as a phone number or an address). This can be a combination of several types to reduce data duplication. For example, email and instant messaging fields could have the same value.

- A storage type, which identifies the kind of data stored in the field: an integer, a string, and so on.

- The actual data.

- An identifier. An item can have several fields with the same mapping and label; for example, several home landline numbers, and these are distinguished by identifier.

- An optional 'mapping', which is used when exporting the contact to a vCard.

- An optional label, which can be used to further specify the meaning of the data. For example, a 'home' phone number, a 'work' address, and so on.

You can find the mappings for the contact fields in your SDK (in epoc32\include\cntdef.h) or search for KUidContactField in the Symbian Developer Library.

On your handset, each contact card can belong to one or more groups, to represent particular collections of contacts. You can create as many groups as you like. A contact can be a friend, a colleague, a member of your family or belong to no group, or one or more. While you are able to add your own contact groups to the database, there may be some system groups that you will not be able to remove. In addition, do not confuse groups with a folder hierarchy: deleting a group will not delete the contact cards in the group.

To speed up the execution of your code, views and filters can be used to retrieve a limited amount of data when accessing the database. Indexing and other internal configuration options allow each database to be optimized for specific common operations, such as sorting contacts by first or last names.

For testing purposes, the code samples of this book contain \PIM\ PopulateContact, which makes sure that your development environment contains a Contact database initialized with a few contact items.

4.2.2   Before You Start with Calendar

Symbian OS v9.1 deprecated the original Agenda Model API and added a new Calendar Interim API, to reflect the push toward the iCalendar standard. You should definitely familiarize yourself with iCalendar before developing any kind of value-added application using this API. The specification can be found at **www.faqs.org/rfcs/rfc2445.html**.

The Calendar database contains calendar entries, which can be appointments, meetings, anniversaries, to-do notes, and so on. For the purpose of this text, we are going to refer to any one of these entries as an 'event'. Each event can belong to one or several categories.

Each calendar entry has an identifier during its lifetime in the database. An entry can be repeated. It would then have several calendar instances.

Typically, these are calculated dynamically. A repeat rule defines when an entry is repeated. Several granularities are available: daily, weekly, monthly. These can be combined.

Access to the Calendar database usually requires a calendar server session and a calendar view. Parts of the view API are asynchronous and it is recommended that any application using the Calendar API uses active objects to handle events (see Chapter 3 for further details).

When dealing with the Calendar APIs, you need to familiarize yourself with how time is represented in Symbian OS. Unless otherwise specified, we use a signed 64-bit integer, which counts the number of microseconds since midnight, January 1st, 0 AD. For more information, the classes of interest are `TTime`, `TDateTime` and all the `TTimeIntervalXyz`, and a good starting point is in the Symbian Developer Library documentation: *Symbian OS Guide > Base > Using User Library (E32) > Date and Time Handling.*

One of the trickiest issues you will face with the Calendar APIs is dealing with phones moving across time zones, or changes to daylight saving hours. Different people and organizations have different requirements about what should happen to the times recorded in your entries when the system time changes. We don't address this further here, since this is an issue every mobile application developer has to deal with in his or her own way. You can easily end up building several versions of your application based purely on this issue and based on the different requirements of each of your customers. The best advice we can offer is to create a flexible solution and get your customer's requirements early on.

For testing purposes, the code samples of this book contain \PIM\ PopulateAgenda, which makes sure that your development environment contains an Agenda database initialized with a few calendar entries.

4.2.3 Easy Recipes

4.2.3.1 Write Data to a Contact

Amount of time required: 40 minutes
Location of example code: \PIM\ContactWriteNewField
Required library(s): cntmodel.lib
Required header file(s): cntdb.h, cntitem.h, cntfield.h, cntfldst.h
Required platform security capability(s): ReadUserData WriteUser-Data

Problem: You want to add a text field to an existing contact item.

Solution: Modifying a contact data is not difficult in itself. You could think of it as executing an SQL UPDATE statement. Several of the next recipes in this section will show you ways of finding a contact to modify. For simplicity's sake, the code sample shows how to use the result of `CContactDatabase::OwnCardId()` as a parameter for the following `AddEmployerL()` method:

```
#include <cntdb.h> // and link to cntmodel.lib
#include <cntitem.h>
#include <cntfield.h>
#include <cntdef.h>
#include <cntfldst.h>

class CContactWrite : public CBase
  {
public:
  static CContactWrite* NewL();
  ~CContactWrite(); // to delete iCntDb
  // The item id for a search.
  void AddEmployerL(TContactItemId aCntId,
                    const TDesC& aCompany);
private:
  void ConstructL();
private:
  CContactDatabase* iCntDb;
  };

  // You need an opened contact database: usually the default
  // database on the phone. You should always assume that it
  // may not have been created before.
void CContactWrite::ConstructL()
  {
  TRAPD(error, iCntDb = CContactDatabase::OpenL());
  if (KErrNotFound == error)
    {
    iCntDb = CContactDatabase::CreateL();
    }
  else
    {
    User::LeaveIfError(error);
    }
  }


void CContactWrite::AddEmployerL(TContactItemId aCntId,
                                 const TDesC& aCompany)
  {
  // Open the contact item and lock it for exclusive use
  CContactItem* item = iCntDb->OpenContactLX(aCntId);
  CleanupStack::PushL(item);

  // Make a Company Name field to add to the contact
  CContactItemField* field =
  CContactItemField::NewLC(KStorageTypeText);
  field->AddFieldTypeL(KUidContactFieldCompanyName);
  field->TextStorage()->SetTextL(aCompany);

  item->AddFieldL(*field); // takes ownership of field
  CleanupStack::Pop(field);// so pop it off the cleanup stack
```

```
iCntDb->CommitContactL(*item);
CleanupStack::PopAndDestroy(item);
CleanupStack::PopAndDestroy(); // Release exclusive lock on item
  }
```

> **Advanced Tip:** What remains on the cleanup stack after a successful call to `OpenContactLX` is not the item it returns. It is a `TCleanupItem` that will release the exclusive lock on the item when destroyed.

> **What may go wrong when you do this:** The field you added may not be easily accessible to the default Contact application on your phone if you don't also specify a vCard mapping for it.

4.2.3.2 Read Data from a Contact

Amount of time required: 40 minutes
Location of example code: `\PIM\ContactReadField`
Required library(s): `cntmodel.lib`
Required header file(s): `cntdb.h`, `cntitem.h`, `cntfield.h`, `cntfldst.h`
Required platform security capability(s): `ReadUserData WriteUserData`

Problem: You want to retrieve the value of a text field from an existing contact item.

Solution: We are just going to write some code to extract all the values for a given content type into a descriptor array. It is very easy to modify the code so that it returns a descriptor containing only the first value, if that is what you require. We don't show the error handling in the code below, but you should remember to handle the case where contacts don't have the requested field.

```
#include <cntdb.h> // and link to cntmodel.lib
#include <cntitem.h>
#include <cntfield.h>
#include <cntdef.h>
#include <cntfldst.h>
#include <badesca.h> // and link to bafl.lib (descriptor arrays)

class CContactRead : public CBase
  {
public:
  static CContactRead* NewL();
```

```
~CContactRead(); // to delete iCntDb
  CDesCArray* ReadTextFieldL(TContactItemId aCntId,
                                 TFieldType aType);
private:
  void ConstructL();
private:
  CContactDatabase* iCntDb;
  };

// You need an opened contact database: usually the default
// database on the phone. You should always assume that it
// may not have been created before.

void CContactRead::ConstructL()
 {
  TRAPD(error, iCntDb = CContactDatabase::OpenL());
  if (KErrNotFound == error)
    {
    iCntDb = CContactDatabase::CreateL();
    }
  else
    {
    User::LeaveIfError(error);
    }
  }

CDesCArray* CContactRead::ReadTextFieldL(TContactItemId aCntId,
                                            TFieldType aType)
  {
  // Create descriptor array to store result
  // Use arbitrary graularity
  CDesCArray* result = new (ELeave) CDesCArrayFlat(2);
  CleanupStack::PushL(result);

  // Use the database engine to read only
  // the fields we are interested in

  CContactItemViewDef* viewDef = CContactItemViewDef::NewLC(
                         CContactItemViewDef::EIncludeFields,
                      CContactItemViewDef::EMaskHiddenFields);
  viewDef->AddL(aType);

  // Get the contact item
  CContactItem* item = iCntDb->ReadContactLC(aCntId, *viewDef);

  // Get all the fields
  CContactItemFieldSet& fieldSet = item->CardFields();

  // Go through all of them, add the values to the result

  for(TInt ii = 0 ; ii < fieldSet.Count() ; ++ii)
    {
    CContactItemField& field = fieldSet[ii];
    if (KStorageTypeText == field.StorageType())
      {
      if (field.TextStorage()->IsFull())
        {
        const TPtrC value = field.TextStorage()->Text();
```

```
        result->AppendL(value);
        }
      }
    }

  CleanupStack::PopAndDestroy(2, viewDef); // item, viewDef
  CleanupStack::Pop(result);
  return result; // transfers owernship to caller
  }
```

> **Tip:** If, instead, you already have a `CContactItem` loaded with all its fields, you can use `CContactItemFieldSet::FindNext()` to iterate through the set.

4.2.3.3 Add a New Contact

Amount of time required: 15 minutes
Location of example code: `\PIM\ContactAddNew`
Required library(s): `cntmodel.lib`
Required header file(s): `cntdb.h`, `cntitem.h`, `cntfield.h`, `cntfldst.h`
Required platform security capability(s): `ReadUserData WriteUserData`

Problem: You want to add a brand new contact to the database.

Solution: You will probably want to use Recipe 4.2.3.1 to add fields to the new contact card, once you are done with this.

You must first open the database, as you did in Recipe 4.2.3.1:

```
#include <cntdb.h> // and link to cntmodel.lib
#include <cntitem.h>
#include <cntfield.h>
#include <cntdef.h>
#include <cntfldst.h>

class CContactWrite : public CBase
  {
public:
  static CContactWrite* NewL();
  ~CContactWrite(); // to delete iCntDb
  void AddCardL(const TDesC& aFirstName, const TDesC& aLastName,
                                         const TDesC& aPhone);
private:
  void ConstructL();
private:
  CContactDatabase* iCntDb;
  };

void CContactWrite::AddCardL(const TDesC& aFirstName,
```

```
                                const TDesC& aLastName,
                                const TDesC& aPhone)
{// Create a contact card
CContactCard* contactCard = CContactCard::NewLC();

// First name
CContactItemField* firstName =
                CContactItemField::NewLC(KStorageTypeText);
firstName->AddFieldTypeL(KUidContactFieldGivenName);
firstName->TextStorage()->SetTextL(aFirstName);
contactCard->AddFieldL(*firstName); // takes ownership of field
CleanupStack::Pop(firstName);

// Last name
CContactItemField* lastName =
                CContactItemField::NewLC(KStorageTypeText);
lastName->AddFieldTypeL(KUidContactFieldFamilyName);
lastName->TextStorage()->SetTextL(aLastName);
contactCard->AddFieldL(*lastName); // takes ownership of field
CleanupStack::Pop(lastName);

// Phone number
CContactItemField* phone =
                    CContactItemField::NewLC(KStorageTypeText);
phone->AddFieldTypeL(KUidContactFieldPhoneNumber);
phone->TextStorage()->SetTextL(aPhone);
contactCard->AddFieldL(*phone); // takes ownership of field
CleanupStack::Pop(phone);

// Add the card to the database, which takes a copy
iCntDb->AddNewContactL(*contactCard);
CleanupStack::PopAndDestroy(contactCard); // destroy local version
}
```

4.2.3.4   Remove a Contact

Amount of time required: 15 minutes
Location of example code: \PIM\ContactRemove
Required library(s): cntmodel.lib
Required header file(s): cntdb.h, cntitem.h, cntfield.h, cntfldst.h
Required platform security capability(s): ReadUserData WriteUser-Data

Problem: You want to remove an existing contact from the database.

Solution: You must first open the database, just like in Recipe 4.2.3.1:

```
#include <cntdb.h> // and link to cntmodel.lib
#include <cntitem.h>
#include <cntfield.h>
#include <cntdef.h>

class CContactWrite : public CBase
```

```
  {
public:
  static CContactWrite* NewL();
  ~CContactWrite(); // to delete iCntDb
  void RemoveContactL(TContactItemId aCntId);
private:
  void ConstructL();
private:
  CContactDatabase* iCntDb;
  };

void CContactWrite::RemoveContactL(TContactItemId aCntId)
  {// just delete it
  iCntDb->DeleteContactL(aCntId);
  }
```

> **Tip:** After deleting contacts, it is good practice to call `CContact-Database::CompactL()`, which may reduce the contact database size. It is not necessary to call `CompactL()` after each deletion, but a good idea to do so after you have removed a few.

4.2.3.5 Modify a Calendar Event

Amount of time required: 15 minutes
Location of example code: `\PIM\AgendaUpdate`
Required library(s): `calinterimapi.lib`
Required header file(s): `calsession.h`, `calentryview.h`, `calprogresscallback.h`
Required platform security capability(s): `ReadUserData WriteUser-Data`

Problem: You want to reschedule an event to start at a new time.

Solution: The first step is to open the Calendar database so it can be modified. Modifying the content of one item is not complex in itself. Think of it as executing an SQL UPDATE statement.

```
#include <calsession.h> // and link to calinterimapi.lib
#include <calentryview.h>
#include <calprogresscallback.h>

class CCalWrite : public CBase, public MCalProgressCallBack
  {
public:
  static CCalWrite* NewL();
  ~CCalWrite(); // to delete iCalSes and iCalView
  void RescheduleL(TCalLocalUid aEventId, TTime aNewTimeUtc);
public: // from MCalProgressCallBack
  void Progress(TInt){};
```

```
  void Completed(TInt){};
  TBool NotifyProgress(){return EFalse;};
private:
  void ConstructL();
private:
  CCalSession* iCalSes;
  CCalEntryView* iCalView;
  };

// You need an opened calendar database (often this
// is the default calendar database on the phone).
// You should always assume that it may not have been created before.

void CCalWrite::ConstructL()
  {
  iCalSes = CCalSession::NewL();
  const TDesC& name = iCalSes->DefaultFileNameL();
  TRAPD(error, iCalSes->CreateCalFileL(name));
  if (KErrAlreadyExists != error)
    {// Leave if an error occurs (but not if it already exists)
    User::LeaveIfError(error);
    }

  iCalSes->OpenL(KNullDesC());
  // Create a calendar view
  iCalView = CCalEntryView::NewL(*iCalSes, *this);
  }

void CCalWrite::RescheduleL(TCalLocalUid aEventId, TTime aNewTimeUtc)
  {
  // find the event
  CCalEntry* entry = iCalView->FetchL(aEventId);
  if (NULL == entry)
    {
    User::Leave(KErrNotFound);
    }
  else
    {// Reschedule it, but keep original duration.
    CleanupStack::PushL(entry);
    TCalTime start = entry->StartTimeL();
    TCalTime end = entry->EndTimeL();
    TTime startUtc = start.TimeUtcL();
    TTime endUtc = end.TimeUtcL();
    TTimeIntervalMicroSeconds duration =
        endUtc.MicroSecondsFrom(startUtc);
    start.SetTimeUtcL(aNewTimeUtc);
    end.SetTimeUtcL(aNewTimeUtc + duration);
    entry->SetStartAndEndTimeL(start, end);

    // Commit it to the database
    RPointerArray<CCalEntry> array;
    CleanupClosePushL(array);
    array.AppendL(entry);

    // We are doing something weird here because we are
    // dealing with only one entry.
    // We don't transfer ownership of entry
    // to the array. When array is closed
```

```
    // it won't delete entry.
    // So we keep entry on the cleanup stack.

    TInt success=0;
    // Update the view
    iCalView->UpdateL(array, success);
    if (success < 1)
      {// Partial success is possible when updating
       // several calendar entries at once.
      User::Leave(KErrGeneral);
      }
    CleanupStack::PopAndDestroy(2, entry); // array, entry
    }
}
```

> **What may go wrong when you do this:** There are some modifications you can apply to a `CCalEntry` that `CCalEntryView::UpdateL()` may not fully commit to the Calendar database. You will need to experiment a little, and you may have to write a method that will copy an entry, modify the copy, store the new entry and delete the old one from the Calendar database. At this point, atomicity of updates becomes an issue.

4.2.3.6 Add a New Calendar Event

Amount of time required: 30 minutes
Location of example code: `\PIM\AgendaAdd`
Required library(s): `calinterimapi.lib`
Required header file(s): `calsession.h`, `calentryview.h`,
`calprogresscallback.h`
Required platform security capability(s): `ReadUserData WriteUser-Data`

Problem: You want to add a new appointment to your calendar.

Solution: You will need a GUID, which is a globally unique string, to permanently identify your calendar entry. S60 provides an API for this purpose (`CalenInterimUtils::GlobalUidL()`) in `caleninter-imutils.h` (you need to link to `caleninterimutils.lib`), but it is not available to UIQ developers. RFC 2445 (***www.faqs.org/rfcs/rfc2445.html***) gives some recommendations on how to obtain a globally unique ID in section 4.8.4.7 (search for 'Unique Identifier').

  Since there is no enforced standard in the matter, there is technically no way to make sure any string you come up with won't be duplicated by another application, but there are a few basic techniques that can be used to greatly reduce the probability of a conflict.

Here are a few useful techniques that can be used to create a GUID:

- Use your application's Symbian Signed UID and your company name.
- Use random number generation.
- Use the current time (introduce a delay between the creation of two GUIDs).
- Use a dedicated GUID-generation server, either remote or local.
- Use the device's Bluetooth MAC address, its phone and IMEI number (there may be a cost to the user if you open a network connection).
- Use a cryptographic hash and your public key.

It is recommended that you use a combination of several of these techniques.

In order to add a new calendar event, you must first open the database as described in Recipe 4.2.3.1:

```cpp
#include <calsession.h> // and link to calinterimapi.lib
#include <calentryview.h>
#include <calprogresscallback.h>

class CCalWrite : public CBase, public MCalProgressCallBack
  {
public:
  static CCalWrite* NewL();
  ~CCalWrite(); // to delete iCalSes and iCalView
  void AddNewL(TTime aStartUtc, const TDesC& aDescription);
public: // from MCalProgressCallBack
  void Progress(TInt){};
  void Completed(TInt){};
  TBool NotifyProgress(){return EFalse;};
private:
  void ConstructL();
  HBufC8* MakeGuidLC();
private:
  CCalSession* iCalSes;
  CCalEntryView* iCalView;
  };

void CCalWrite::AddNewL(TTime aStartUtc, const TDesC& aDescription)
  {
  // create a new entry
  HBufC8* guid = MakeGuidLC();
  CCalEntry* entry = CCalEntry::NewL(CCalEntry::EAppt, guid,
                                     CCalEntry::EMethodNone, 0);
  CleanupStack::Pop(guid);
  CleanupStack::PushL(entry);

  // set some values
  TCalTime start;
  start.SetTimeUtcL(aStartUtc);
  TTime endUtc = aStartUtc;
```

```
  endUtc += TTimeIntervalHours(1);
  TCalTime end;
  end.SetTimeUtcL(endUtc);
  entry->SetStartAndEndTimeL(start, end);
  entry->SetDescriptionL(aDescription);

  // add the entry to the database
  RPointerArray<CCalEntry> array;
  CleanupClosePushL(array);
  array.AppendL(entry);
  // Don't transfer ownership of entry to array.
  TInt success = 0;
  iCalView->StoreL(array, success);
  if (success < 1)
    {
    User::Leave(KErrGeneral);
    }
  CleanupStack::PopAndDestroy(2, entry); // array, entry
  }

// A simplified version of a unique Id generator.
// It transfers the ownership of its result to the caller.
// You can roll your own or use
// CalenInterimUtils::GlobalUidL() in S60 code

const TInt KMaxGuidSize = 64;
_LIT(KDateFormat,"%F%Y%M%D");
_LIT(KTimeSeparator,"T");
_LIT(KTimeFormat,"%F%H%T%S");
_LIT(KTimeDivider,"-");
_LIT(KAddress,"0x2000DF18_QuickRecipes@SymbianPress.com");

HBufC8* CCalWrite::MakeGuidLC()
  {
  TTime now;
  now.UniversalTime();
  TBuf<KMaxGuidSize> time;
  now.FormatL(time,KTimeFormat);
  TBuf<KMaxGuidSize> date;
  now.FormatL(date,KDateFormat);

  HBufC8* guid = HBufC8::NewLC(KMaxGuidSize);

  TPtr8 guidPtr = guid->Des();
  guidPtr.Zero();
  guidPtr.Append(date);
  guidPtr.Append(KTimeSeparator());
  guidPtr.Append(time);
  guidPtr.Append(KTimeDivider());
  guidPtr.Append(KAddress());

  return guid;
  }
```

What may go wrong when you do this: Given that you may be writing your own GUID generation function, you need to deal with the fact

> that `CCalEntry::NewL()` could fail if another item already has the same GUID.
>
> You also need to be careful with the amount of data you append to the GUID descriptor or you will get a descriptor overflow panic.

4.2.3.7 Remove a Calendar Event

Amount of time required: 10 minutes
Location of example code: `\PIM\AgendaRemove`
Required library(s): `calinterimapi.lib`
Required header file(s): `calsession.h`, `calentryview.h`, `calprogresscallback.h`
Required platform security capability(s): `ReadUserData WriteUserData`

Problem: You want to delete an event from the Calendar database.

Solution: You must first open the database as you did in Recipe 4.2.3.1:

```cpp
#include <calsession.h> // and link to calinterimapi.lib
#include <caltime.h>
#include <calentryview.h>
#include <calentry.h>
#include <calprogresscallback.h>

class CCalWrite : public CBase, public MCalProgressCallBack
  {
public:
  static CCalWrite* NewL();
  ~CCalWrite(); // to delete iCalSes and iCalView
  void RemoveL(TCalLocalUid aEventId);
public: // from MCalProgressCallBack
  void Progress(TInt){};
  void Completed(TInt){};
  TBool NotifyProgress(){return EFalse;};
private:
  void ConstructL();
private:
  CCalSession* iCalSes;
  CCalEntryView* iCalView;
  };

void CCalWrite::RemoveL(TCalLocalUid aEventId)
  {
  RArray<TCalLocalUid> array;
  CleanupClosePushL(array);
  array.AppendL(aEventId);
  TInt success = 0;
  iCalView->DeleteL(array, success);
  // no real need to deal with failure here
  CleanupStack::PopAndDestroy(&array);
  }
```

4.2.4 Intermediate Recipes

4.2.4.1 Sort Contacts

Amount of time required: 40 minutes
Location of example code: \PIM\ContactSort
Required library(s): cntmodel.lib
Required header file(s): cntdb.h, cntitem.h, cntfield.h, cntdef.h
Required platform security capability(s): ReadUserData WriteUserData

Problem: You want to sort the contacts in the database, by name, in alphabetical order.

Solution: What you want is a collection of TContactItemId objects. The elements are sorted according to your criteria. Once returned, the collection can be used to retrieve data from each element individually. Remember to use a CContactItemViewDef, like in Recipe 4.2.3.2.

The Contact database supports several layers of sorting folded into one operation. This means that you can set up the sort on one field first. If several items have the same order for that sort, a second field is used to order these items amongst themselves. You can specify as many fields as you want to refine how the items will be sorted.

We are going to sort all contacts by their last name. Those with the same last name will then be further sorted by first name.

You could imagine the same kind of sorting by country first, then by city or by more than two parameters.

Open the database as you did in Recipe 4.2.3.1:

```
#include <cntdb.h> // and link to cntmodel.lib
#include <cntitem.h>
#include <cntfield.h>
#include <cntdef.h>

class CContactRead : public CBase
  {
public:
  static CContactRead* NewL();
  ~CContactRead(); // to delete iCntDb
  CContactIdArray* SortByNameL();
private:
  void ConstructL();
private:
  CContactDatabase* iCntDb;
  };

CContactIdArray* CContactRead::SortByNameL()
  {
  CArrayFix<CContactDatabase::TSortPref>* sortOrder=new(ELeave)
             CArrayFixSeg<CContactDatabase::TSortPref>(2);
```

```
CleanupStack::PushL(sortOrder);
CContactDatabase::TSortPref lastNameSort(
                        KUidContactFieldFamilyName);
CContactDatabase::TSortPref firstNameSort(
                        KUidContactFieldGivenName);
sortOrder->AppendL(lastNameSort);
sortOrder->AppendL(firstNameSort);
iCntDb->SortL(sortOrder); // takes ownership of sortOrder
CleanupStack::Pop(sortOrder);
return CContactIdArray::NewL(iCntDb->SortedItemsL());
}
```

> **Tip:** The Contact database is the most optimized to deal with this partic-
> ular type of sorting. Even with several hundred contacts, it will not take
> more than a couple of seconds on your phone. There is an additional
> asynchronous overload that can be used inside an active scheduler
> using `CContactDatabase::SortAsynchL()`, which is the one
> you should use inside a GUI application. For an example of how to
> do so, please see the code sample in `\PIM\ContactAsynchSort`.

> **What may go wrong when you do this:** On UIQ, you may get strange
> results using the synchronous sort, because a contact with an empty
> field of the right type will be considered first in alphabetical order. The
> asynchronous sort seems to filter these out, and both return correct
> results on S60.

4.2.4.2   Use the vCard Format

Amount of time required: 40 minutes
Location of example code: `\PIM\ContactStandard`
Required library(s): `cntmodel.lib`
Required header file(s): `cntdb.h`, `cntitem.h`, `cntfield.h`,
`cntdef.h`
Required platform security capability(s): `ReadUserData WriteUser-
Data`

Problem: You want to send and receive contacts between different
devices.

Solution: The vCard standard is supported by many devices, mobile or
not, regardless of their operating system. The vCard specification can
be found at ***www.imc.org/pdi/vcard-21.txt*** (Symbian OS v9.1 supports
vCard 2.1).

Our aim is to convert text data into a contact in the Contacts database, and then convert it back again. The actual data transfer between devices is outside the scope of this book. Section 4.3 on Networking and Section 4.9 on Connectivity should be a useful reference however.

Symbian OS streams have the advantage of exposing the same API, regardless of where the data is actually stored (file, descriptor, database, etc.), so they are perfect for our purpose here. You will find further discussion of streams in the file handling recipes given in Section 4.1.

Remember to open the database as you did in Recipe 4.2.3.1:

```
#include <cntdb.h> // and link to cntmodel.lib
#include <cntitem.h>
#include <cntfield.h>
#include <cntdef.h>
#include <s32strm.h> // and link to estor.lib

class CContactWrite : public CBase
  {
public:
  static CContactWrite* NewL();
  ~CContactWrite(); // to delete iCntDb
  void ExportContactL(TContactItemId aCntId,
                      RWriteStream& aOutput);
  void ImportContactL(RReadStream& aInput);
private:
  void ConstructL();
private:
  CContactDatabase* iCntDb;
};

void CContactWrite::ExportContactL(TContactItemId aCntId,
                                    RWriteStream& aOutput)
  {// this only works with a collection of contact ids.
  CContactIdArray* array = CContactIdArray::NewLC();
  array->AddL(aCntId);
  TUid uid;
  uid.iUid = KVersitEntityUidVCard;
  iCntDb->ExportSelectedContactsL(uid, *array, aOutput,
                                  CContactDatabase::EDefault);
  CleanupStack::PopAndDestroy(array);
  }

void CContactWrite::ImportContactL(RReadStream& aInput)
  {
  TBool success;
  CArrayPtr<CContactItem>* importedContacts =
              iCntDb->ImportContactsL
          (
          TUid::Uid(KVersitEntityUidVCard),
          aInput,
          success,
          CContactDatabase::EImportSingleContact |
          CContactDatabase::EIncludeX |
          CContactDatabase::ETTFormat
          );
```

```
if (success)
  {
  // use the cleanupstack if you intend to commit
  // the imported contact to the database.
  delete importedContacts->At(0);
  // because CArrayPtr::Reset() isn't enough
  delete importedContacts;
  }
  else
  {
  delete importedContacts; // just in case
  User::Leave(KErrGeneral);
  }
}
```

Tip: Using `EImportSingleContact` is important here so success is meaningful. Otherwise, you risk reading more of the stream than you meant to or missing an error report. You should also have a look at the `CParserVCard` API.

What may go wrong when you do this: The Symbian OS contact engine allows developers to create contact items that cannot be fully converted into vCard data. The pitfalls of this are too numerous to enumerate here, so experimentation will be required if you start using advanced contact functionalities. Field mappings and `CContact-Database::EIncludeXyz` are here to help.

What may go wrong when you do this: If you have gone through this section in order and run each set of sample code, the test contact database may be without an own card, because you removed it in Recipe 4.2.3.4. Just run the `\PIM\PopulateContact` sample code again to add it back to the database.

4.2.4.3   Use the vCal Format

Amount of time required: 40 minutes
Location of example code: `\PIM\AgendaStandard`
Required library(s): `calinterimapi.lib`
Required header file(s): `calsession.h`, `calentryview.h`, `calprogresscallback.h`, `caldataexchange.h`
Required platform security capability(s): `ReadUserData WriteUser-Data`

Problem: You want to send and receive calendar entries across different devices.

Solution: The vCal standard is supported by many devices, mobile or not, regardless of their operating system. The vCal specification can be found at ***www.imc.org/pdi/vcal-10.txt*** (Symbian OS v9.1 supports vCal 1.0). However, from Symbian OS v9.1, there has been a clear push toward the iCalendar standard, which is specified at ***www.faqs.org/rfcs/rfc2445.html***.

In effect, we need to convert text data into an event in the Calendar database, and then convert it back again.

Symbian OS streams have the advantage of exposing the same API, regardless of where the data is actually stored (file, descriptor, DBMS, etc.), so they are perfect for our purpose here. You will find further discussion of streams in the file handling recipes given in Section 4.1.

You must first open the Calendar database as you did in Recipe 4.2.3.1:

```
#include <calsession.h> // and link to calinterimapi.lib
#include <calentryview.h>
#include <calprogresscallback.h>
#include <caldataexchange.h>
#include <CalDataFormat.h>
#include <s32strm.h> // and link to estor.lib
#include <mmf\common\mmfcontrollerpluginresolver.h>
// this last one is for the ResetAndDestroy TCleanupItem

class CCalWrite : public CBase, public MCalProgressCallBack
  {
public:
  static CCalWrite* NewL();
  ~CCalWrite(); // to delete iCalSes and iCalView
  void ExportEventL(TCalLocalUid aEventId,
                    RWriteStream& aOutput);
  void ImportEventL(RReadStream& aInput);
public: // from MCalProgressCallBack
  void Progress(TInt){};
  void Completed(TInt){};
  TBool NotifyProgress(){return EFalse;};
private:
  void ConstructL();
private:
  CCalSession* iCalSes;
  CCalEntryView* iCalView;
  };

void CCalWrite::ExportEventL(TCalLocalUid aEventId,
                             RWriteStream& aOutput)
  {
  CCalEntry* entry = iCalView->FetchL(aEventId);
  if (NULL == entry)
    {
    User::Leave(KErrNotFound);
    }
  else
    {
    CleanupStack::PushL(entry);
```

```
    CCalDataExchange* exch =
                    CCalDataExchange::NewL(*iCalSes);
    CleanupStack::PushL(exch);
    RPointerArray<CCalEntry> array;
    CleanupClosePushL(array);
    array.AppendL(entry);
    // as in [1.5.], we don't transfer ownership of entry
    // to array.
    exch->ExportL(KUidVCalendar, aOutput, array);
    // Clean up array, exch, entry
    CleanupStack::PopAndDestroy(3, entry);
    }
}

void CCalWrite::ImportEventL(RReadStream& aInput)
  {
  RPointerArray<CCalEntry> array;
  CleanupResetAndDestroyPushL(array);
  CCalDataExchange* exch = CCalDataExchange::NewL(*iCalSes);
  CleanupStack::PushL(exch);
  exch->ImportL(KUidVCalendar, aInput, array, 0, 1);
  CleanupStack::PopAndDestroy(exch);
  // do something with the imported event here (code omitted)
  ...
  CleanupStack::PopAndDestroy(&array);
  }
```

What may go wrong when you do this: The Symbian OS Calendar
APIs allow developers to create calendar entries that cannot be fully
converted into vCal data. The pitfalls of this are too numerous to
enumerate here, so experimentation may be required.

Tip: You should also have a look at the `CParserVCal` API.

4.2.4.4   Create a Repeating Calendar Event

Amount of time required: 45 minutes
Location of example code: \PIM\AgendaRepeat
Required library(s): calinterimapi.lib
Required header file(s): calsession.h, calentryview.h,
calrrule.h, calprogresscallback.h
Required platform security capability(s): ReadUserData WriteUser-
Data

Problem: You want to create a new calendar event that repeats daily and
every other week.

Solution: Much of this example repeats what we described in Recipe 4.2.3.6 (for example, the GUID generator, which we won't discuss again here).

First of all, open the database as described in Recipe 4.2.3.1:

```
#include <calsession.h> // and link to calinterimapi.lib
#include <calentryview.h>
#include <calrrule.h>
#include <calprogresscallback.h>
#include <e32const.h>

class CCalWrite : public CBase, public MCalProgressCallBack
  {
public:
  static CCalWrite* NewL();
  ~CCalWrite(); // to delete iCalSes and iCalView
  void AddRepeatL(const TDesC& aDescription,
                    TInt aWeeklyInterval);
public: // from MCalProgressCallBack
  void Progress(TInt){};
  void Completed(TInt){};
  TBool NotifyProgress(){return EFalse;};
private:
  void ConstructL();
  HBufC8* MakeGuidLC();
private:
  CCalSession* iCalSes;
  CCalEntryView* iCalView;
  };

void CCalWrite:: AddRepeatL(const TDesC& aDescription,
                                TInt aWeeklyInterval)
  {// create a new entry
  HBufC8* guid = MakeGuidLC();
  CCalEntry* entry = CCalEntry::NewL(CCalEntry::EAppt, guid,
                                      CCalEntry::EMethodNone, 0);
  CleanupStack::Pop(guid);
  CleanupStack::PushL(entry);

  // set some values
  TTime now;
  now.UniversalTime();
  now += TTimeIntervalHours(1); // start in an hour
  TCalTime start;
  start.SetTimeUtcL(now);
  now += TTimeIntervalHours(1); // lasts an hour
  TCalTime end;
  end.SetTimeUtcL(now);
  entry->SetStartAndEndTimeL(start, end);
  entry->SetDescriptionL(aDescription);

  // make the repeat rule
  TCalRRule rule(TCalRRule::EWeekly);
  rule.SetDtStart(start);
  rule.SetCount(52/aWeeklyInterval); // for a year
  rule.SetInterval(aWeeklyInterval);
```

```
RArray<TDay> days;
CleanupClosePushL(days);
days.AppendL(EMonday);
days.AppendL(ETuesday);
days.AppendL(EWednesday);
days.AppendL(EThursday);
days.AppendL(EFriday);

rule.SetByDay(days); // every weekday
CleanupStack::PopAndDestroy(&days);
entry->SetRRuleL(rule);

// add the entry to the database
RPointerArray<CCalEntry> array;
CleanupClosePushL(array);
array.AppendL(entry);
// Don't transfer ownership of entry to array
TInt success = 0;
iCalView->StoreL(array, success);
if (success < 1)
  {
  User::Leave(KErrGeneral);
  }
CleanupStack::PopAndDestroy(2, entry); // array, entry
  }
```

4.2.5   Advanced Recipes

4.2.5.1   Find a Contact

Amount of time required: 1 hour
Location of example code: \PIM\ContactFind
Required library(s): cntmodel.lib
Required header file(s): cntdb.h, cntitem.h, cntfield.h,
cntdef.h
Required platform security capability(s): ReadUserData WriteUser-
Data

Problem: You want to find all the contacts that match a given search criterion.

Solution: What you want is a collection of TContactItemId objects. All the elements it contains will match your search criterion, but they are added to the collection in no particular order.

Once returned, the collection can be used to retrieve data from each element individually. Remember to use a CContactItemViewDef, as in Recipe 4.2.3.2.

The recipe is used to find out which contacts contain some string in one (or any) of their fields. The API we are going to use requires you to implement a word-parsing method. You can look for contacts using a full sentence but the internal engine only supports single words. So it is up to you to tell the engine how to extract single words out of a sentence, according to your own set of rules. The code is implemented using a `TCallback`, but it doesn't require an observer interface.

First open the database as in Recipe 4.2.3.1:

```
#include <cntdb.h> // and link to cntmodel.lib
#include <cntitem.h>
#include <cntfield.h>
#include <cntdef.h>
#include <badesca.h> // and link to bafl.lib (for descriptor arrays)

class CContactRead : public CBase
  {
public:
  static CContactRead* NewL();
  ~CContactRead(); // to delete iCntDb
public:
  static TInt ParseWord(TAny*);
  CContactIdArray* FindWithCallbackLC(TFieldType aField,
                                      const TDesC& aMatch);
private:
  void ConstructL();
  CContactRead();
private:
  TCallBack iCallback;
  CContactDatabase* iCntDb;
  };

// we need to setup the callback.
CContactRead::CContactRead()
  : iCallback(&CContactRead::ParseWord)
  {}

// runs the search and transfer ownership of
// the returned object to the caller.
CContactIdArray* CContactRead::FindWithCallbackL(TFieldType aField,
                                                 const TDesC& aMatch)
  {
  TContactTextDefItem field(aField);
  CContactTextDef* textDef = CContactTextDef::NewL();
  CleanupStack::PushL(textDef);
  textDef->AppendL(field);

  // we need a descriptor array to setup the search
  CDesCArray* match = new (ELeave) CDesCArrayFlat(1);
  CleanupStack::PushL(match);
      match->AppendL(aMatch);

  CContactIdArray* result = iCntDb->FindInTextDefLC(*match,
                                                    textDef, iCallback);
  CleanupStack::Pop(result);
  CleanupStack::PopAndDestroy(2, textDef);
      return result;
  }
```

```
// The whole purpose of the callback at this point is to take the
// content of the aMatch parameter in CContactRead::FindByCallbackL()
// and split it into words, presumably using punctuation and spaces.
// This is just a sample implementation designed for illustration.
// Note that ParseWord can't leave.
TInt CContactRead::ParseWord(TAny* aParam)
    {
  SFindInTextDefWordParser* parserStruct =
                            (SFindInTextDefWordParser*)aParam;
  TPtrC searchString(*(parserStruct->iSearchString));
  TInt index = KErrNotFound;
  TInt error = KErrNone;
  while(0 <= (index = searchString.Locate(' ')))
    {
    if (index > 0)
      {
      TRAP(error,
      parserStruct->iWordArray->AppendL(
      searchString.Left(index)));
      if (error != KErrNone)
        return error;
      if (searchString.Length() > index + 1)
        {
        searchString.Set(searchString.Mid(index + 1));
        }
      else
        {
        searchString.Set(KNullDesC());
        break;
        }
      }
    else
      {
      // remove first character as it is a space
      searchString.Set(searchString.Mid(1));
      }

    }
  if(searchString.Length() > 0) // the last word
    {
    TRAP(error,
    parserStruct->iWordArray->AppendL(searchString));
    if (error != KErrNone)
      return error;
    }
  return KErrNone;
    }
```

Tip: On large contact databases, a search can end up taking some time. This is why there is an asynchronous method you can use: `CContactDatabase::FindInTextDefAsyncL()`. See the code sample in `\PIM\ContactAsynchFind` for more details.

> **What may go wrong when you do this:** Well, searching itself is not much of a problem. Reading all the contacts you found afterwards can take a huge amount of time if there are too many. Depending on the circumstances, you may want to discover them in smaller batches (i.e., using CIdle).

4.2.5.2 Move a Contact to Another Group

Amount of time required: 1 hour
Location of example code: \PIM\ContactMove
Required library(s): cntmodel.lib
Required header file(s): cntdb.h, cntitem.h, cntfield.h, cntdef.h
Required platform security capability(s): ReadUserData WriteUser-Data

Problem: You want to remove a contact card from one group and then add it to another group.

Solution: In order to make the problem a little more challenging, we are going to assume that the group we want to add the contact to is only known by its name (or label). That way, we also have to find it first.

However, even though contacts can belong to several groups at once, we are just going to remove the contact from the first group we find it belonging to. Adding a loop to handle multiple groups is trivial.

First of all, open the database as you did in Recipe 4.2.3.1:

```cpp
#include <cntdb.h> // and link to cntmodel.lib
#include <cntitem.h>
#include <cntfield.h>
#include <cntdef.h>

class CContactWrite : public CBase
    {
public:
  static CContactWrite* NewL();
  ~CContactWrite(); // to delete iCntDb
  void MoveContactL(TContactItemId aCntId,
                 const TDesC& aNewGroup);
private:
  void ConstructL();
private:
  CContactDatabase* iCntDb;
  };

void CContactWrite::MoveContactL(TContactItemId aCntId,
                                const TDesC& aNewGroup)
  {// open the contact item for exclusive use
  CContactItem* item = iCntDb->OpenContactLX(aCntId);
  CleanupStack::PushL(item);
```

```
// Let's find out what group the contact already belongs to
TContactItemId groupId = KNullContactId;
CContactItem* group = NULL;
if (KUidContactCard == item->Type())
  {
  CContactCard* card = (CContactCard*)item;
  CContactIdArray* ids = card->GroupsJoinedLC();
  if (0 < ids->Count())
    {
    groupId = (*ids)[0];
    }
  CleanupStack::PopAndDestroy(ids);
  }
if (KNullContactId != groupId)
  {
  // let's remove the contact from the group
  group = iCntDb->OpenContactLX(groupId);
  CleanupStack::PushL(group);
  iCntDb->RemoveContactFromGroupL(*item, *group);
  CleanupStack::PopAndDestroy(group);
  CleanupStack::PopAndDestroy(); // exclusive lock on group
  group = NULL;
  }

CleanupStack::PopAndDestroy(2); // item, exclusive lock on item

// let's find the new group in the database, or create it

groupId = KNullContactId;
CContactIdArray* groupArrayId = iCntDb->GetGroupIdListL();
  if (NULL != groupArrayId)
  {
  CleanupStack::PushL(groupArrayId);
  for (TInt ii = 0 ; ii < groupArrayId->Count() ; ++ii)
  {
  group = iCntDb->ReadContactLC((*groupArrayId)[ii]);
  TPtrC label = ((CContactGroup*)group)->
                        GetGroupLabelL();
  if (aNewGroup.MatchC(label))
  {
  groupId = (*groupArrayId)[ii];
  ii = groupArrayId->Count(); // break
  }
  CleanupStack::PopAndDestroy(group);
  group = NULL;
  }
  CleanupStack::PopAndDestroy(groupArrayId);
  }
if (KNullContactId == groupId)
  {
  group = iCntDb->CreateContactGroupLC(aNewGroup);
  groupId = group->Id();
  CleanupStack::PopAndDestroy(group);
  }
    // let's add the contact to the group
iCntDb->AddContactToGroupL(aCntId, groupId);
}
```

> **Tip:** Here, we face the issue of non-atomic operations. If the method fails halfway through, the contact may become an orphan. Rolling the changes back requires a considered approach, which should be added explicitly because you cannot rely on the cleanup stack to unwind every transaction.

4.2.5.3 Find Out If You are Available

Amount of time required: 45 minutes
Location of example code: \PIM\AgendaSearch
Required library(s): calinterimapi.lib
Required header file(s): calsession.h, calinstanceview.h, calinstance.h, calprogresscallback.h
Required platform security capability(s): ReadUserData WriteUser-Data

Problem: You want to know what is in the calendar at a given time slot.

Solution: At this level, we don't care that much about calendar entries but rather about entry instances (an instance exists every time an entry is repeated). The API that allows us to filter the database using a time slot is CalCommon::TCalViewFilter, which has several subclasses, for different purposes.

```cpp
#include <calsession.h> // and link to calinterimapi.lib
#include <calinstanceview.h>
#include <calinstance.h>
#include <calprogresscallback.h>
#include <mmf\common\mmfcontrollerpluginresolver.h>
// this last on is for the ResetAndDestroy TCleanupItem

class CCalRead : public CBase, public MCalProgressCallBack
  {
public:
  static CCalRead* NewL();
  ~CCalRead(); // to delete iCalSes and iCalView
  TBool CheckFreeL(TTime aStartUtc, TTimeIntervalMinutes aSlot);
public: // from MCalProgressCallBack
  void Progress(TInt){};
  void Completed(TInt){};
  TBool NotifyProgress(){return EFalse;};
private:
  void ConstructL();
private:
  CCalSession* iCalSes;
  CCalInstanceView* iCalView;
  };

// You need an opened calendar database, which is typically
// the default database in the phone.
```

```
// You should assume that it may not have been created before.
void CCalRead::ConstructL()
  {
  iCalSes = CCalSession::NewL();
      const TDesC& name = iCalSes->DefaultFileNameL();
  TRAPD(error, iCalSes->CreateCalFileL(name));
  if (error != KErrAlreadyExists)
    {
    User::LeaveIfError(error);
    }
  iCalSes->OpenL(KNullDesC);
  iCalView = CCalInstanceView::NewL(*iCalSes, *this);
      }


TBool CCalRead::CheckFreeL(TTime aStartUtc,
                                            TTimeIntervalMinutes aSlot)
  {
  TBool result = ETrue;
  TCalTime start;
  TCalTime end;
  start.SetTimeUtcL(aStartUtc);
  TTime endUtc = aStartUtc + aSlot;
  end.SetTimeUtcL(endUtc);
  CalCommon::TCalTimeRange range(start, end);
  RPointerArray<CCalInstance> array;
  CleanupResetAndDestroyPushL(array);
  iCalView->FindInstanceL(array, CalCommon::EIncludeAll, range);
  result = (0 == array.Count());
  CleanupStack::PopAndDestroy(&array);
  return result;
  }
```

4.2.5.4   Get Attendee List

Amount of time required: 45 minutes
Location of example code: \PIM\AgendaPeople
Required library(s): calinterimapi.lib
Required header file(s): calsession.h, calentryview.h,
calprogresscallback.h, caluser.h
Required platform security capability(s): ReadUserData WriteUser-
Data

Problem: You want to find the addresses of the attendees who accepted an invitation.

Solution: What you want is a descriptor array that will contain the email addresses of everybody who is going to attend the meeting. Once you have selected the meeting you are interested in, you need to go through its list of attendees and read the stored address of each one.

```
#include <calsession.h> // and link to calinterimapi.lib
#include <calentryview.h>
```

```
#include <calprogresscallback.h>
#include <caluser.h>
#include <badesca.h> // and link to bafl.lib

class CCalRead : public CBase, public MCalProgressCallBack
  {
public:
  static CCalRead* NewL();
  ~CCalWrite(); // to delete iCalSes and iCalView
  CDesCArray* GetAttendeesL(TCalLocalUid aEventId);
public: // from MCalProgressCallBack
  void Progress(TInt){};
  void Completed(TInt){};
  TBool NotifyProgress(){return EFalse;};
private:
  void ConstructL();
private:
  CCalSession* iCalSes;
  CCalEntryView* iCalView;
  };

// You need an opened calendar database, which is typically
// the default database in the phone.
// You should assume that it may not have been created before.
void CCalRead::ConstructL()
  {
  iCalSes = CCalSession::NewL();
  const TDesC& name = iCalSes->DefaultFileNameL();
  TRAPD(error, iCalSes->CreateCalFileL(name));
  if (error != KErrAlreadyExists)
    {
    User::LeaveIfError(error);
    }
  iCalSes->OpenL(KNullDesC);
  iCalView = CCalEntryView::NewL(*iCalSes, *this);
  }

// Transfers ownership of result to caller
CDesCArray* CCalRead::GetAttendeesL(TCalLocalUid aEventId)
  {
  CDesCArray* result = NULL;
  // find the event
  CCalEntry* entry = iCalView->FetchL(aEventId);
  // get attendees
  if (NULL != entry)
    {
    CleanupStack::PushL(entry);
    RPointerArray<CCalAttendee>& list = entry->AttendeesL();
    if (list.Count() > 0)
      {
      result = new (ELeave) CDesCArrayFlat(list.Count());
      CleanupStack::PushL(result);
      for (TInt ii = 0 ; ii < list.Count() ; ++ii)
        {
        result->AppendL(list[ii]->Address());
        }
      CleanupStack::Pop(result);
      }
```

```
  CleanupStack::PopAndDestroy(entry);
  }
return result;
}
```

What may go wrong when you do this: `CCalAttendee` is basically a placeholder for contact information and the format of the data it contains is not as strictly enforced as it could be. Retrieving the address will work fine as long as it is indeed the email address that was stored as attendee data when it was created.

What may go wrong when you do this: If you have gone through this section in order, the last calendar entry you modified is from the `\PIM\AgendaRepeat` code sample and it doesn't have any attendees. Just run the `\PIM\PopulateAgenda` code sample again to find some attendees.

4.3   Networking

Symbian OS has comprehensive support for IP networking protocols for developing applications that can run over a variety of IP-capable bearers, whether it is Wireless LAN or GPRS.

The networking stack is implemented using client–server architecture, in the ESOCK component, just like many other framework service providers in Symbian OS. The client side of ESOCK exposes a generic, protocol-independent API; the server side provides a plug-in-based interface to load and manage various protocols, each of which can be run in a separate thread and are accessible through the client APIs. Examples of protocols loaded by ESOCK include Bluetooth, IrDA and IP.

The IP thread hosts the TCP/IP stack, which implements the popular TCP (RFC 793) and UDP (RFC 768) protocols running over IP (RFC 791). The TCP/IP stack in turn communicates with low-level bearers representing link layer technologies such as WLAN and GPRS through network interfaces.

CommsDat, which is a separate client library, is used to store and retrieve various settings relating to the networking subsystem and is used by both the IP-subsystem and client applications for settings retrieval and storage. See Figure 4.3.1.

In order to keep them as simple as possible, the code samples in these recipes use as few active objects as possible. Most asynchronous method calls are simply followed by `User::WaitForRequest()`. This

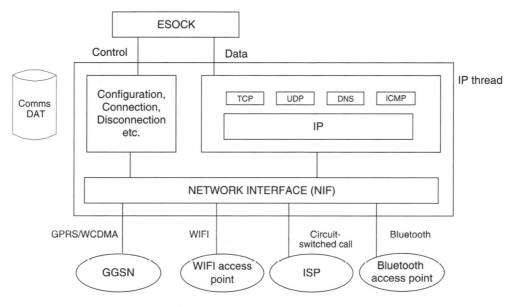

Figure 4.3.1   Symbian OS Networking Subsystem and Bearer Technologies

is not how production-quality code should behave, and the code samples provided for download to accompany this book will illustrate how to call asynchronous APIs correctly using active objects. You can also read more about asynchronous calls and event handling on Symbian OS in Chapter 3.

4.3.1   Getting Started

The three most important APIs for developing IP-enabled applications are RConnection, RSocket and RHostResolver – all of which are declared in es_sock.h. The RConnection API is used for connection selection/startup and management. The RSocket and RHostResolver APIs implement socket and host resolver functionality respectively, similar to the BSD-style socket and host resolver APIs found on other operating systems.

IP-enabled applications require NetworkServices capability to be present, since it is required for initiating a network connection and sending and receiving data over protocols such as TCP and UDP.

On a mobile device, where multiple bearers are available and can be active at the same time – for example, GPRS and WLAN – it is important to have a mechanism that allows applications to choose over which bearer IP data is sent and received; not only because of potential cost issues involved (WLAN might be cheaper than using GPRS), but also for potential routing issues. The RConnection API facilitates an explicit way to start a particular network connection on a bearer to remove all ambiguity.[1] Once the network connection has been initiated, the socket and host resolver API can use that particular connection to send and receive data. Besides selection and tearing down of a network connection, RConnection can be used to gather information about the active network connection such as connection status, how much data was sent and received at link layer, and so on.

An Internet Access Point (IAP) is a collection of settings that enables selection of a particular network connection on a particular bearer, which is specified as a selection parameter when starting a connection using the RConnection API.

The CommsDat API enables retrieval of configuration information from the settings database, known as the CommsDat database. Examples of configuration information stored in CommsDat include the list of available IAPs, default connection preferences and settings specific to an IAP, which could be the phone number in case of a dial-up ISP, the access point name (APN) in case of a GPRS network or the SSID of a WLAN access point in case the IAP is configured to use WLAN as a bearer.

In most cases, barring sensitive data like passwords, reading information from the CommsDat does not require any platform security capability.

The common pattern for any IP-enabled application connecting to an IP network and using its services would normally be:

Configure – select the correct IAP; programmatically, by asking the user or letting the system choose one.
Connect – start connection using selected connection parameters.
Use – send and receive data using sockets and finally.
Disconnect – close socket connection and indicate that the application has finished using the connection by closing it.

We will use the above pattern throughout for example code.

4.3.2 Setting Up the Environment

Running your IP-enabled application under the emulator usually requires some extra steps beyond installing the SDK. In this subsection we will look at some of the most common methods for enabling IP networking connectivity on the emulator, listed in Table 4.3.1.

---

[1] How Symbian OS facilitates establishing simultaneous, independent, network connections to multiple bearers (or even the same bearer using different networks), known as multihoming, is discussed in depth in chapter 6 of *Symbian OS Communication Programming*, 2nd Edition, by Iain Campbell.

Table 4.3.1 Common Methods for Enabling IP Network Connectivity

Technology	Requirement
WinPCap	A wired Ethernet card on your PC connected to a network
WinTAP	Any IP connection from your PC and enabling Internet Connection Sharing (ICS) on your PC
WinSock	Any IP connection from your PC

4.3.2.1 Using the SDK Configuration Tools

If you are using the S60 emulator, it already comes configured with the WinSock method, which should just work out of the box, since it is going to simply use the Windows networking stack for connectivity.

In the case of UIQ, the SDK installer will ask during installation to install WinPCap, a free packet capture library for Windows. If you accept, the WinPCap method will be available for the UIQ installer. After installation, you will need to finalize the WinPCap setup by going to (from the Windows Start menu) UIQ 3 SDK -> SDKConfig -> Communications tab and click 'Apply Ethernet'. Note that the UIQ 3.0 SDK can be picky about the version of Perl installed and can prevent the SDKConfig application from running. It is recommended you install the one that comes with the SDK installer (version 5.6.1.635).

4.3.2.2 Using **WinPCap**

As we saw earlier, the SDKConfig application can be used to configure WinPCap-based IP connectivity for the UIQ SDK. What the SDKConfig application really does is set up a virtual Ethernet driver for the emulator, which shares your PC's Ethernet interface. The configuration option for the virtual Ethernet driver is stored in the epoc.ini file (stored in sdk_installation_path\epoc32\data), and looks like this:

```
ETHER_NIF=\Device\NPF_{80FA5794-DAC8-4BAA-94C9-A0FAB2DE04D8}
ETHER_MAC=020702b68886
ETHER_SPEED=100Mbps
```

In case the SDKConfig application fails to update the epoc.ini file, or you would like to use Ethernet connectivity in the S60 SDK, you will need to edit epoc.ini to add the lines above, with the appropriate parameters.

ETHER_NIF specifies which Ethernet network card to use on your PC. The best way to get this is to install a free protocol analysis tool like WireShark or Ethereal and use the 'Capture Options' dialog's 'Interface' dropdown list to select the appropriate adapter and copy the part starting with '\Device...' and specify that in the ETHER_NIF option.

ETHER_MAC specifies the MAC address of your virtual adapter. This is the same as the MAC address of the selected adapter in ETHER_NIF, with the top byte changed from 00 to 02 (that is, if the original MAC was 000702b68886, it becomes 020702b68886), which means locally administered MAC according to IEEE. Certain networks, for example corporate LANs, sometimes use MAC address filtering to only allow packets from registered LAN adapters. Make sure that this virtual MAC is registered with the network (ask your network admin) if that is the case.

Once you have finished making the changes to the epoc.ini file, you are ready to generate the CommsDat database that will use the settings. However, before you generate the new database, it is better that you back up the existing one, so that you can go back if the new settings don't work. Backing up of the existing database is achieved through running a tool called ceddump.exe from the command line, which when invoked creates a file called cedout.cfg in the emulator's C: drive (i.e., sdk_path\epoc32\winscw\c\ folder). To apply the Ethernet settings, you will need a CommsDat database that is already configured with appropriate Ethernet settings; fortunately, one already ships with the SDK, ethernetced.xml, again found in the emulator's C: drive. Now run ced.exe from the command line, specifying the emulator path of ethernetced.xml as an argument (e.g., ced c:\ethernetced.xml). Once ced has finished running, check the emulator's C: drive for ced.log. If there was any problem generating the new database, you should be able to spot it here; look for words like failure, failed and error. Once the database is generated, there should be multiple IAPs set up for use. For the vast majority, the one called 'Ethernet with Daemon Dynamic IP' should work out of the box, since it is configured to use DHCP to allocate IP address and name server for the virtual Ethernet adapter. If you would like to use a statically allocated IP address for some reason and know other configuration information like name server address(s), you can use the IAP 'Ethernet No Daemon Static IP', however you will have to change the relevant fields in the service table in ethernetced.xml and regenerate CommsDat, using the above procedure.

Note that on UIQ 3.0 SDK installation, the ethernetced.xml file is missing. You can get a copy from the S60 SDK 3rd Edition SDK.

Tip: ced.exe supports an additional commandline option -v that reports all errors encountered while generating the CommsDat database from a configuration file at the end of the ced.log file, which is quite helpful. However, using the -v option will require using the -i option to specify the input configuration file (e.g., ced -v -i c:\ethernetced.xml).

4.3.2.3 Using `WinTAP`

`WinTAP` is a relatively new connectivity method available to Symbian OS emulators. Instructions on how to install and use it can be found at: ***www.developer.symbian.com/main/tools/devtools***. The main advantage of `WinTAP` is that it doesn't require the elaborate setup involving `WinPCap` and creates a virtual Ethernet adapter that is visible on a Windows PC too. The slight downside of this method is that it requires enabling of Internet Connection Sharing on your PC, since the virtual adapter accesses the IP network through the physical adapter on which ICS was enabled; for example, the PC LAN card. Note that problems associated with network access over ICS will apply to your application too.

4.3.2.4 Using `WinSock`

The `WinSock` method is the default connectivity solution in the S60 SDK and uses Windows sockets directly, bypassing the Symbian OS TCP/IP stack. The biggest advantage is that there is no special setup required at all, since the Symbian OS applications running under the emulator are just clients to the Windows networking stack. The downside is that setting or retrieval of protocol-level options supported by the Symbian OS TCP/IP stack which are not present in the Windows stack will fail, besides features that are not supported on `WinSock`, like IP multicasting. Hence, be sure to pick the right connectivity method depending on the application you are developing.

At the time of writing, there is no `WinSock` connectivity method available for the UIQ 3 SDKs based on Symbian OS v9.x.

4.3.3 HTTP

The HTTP framework in Symbian OS provides a HTTP client stack, supporting all standard HTTP 1.1 services and protocol-defined requests, including GET and POST. The framework also supports compatibility with HTTP 1.0 servers, authentication (basic and digest) and secure connections. Notable omissions include cookie management, caching and content encoding. However, the framework supports an extensible filter mechanism that can be used to provide support for the above. Check your SDK documentation for more information.

The HTTP framework is implemented as a client-side library in `http.lib`. The framework-related classes and so on are defined in `http.h`. HTTP requires access to a network connection; hence applications using the HTTP framework need `NetworkServices` platform security capability.

4.3.4 `InetProtUtils`

The `InetProtUtils` API is used to handle URIs, including constructing and modifying a URI, extracting URI components and utility parsing methods.

The Universal Resource Identifier (URI), described in RFC 2396, is a formatted string that identifies the location and name of a resource; for example, a web address (in fact, a URI can be seen as an extended URL) or a file in the local file system.

The `InetProtUtils` API is implemented in `InetProtUtils.lib` and requires no platform security capability for usage.

Note that all URI-related methods in `InetProtUtils` operate on 8-bit descriptors, since a URI, by definition, can only be 8-bit UTF-8 encoded text. For convenience, the URI classes support a method called `DisplayFormL()` where applicable, which returns the 16-bit Unicode equivalent.

4.3.5 Easy Recipes

4.3.5.1 Send/Receive Data Using TCP Sockets

Amount of time required: 15 minutes
Location of example code: `\Networking\TCPSendReceive`
Required library(s): `esock.lib`, `insock.lib`
Required header file(s): `es_sock.h`, `in_sock.h`
Required platform security capability(s): `NetworkServices`

Problem: You want to send and receive data using TCP sockets.

Solution: Use `RSocket::Connect()` to connect to a remote peer and use `RSocket::Send()` and `RSocket::RecvOneOrMore()` to exchange data with the remote peer.

```
// RSocketServ, RConnection et al. (link to esock.lib)
#include <es_sock.h>
// KAfInet et al (link to insock.lib)
#include <in_sock.h>

void TCPSendReceiveL()
  {
  // Open socket server session
  RSocketServ ss;
  CleanupClosePushL(ss);
  User::LeaveIfError(ss.Connect());

  // Open connection on the socket server session
  RConnection conn;
  CleanupClosePushL(conn);
  User::LeaveIfError(conn.Open(ss));

  // Start the default connection
```

```
TRequestStatus status;
conn.Start(status);

// Wait for the connection to start
User::WaitForRequest(status);

// Check if Start succeed
User::LeaveIfError(status.Int());

// Open TCP socket on the started connection
RSocket sock;
CleanupClosePushL(sock);
User::LeaveIfError(
sock.Open(ss, KAfInet, KSockStream, KProtocolInetTcp, conn));

// Connect to the remote peer (symbian.com)
TInetAddr remoteAddr(INET_ADDR(81, 89, 143, 203), 80);
sock.Connect(remoteAddr, status);
User::WaitForRequest(status);
User::LeaveIfError(status.Int());

// Now that we are connected,
// exchange some data...
// Make a HTTP GET request to the remote peer
_LIT8(KHTTPGetRequest, "GET / HTTP/1.0\r\n
        host: www.symbian.com\r\n\r\n");
sock.Write(KHTTPGetRequest(), status);
User::WaitForRequest(status);
// Did we manage to queue the data?
User::LeaveIfError(status.Int());

// Request made, now read the response
RBuf8 response;
response.CreateL(512);
response.CleanupClosePushL();
TSockXfrLength len;
sock.RecvOneOrMore(response, 0, status, len);
User::WaitForRequest(status);
// Did read fail or the remote peer closed the
// connection?
User::LeaveIfError(status.Int());

// Check the length of the data received
TInt lenRecv = response.Length();

// Shutdown the socket.
// Discard any pending read/write
sock.Shutdown(RSocket::EImmediate, status);
User::WaitForRequest(status);

// Close the response buffer,
// socket, connection and socket server session
CleanupStack::PopAndDestroy(4);
}
```

Discussion: The above code snippet demonstrates usage of a TCP socket to send and receive some data. Even though it is a simple example, it still demonstrates how the vast majority of applications will use TCP sockets.

This code starts a network connection with the system default settings. On the S60 platform, the standard behavior is to display a dialog with the list of IAPs available and let the user select one. On UIQ, calling `RConnection::Start()` without a parameter will start the preferred IAP, if there is one – which is defined through the Internet account settings in the control panel. As a result, an IAP list dialog may not be displayed.

The `TInetAddr` class encapsulates an IP4 or IP6 address and any application using IP-based sockets, whether it is TCP or UDP, will use this class to specify an address and port for the endpoint to connect to.

We use `RSocket::RecvOneOrMore()` to receive data from the remote peer; unlike `RSocket::Read()` and `RSocket::Recv()`, which wait to return till the buffer (i.e., descriptor) has been filled to its `MaxLength()` and can potentially be confusing, `RSocket::RecvOneOrMore()` returns whenever there is some data to be read from the TCP stack's receive queue. The length of the data received can be identified by checking the `TSockXfrLength` parameter or the length of the buffer; in the case of TCP, both are always the same. The `RecvXyz()`/`Read()` methods complete with `KErrEof` if the remote peer disconnected or the socket was shut down with `TShutdown::EStopInput` (see below).

`RSocket::Close()` ensures that all data that is queued for sending/receiving is processed first. This might create a problem in certain cases, because a seemingly harmless call to `Close()` can block the thread as it completes normal disconnection. The `RSocket` class provides two ways to mitigate this issue. The first method, `Shutdown()`, asynchronously disconnects the TCP connection. `Shutdown()` takes a parameter of type `TShutdown` which directs how the TCP disconnection takes place. The second method is to set the TCP linger option using `TSoTcpLingerOpt` (defined in `in6_opt.h`) on the socket before it is closed. In fact, the Symbian OS implementation of the TCP/IP stack supports a comprehensive range of configuration options as found in other platforms. See code sample for download accompanying this book to see how socket/protocol-level options are specified.

Tip: Always ensure that the buffer passed in the `RecvXyz()`/`Read()` methods is ample and tailored to your protocol. Otherwise you will end up calling the receive methods multiple times to get data, which is inefficient. Also, it is a common mistake to assume that the `Send()`/`Write()` methods complete when the data has been delivered to the remote endpoint. In reality, they return after data is queued in the TCP/IP stack's internal buffer.

4.3.5.2 Force a Connection to Use a Specific Bearer

Amount of time required: 15 minutes
Location of example code: \Networking\StartConnectionWith-Prefs
Required library(s): esock.lib, commdb.lib
Required header file(s): es_sock.h, commdbconnpref.h
Required platform security capability(s): NetworkServices

Problem: You want to force a connection to use a particular bearer.

Solution: Use TCommDbConnPref to specify a bearer selection preference for RConnection::Start().

```cpp
#include <es_sock.h> // RSocketServ, RConnection (link to esock.lib)
#include <commdbconnpref.h> // TCommDbConnPref (link to commdb.lib)

void StartConnectionWithPrefsL()
  {
  // Open socket server session
  RSocketServ ss;
  CleanupClosePushL(ss);
  User::LeaveIfError(ss.Connect());

  // Open connection on the socket server session
  RConnection conn;
  CleanupClosePushL(conn);
  User::LeaveIfError(conn.Open(ss));

  // Define the selection preferences...
  TCommDbConnPref startPrefs;
  // Select bearers of type
  // GPRS and Wireless LAN only
  startPrefs.SetBearerSet(ECommDbBearerGPRS| ECommDbBearerWLAN);
  // Make sure the user is prompted with a list
  // of IAPs matching the preferences
  startPrefs.SetDialogPreference(ECommDbDialogPrefPrompt);

  // Start connection using our preference
  TRequestStatus status;
  conn.Start(startPrefs, status);

  // Wait for the connection to start
  User::WaitForRequest(status);
  // Check if Start succeed

  TInt error = status.Int();

  // Do something...

  // Close the connection and socket server session
  CleanupStack::PopAndDestroy(2);
  }
```

Discussion: The complete list of bearer sets is defined as part of the TCommDbBearer enumeration, defined in cdbcols.h.

Note that, on UIQ, it is necessary to explicitly specify that the user will be prompted with an IAP list dialog, done by setting the dialog preference to ECommDbDialogPrefPrompt in SetDialogPreference(). This avoids having the system automatically select the 'preferred' IAP, unlike S60, where a list is always displayed.

4.3.5.3   Force a Connection to Use a Specific IAP

Amount of time required: 15 minutes
Location of example code: \Networking\StartConnectionWith-Prefs
Required library(s): esock.lib, commdb.lib, commsdat.lib
Required header file(s): es_sock.h, commdbconnpref.h, metadatabase.h, commsdattypesv1_1.h
Required platform security capability(s): NetworkServices

Problem: You want to force a connection to use a specific Internet access point (IAP).

Solution: Load the IAP recordset and iterate through the recordset to retrieve information about each IAP record in CommsDat. Set the user-selected IAP id as a connection preference.

```cpp
#include <metadatabase.h> // CMDBSession (link to commsdat.lib)
#include <commsdattypesv1_1.h> // CCDIAPRecord (link to commsdat.lib)

using namespace CommsDat;

void DisplayIAPListL()
  {
  // Open the comms repository
  CMDBSession* db = CMDBSession::NewLC(KCDVersion1_1);
  // Create a recordset (table) of IAPs
  CMDBRecordSet<CCDIAPRecord>* iapRecordSet
    = new(ELeave) CMDBRecordSet<CCDIAPRecord>(KCDTIdIAPRecord);
  CleanupStack::PushL(iapRecordSet);

  // Load the IAP recordset from the comms repository
  iapRecordSet->LoadL(*db);

  // Iterate through the recordset
  CCDIAPRecord* iap = NULL;
  for (TInt i = 0; i < iapRecordSet->iRecords.Count(); ++i)
    {
    // Get the IAP record (CCDIAPRecord)
    iap = static_cast<CCDIAPRecord*>(iapRecordSet->iRecords[i]);
    // We can now get information about the IAP.
    // For example,
    // iap->RecordId() gives us the IAP id and
    // iap->iRecordName gives us the human
```

```
  // readable name of the IAP
  }
// Close the IAP recordset and the database session
CleanupStack::PopAndDestroy(2); // iapRecordSet, db
}

void StartConnectionWithPrefsL(TInt aIapId)
{
// Open socket server session
RSocketServ ss;
CleanupClosePushL(ss);
User::LeaveIfError(ss.Connect());

// Open connection on the socket server session
RConnection conn;
CleanupClosePushL(conn);
User::LeaveIfError(conn.Open(ss));

// Define the selection preferences...
TCommDbConnPref startPrefs;
// Specify the IAP to use
startPrefs.SetIapId(aIapId);
// Since we know which IAP we are using, it pays to
// disable prompting
startPrefs.SetDialogPreference(ECommDbDialogPrefDoNotPrompt);

// Start connection using our preference
TRequestStatus status;
conn.Start(startPrefs, status);

// Wait for the connection to start
User::WaitForRequest(status);

// Check if Start succeed
TInt error = status.Int();

// Close the connection and socket server session
CleanupStack::PopAndDestroy(2);
}
```

Discussion: By implementing this in your application, you can store the id of the IAP selected by the user and reuse it without prompting again. Note how IAP selection prompting has been disabled through `TCommDbConnPref::SetDialogPreference()`.

Check `commsdattypesv1_1.h` for a list of standard records, including each record's attributes.

Note that, even though we explicitly created a recordset of type `CCDI-APRecord`, elements in `iRecords` need to be cast to the appropriate type before usage, since `iRecords` is an `RPointerArray` of type `CMDBRecordBase`.

On the UIQ 3.0 SDK, `commsdat.lib` is missing for both `winscw` and `armv5` targets. You can get hold of the library for both the targets from the S60 3rd Edition SDK and use them in the UIQ SDK, which should work just fine.

> **What may go wrong when you do this:** Care should be taken when storing and reusing the IAP id, since the stored IAP can be deleted by the user or not available, in which case, `RConnection::Start()` will fail. In such a scenario, the application should have an option for the user to select another IAP.

4.3.5.4   Resolve Domain Name

Amount of time required: 15 minutes
Location of example code: `\Networking\HostResolver`
Required library(s): `esock.lib`, `insock.lib`
Required header file(s): `es_sock.h`
Required platform security capability(s): `NetworkServices`

Problem: You want to resolve a domain name to its corresponding IP address, or resolve an IP address to its corresponding domain name, if it has one.

Solution: Use `RHostResolver::GetByName()` to resolve a domain name to its corresponding IP address and `RHostResolver::GetBy-Address()` to resolve an IP address to its corresponding domain name, if it has one.

```
// RSocketServ, RConnection et al (link to esock.lib)
#include <es_sock.h>
// KAfInet et al (link to insock.lib)
#include <in_sock.h>
// Host resolver daemon error codes
#include <networking/dnd_err.h>

void HostNameToAddressL()
  {
  // Open socket server session
  RSocketServ ss;
  CleanupClosePushL(ss);
  User::LeaveIfError(ss.Connect());

  // Initiate a connection

  // Open connection on the socket server session
  RConnection conn;
  CleanupClosePushL(conn);
  User::LeaveIfError(conn.Open(ss));

  TRequestStatus status;
  // Start the default connection
  conn.Start(status);

  // Wait for the connection to start
  User::WaitForRequest(status);
```

```
// Check if Start succeed
User::LeaveIfError(status.Int());

// Connection started

// Open the host resolver on the started connection
RHostResolver res;
CleanupClosePushL(res);
User::LeaveIfError(res.Open(ss, KAfInet, KProtocolInetUdp, conn));
// Host name to resolve
_LIT(KHostName, "www.symbian.com");
// Define a TNameEntry instance that will receive the
// resolved address.
// TNameEntry is actually a packaged buffer that
// wraps up TNameRecord in es_sock.h
TNameEntry entry;
User::LeaveIfError(res.GetByName(KHostName, entry));

// Get the IP address of the host
TInetAddr hostAddr = entry().iAddr;

// Now do the opposite, resolve host name using IP
// address provided
User::LeaveIfError(res.GetByAddress(hostAddr, entry));

// hostname and KHostName should be equal, if the reverse
// DNS entry (PTR record) is correctly setup
// for www.symbian.com
THostName hostName = entry().iName;

// Close the host resolver, connection and socket server session
CleanupStack::PopAndDestroy(3);
}
```

Discussion: The TNameEntry object passed on to the resolver functions is a packaged buffer of type TNameRecord. Besides returning the address/name, TNameRecord has an iFlags member of type TNameRecordFlags that can be used to determine the origin of the query response (see RFC1034).

We can examine the error returned by the address/name functions to determine whether the error was specific to DNS, listed in networking/dnd_err.h. KErrDndNameNotFound (-5120) implies the DNS server could not be contacted, possibly because an incorrect DNS server address had been specified. KErrDndAddrNotFound (-5121) implies the address was not found in DNS records, possibly because an incorrect host name was specified.

RHostResolver::Next() can be called repeatedly till it returns KErrNotFound to retrieve additional address(s)/name(s) associated with a host after the main name/address methods have been called.

What may go wrong when you do this: The S60 3rd Edition SDK is missing the networking/dnd.h file. A simple solution is to copy

it from the UIQ 3 SDK and place it in `<s60_sdk_install_path>`
`\epoc32\include\networking`. The address family and protocol
fields specified in `RHostResolver::Open()` must be `KAfInet` and
`KProtocolInetUdp` respectively.

4.3.5.5   Use HTTP GET Request

Amount of time required: 20 minutes
Location of example code: `\HTTP\HTTPGet`
Required library(s): `http.lib, bafl.lib, inteprotutil.lib`
Required header file(s): `http.h`
Required platform security capability(s): `NetworkServices`

Problem: You want to use HTTP GET requests.

Solution: Create a transaction, specifying HTTP GET as method, along
with the URI of the resource requested.

```
// RHTTPSession et al. (link to http.lib, bafl.lib, inetprotutil.lib)
#include <http.h>

void CGetPage::ConstructL()
    {
    // Open the HTTP session with
    // default protocol, e.g. HTTP over TCP
    iSession.OpenL();
    // Set generic headers, applicable to all
    // transactions
    RHTTPHeaders httpHeaders = iSession.RequestSessionHeadersL();
    SetHeaderL(httpHeaders, HTTP::EUserAgent, KUserAgent);
    SetHeaderL(httpHeaders, HTTP::EAccept, KAccept);
    }
```

```
void CGetPage::SetHeaderL(RHTTPHeaders aHeaders,
        TInt aHeaderField, const TDesC8& aHeader)
    {
    RStringPool stringPool = iSession.StringPool();
    // Note that aHeader is user defined string, hence we
    // are responsible for freeing up the associated
    // RStringF object once we are done with it!
    RStringF header = stringPool.OpenFStringL(aHeader);
    CleanupClosePushL(header);
    THTTPHdrVal headerVal(header);
    aHeaders.SetFieldL(stringPool.StringF(aHeaderField,
                RHTTPSession::GetTable()), headerVal);
    CleanupStack::PopAndDestroy(&header);
    }
```

```
void CGetPage::GetPageL(const TDesC& aURL,
     MHTTPTransactionCallback& aTransCallback)
  {
  // Convert URL to RFC3629 compliant
  // 8 bit UTF-8 encoded URI
  RBuf8 url8;
  CleanupClosePushL(url8);
  url8.CreateL(aURL.Length());
  url8.Copy(aURL);
  TUriParser8 uri;
  User::LeaveIfError(uri.Parse(url8));

  // Set method to HTTP GET and submit
  // the transaction.
  // Note that method is a pre-defined string in
  // the string pool, hence we don't need to worry about
  // freeing it up, unlike user defined strings, see
  // SetHeaderL()
  RStringF method = iSession.StringPool().StringF(
           HTTP::EGET, RHTTPSession::GetTable());
  RHTTPTransaction transaction = iSession.OpenTransactionL(
                               uri, aTransCallback, method);
  transaction.SubmitL();

  CleanupStack::PopAndDestroy(&url8);
  }
```

```
void CHTTPGetPageAppUi::MHFRunL(RHTTPTransaction aTransaction,
     const THTTPEvent& aEvent)
  {
  switch (aEvent.iStatus)
    {
    case THTTPEvent::EGotResponseHeaders:
      // Examine the header received
      RHTTPResponse resp = aTransaction.Response();
      // Check status code. See httperr.h
      TInt status = resp.StatusCode();
      // For secure HTTP transaction
      // e.g. URI scheme is https://,
      // we can examine the server certificate
      // here too
      break;

    case THTTPEvent::EGotResponseBodyData:
      MHTTPDataSupplier* body = aTransaction.Response().Body();
      TPtrC8 bodyData;
      TBool noMoreData = body->GetNextDataPart(bodyData);

      // Do something with the body data

      // Check noMoreData to verify there's
      // no more data to be received

      // Must call ReleaseData on the body
      // once done
      body->ReleaseData();
      break;
```

```
case THTTPEvent::EResponseComplete:
  // The transaction's response is complete
  break;

case THTTPEvent::ESucceeded:
  // Transaction completed successfully,
  // we can close it now
  aTransaction.Close();
  break;

case THTTPEvent::EFailed:
  // Transaction failed for some reason
  aTransaction.Close();
  break;

default:
  // Check if there was any framework
  // specific error
  if (aEvent.iStatus < 0)
    {
    aTransaction.Close();
    }
  break;
  }
}
```

```
TInt CHTTPGetPageAppUi::MHFRunError(TInt /*aError*/, RHTTPTransaction
    /*aTransaction*/, const THTTPEvent& /*aEvent*/)
  {
  // Cleanup any resources in case MHFRunL() leaves
  return KErrNone;
  }
```

Discussion: Any header added to the session automatically applies to all transactions and is used in all requests sent using the session.

All events regarding the transaction response are received through the transaction callback object, which implements `MHTTPTransaction-Callback::MHFRunL()` and `MHTTPTransactionCallback::MHFRunError()`. Both methods are essentially calls from the transaction's internal active object.

From the HTTP framework developer's perspective, `MHFRunL()` is where the bulk of the action takes place. `MHFRunL()` is essentially used by the framework to notify the client of incoming and outgoing events through the `THTTPEvent::iStatus` parameter. Incoming events are the transaction's current status; for example, header received, body data received, and so on. Outgoing events are events that originate due to client actions, for example when a transaction is cancelled. Check out the `THTTPEvent` class in `http/httpevent.h` for the full list of events and the Symbian Developer Library for detailed documentation on the events. For normal usage scenarios, handling only a few is sufficient.

Receiving `EGotResponseHeaders` indicates the HTTP status code, for example 404 and response header fields have been received. For secure HTTP transactions (transaction URI scheme was `https://`), it is possible to inspect the server certificate when this event is received, using `RHTTPTransaction::ServerCert()`, which returns a `CCertificate` object. This can be used to determine the serial, validity period, and so on of the server certificate.

Receiving `EGotResponseBodyData` indicates body data is available. Since a response might not be received in one go, the framework may generate this event multiple times. We will need to read the body data each time using `GetNextDataPart()`, which essentially gives us a pointer to the buffer received. The body data ownership lies with the framework and we must call `ReleaseData()` once we have finished using the buffer. When the full body is received, `GetNextDataPart()` returns `ETrue` to indicate there is no more body data.

Receiving `EResponseComplete` indicates that all body data has been received. It is useful to handle this event in case `GetNextDataPart()` fails to return `ETrue`.

Receiving `ESucceeded/EFailed` indicates success of the transaction and you should close it once you receive any one of the events.

Receiving a negative `THTTPEvent::iStatus` indicates a general framework failure and usually is a standard Symbian OS error code. You should close the transaction if that is the case.

4.3.5.6 Parse a URI

Amount of time required: 10 minutes
Location of example code: `\InetProtUtils\InetProtUtilsDemo`
Required library(s): `intetprotutils.lib`
Required header file(s): `uri8.h`
Required platform security capability(s): None

Problem: You want to parse a URI.

Solution: Test the presence of individual URI components using `TUriParser8::IsPresent()` and retrieve the component using `TUriParser8::Extract()`.

```
#include <uri8.h> // TUriParser8 (link to intetprotutils.lib)

void ExtractUriComponents()
  {
  // The URI to test
  // Note, the user info, query and fragment isn't present
  _LIT8(KUri, "http://www.symbian.com/developer/index.htm");
  TUriParser8 parser;
  TInt ret = parser.Parse(KUri);
  if (KErrNone == ret) // URI is valid
    {
    if (parser.IsPresent(EUriScheme))
```

```
      {
      const TDesC8& scheme = parser.Extract(EUriScheme);
      }
  if (parser.IsPresent(EUriUserinfo))
      {
      const TDesC8& scheme = parser.Extract(EUriUserinfo);
      }
  if (parser.IsPresent(EUriHost))
      {
      const TDesC8& host = parser.Extract(EUriHost);
      }
  if (parser.IsPresent(EUriPort))
      {
      const TDesC8& port = parser.Extract(EUriPort);
      }
  if (parser.IsPresent(EUriPath))
      {
      const TDesC8& path = parser.Extract(EUriPath);
      }
  if (parser.IsPresent(EUriQuery))
      {
      const TDesC8& query = parser.Extract(EUriQuery);
      }
  if (parser.IsPresent(EUriFragment))
      {
      const TDesC8& fragment = parser.Extract(EUriFragment);
      }
  }
}
```

Discussion: The list of components that can be used with `IsPresent()` and `Extract()` is defined in `TUriComponent`.

What may go wrong when you do this: Parsing is a precondition for most operations on the `TUriParser8` object, hence make sure you call `Parse()` before performing additional operations.

4.3.5.7   Create a URI

Amount of time required: 15 minutes
Location of example code: `\InetProtUtils\InetProtUtilsDemo`
Required library(s): `intetprotutils.lib`
Required header file(s): `uri8.h`
Required platform security capability(s): None

Problem: You want to create a URI.

Solution: The three most common ways of generating a URI are:

- Use `CUri8::CreateFileUriL()` and `CUri8::CreatePrivateFileUriL()` to create a file URI from an existing filename.

```cpp
#include <uri8.h> // CUri8 (link to intetprotutils.lib)

void CreateUriFromFileL()
  {
  // File is on a fixed drive
  _LIT(KFileOnFixedDrive, "c:\\data\\test.txt");
  // Create URI from the filename
  CUri8* uri8 = CUri8::CreateFileUriL(KFileOnFixedDrive());
  // uriFixed should be file:///c/data/test.txt
  const TDesC8& uriFixed = uri8->Uri().UriDes();
  delete uri8;

  // File is on a fixed drive
  _LIT(KFileOnremovableDrive, "e:\\data\\test.txt");
  // Create URI from the filename
  uri8 = CUri8::CreateFileUriL(KFileOnremovableDrive(), EExtMedia);
  // uriRemovable should be file:///ext-media/data/test.txt
  const TDesC8& uriRemovable = uri8->Uri().UriDes();
  delete uri8;

  // File is in private directory, on a fixed drive
  _LIT(KPrivateFileOnFixedDrive, "data\\test.txt");
  // Create URI from the filename
  uri8 = CUri8::CreatePrivateFileUriL(KPrivateFileOnFixedDrive(),
                          EDriveC);
  // uriPrivateFixed should be file:///private/c/data/test.txt
  const TDesC8& uriPrivateFixed = uri8->Uri().UriDes();
  delete uri8;

  // File is in private directory, on a removable drive
  _LIT(KPrivateFileOnremovableDrive, "data\\test.txt");
  // Create URI from the filename
  uri8 = CUri8::CreatePrivateFileUriL( KPrivateFileOnremovableDrive(),
      EDriveE, EExtMedia);
  // uriPrivateRemovable should be
  // file:///private/ext-media/data/test.txt
  const TDesC8& uriPrivateRemovable = uri8->Uri().UriDes();
  delete uri8;
  }
```

- Use `CUri8::ResolveL()` to convert a relative URI to its absolute form.

```cpp
#include <uri8.h> // TUriParser8 et al. (link to intetprotutils.lib)

void ResolveUriL()
  {
  // The base URI
  _LIT8(KBaseUri,"http://www.symbian.com/dev/tools/wintap/index.html");
  TUriParser8 baseUri;
  User::LeaveIfError(baseUri.Parse(KBaseUri));
```

```
// The reference URI
_LIT8(KRefUri, "../analyseheap/index.html");
TUriParser8 refUri;
User::LeaveIfError(refUri.Parse(KRefUri));

// Create the resolved URI
CUri8* uri = CUri8::ResolveL(baseUri, refUri);
// resolvedUri should now be
// http://www.symbian.com/dev/tools/analyseheap/index.html
const TDesC8& resolvedUri = uri->Uri().UriDes();
// Do something...
delete uri;
}
```

- Use `CUri8::SetComponentL()` to specify each component and get the full URI.

```
#include <uri8.h> // CUri8 (link to intetprotutils.lib)

void URIFromComponentL()
    {
    // The URI components
    _LIT8(KScheme, "http");
    _LIT8(KHost, "www.symbian.com");
    _LIT8(KPort, "80");
    _LIT8(KPath, "/index.htm");

    // Create the URI object
    CUri8* uri = CUri8::NewLC();
    // Set the components
    uri->SetComponentL(KScheme, EUriScheme);
    uri->SetComponentL(KHost, EUriHost);
    uri->SetComponentL(KPort, EUriPort);
    uri->SetComponentL(KPath, EUriPath);
    // Get the final URI
    const TDesC8& fullUri = uri->Uri().UriDes();

    // Get the final URI in 16 bit descriptor
    HBufC* displayName = uri->Uri().DisplayFormL();
    // Use it...
    delete displayName;

    CleanupStack::PopAndDestroy(uri);
    }
```

Discussion: The `CreateXyzFileUriL()` methods automatically encode any URI unsafe characters, for example "'", when generating the URI. Also note, they won't actually check if the filename specified exists in the file system.

The base URI specified as the first parameter for `CUri8::ResolveL()` must either be empty or in absolute form, otherwise `ResolveL()` will leave with `KUriErrBadBasePath`.

`CUri8::SetComponentL()` does not automatically encode the components specified. Applications specifying components with reserved

URI characters must call `EscapeUtils::EscapeEncodeL()` to ensure proper encoding. Interestingly, components can also be removed from a URI with `CUri8::RemoveComponentL()`.

A fourth alternative way of creating a URI is to use `UriUtils::CreateUriL()`, which takes a 16-bit descriptor as parameter. More information about this method can be found in the Symbian Developer Library.

4.3.6 Intermediate Recipes

4.3.6.1 Listen for an Incoming Connection Using TCP

Amount of time required: 20 minutes
Location of example code: \Networking\TCPListen
Required library(s): esock.lib, insock.lib
Required header file(s): es_sock.h, in_sock.h
Required platform security capability(s): NetworkServices

Problem: You need to listen for an incoming connection using TCP.

Solution: Use `RSocket::Listen()` and `RSocket::Accept()` on an opened socket to listen for incoming TCP requests and establish connection with a remote peer.

```
#include <es_sock.h> // RSocketServ, RSocket et al. (link to esock.lib)
#include <in_sock.h> // KAfInet et al (link to insock.lib)

void SetupListeningSocketL()
    {
    // Open the listening socket
    User::LeaveIfError(iSockListen.Open
        (iSockServ, KAfInet, KSockStream, KProtocolInetTcp, iConn));

    // Bind the listening socket to a local address
    TInetAddr localAddr(INET_ADDR(127, 0, 0, 1), 8000);
    User::LeaveIfError(iSockListen.Bind(localAddr));

    // Put the socket in listening mode
    User::LeaveIfError(iSockListen.Listen(4));
    }
```

```
#include <es_sock.h> // RSocketServ, RSocket et al. (link to esock.lib)
#include <in_sock.h> // KAfInet et al (link to insock.lib)

void SetupActiveSocketL()
    {
    // Open the connecting socket
    User::LeaveIfError(iSockActive.Open(
        iSockServ, KAfInet, KSockStream, KProtocolInetTcp, iConn));

    // Connect to the listening socket
```

```
  // already running on 127.0.0.1:8000
  TInetAddr connectAddr(INET_ADDR(127, 0, 0, 1), 8000);
  TRequestStatus status;
  iSockActive.Connect(connectAddr, status);
  // Wait for Connect to finish
  User::WaitForRequest(status);
  // Check if there was any error
  User::LeaveIfError(status.Int());
  }
```

```
#include <es_sock.h> // RSocketServ, RSocket et al. (link to esock.lib)
#include <in_sock.h> // KAfInet et al (link to insock.lib)

void AcceptConnectionL()
  {
  // Create a 'blank' socket.
  // This will be used to accept
  // the connect request from iSockActive
  RSocket sockBlank;
  User::LeaveIfError(sockBlank.Open(iSockServ));
  CleanupClosePushL(sockBlank);

  // Accept any incoming connect request
  // This will connect sockPassive with
  // sockActive
  TRequestStatus status;
  iSockListen.Accept(sockBlank, status);
  // Wait for Accept to complete
  User::WaitForRequest(status);
  // Check if there was an error
  User::LeaveIfError(status.Int());

  // iSockActive is now connected
  // with sockBlank, so we can exchange data

  _LIT8(KHello, "hello");
  iSockActive.Write(KHello, status);
  User::WaitForRequest(status);
  User::LeaveIfError(status.Int());

  TBuf8<10> recvBuf;
  TSockXfrLength len;
  sockBlank.RecvOneOrMore(recvBuf, 0, status, len);
  User::WaitForRequest(status);
  User::LeaveIfError(status.Int());

  ASSERT(recvBuf == KHello);

  CleanupStack::PopAndDestroy(&sockBlank);
  }
```

Discussion: RSocket::Listen() takes an integer parameter that specifies how many incoming TCP connection requests can be queued. Any incoming request crossing the listen queue limit will be rejected. You will need to tweak the listen queue size depending on the application you are writing.

RSocket::Accept() takes what is known as a 'blank' socket as a parameter. The blank socket is an RSocket instance that is opened without specifying any protocol attributes. Once Accept() completes without any error, the blank socket becomes a full-fledged TCP socket, connected to the remote peer that requested the connection and ready to exchange data. If multiple incoming socket requests are queued in the listening socket's listen queue, the application can call Accept() multiple times, passing a new 'blank' socket each time to establish connection with the remote peers in waiting.

4.3.6.2 Observe Connection Status

Amount of time required: 20 minutes
Location of example code: \Networking\ConnectionStatus
Required library(s): esock.lib
Required header file(s): es_sock.h, nifvar.h
Required platform security capability(s): None

Problem: You want to monitor the status of a connection.

Solution: Use RConnection::ProgressNotification() to monitor the status of a connection.

```
#include <nifvar.h> // link to esock.lib

void CConnectionProgressObserver:: RequestProgressNotification()
  {
  ASSERT(!IsActive());
  iConnection.ProgressNotification(iProgressBuf, iStatus);
  SetActive();
  }
```

```
void CConnectionProgressObserver::RunL()
  {
  TInt error = iStatus.Int();
  if (KErrNone == error)
    {
    iConnection.ProgressNotification(iProgressBuf, iStatus);
    SetActive();
    }
  iNotify->OnProgressNotificitionL(iProgressBuf(), error);
  }
```

```
void CConnectionStatusAppUi::ProgressNotificitionL(const TNifProgress&
                                           aProgress, TInt aError)
  {
  if (KErrNone != aError)
    {
```

```
    // Error calling ProgressNotification. Check if the
    // connection is open
    }
else
    {
    // Examine generic progress received.
    // See nifvar.h
    switch (aProgress.iStage)
        {
    case KConnectionUninitialised:
        // The connection has closed and returned to
        // uninitialized state. Retrieve the
        // last progress and decide whether to
        // restart the connection
        TNifProgress progress;
        User::LeaveIfError(iConnection.LastProgressError(progress));
        ...
        break;

    case KLinkLayerClosed:
    case KConnectionClosed:
    case KConnectionFailure:
        // Connection disconnected/closed. We'll eventually hit
        // KConnectionUninitialised stage
        ...
        break;

    case KLinkLayerOpen:
        // Link layer opened, note this doesn't mean
        // the connection is ready for data transfer
        // as it still might be busy acquiring a network
        // address, e.g. WLAN
        ...
        break;

        }
    }
}
```

Discussion: It is common for a connection state to change faster than it can be handled. RConnection::LastProgressError() can be used to determine any reason for disconnection, along with the stage when it happened.

When a connection fails, care must be taken to determine the feasibility of retrying the connection (by checking TNifProgress::iError), not only because it might potentially be a CPU-intensive, hence battery-draining, operation, but also because the user of the phone can explicitly request the connection termination, for example using a connection manager tool, found in both UIQ and S60. Unfortunately, there is no all-encompassing guideline. However, for certain errors, like KErr-AccessDenied (-21) or KErrConnectionTerminated (-17210), the application should not retry at all, since this usually indicates a user-initiated disconnect through a connection manager.

Note that besides the generic progress values defined in `nifvar.h`, each bearer technology, for example WLAN/GPRS implementation, is free to provide its own set of progress values.

4.3.6.3   Get Active Connection Information

Amount of time required: 15 minutes
Location of example code: \Networking\ConnectionStatus
Required library(s): esock.lib
Required header file(s): es_sock.h
Platform security capability(s): None

Problem: You want to retrieve information about an existing connection.

Solution: Use `RConnection::GetXyzSetting()` methods to retrieve information about an existing connection.

```
#include <es_sock.h> // link to esock.lib

void DisplayConnectionInfo()
    {
  TUint32 aIntValue;
  TBuf<70> aDesValue;

  // Read IAP Id
  _LIT(KIAPId, "IAP\\ID");
  User::LeaveIfError(iConnection.GetIntSetting(KIAPId, aIntValue));

  // Read IAP Name
  _LIT(KIAPName, "IAP\\Name");
  User::LeaveIfError(iConnection.GetDesSetting(KIAPName, aDesValue));

      // Read the service type, e.g. IAP_SERVICE_TYPE
  _LIT(KIAPServiceType, "IAP\\IAPServiceType");
  User::LeaveIfError(iConnection.GetDesSetting(KIAPServiceType,
                                               aDesValue));

  // Read the name of the service table
  TBuf<100> serviceTableName;
  _LIT(KServiceTableName, "%S\\Name");
  serviceTableName.Format(KServiceTableName, &aDesValue);
  User::LeaveIfError(iConnection.GetDesSetting(serviceTableName,
                                               aDesValue));
  }
```

Discussion: The `GetXyzSetting()` methods read the `CommsDat` settings using `<table name>\<field name>` format. The table and field names are defined in `cdbcols.h`.

As an example, reading 'IAP\ID' gives the id of the IAP and 'IAP\IAPServiceType' gives the service type, for example LANBearer.

> **What may go wrong when you do this:** During testing, the S60 3rd Edition Maintenance Release 3 emulator failed to retrieve the IAP id using `GetIntSetting()`. The other settings retrieval worked just fine.

4.3.6.4   Use Secure Socket

Amount of time required: 20 minutes
Location of example code: `\Networking\SecureSockets`
Required library(s): `esock.lib, securesocket.lib`
Required header file(s): `es_sock.h, in_sock.h, securesocket.h`
Platform security capability(s): `NetworkServices`

Problem: You want to use a secure connection.

Solution: Use `CSecureSocket` to establish a secure connection and exchange data with a remote peer.

```cpp
// RSocketServ, RConnection et al (link to esock.lib)
#include <es_sock.h>
// KAfInet et al (link against insock.lib)
#include <in_sock.h>
// CSecureSocket (link against securesocket.lib)
#include <securesocket.h>

void CSecureSocketAppUi::RunL()
  {
  User::LeaveIfError(iStatus.Int());
  switch (iState)
    {
    case EStartingConnection:
      User::LeaveIfError(iSocket.Open(iSockServ,
        KAfInet, KSockStream, KProtocolInetTcp, iConn));
      iSocket.Connect(iAddress, iStatus);
      iState = EConnecting;
      SetActive();
      break;


    case EConnecting:
      iSecureSocket = CSecureSocket::NewL(iSocket, KSSLProtocol);
    // Set the domain name of the host that we are connecting to.
    // Note usage of name as opposed to IP address.
      User::LeaveIfError(iSecureSocket->SetOpt(KSoSSLDomainName,
        KSolInetSSL, KSecureHostName));

      // Enable user prompting when an
      // un-trusted certificate is received
      User::LeaveIfError(
        iSecureSocket->SetDialogMode(EDialogModeAttended));
      iSecureSocket->StartClientHandshake(iStatus);
      iState = EHandShaking;
      SetActive();
```

```
      break;

  case EHandShaking:
    iSecureSocket->Send(KSendData, iStatus);
    iState = ESendData;
    SetActive();
    break;

  case ESendData:
    iSecureSocket->RecvOneOrMore(iRecvBuf, iStatus, iRecvLen);
    iState = EReceiveData;
    SetActive();
    break;

  case EReceiveData:
    // Do something with the received data...
    // Then cleanup
    iSecureSocket->Close();
    delete iSecureSocket;
    iSecureSocket = NULL;
    iState = EUninitialized;
    break;

  default:
    User::LeaveIfError(KErrUnknown);
    break;
  }
}
```

Discussion: The `CSecureSocket` implementation requires a TCP socket already connected to the remote peer before a secure session can be initiated with that peer. The session is established by calling `CSecure-Socket::StartClientHandshake()`. Once client handshake is complete, the application can use a subset of the `RSocket` send/receive methods implemented in `CSecureSocket` to exchange data.

Note that calling `StartClientHandshake()` may result in a dialog prompt asking for permission to establish the connection (since we have set the dialog mode to `EDialogModeAttended`) in case an untrusted certificate was received. By default, any untrusted certificate is rejected and client handshake completed with an error.

At the time of writing, `CSecureSocket` supports both TLS 1.0 and SSL 3.0 protocols.

Tip: Besides providing the basic communication methods, as we have seen already, the `CSecureSocket` class provides various utility methods that allow the application to get the server–client certificate in use, the cipher suites currently available in the system for use, or set which ones to use, and so on. Be sure to check `securesocket.h` and its associated documentation in the Symbian Developer Library.

> **What may go wrong when you do this:** The CSecureSocket instance effectively takes ownership of the RSocket instance passed during creation and closes the socket when the secure socket is closed. Any attempt to use the RSocket instance without reopening it again will result in the application being panicked!

4.3.6.5   Use HTTP POST Request

Amount of time required: 20 minutes
Location of example code: \HTTP\HTTPPost
Required library(s): http.lib, bafl.lib, inteprotutil.lib
Required header file(s): http.h
Platform security capability(s): NetworkServices

Problem: You want to use a HTTP POST request.

Solution: Create a transaction, specifying HTTP POST as method, along with the URI of the resource requested.

You should be familiar with the HTTP GET Recipe (4.3.5.5) before trying a POST as we reuse a lot of its code.

```
#include <http.h> // link to http.lib, bafl.lib, inetprotutil.lib
void CHTTPPostMultipart::PostMultipartDataL(const TDesC& aActionURI,
     RFile& aPostData, MHTTPTransactionCallback& aTransCallback)
 {
 // Convert URL to RFC3629 compliant
 // 8 bit UTF-8 encoded URI
 RBuf8 uri8;
 CleanupClosePushL(uri8);
 uri8.CreateL(aActionURI.Length());
 uri8.Copy(aActionURI);
 TUriParser8 uri;
 User::LeaveIfError(uri.Parse(uri8));

 // Set method to HTTP POST and submit
 // the transaction
 RStringF method = iSession.StringPool().StringF(
     HTTP::EGET, RHTTPSession::GetTable());
 iTransaction = iSession.OpenTransactionL(uri, aTransCallback,
                                                     method);

 // Store the file handle for
 // reading file content later
 iPostData = aPostData;

 // Assign the data supplier
 iTransaction.Response().SetBody(*this);

 iTransaction.SubmitL();

 CleanupStack::PopAndDestroy(&uri8);
 }
```

```
TBool CHTTPPostMultipart::GetNextDataPart(TPtrC8& aDataPart)
  {
  // Read from the post data file
  iNoMoreData = EFalse;
  TInt err = iPostData.Read(iDataPart);
  if (KErrNone == err)
    {
    aDataPart.Set(iDataPart);
    iNoMoreData = (iDataPart.Length() == 0);
    }
  return iNoMoreData;
  }

void CHTTPPostMultipart::ReleaseData()
  {
  iDataPart.Zero();
  // We still haven't posted the whole file yet;
  // notify the transaction
  if (!iNoMoreData)
    {
    TRAP_IGNORE(iTransaction.NotifyNewRequestBodyPartL());
    }
  }

TInt CHTTPPostMultipart::OverallDataSize()
  {
  TInt dataSize = 0;
  // Ignore error return from Size()
  iPostData.Size(dataSize);
  return (dataSize == 0 ? KErrNotFound : dataSize);
  }

TInt CHTTPPostMultipart::Reset()
  {
  TInt pos = 0;
  return iPostData.Seek(ESeekStart, pos);
  }
```

Discussion: The framework calls `MHTTPDataSupplier::GetNext-DataPart()` to request the post body data. For small post requests, the application can return the whole body data in one go. However, for larger requests, it is recommended that the application returns the data in chunks, as seen in our example code. No matter what, the data (buffer) supplied in `GetNextDataPart()` must remain valid until the framework calls `ReleaseData()`.

`ReleaseData()` is called by the framework to indicate that the post data supplied earlier in `GetNextDataPart()` has been processed by the framework and can be freed. Applications supplying post data in chunks need to call `NotifyNewRequestBodyPartL()` on the transaction object if there is data still to be posted.

If the framework encountered some problem posting the data, it calls `Reset()` to indicate that it would like to restart the post request. The application can choose to comply or decline the request, by returning `KErrNone` or an error code, respectively.

OverallDataSize() is used by the framework to determine the length of the post request data. Applications should return the length of the post request data if known, or KErrNotFound otherwise.

The HTTP framework provides a utility class, CHTTPFormEncoder, defined in chttpformencoder.h for posting requests where the content type is 'application/x-www-form-urlencoded', for example a search engine query submission form. CHTTPFormEncoder implements the MHTTPDataSupplier interface described above and simplifies request posting, as the example below illustrates:

```cpp
void CPostForm::SubmitFormL(const TDesC& aActionURI, const TDesC& aField,
      const TDesC& aValue, MHTTPTransactionCallback& aTransCallback)
 {
 // Convert URL to RFC3629 compliant
 // 8 bit UTF-8 encoded URI
 RBuf8 uri8;
 CleanupClosePushL(uri8);
 uri8.CreateL(aActionURI.Length());
 uri8.Copy(aActionURI);
 TUriParser8 uri;
 User::LeaveIfError(uri.Parse(uri8));

 // Set method to HTTP POST and submit
 // the transaction
 RStringF method = iSession.StringPool().StringF(
     HTTP::EPOST, RHTTPSession::GetTable());
 RHTTPTransaction transaction = iSession.OpenTransactionL(uri,
                                    aTransCallback, method);

 // Create the form encoder
 if (iFormEncoder)
   {
   delete iFormEncoder;
   iFormEncoder = NULL;
   }
 iFormEncoder = CHTTPFormEncoder::NewL();

 // Convert field and value to 8 bit counterparts
 // and add to the form encoder
 RBuf8 field8;
 field8.CreateL(aField.Length());
 field8.CleanupClosePushL();
 field8.Copy(aField);

 RBuf8 value8;
 value8.CreateL(aValue.Length());
 value8.CleanupClosePushL();
 value8.Copy(aValue);

 // Add field/value pair
 iFormEncoder->AddFieldL(field8, value8);

 // Assign form encoder as the data supplier
 transaction.Response().SetBody(*iFormEncoder);
```

```
transaction.SubmitL();

CleanupStack::PopAndDestroy(3); // uri8, field8, value8
}
```

4.3.6.6   Set Advanced HTTP Properties

Amount of time required: 20 minutes
Location of example code: \HTTP\HTTPConnectionConfiguration
Required header(s): http.h
Required library(s): http.lib, bafl.lib, inteprotutil.lib
Required platform security capability(s): None

Problem: You need to override the default system settings for a network connection.

Solution: Set some commonly used connection parameters, including proxy information and network connection.

```
void CGetPage::SetConnectionInfoL(RSocketServ& ss, RConnection& conn)
{
RStringPool strPool = iSession.StringPool();
RHTTPConnectionInfo connInfo = iSession.ConnectionInfo();

connInfo.SetPropertyL(strPool.StringF(HTTP::EHttpSocketServ,
    RHTTPSession::GetTable()), THTTPHdrVal(ss.Handle()));

connInfo.SetPropertyL(strPool.StringF(HTTP::EHttpSocketConnection,
                                      RHTTPSession::GetTable()),
                  THTTPHdrVal(reinterpret_cast<TInt>(&conn)));
}
```

Discussion: The HTTP framework uses the system defaults for establishing the network connection, which is similar to using `RConnection::Start()` with no preferences set. This recipe allows you to override this behavior.

Note that when using an external connection, the framework assumes it has already been started. The framework also does not take ownership of the specified connection; hence it is up to the application developer to ensure the lifetime of the connection is longer than the HTTP session. Apart from that, the `RConnection` object specified must have been opened as a sub-session of the `RSocketServ` session object specified.

The downside of using a user-specified connection is that the HTTP framework won't automatically restart the connection once it has gone down (signs for this are transaction fails with `KErrNotReady`). It is recommended that the application monitors the status of the connection (see Recipe 4.3.6.2) to handle resubmission of any failed transaction.

The connection proxy settings can also be overridden, both at the HTTP session level and at the HTTP transaction level:

```
void CGetPage::SetProxyInfoL(const TDesC& aProxyAddr)
  {
  RStringPool strPool = iSession.StringPool();
  RHTTPConnectionInfo connInfo = iSession.ConnectionInfo();

  RBuf8 proxyAddr8;
  proxyAddr8.CreateL(aProxyAddr.Length());
  proxyAddr8.CleanupClosePushL();
  proxyAddr8.Copy(aProxyAddr);

  RStringF proxyAddr = strPool.OpenFStringL(proxyAddr8);
  CleanupClosePushL(proxyAddr);

  connInfo.SetPropertyL(strPool.StringF(HTTP::EProxyUsage,
      RHTTPSession::GetTable()), strPool.StringF(HTTP::EUseProxy,
                                    RHTTPSession::GetTable()));

  connInfo.SetPropertyL(strPool.StringF(HTTP::EProxyAddress,
        RHTTPSession::GetTable()), THTTPHdrVal(proxyAddr));

  CleanupStack::PopAndDestroy(2); // proxyAddr8, proxyAddr
  }
```

```
void CGetPage::SetTransactionProxyInfoL(const TDesC& aProxyAddr,
      RHTTPTransaction aTransaction)
  {
  RStringPool strPool = iSession.StringPool();
  RHTTPTransactionPropertySet propertySet = aTransaction.PropertySet();

  RBuf8 proxyAddr8;
  proxyAddr8.CreateL(aProxyAddr.Length());
  proxyAddr8.CleanupClosePushL();
  proxyAddr8.Copy(aProxyAddr);

  RStringF proxyAddr = strPool.OpenFStringL(proxyAddr8);
  CleanupClosePushL(proxyAddr);

  propertySet.SetPropertyL(strPool.StringF(HTTP::EProxyUsage,
      RHTTPSession::GetTable()), strPool.StringF(HTTP::EUseProxy,
                                    RHTTPSession::GetTable()));

  propertySet.SetPropertyL(strPool.StringF(HTTP::EProxyAddress,
          RHTTPSession::GetTable()), THTTPHdrVal(proxyAddr));

  CleanupStack::PopAndDestroy(2); // proxyAddr8, proxyAddr
  }
```

4.3.6.7   Extract Local Filename from URI

Amount of time required: 10 minutes
Location of example code: \InetProtUtils\InetProtUtilsDemo

Required library(s): `intetprotutils.lib`
Required header file(s): `uri8.h`
Required platform security capability(s): None

Solution: Get the filename from a URI using `TUriParser8::GetFileNameL()`.

```cpp
#include <uri8.h>

void CInetProtUtilsDemoAppUi::UriToFileNameL()
  {
  TUriParser8 uriParser;

  _LIT8(KFixedFile, "file:///c/data/test.txt");
  User::LeaveIfError(uriParser.Parse(KFixedFile));
  // fixedFileName should now be
  // c:\data\test.txt, if the file exists
  HBufC* fixedFileName = uriParser.GetFileNameL();
  // Do something...
  delete fixedFileName;

  _LIT8(KRemovableFile, "file:///ext-media/data/test.txt");
  User::LeaveIfError(uriParser.Parse(KRemovableFile));
  // removableFileName should now be
  // e:\data\test.txt, if the file exists
  HBufC* removableFileName = uriParser.GetFileNameL();
  // Do something...
  delete removableFileName;

  _LIT8(KPrivateFixedFile, "file:///private/c/data/test.txt");
  User::LeaveIfError(uriParser.Parse(KPrivateFixedFile));
  // pvtFixedFileName should now be
  // c:\private\0xE34E47D5\data\test.txt, if the file exists
  HBufC* pvtFixedFileName = uriParser.GetFileNameL();
  // Do something...
  delete pvtFixedFileName;
  }
```

Discussion: Earlier in Recipe 4.3.5.7 we saw how to get the URI, given a filename. The code snippet above does the reverse, by getting the actual file system path of the URI given. Unlike the `CreateXyzFileUriL()` methods, `GetFileNameL()` actually resolves the filename by looking it up in the physical file system; if the file specified by the URI does not exist, it leaves with `KErrNotFound`.

4.3.7 Advanced Recipes

4.3.7.1 Retrieve HTTP Proxy Information

Amount of time required: 20 minutes
Location of example code: `\HTTP\HTTPConnectionConfiguration`
Required library(s): `commsdat.lib`

Required header file(s): `metadatabase.h`, `commsdattypeinfov1_`
`1.h`, `commsdattypesv1_1.h`
Required platform security capability(s): None

Problem: You need to retrieve the HTTP proxy information.

Solution: Read proxy server address and port information from `CommsDat`
using 'priming' search technique.

```cpp
#include <metadatabase.h> // CMDBSession
#include <commsdattypeinfov1_1.h> // CCDIAPRecord, CCDProxiesRecord
#include <commsdattypesv1_1.h> // KCDTIdIAPRecord, KCDTIdProxiesRecord

void CGetProxyInfo::ProxyServerL(TInt aIAPId, TDes& aProxyServer)
  {
  // Create session to CommsDat first
  CommsDat::CMDBSession* dbs =
    CMDBSession::NewLC(CMDBSession::LatestVersion());

  // Load the IAP with record id aIAPId
  CCDIAPRecord* iap = static_cast<CCDIAPRecord*>
    (CCDRecordBase::RecordFactoryL(KCDTIdIAPRecord));
  CleanupStack::PushL(iap);
  iap->SetRecordId(aIAPId);
  iap->LoadL(*dbs);

  // Read service table id and service type
  // from the IAP record found
  TUint32 serviceId = iap->iService;
  RBuf serviceType;
  serviceType.CreateL(iap->iServiceType);
  CleanupClosePushL(serviceType);

  // Create a recordset of type CCDProxiesRecord
  // for priming search.
  // This will ultimately contain record(s)
  // matching the priming record attributes
  CMDBRecordSet<CCDProxiesRecord>* proxyRecords = new(ELeave)
    CMDBRecordSet<CCDProxiesRecord>(KCDTIdProxiesRecord);
  CleanupStack::PushL(proxyRecords);

  // Create the priming record and set attributes
  // that will be the search criteria
  CCDProxiesRecord* primingProxyRecord =
      static_cast<CCDProxiesRecord*>
      (CCDRecordBase::RecordFactoryL(KCDTIdProxiesRecord));
  CleanupStack::PushL(primingProxyRecord);

  primingProxyRecord->iServiceType.SetMaxLengthL(serviceType.Length());
  primingProxyRecord->iServiceType = serviceType;
  primingProxyRecord->iService = serviceId;
  primingProxyRecord->iUseProxyServer = ETrue;

  // Append the priming record to the priming recordset
  proxyRecords->iRecords.AppendL(primingProxyRecord);
  // Ownership of primingProxyRecord is transferred to
  // proxyRecords, just remove it from the CleanupStack
```

```
CleanupStack::Pop(primingProxyRecord);

// All done!

// Now to find a proxy table matching our criteria
if (proxyRecords->FindL(*dbs))
    {
    // Use the first record found
    CCDProxiesRecord* proxyRecord = static_cast<CCDProxiesRecord*>
                                    (proxyRecords->iRecords[0]);

    // Get proxy server name
    TPtrC serverName(proxyRecord->iServerName);
    if (serverName.Length() == 0)
        {
        User::Leave(KErrNotFound);
        }
    // Get port number
    TInt port = proxyRecord->iPortNumber;

    // Finally, create buffer in the form of
    // proxy_server_name:port format
    aProxyServer.Zero();
    aProxyServer.Append(serverName);
    aProxyServer.Append(':');
    aProxyServer.AppendNum(port);
    }
else
    {
    // Didn't find a proxy table with
    // specified service type, id and proxy attribute set
    User::Leave(KErrNotFound);
    }

// dbs, iap, serviceType, proxyRecords
CleanupStack::PopAndDestroy(4);
}
```

Discussion: CommsDat stores proxy information in the CCDProxies-Record table (see commsdattypesv1_1.h), which along with server name and port number, stores service information, linking it to a service table. By loading the IAP, given by aIAPId, we retrieve the associated service table name and id for our IAP, which we subsequently use to perform a 'priming' search on the proxy records to get the matching proxy record.

4.3.8 Resources

- *Symbian OS Communications Programming*, 2nd Edition: **developer.symbian.com/commsbook**.

- Symbian Developer Library:

  ○ *Symbian OS Guide > Communications Infrastructure > CommDb.*

- ○ *Symbian OS Guide > Communications Infrastructure > Using Sockets Server (ESOCK).*
- ○ *Symbian OS Guide > Networking > Using TCP/IP (INSOCK).*
- ○ *Symbian OS Guide > Networking > Using Secure Sockets (TLS).*
- ○ *Symbian OS Guide > Application Protocols > Using HTTP Client.*
- ○ *Symbian OS Guide > Application Protocols > Using InetProtUtils.*

4.4 Messaging

The ability to send and receive information in asynchronous forms, such as text messaging, multimedia messaging and email, has become a key feature of modern mobile phone communications. The ability to communicate with someone via phone or computer, without requiring them to be available at the time, has become very popular. Growing with this worldwide trend, messaging has evolved to make use of the multimedia capabilities of today's phones, providing users with even more ways to communicate.

Messaging can be an efficient and cheap form of mobile communication, as it is only necessary to connect to the network while a message is actually being transmitted or received. This has made it a particularly suitable candidate for relatively infrequent ('bursty') streams of communication, such as traffic updates or automatic reporting of medical data.

Messages are easy to store for future reference, it is a simple task to send a message more than once, or to more than one recipient, or to schedule the sending of a message. Such functionality is not so readily available with a synchronous means of communication, such as a phone call.

4.4.1 Supported Bearers

Symbian provides support for:

- Short Message Service (SMS, also known as text messaging).
- Multimedia Message Service (MMS).
- Post Office Protocol version 3 (POP3) for receiving email.
- Internet Message Access Protocol version 4 (IMAP4) for receiving email.
- Simple Mail Transfer Protocol (SMTP) for sending email.

They all require a connection to an operator's network, and in the case of email, the Internet, when sending or receiving messages.

Symbian provides support for receiving Cell Broadcast and Unstructured Supplementary Service Data (USSD). There is also a 'BIO messaging' component for handling messages which are meant to update some aspect of the device, such as vCards, vCalendars, over-the-air configuration messages and Nokia Smart Messages. All of these areas are outside the scope of this book.

Symbian has abstracted the common functionality into a client–server messaging subsystem, which exposes a framework API for receiving, sending, creating and manipulating messages. The message server manages access to the different transports via a plug-in architecture, as well as the Symbian OS message store.

In the messaging plug-in architecture, each protocol bearer is represented by a client Message Type Module (MTM).

4.4.2   SendAs

Since it is not guaranteed that all bearers will be available on every Symbian phone, Symbian provides the SendAs server, which allows applications to dynamically discover and choose a message type that is appropriate for their data, based on the transports available; the SendAs server will then create and send the message for you.

The SendAs server is described in more detail in the Sending Messages chapter of the Symbian Press book by Iain Campbell, *Symbian OS Communications Programming*, 2nd Edition. In these recipes, we show you how to use the message server itself to add email, SMS or MMS messaging to your application.

4.4.3   Services

The purpose of a service is to handle communications, via lower-level comms components such as Telephony and Networking, with an external messaging service provider (known as a remote service); for example, sending an SMS to a Short Message Service Center (SMSC), or receiving emails from a mailbox on a POP3 server. A remote service is frequently associated with a remote store – for instance, the SIM's SMS store, or a user's email server mailbox. There is also a local service which manages operations performed on the phone's message store itself, such as reading or deleting messages.

4.4.4   The Message Store

4.4.4.1   Structure and Main Classes

In the Symbian OS message store, messages, folders and services are organized in a tree structure, as shown in Figure 4.4.1. The tree's nodes, or entries, are accessible to message server clients through the CMsvEntry

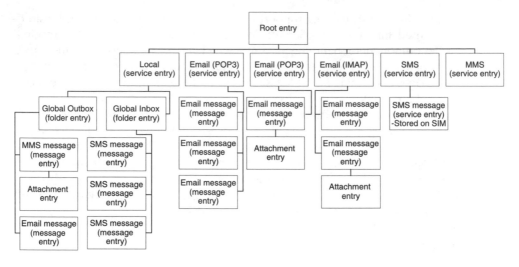

Figure 4.4.1 Simplified Version of the Contents of a Typical Message Store

class. An object of this type caches its children and has a relatively high RAM usage, so creating and destroying them often is not recommended. Instead, it is better to maintain only a small number (ideally one) of pointers to CMsvEntry objects, and change which entry they point to (known as the current context) only when necessary, to improve performance and keep memory usage as low as possible.

Each entry has a header which stores the entry's metadata. The header class, TMsvEntry, is most useful in the context of message entries, as it is capable of holding information such as whether a message is unread, is scheduled for sending, has an attachment, and other generic message attributes. Depending on the actual protocol used, you may be able to use more specialized subclasses, such as TMsvEmailEntry. An important field for all types of entry is the ID (TMsvId), which allows you to nominate a specific message, folder or service. For a message entry to be valid, the iType and iMtm data members must be set. For a service entry, those and the iServiceId data members must be set; other than these, it is not guaranteed that any other data members will be set for a particular entry.

An entry's header object can be retrieved from CMsvEntry; however, it is recommended that you use TMsvEntry (or one of its derived classes) directly, whenever possible – that is, if only the header data is required.

4.4.4.2 Types of Entry

When navigating the message store, it is common for a client not to know the IDs of the entries it wants to access in advance, but instead to ask for the child entries of a known parent – for instance, listing all the messages in the inbox. By repeating that procedure, all entries can be obtained from the root entry of the tree.

The next level of the tree consists of service entries. The `TMsvId` values for a number of common services are defined in `msvids.h`.

Below each service entry are any folders relating to that service. When the message server starts, it creates the standard folders stated in the file `msgs.rsc` under the local service. These will generally be:

- A global inbox – most SMS and MMS messages are stored here when they are received by the device. Class 2 SMS messages are the common exception; they are usually stored on the SIM.

- A global outbox – messages are stored here temporarily before being sent, or if sending fails.

- A draft folder – unfinished messages are stored here until they are ready to be sent.

- A sent folder – messages are stored here after they have successfully been sent.

- A deleted folder – messages are stored here once they have been deleted. This folder is invisible to the user.

The `TMsvId` values for the above folders are also defined in `msvids.h`.

Following this, the message store may be customized further – for example, some phone manufacturers use a templates folder which stores a set of pre-composed messages. The user may also define its own local folders. Remember, it is possible to get a list of all the available services by requesting the children of the root entry, and the available folders under a service by requesting the children of that service.

Remote service entries may not use child folder entries, if there is only one remote storage area which is relevant to those service settings, such as a POP3 email mailbox, or the SIM for storing class 2 SMS messages. In this case the message entries are stored directly under the remote service entry, as shown in Figure 4.4.1. However, IMAP4 does use child folder entries under the remote service to represent the different folders on the remote server. The UI messaging application controls which folders are displayed to the user, and how (for instance a service entry may be displayed to the user as a POP3 'mailbox' folder, even though no such folder exists in the message store).

Under each folder (or service entry) are the entries for the messages stored in that folder. These contain the message metadata as well as body text and any data specific to the message type. If the message type supports attachments, the message entries may have child attachment entries to hold files such as multimedia clips or pictures.

4.4.3   Tips for Writing Messaging Applications

4.4.3.1   Messaging Libraries

There are two versions of the messaging library, `msgs.lib` and `msgs_autoshutdown.lib`. With the latter, the message server automatically shuts down when no sessions exist.

4.4.3.2   Multimode SMS

Your application should use the multimode version of the messaging APIs, the header files for which are in `\epoc32\include\messaging`.

If writing an application which makes explicit use of CDMA SMS functions (not needed for the examples here), you may require the following macros:

```
MACRO   CDMA_API_ENABLED
MACRO   GSM_COMPATIBILITY_MODE
```

4.4.3.3   UI Implementation Differences

It is important to remember that there may be implementation differences between different UI versions, especially when it comes to the phone's own messaging application, service entry, folders, etc. and its own way of creating, handling and displaying messages. You may be able to use some of the functionality provided by the UI in your application, such as the message editor, but be aware of such differences.

You can use SendAs to help shield you from some dependencies on UI implementations, but its functionality only extends to creating and sending messages.

4.4.3.4   Mail Store Debugging

You can view the emulator's message store tree by going to `epoc32\winscw\c\private\1000484b\Mail2` in a Windows command prompt and using the Windows `tree` command. The message, folder and attachment entries are identified by their `TMsvId` (hexadecimal) values and you can see the message text and attachment files. It is worth experimenting with this to improve your understanding of how the message store works – try creating or deleting some messages in the emulator and see what happens to the tree. It can be a useful debugging tool once you know what you are looking at.

4.4.4   About the Recipes

We will use SMS to illustrate how to use the message server to carry out common messaging tasks. For other transports, these tasks are performed in a very similar way, as they use the same common interface (for instance, see *Symbian OS Communications Programming*, 2nd Edition for an example using email).

However, the implementations of some CMsvEntry functions differ between message types – for instance, copying messages from a remote server to the local service is allowed for email (to download emails from a mailbox) but is not supported (returns KErrNotSupported) for SMS, because SMS messages are automatically received by the SMS watcher. Information on these differences can be found in the Symbian Developer Library, for example see *Symbian OS Guide ≫ Messaging ≫ Using email ≫ CMsvEntry functions for IMAP4 message entries*. Under the same categories you will also find specific information on how the TMsvEntry class is used by each type of messaging.

4.4.4.1 Required Capabilities

The capabilities required for each task depend on various factors, like which bearer you are using, whether you are using SendAs, and which folder you are creating a message in. Therefore, we have not stated the capabilities on a per-recipe basis as your application is likely to have different needs to the example application. However, there are three main user capabilities your application is most likely to need: ReadUserData, WriteUserData and NetworkServices.

4.4.5 Recipes

4.4.5.1 Initialize your Application to Use Messaging

Amount of time required: 30 minutes
Location of example code: \Messaging\SmsManager
Required libraries: msgs.lib, smcm.lib
Required header file(s): msvapi.h, smsclnt.h, msvids.h, smut.h
Required platform security capability(s): Platform-dependent (see example code)

Problem: You want to start using messaging services.

Solution: We open a session with the message server and create member variables for classes which are heavy on RAM usage, like CMsvEntry and CSmsClientMtm.

Description: It is good practice to call asynchronous versions of messaging functions and make your own messaging functions asynchronous, so that the thread remains responsive to user input, because they can be long-running. In some cases, the synchronous versions are not supported for non-local contexts, for exactly this reason. We therefore make CSmsManager an active object with a RunL() function which breaks up the functionality into a number of relatively short tasks, many of them asynchronous themselves (though the order of events within RunL() is controlled by a state machine).

```
#include <msvapi.h> // CMsvSession, MMsvSessionObserver, CMsvEntry
#include <smsclnt.h> // CSmsClientMtm

class CSmsManager : public CActive, public MMsvSessionObserver
  {
public: // methods
  // MMsvSessionObserver
  void HandleSessionEventL(TMsvSessionEvent aEvent, TAny* aArg1, TAny*
                                               aArg2, TAny* aArg3);

private: // enum
enum TSmsManagerState
  {
  EIdle,
  EConnectingToServer,
  ...
  };

private: // methods
  void Start(TInt aError);
  // CActive
  void RunL();
  TInt RunError(TInt aError);
  void DoCancel();

private: // data
  CMsvSession* iMsvSession;
  CMsvEntry* iEntry;
  CSmsClientMtm* iSmsMtm;
  };
```

To open a session to the message server asynchronously, we use CMsvSession::OpenAsyncL().

Applications need to implement HandleSessionEventL() to respond to events from the message server. The possible events are documented in the MMsvSessionObserver class – you must decide which are appropriate for your application to handle. All applications must close their session upon receiving the EMsvCloseSession event.

When the connection is ready, the message server calls the MMsv-SessionObserver:: HandleSessionEventL() callback function with the event EMsvServerReady. We then call Start() to send us into RunL(), where we can begin to use messaging. If the connection failed, the event given is EMsvServerFailedToStart; and we call Start() with an error, which will cause us to retry a few times (this is the application's main error-handling strategy).

```
/**
In this example application, some of the events are not handled. However,
have a look at the inline comments for some things to
```

```
consider when writing your application.
*/
void CSmsManager::HandleSessionEventL(TMsvSessionEvent aEvent, TAny*
                                aArg1, TAny* aArg2, TAny* /*aArg3*/)
  {
    switch (aEvent)
    {
    case (EMsvServerReady):
      {
      Start(KErrNone);
      break;
      }
    case (EMsvServerFailedToStart): // do you want to retry?
      {
      Start (KErrCouldNotConnect );
      break;
      }
    case (EMsvCloseSession):
    case (EMsvServerTerminated):
      // delete objects relying on the session and
      // then the session itself
      {
      CloseSession();
      break;
      }
    case (EMsvEntriesCreated): // to be discussed later
      ...
      break;
      // other cases relevant to our application
      // are already handled in RunL()
    default:
      {
      break;
      }
    }
  }
```

In order to access and manipulate entries in the messaging store, we create a CMsvEntry object as a member variable (remembering that it is best to only have one of these objects per application). The object's initial context is set to KMsvNullIndexEntryId, so as not to use up memory or lock any message entries while the object is not in use. (Note that the Cancel() function also finishes by setting the CMsvEntry and CSmsClientMtm objects to point to KMsvNullIndexEntryId, for the same reason.)

The functions in the SMS client MTM class, CSmsClientMtm, provide a useful interface to SMS-specific messaging functionality. There are equivalent client MTM classes for email (such as CSmtpClientMtm) and MMS (CMmsClientMtm), although the latter is part of the UI, so may be implementation-dependent.

We construct the CMsvEntry and CSmsClientMtm classes in the ConstructL() function, once we know the session is ready; those classes take a reference to the opened session as a parameter. The SMS

MTM is accessed by casting from the base class pointer returned by
`CClientMtmRegistry::NewMtmL()`.

```
#include <msvids.h> // TMsvIds for standard folders
#include <smut.h> // KUidMsgTypeSMS

void CSmsManager::ConstructL()
  {
  TMsvSelectionOrdering noOrdering;
  iEntry = CMsvEntry::NewL(*iSession,
  KMsvNullIndexEntryId, noOrdering);

  CClientMtmRegistry* mtmReg = CClientMtmRegistry::NewL(*iSession);
  CleanupStack::PushL(mtmReg);
  CBaseMtm* mtm = mtmReg->NewMtmL(KUidMsgTypeSMS);
  iSmsMtm = static_cast<CSmsClientMtm*>(mtm);
  CleanupStack::PopAndDestroy(mtmReg);
  }
```

4.4.5.2   Create a Folder

Amount of time required: 10 minutes
Location of example code: \Messaging\SmsManager
Required libraries: msgs.lib, smcm.lib
Required header file(s): msvapi.h, msvids.h, msvuids.h
Required platform security capability(s): Platform-dependent (see
example code)

Problem: You want to create a custom folder for your application.

Solution: We call the `CMsvEntry::CreateL()` function, specifying
the `KUidMsvFolderEntry` type.

Description: We use an active object class because we are using an asynchronous overload of `CreateL()`. Asynchronous `CMsvEntry` functions
return a `CMsvOperation` object, an interface which allows us to get
information on how the function is progressing (particularly useful when
acting on more than one entry), and cancel the function.
    Note that we do not create a new `CMsvEntry` object, but store a
reference to the one owned by `CSmsManager`.

```
#include <msvapi.h> // CMsvOperation

class CSmsCreator : public CActive
  {
public:  // methods
  void CreateFolderEntryL(TRequestStatus& aStatus);
private: // data
  CMsvEntry& iEntry;
  CMsvOperation* iOperation;
  TMsvEntry iFolderHeader;
  };
```

We set our CMsvEntry to the parent of the new entry; in this case, to the local service entry as we want to create a local folder. We set the relevant attributes in our TMsvEntry object (remember that iType and iMtm must be set for a non-service entry to be valid); the entry should be marked as in preparation and not visible at this point to show that it is not yet ready to be displayed. Finally we start the folder creation by calling CreateL() and SetActive().

```
#include <msvids.h> // TMsvIds for standard folders
#include <msvuids.h> // KUidMsvFolderEntry, KUidMsvLocalServiceMtm

void CSmsCreator::CreateFolderEntryL(TRequestStatus& aStatus)
  {
  iEntry.SetEntryL(KMsvLocalServiceIndexEntryId);
  iFolderHeader.SetInPreparation(ETrue);
  iFolderHeader.SetVisible(EFalse);
  iFolderHeader.iType = KUidMsvFolderEntry;
  iFolderHeader.iServiceId = KMsvLocalServiceIndexEntryId;
  iFolderHeader.iMtm = KUidMsvLocalServiceMtm;
  iFolderHeader.SetReadOnly(EFalse);

  iOperation = iEntry.CreateL(iFolderHeader, iStatus);
  SetActive ();
  }
```

Following good practice, we check the value of iStatus upon completion of CreateL(); if it is KErrNone, the message has been successfully created. We then set iEntry to point to the new folder entry so that the SMS Manager can store the folder's TMsvId. If this failed, we would lose track of the new entry, and although it would be retrievable by enumerating the children of the local service entry, we have chosen to use the functions CleanupEntryPushL() and CleanupEntryPop() from the CMsvSession class, which, as well as performing normal cleanup, would also remove the folder from the message store in the event that SetEntryL() was to leave. Once we have done this, we update the InPreparation and Visible flags and call CMsvEntry::ChangeL() to commit these changes to the message store.

```
void CSmsCreator::RunL()
  {
  User::LeaveIfError(iStatus.Int());
  ...
  iEntry.Session().CleanupEntryPushL(iFolderHeader.Id());
  iEntry.SetEntryL(iFolderHeader.Id());
  iEntry.Session().CleanupEntryPop(1);
  iFolderHeader.SetVisible(ETrue);
  iFolderHeader.SetInPreparation(EFalse);
  iEntry.ChangeL(iFolderHeader);
  ...
  }
```

4.4.5.3 Create a Message

Amount of time required: 10 minutes
Location of example code: \Messaging\SmsManager
Required libraries: msgs.lib, smcm.lib, etext.lib
Required header file(s): msvapi.h, smsclnt.h, txtrich.h, mtmdef.h
Required platform security capability(s): Platform-dependent (see example code)

Problem: You want to create a new outgoing message.

Solution: We use the client MTM's CreateMessageL() function, add recipient addresses and attachments as required, and set any other relevant settings such as the message subject.

Description: It is possible to create message entries in a similar way to the folder entry from Recipe 4.4.5.2, but the client MTM you are using should have a CreateMessageL() function which will do the work for you; for instance, it sets the protocol-specific message settings such as the service center address for SMS, and sets at least iType and iMtm to make the entry valid. This is recommended because it reduces the chance of leaving something out or making a mistake; however, be aware that this is a synchronous function, so if you are using it repeatedly (as in our application) you should wrap it in an active object and make sure that the RunL() can complete relatively quickly.

Again, we do not create a new CSmsClientMtm object, but store a reference to the one owned by CSmsManager (and the same idea is used throughout the recipes). We reuse iOperation and iFolderHeader from Recipe 4.4.5.2.

```cpp
#include <smsclnt.h> // CSmsClientMtm
#include <msvapi.h> // CMsvOperation

_LIT(KExampleRecipientAddress, "+440123456789");

class CSmsCreator : public CActive
  {
public:
  void CreateMessageEntriesL(TRequestStatus& aStatus);
private:
  void CreateMessageL();
private:
  CSmsClientMtm& iSmsMtm;
  };
```

To initialize the message creation, CreateMessageEntriesL() sets the context of the SMS client MTM to the folder entry from Recipe 4.4.5.2 (this is the parent entry for our new message).

```
void CSmsCreator::CreateMessageEntriesL(TRequestStatus& aStatus)
  {
  ...
  iSmsMtm.SwitchCurrentEntryL(iFolderHeader.Id());
  ...
  }
```

The actual message creation takes place in our `CreateMessageL()` function, using the function of the same name in the SMS client MTM. We retrieve the `TMsvEntry` of the new message entry in order to push it to the entry cleanup stack so that it will be removed if something goes wrong; we then retrieve the body of the message and insert some text.

Next we add a message recipient address; this is also the time to add attachments, set the subject or change any other settings for the entry which are relevant to the type of message you are using. We can call the client MTM's `ValidateMessage()` function to validate the address format – the implementation of this function is dependent on the MTM you are using.

Finally, we call `CSmsClientMtm::SaveMessageL()` to commit the changes (this also updates the `Visible` and `InPreparation` attributes), and pop the message from the entry cleanup stack.

```
#include <txtrich.h> // CRichText
#include <mtmdef.h> // TMsvPartList, KMsvMessagePartRecipient

void CSmsCreator::CreateMessageL()
  {
  iSmsMtm.CreateMessageL(0);
  TMsvEntry header = iSmsMtm.Entry().Entry();
  iSmsMtm.Session().CleanupEntryPushL(header.Id());
  CRichText& body = iSmsMtm.Body();
  // Create some body text in a descriptor
  ...
  body.InsertL(0, bodyText);
  iSmsMtm.AddAddresseeL(KExampleRecipientAddress);
  User::LeaveIfError(
          iSmsMtm.ValidateMessage(KMsvMessagePartRecipient));
  header.SetUnread(ETrue);
  iSmsMtm.SaveMessageL(); // sets visible and not in preparation
  iSmsMtm.Session().CleanupEntryPop(1);
  }
```

4.4.5.4 Read Message Details

Amount of time required: 10 minutes
Location of example code: `\Messaging\SmsManager`
Required libraries: `msgs.lib`, `smcm.lib`
Required header file(s): `smsclnt.h`, `msvstd.h`, `msvids.h`
Required platform security capability(s): Platform-dependent (see example code)

Problem: You want to display a summary of an unread message.

Solution: We set our `CMsvEntry` to point to our folder entry in order to find the child entry we are interested in. We retrieve the message description and details from the header metadata using the `TMsvEntry` class.

Description: Our application reads data for a number of messages, so, just as for Recipe 4.4.5.3, we wrap the reads in a long-running active object. `CMsvEntrySelection` is an array of `TMsvId` values – an object of this type is often returned from, or passed to, messaging functions.

```
#include <smsclnt.h> // CSmsClientMtm
#include <msvstd.h> // CMsvEntrySelection

class CSmsReader : public CActive
  {
public:
  void DisplayUnreadMessageSummariesL(TMsvId aFolderId,
                            TRequestStatus& aStatus);
private:
  void InitializeL(TMsvId aFolderId, TRequestStatus& aStatus);
  void DisplayMessageSummaryL();
private:
  CMsvEntry& iEntry;
  CMsvEntrySelection* iMessages;
  TInt iMessageCount;
  TInt iCounter;
  };
```

`DisplayUnreadMessageSummariesL()` calls `InitializeL()` which sets `iEntry` to our example folder and retrieves the list of children of type SMS, using `ChildrenWithMtmL()`, clearing the `New` flag for these messages.

```
#include <msvids.h> // TMsvIds for common folders

void CSmsReader::InitializeL(TMsvId aFolderId, TRequestStatus& aStatus)
  {
  if (aFolderId != KMsvNullIndexEntryId)
    {
    iEntry.SetEntryL(aFolderId);
    iMessages = iEntry.ChildrenWithMtmL(KUidMsgTypeSMS);
    iMessageCount = iMessages->Count();
    if (iMessageCount > 0)
      {
      iEntry.ChangeAttributesL(*iMessages, 0, KMsvNewAttribute);
      }
    }
  }
```

We set `iEntry` to point to the message we want to read and check that the message is unread (we set this attribute when we created or edited the message). If so, we display the message description and details. The meaning of these depends on message type: for SMS, `iDescription` is the beginning of the message, disregarding leading white space (the length of which is given by the `DescriptionLength()` setting in the SMS settings) and `iDetails` is the address of the first recipient. For other message types, see the documentation in the OS Library, for example *Symbian OS Guide ≫ Messaging ≫ Using email ≫ TMsvEntry functions and members used in SMTP message entries*. To finish, we update the `Unread` flag.

```
void CSmsReader::DisplayMessageSummaryL()
  {
  iEntry.SetEntryL(iMessages->At(iCounter ));
  TMsvEntry header = iEntry.Entry();
  if (header.Unread())
    {
    DisplayInfo(header.iDescription);
    DisplayInfo(header.iDetails);
    header.SetUnread(EFalse);
    iEntry.ChangeL(header );
    }
  ...
  }
```

4.4.5.5 Edit a Message

Amount of time required: 10 minutes
Location of example code: `\Messaging\SmsManager`
Required libraries: `msgs.lib`, `smcm.lib`, `etext.lib`
Required header file(s): `smsclnt.h`, `msvids.h`, `txtrich.h`
Required platform security capability(s): Platform-dependent (see example code)

Problem: You want to edit aspects of a message such as the body text and the addressee list.

Solution: We use the client MTM to add an addressee, edit body text and save the changes.

Description: The `EditMessageL()` function calls the `Initialize()` function and then uses the `CSmsClientMtm` class to edit the message as described.

```
#include <smsclnt.h> // CSmsClientMtm

_LIT(KExampleSmsBodyTextExtension,
"This text extends the SMS message text. ");
_LIT(KExampleRecipientAddress2, "+449876543210");
```

```
class CSmsEditor : public CBase
  {
public:
  void EditMessageL(TMsvId aFolderId);
private:
  void InitializeL(TMsvId aFolderId);
private:
  CSmsClientMtm& iSmsMtm;
  };
```

To initialize, we retrieve the child entries of the folder as for Recipe 4.4.5.4, only this time using `CSmsClientMtm` instead of `CMsvEntry`. In this case, the client MTM class is preferable, as we need to use it later.

```
void CSmsEditor::InitializeL(TMsvId aFolderId)
  {
  if (aFolderId != KMsvNullIndexEntryId)
    {
    iSmsMtm.SwitchCurrentEntryL(aFolderId);
    CMsvEntrySelection* selection = iSmsMtm.Entry().
            ChildrenWithMtmL(KUidMsgTypeSMS);
    CleanupStack::PushL(selection);
    if (selection->Count() > 0)
      {
      iSmsMtm.SwitchCurrentEntryL(selection->At(0));
      iSmsMtm.LoadMessageL();
      }
    CleanupStack::PopAndDestroy(selection);
    }
  ...
  }
```

After initializing, we add another addressee and validate the address format, just as in Recipe 4.4.5.3. We then retrieve the body text of the message using the client MTM's `Body()` function in order to insert another line. We set the message `Unread` attribute to true (so that the changes may be picked up by the SMS reader) and save the changes.

```
void CSmsEditor::EditMessageL(TMsvId aFolderId)
  {
  InitializeL(aFolderId);
  iSmsMtm.AddAddresseeL(KExampleRecipientAddress2);
  User::LeaveIfError(
            iSmsMtm.ValidateMessage(KMsvMessagePartRecipient));
  CRichText& body = iSmsMtm.Body();
  body.InsertL(0, KExampleSmsBodyTextExtension);
  TMsvEntry header = iSmsMtm.Entry().Entry();
  header.SetUnread(ETrue);
  iSmsMtm.SaveMessageL();
  }
```

4.4.5.6 Retrieve and Edit Message Settings

Amount of time required: 15 minutes
Location of example code: \Messaging\SmsManager
Required libraries: msgs.lib, smcm.lib
Required header file(s): smsclnt.h, csmsaccount.h, smutset.h
Required platform security capability(s): Platform-dependent (see example code)

Problem: You want to edit settings common to all SMS messages, such as the length of the description.

Solution: We use the CSmsAccount class to access the CSmsSettings, which is the interface to allow us to edit the SMS settings.

Description: The CSmsAccount and CSmsSettings classes allow us to access the account information and settings which are stored in the Central Repository. For email, the equivalent classes are CEmailAccounts, CImPop3Settings, CImImap4Settings and CImSmtpSettings, and for MMS they are CMmsAccounts and CMmsSettings.

```
#include <smsclnt.h>

class CSmsEditor : public CBase
  {
public:
  void EditSettingsL();
  // same as the Edit a Message recipe
  ...
  };
```

It is simple to edit the settings – we create a CSmsAccount and load the settings into a CSmsSettings object. We can then retrieve and edit settings such as the description length, and must call CSmsAccount::SaveSettingsL() to commit the changes.

```
#include <csmsaccount.h> // CSmsAccount
#include <smutset.h> // CSmsSettings

void CSmsEditor::EditSettingsL( )
  {
  CSmsAccount* smsAccount = CSmsAccount::NewLC();
  CSmsSettings* smsSettings = CSmsSettings::NewLC();
  smsAccount->LoadSettingsL(*smsSettings);
  TInt descriptionLength = smsSettings->DescriptionLength();
  smsSettings->SetDescriptionLength(descriptionLength + 40);
  smsAccount->SaveSettingsL(*smsSettings);
  CleanupStack::PopAndDestroy(2, smsAccount); // smsSettings, smsAccount
  }
```

4.4.5.7   Copy a Message

Amount of time required: 15 minutes
Location of example code: \Messaging\SmsManager
Required libraries: msgs.lib, smcm.lib
Required header file(s): msvapi.h, smsclnt.h, smut.h
Required platform security capability(s): Platform-dependent (see example code)

Problem: You want to create a copy of a message.

Solution: Use the CMsvEntry::CopyL() function.

Description: CopyMessageL() calls Initialize() and then uses the asynchronous version of CopyL() to create a copy of a message in the draft folder. We therefore make the CSmsTransporter class an active object.

```cpp
#include <msvapi.h> // CMsvOperation
#include <smsclnt.h> // CSmsClientMtm

class CSmsTransporter : public CActive
  {
public:
  void CopyMessageL(TMsvId aFolderId, TRequestStatus& aStatus);

private:
  void InitializeL(TMsvId aFolderId, TRequestStatus& aStatus);

private:
  CSmsClientMtm& iSmsMtm;
  CMsvOperation* iOperation;
  TMsvId iMessageId;
  };
```

As in Recipe 4.4.5.5, we find a message entry by enumerating the child entries of our folder (this is done using the client MTM but could equally be done using CMsvEntry). In this case, we only need the TMsvId of the message in order to copy it.

```cpp
#include <msvids.h> // TMsvIds for standard folders
#include <smut.h> // KUidMsgTypeSMS

void CSmsTransporter::InitializeL(TMsvId aFolderId,
      TRequestStatus& aStatus)
  {
  ...
  if (aFolderId != KMsvNullIndexEntryId)
    {
    iSmsMtm.SwitchCurrentEntryL(aFolderId);
    CMsvEntrySelection* selection = iSmsMtm.Entry().
            ChildrenWithMtmL(KUidMsgTypeSMS);
    if (selection->Count() > 0)
      {
```

```
        iMessageId = selection->At(0);
        }
    delete selection;
    }
...
}
```

We then call `CMsvEntry::CopyL()` and `SetActive()` to initiate the asynchronous copy. Note that there is also an overload of `CopyL()` which takes a `CMsvEntrySelection` array of entry IDs. When copying is complete, the `RunL()` function is called, in which we check the value of `iStatus`.

```
void CSmsTransporter::CopyMessageL(TMsvId aFolderId,
     TRequestStatus& aStatus)
    {
    InitializeL(aFolderId, aStatus);
    iOperation = iSmsMtm.Entry().CopyL(iMessageId,
                     KMsvDraftEntryId, iStatus);
    ...
    SetActive();
    }
```

Whether a copy operation can involve two remote entries is dependent on the MTM.

4.4.5.8 Move a Message

Amount of time required: 15 minutes
Location of example code: \Messaging\SmsManager
Required libraries: msgs.lib, smcm.lib
Required header file(s): msvapi.h, msvids.h, smsclnt.h
Required platform security capability(s): Platform-dependent (see example code)

Problem: You want to move a message to another folder.

Solution: Use the `CMsvEntry::MoveL()` function.

Description: `MoveMessageL()` calls `Initialize()`, exactly as in Recipe 4.4.5.7, and then uses the asynchronous version of `MoveL()` to move a message to the global outbox.

```
#include <msvapi.h> // CMsvOperation
#include <smsclnt.h> // CSmsClientMtm

class CSmsTransporter : public CActive
    {
public:
    ...
    void MoveMessageL(TMsvId aFolderId, TRequestStatus& aStatus );
```

```
// same as the Copy a Message recipe
...
};
```

We then call `CMsvEntry::MoveL()` and `SetActive()` to initiate the asynchronous move. Again, there is also an overload of `MoveL()` which takes a `CMsvEntrySelection` array of entry IDs. When moving is complete, the `RunL()` function is called, in which we check the value of `iStatus`.

```
void CSmsTransporter::MoveMessageL(TMsvId aFolderId,
    TRequestStatus& aStatus)
{
InitializeL(aFolderId, aStatus);
iOperation = iSmsMtm.Entry().MoveL(iMessageId,
    KMsvGlobalOutBoxIndexEntryId, iStatus);
...
SetActive();
}
```

Whether a move operation can involve two remote entries is dependent on the MTM.

4.4.5.9   Send a Message

Amount of time required: 15 minutes
Location of example code: `\Messaging\SmsManager`
Required libraries: `msgs.lib`, `smcm.lib`
Required header file(s): `msvapi.h`, `smsclnt.h`
Required platform security capability(s): Platform-dependent (see example code)

Problem: You want to send a message.

Solution: Use the `CMsvEntry::CopyL()` function to copy the message to the remote service which is responsible for the type of message you are using.

Description: This is very similar to the copy functionality in Recipe 4.4.5.7, except that the target ID is the `TMsvId` of the remote service entry.

```
#include <msvapi.h> // CMsvOperation
#include <smsclnt.h> // CSmsClientMtm

class CSmsTransporter : public CActive
  {
public:
```

```
void SendMessageL(TMsvId aFolderId, TRequestStatus& aStatus);
// same as the Copy a Message recipe
...
};
```

Initialize() is the same as in Recipe 4.4.5.7.

```
void CSmsTransporter::SendMessageL(TMsvId aFolderId,
     TRequestStatus& aStatus)
{
InitializeL(aFolderId, aStatus);
TMsvId smsServiceId = iSmsMtm.ServiceId();
iOperation = iSmsMtm.Entry().CopyL(iMessageId,
         smsServiceId, iStatus);
...
SetActive();
}
```

It is also possible to use CMsvEntry::MoveL() to send a message – the difference is that the message will be deleted from the local store after the message is sent.

When the SMS or IMAP4 MTM is sending a message, it checks the value of TMsvEntry::SendingState() for all the other messages of the same type in the outbox. The result will be one of the values in TMsvSendState; if it is KMsvSendStateWaiting, KMsvSendStateUponRequest or KMsvSendStateResend, that message will also be sent at the same time.

Some MTMs support scheduled sending of messages – to activate this for SMS, use CSmsSettings::SetDelivery(ESmsDeliveryScheduled). To ensure that a particular message will be sent by the scheduler, you must set the sending state of that message to KMsvSendStateScheduled, otherwise the behavior described above will still apply.

4.4.5.10   Delete Messages

Amount of time required: 15 minutes
Location of example code: \Messaging\SmsManager
Required libraries: msgs.lib, smcm.lib
Required header file(s): msvapi.h, msvstd.h, msvids.h, smut.h
Required platform security capability(s): Platform-dependent (see example code)

Problem: You want to delete messages.

Solution: Use CMsvEntry::DeleteL().

Description: In this case we are not using the client MTM, only CMsvEntry. There is not much initializing to be done, so there is no separate Initialize() function.

```
#include <msvapi.h> // CMsvEntry, CMsvOperation
#include <msvstd.h> // CMsvEntrySelection

class CSmsDeleter : public CActive
  {
public:
  void DeleteMessagesL(CMsvEntry& aEntry, TMsvId aFolderId,
                                  TRequestStatus& aStatus);

private:
  CMsvEntrySelection* iSelection;
  CMsvOperation* iOperation;
  };
```

In this case, we are deleting all the SMS messages in a folder, which is a simple task – call `CMsvEntry::DeleteL()` passing in the `CMsvEntrySelection` of message IDs and `SetActive()`. However, it is also possible to delete just one message, passing in its `TMsvId`.

```
#include <msvids.h> // TMsvIds for standard folders
#include <smut.h>   // KUidMsgTypeSMS

void CSmsDeleter::DeleteMessagesL(CMsvEntry& aEntry, TMsvId aFolderId,
                                            TRequestStatus& aStatus)
  {
  if (aFolderId != KMsvNullIndexEntryId)
    {
    aEntry.SetEntryL(aFolderId)
    iSelection = aEntry.ChildrenWithMtmL(KUidMsgTypeSMS);
    }
  ...
  iOperation = aEntry.DeleteL(*iSelection, iStatus);
  SetActive();
  }
```

4.4.5.11　Handle Incoming Messages

Amount of time required: 15 minutes
Location of example code: `\Messaging\SmsManager`
Required header file(s): `msvapi.h`, `msvids.h`, `smsclnt.h`
Required libraries: `msgs.lib`, `smcm.lib`

Problem: You want your application to be informed when new messages are received by the device, or created locally, so that we can handle these events.

Solution: When new entries are created, we are notified by `MMsvSessionObserver::HandleSessionEventL()`.

Description: New incoming SMS messages are received automatically by an SMS watcher and placed in the global inbox or class 2 folder (usually the SIM, accessible through the SMS client MTM). Email and MMS messages, in contrast, must be downloaded from the server using the `Copy()` function (this is similar to Recipe 4.4.5.7, except that you must copy from the remote service to a local folder).

Once a new entry has been created in either of these ways, our application is notified through `HandleSessionEventL()`. In fact, new entries of all types (not just messages) will cause the callback to be called, so we need to check whether the new entries are of a type that we are interested in. To help with this, we are given the `TMsvId` of the parent entry and a `CMsvEntrySelection` containing the IDs of the new messages. Our application handles entries of all types which have been created in the global inbox (which means they must be message entries). You may want to add more checks to your own application, such as checking for a specific type of message (using the `iType` member of `TMsvEntry`), or only checking for complete messages – the latter is important in the cases of email and MMS, and in fact in these cases it may be better to check the `EMsvEntriesChanged` case instead, as seen in the Summary Screen application example in *Symbian OS Communications Programming*, 2nd Edition.

As an example, our application provides a basic `HandleNew-IncomingMessagesL()` function which just clears the `TMsvEntry New()` attribute for all of the messages. The `CMsvEntry::Change-AttributesL()` function is a convenient way to set and clear a number of `TMsvEntry` attributes for a number of messages at once. You might refresh any cached lists of messages, update the user view of the inbox, display the new messages, forward the messages – whatever is appropriate for your application.

```
void CSmsManager::HandleSessionEventL(TMsvSessionEvent aEvent, TAny*
                                aArg1, TAny* aArg2, TAny* /*aArg3*/)
  {
  switch (aEvent)
    {
    ...
    case (EMsvEntriesCreated):
    // what kind of entries are they?
      {
      if (iState == EWaitingForNewMessages)
        {
        TMsvId* parentId = static_cast<TMsvId*>(aArg2);
        if (*parentId == KMsvGlobalInBoxIndexEntryId)
          {
          CMsvEntrySelection* newMessageSelection =
                  static_cast<CMsvEntrySelection*>(aArg1);
          CleanupStack::PushL(newMessageSelection);
          HandleNewIncomingMessagesL(*newMessageSelection);
          CleanupStack::PopAndDestroy(newMessageSelection);
          }
        }
      }
      break;
```

```
      }
    ...
    }
  }

void CSmsManager::HandleNewIncomingMessagesL(CMsvEntrySelection&
                                             aSelection)
  {
  iEntry->ChangeAttributesL(aSelection, 0, KMsvNewAttribute);
  // other handling, as appropriate for your application
  }
```

Taking things further: You may wish to receive SMS messages destined specifically for your application, indicated by a specific text prefix; for instance, a traffic report where the first words are 'Traffic update'. It is desirable to intercept these messages before they are written to the message store in the normal way, so that other applications, such as the phone's messaging application, are not notified of your message. This is particularly useful if the message is not a 'standard' class 1 SMS message, and you do not want the user to be notified that there is a new message, or attempt to read it. To do this, rather than receiving a notification and then checking whether the message was intended for your application, it is preferable to listen on a specific socket. Refer to the example titled *Easy API for sending and receiving SMS datagrams* on the Symbian Developer Network at ***developer.symbian.com/main/tools/utilities***.

4.4.6   Resources

- *Symbian OS Communications Programming*, 2nd Edition: ***developer. symbian.com/commsbook***.

4.5   Graphics and Drawing

On Symbian OS, applications do not draw directly to the window, but use a graphics context (GC) for drawing to the window. An area inside the physical screen (the device's display) first needs to be defined, any drawing occurs inside that defined window area, thus preventing an application from drawing outside its window area.

In principle, all normal graphics drawing in Symbian OS takes place in an `RWindow`-derived window, owned by the window server (WSERV). WSERV uses the font and bitmap server (FBSERV) for effective handling of fonts and bitmaps. It also manages other aspects of the user interaction (such as key input handling, pointer events, and so on). FBSERV is highly optimized for speed and memory consumption and all fonts and bitmaps are loaded only once into memory, and then reference counted to determine when they can be unloaded. The optimization can occasionally cause problems. For example, if an application loads a font and forgets to release it after use, it could lead to situations where the font file is left open. If the user tries to remove the font file from the file system, the installer returns an 'In use' error and removal is prevented. Another potential error situation comes with scalable graphics images. These are loaded into the memory once, and all future access is handled by using the cached image. If the content of the MIF file is altered, it might not be reflected when loading images, until the cached image is released from the memory, and the updated file reloaded.

If you need to update the screen a number of times per second, for example when writing a game, drawing through WSERV may be too slow. As an alternative, you can also draw graphics using direct screen access (DSA), which greatly reduces the overhead of communicating with the window server, and increases the drawing speed.

When you create an application using the Symbian OS application framework, drawable windows are created by constructing CCoe-Control-derived container classes for UIs, and the drawing is handled using CWindowGc in the CCoeControl's Draw() function. In case you need to get access to the container's window, you could get a handle to it by using the Window() function defined for CCoe-Control, the area set for the container can be fetched with the Rect() function call and its position in the display is returned by the Position-RelativeToScreen() function. With CCoeControl, there is no need to activate/deactivate the graphics context (and trying to do so might lead to a panic) or to implement active objects for monitoring redraw events, since all of this is already handled by the Symbian OS application framework and the CCoeControl class.

An important issue to understand with Symbian OS – and drawing in it – is that Symbian OS is event-driven, and also all drawing is implemented as event-driven drawing. This means that each redraw is started with an event, usually a WSERV-generated redraw event. WSERV implements a queue for storing redraw events in case they can't be delivered, and this queue holds a maximum of only one redraw event per window. If your application is unable to receive and handle redrawing because it is handling an event of higher priority, subsequent redraw events can be lost. However, as soon as the application can handle events again, it will process exactly one redraw event from the WSERV.

This is important to understand, since if the application is busy handling some other events, it will not be able to receive redraw events until it has finished. This means that no updates to the window will occur until the application has completed processing for the other event. Most often this happens when using tight for or while loops or, for example, when implementing delays with calls to User::After(). It also can happen when using User::WaitForRequest() to wait active object requests to complete. In the worst case scenario the window server will panic the hanging thread with `ViewSrv 11` panic. This is why we have warned you not to use `User::Wait...()` throughout, whenever it has been shown in sample code (it is shown only to make the code snippet simpler).

In case the drawing also has to be handled with these tight-looping functions, the loops should be implemented as active objects where each `RunL` call does one round of the loop and then sleeps for a while. The sleeping could, for example, be implemented as an `RTimer/CPeriodic` type of timer (with idle priority). This method would also allow the drawing loops to be cancelled (since key events can be received and a menu can be shown), and it allows applications to receive redraw events from the WSERV. For more information about active objects, please refer to Chapter 3.

Drawing events are also buffered in the client side. In practice this means that lines inside the `Draw()` function are not executed one-by-one in the WSERV, but instead line commands are collected into a buffer, which will be executed when it is big enough or when it is flushed. For this reason, having `for/while` loops or `User::After()` in the `Draw()` function and trying to do drawing into the same area while changing the drawing content will not work well in practice. Instead, this kind of drawing should be timed or looped outside the `Draw()` function using active objects, drawing one state at a time, and waiting between draws.

The most important feature of the `Draw()` function is that it is non-leaving and constant. This means that no code inside the `Draw()` function may have the potential to leave – in case the leaving code cannot be avoided, it must be TRAPed. Since this function is constant, it cannot modify values so, for example, you can't change state variables belonging to the class inside the `Draw()` function. Instead, you need to change the values outside and then call the `DrawNow()` function to inform WSERV to draw the required content to the container's screen.

All example code for drawing in normal application frameworks in this section assumes that drawing is handled inside `CCoeControl`'s `Draw()` function, where the graphics context (GC) is retrieved as follows:

```
void CMyContainer::Draw(const TRect& aRect,) const
  {
  CWindowGc& gc = SystemGc();
  }
```

The example code in the recipes below shows just the snippets most relevant to the discussion in question. Further information about graphics and drawing on Symbian OS can be found in the Symbian Developer Library documentation, available in each SDK and online. See the Graphics section of the Symbian OS Guide for an overview of using WSERV and FBSERV, and the C++ Component Reference section for details of each API. You will also find a set of recipes for using OpenGL ES, for 3D graphics, later in Section 4.6.

4.5.1   Easy Recipes

4.5.1.1   Draw Lines and Shapes

Amount of time required: 15 minutes
Location of example code: \Graphics_Basics
Required library(s): gdi.lib, ws32.lib
Required header file(s): gdi.h, w32std.h
Required platform security capability(s): None

Problem: You want to draw lines and shapes to the screen.

Solution: When drawing lines, either by using the line-drawing functions or by using the shape-drawing functions, the lines and borders are drawn using the currently set pen. The most important settings for the pen are pen color and style.

You can set the pen color by using the SetPenColor() function, and the pen style can be changed with SetPenStyle(). If you need lines with more than one pixel width, you can also change the pen size with the SetPenSize() function.

The default value for the pen color is black and for the style is solid. The possible styles for the pen are as follows:

- ENullPen (pen does not draw anything – i.e., is transparent).

- ESolidPen (drawn with solid color).

- EDottedPen (drawn as dotted line).

- EDashedPen (drawn as dashed line).

- EDotDashPen (drawn as alternating dashes and dots).

- EDotDotDashPen (drawn as alternating single dashes and pairs of dots).

To draw a straight line you can call DrawLineXyz() functions, for example drawing a line from TPoint(10,10) to TPoint(50,60) could be done like this:

```
gc.SetPenColor(KRgbRed);
gc.SetPenStyle(CGraphicsContext::EDottedPen);
gc.DrawLine(TPoint(10,10), TPoint (50,60));
```

And to draw a rectangular area between these two points could be done like this:

```
gc.DrawRect(TRect(10,10,50,60));
```

For other line- and shape-drawing functionality, check the `Graphics_Basics` example code and also the Symbian Developer Library documentation for the `CWindowGc` class.

4.5.1.2 Draw Background Color or Fill a Shape

Amount of time required: 15 minutes
Location of example code: `\Graphics_Basics`
Required library(s): `gdi.lib`, `ws32.lib`
Required header file(s): `gdi.h`, `w32std.h`
Required platform security capability(s): None

Problem: You want to draw a background color or fill the shapes you have drawn.

Solution: Brushes are used to fill the drawing area. In general, they are used to fill a shape that is drawn onto the screen. Default color for the brush is white and the default style is Null. Null brush means that no filling is used, thus the area is drawn transparent and the original background is shown under the shape drawn to the screen. Styles that can be set for the brush are:

- `ESolidBrush` (background is filled with solid color).

- `EPatternedBrush` (brush image is used as background).

- `EVerticalHatchBrush` (brush fills the shape with vertical hatching lines).

- `EForwardDiagonalHatchBrush` (brush fills the shape with diagonal hatching lines).

- `EHorizontalHatchBrush` (brush fills the shape with horizontal hatching lines).

- `ERearwardDiagonalHatchBrush` (brush fills the shape with rearward diagonal hatching lines).

- `ESquareCrossHatchBrush` (brush fills the shape with horizontal and vertical hatching lines).

- `EDiamondCrossHatchBrush` (brush fills the shape with forward diagonal and rearward diagonal hatching lines).

With brush fillings, the brush color will define the background color and the pen color is used with the lines (if the brush style has lines in it). When using brush patterns, after you have finished using the brush, you should call `DiscardBrushPattern()` to release the brush pattern's memory.

Another notable issue is that if the size of the brush image is smaller than the brush area, the image will be tiled – thus if you want to fill the whole drawing area with the image without having it tiled, you should either scale the image beforehand so it fits the whole screen nicely, or just draw the image as per usual to fill the screen and then use Null brush with all other drawing.

After you have set the brush, you could fill the whole container area with it by calling `gc.Clear()` in the `Draw()` function, or draw it to any selected shape as shown in the following code sample:

```
void Draw( const TRect& aRect) const
  {
  CWindowGc& gc = SystemGc();
  gc.SetBrushColor(KRgbWhite);
  gc.SetBrushStyle(CGraphicsContext::ESolidBrush);
  gc.DrawRect(aRect);
  }
```

What may go wrong when you do this: When using a patterned brush, the brush bitmap needs to be set first by calling the `UseBrush-Pattern()` function. If you call `SetBrushStyle(CGraphics-Context::EPatternedBrush)` without first setting a valid bitmap, it will cause a panic.

Tip: When using bitmaps, an important issue to remember is that even when the pointer for the bitmap is valid, the content could still be invalid – and using this type of image will generate a panic for sure. To avoid such a problem, you should always first check the pointer of the bitmap and then also that it has a valid (that is, a non-NULL) handle.

4.5.1.3 Load and Draw MBM or MIF Images

Amount of time required: 15 minutes
Location of example code: `\Graphics_Images`
Required library(s): `efsrv.lib, bitgdi.lib, w32.lib`
Required header file(s): `f32file.h, bitstd.h, w32std.h`
Required platform security capability(s): None

Problem: You want to load an image that is stored in a Symbian OS proprietary multi-image file (MBM or MIF) and draw it to the screen.

Solution: On Symbian OS, images may be stored in a proprietary multi-image file (MBM for bitmaps and MIF for scalable images).

First, you need to locate the image file. Usually you can't know in which drive the application is installed, thus you don't know from which drive to load the image. To locate the image you could, for example, use `TFindFile` and just specify the full path with filename and extension, and let the API find the drive the file is stored in.

Files can then be loaded directly with a `CFbsBitmap`-type object, by first constructing the object and then calling its `Load()` function. The `Load()` function takes two arguments, of which the first is the image name and the second the index of the image stored in the multi-image file. Note that the index is zero-based, thus the first image's index is 0. The code for locating and loading a bitmap at index 0 in a file called `bitmap.mbm` is shown in the following code sample:

```
_LIT(KtxBitmapFile,"\\private\\A0003139\\bitmap.mbm");
TFindFile imageFile(CCoeEnv::Static()->FsSession());
if(KErrNone == imageFile.FindByDir(KtxBitmapFile, KNullDesC))
  {
  iBrushBitmap = new(ELeave) CFbsBitmap();
  iBrushBitmap->Load(imageFile.File(),0);
  }
```

After loading the image you can draw it to the screen in the `Draw()` function like this:

```
void CMyContainer::Draw(const TRect& aRect) const
  {
  CWindowGc& gc = SystemGc();
  gc.DrawBitmap(Rect(), iBitmap);
  }
```

> **What may go wrong when you do this:** The `Load()` function used for loading the image will return an error code if the loading fails. In case the error is not checked, you need to check the handle for the image before drawing it. Trying to draw an image in which loading failed will generate a panic.

4.5.1.4   Draw an Image with a Transparent Section

Amount of time required: 15 minutes
Location of example code: \Graphics_Images
Required library(s): efsrv.lib, bitgdi.lib, w32.lib
Required header file(s): f32file.h, bitstd.h, w32std.h
Required platform security capability(s): None

Problem: The image you want to draw contains at least partially transparent pixels.

Solution: When you want to draw images with transparent sections, you need to have firstly the bitmap image to show and then a 1-pixel black and white image which masks the background with the image. Thus, this time you need to load two different images:

```
// bitmapFile is a TFindFile
iBall = new(ELeave) CFbsBitmap();
iBall->Load(bitmapFile.File(),1);
iMask = new(ELeave) CFbsBitmap();
iMask->Load(bitmapFile.File(),2);

void CMyContainer::Draw(const TRect& aRect,) const
  {
  CWindowGc& gc = SystemGc();

  TSize imageSize(iBall->SizeInPixels());
  TRect destRect(0,0, imageSize.iWidth, imageSize.iHeight);
  TRect sourceRect(0,0, imageSize.iWidth, imageSize.iHeight);
  gc.DrawBitmapMasked(destRect, iBall, sourceRect, iMask, ETrue);
  }
```

Discussion: With the mask, usually the black pixels are the ones that will show the image and the white ones are the ones that will show the background, but you can define the mask to work the other way around by changing the last argument in the `DrawBitmapMasked()` function to be `EFalse`.

Tip: The first argument to `DrawBitmapMasked()` is the destination rectangle to which the image is to be drawn. This looks like you could ask for the image to be scaled to your requirements, but using this would not be a good idea. Some phones will do this correctly, but in some devices you would get distorted images. It is advisable to pre-scale all masked images and then draw them the size they are. One way to scale an image is to draw it into an off-screen image that is constructed to the desired size (Recipe 4.5.3.1 explains how to do this in more detail).

The rectangle argument defined between the image and the mask is a source rectangle, defining which part of the image is to be drawn into the target. If you bear in mind the previous advice and change this to anything other than the original rectangle of the image, you need to adjust the destination rectangle size as well.

4.5.2   Intermediate Recipes

4.5.2.1   Load a JPG or PNG Image

Amount of time required: 15 minutes
Location of example code: \Graphics_Images

Required library(s): `bitgdi.lib`, `ws32.lib`, `imageconversion.lib`, `apgrfx.lib`, `apmime.lib`
Required header file(s): `bitstd.h`, `w32std.h`, `ImageData.h`, `imageconversion.h`, `apgcli.h`, `apmrec.h`
Required platform security capability(s): None

Problem: You want to load and draw image files other than those stored in MBM or MIF files.

Solution: To load an image file other than a MBM or MIF image, you need to use the Symbian OS image converter library (ICL), which can convert single and multiframe images stored in files or descriptors to `CFbsBitmap` objects for rendering to the screen. When opening image files, you first need to know which type of image you are dealing with. For this purpose you could use `RApaLsSession` as shown in the `Get-FileType()` function, or simply use the static `GetMimeTypeFileL()` function provided with the `CImageDecoder` class.

The file type defines the internal structure of the image and `CImage-Decoder` requires this to be specified when it is constructed for decoding an image file to a Symbian OS internal bitmap format. After determining the file type you can construct the `CImageDecoder` instance and start decoding the image.

```
iImageDecoder = CImageDecoder::FileNewL(iFsSession, aFileName,
                                                     imageType);
iFrameImg = new(ELeave) CFbsBitmap();
iFrameImg->Create(iImageDecoder->FrameInfo(0).iOverallSizeInPixels,
                  iImageDecoder->FrameInfo(0).iFrameDisplayMode);

iImageDecoder->Convert(&iStatus, *iFrameImg, 0);
SetActive();
```

Note that `CImageDecoder` is asynchronous and requires an active object to notify when the image has decoded. After the image is loaded (or if the loading fails), `RunL()` will be called and you can start using the bitmap image to render it to the screen. Please see the ICL documentation in the Symbian Developer Library (the Multimedia section of the Symbian OS Guide) and the reference documentation for class `CFbsBitmap`.

What may go wrong when you do this: By default, applications have 1 MB heap memory to use. Each pixel takes 3 bytes, so for a 5 megapixels image, the RAM required is 15 MB. You will run out of memory before the image is loaded if you do not increase the maximum heap value by using the `EPOCHEAPSIZE` keyword in your MMP file, as Chapter 3, Section 3.13 described. For this reason (and also because the screen is quite small and you can't show the image in full size), you could define a smaller target size when creating the image to be loaded, and it will be scaled to fit the size when `CImageDecoder` loads it to the bitmap.

4.5.2.2 Draw Text to the Screen

Amount of time required: 15 minutes
Location of example code: `\Graphics_Images`
Required library(s): `gdi.lib`, `ws32.lib`, `eikcore.lib`, `cone.lib`
Required header file(s): `gdi.h`, `ws32std.h`, `eikenv.h`, `coetextdrawer.h`
Required platform security capability(s): None

Problem: You want to draw text onto the screen.

Solution: Before you can draw any text onto the screen, you need to select a font, set that font into use with the `CWindowGc::UseFont()` function and then call the text-drawing functions. After you have finished using the font, you should call `DiscardFont()` to inform WSERV that you have finished using that particular font. When changing the font, you don't need to call `DiscardFont()`, since calling `UseFont()` will automatically discard the previously set font.

To get a font you can use one of the different-sized system fonts accessible through `CEikonEnv::Static()`, such as:

- `AnnotationFont()`

- `TitleFont()`

- `LegendFont()`

- `SymbolFont()`

- `DenseFont()`.

On the S60 platform you can also use `AknLayoutUtils::Font-FromId()` to get the normal system fonts (see the SDK documentation for `AknLayoutUtils` for further details). As an example for text drawing, if you want to draw 'Hello' in the top left corner of your container with the title font, you can do it like this:

```
_LIT(KTextBuffer, "Hello");
gc.UseFont(CEikonEnv::Static()->TitleFont());
gc.DrawText(KTextBuffer,TPoint(0,0));
gc.DiscardFont();
```

Discussion: The text color is defined by the pen color settings. The default color is black and you can change it with the `SetPenColor()` function. In addition, the rectangular area where the text is drawn is filled with the current brush, and if you don't want any fillings, you should set the brush style to Null before drawing any text to the container.

With `CWindowGc`, there are two different variants of horizontal drawing one that renders text from a point, and another that renders text in a box. Each is illustrated in Figure 4.5.1.

```
void CWindowGc::DrawText(const TDesC& aBuf, const TRect& aBox, TInt
        aBaselineOffset, TTextAlign aHoriz=ELeft, TInt aLeftMrg=0)
```

`aBaselineOffset` is the line on which the letters sit (for instance, below r, s, t and above the tail of q and y). `aHoriz` is the alignment (left, right, center). `aLeftMrg` is the text margin value (left margin for left-aligned text, right margin for right-aligned text).

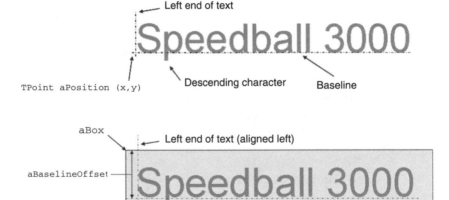

Figure 4.5.1 Rendering Text from a Coordinate Point (Top) and Rendering Text Within a Box (Bottom)

If you want to draw vertical text, `CWindowGc` also defines two versions of the `DrawTextVertical()` function.

What may go wrong when you do this: For text drawing there are no default fonts set, thus you must set a font before attempting to draw any text. Failing this will again generate a panic. Since the fonts are handled by FBSERV, you should always release the font when you are done with it, so the server can decrement the reference count for the font and determine when it can be released from memory.

> **Tip:** With the S60 platform you could also use `AknLayout-Utils::FontFromId()` to get the normal system fonts.
>
> Also note that `CFont` is a generic Symbian OS class that defines plenty of useful functions, as you can see in the system header file `gdi.h`. For example, you could check how many pixels the string needs and then act accordingly when drawing the text into the control's screen.
>
> Characters that do not have a definition in the selected font will be shown as empty rectangles. For example, if you buy a normal British phone, and try displaying Chinese text on it, the phone most likely does not include any characters for Chinese text. The text would show only a sequence of empty rectangles rather than the correct characters.

4.5.2.3   Load Fonts

Amount of time required: 15 minutes
Location of example code: \Graphics_Images
Required library(s): gdi.lib, ws32.lib, eikcore.lib
Required header file(s): gdi.h, ws32std.h, eikenv.h
Required platform security capability(s): None

Problem: You want to use fonts other than those supplied by the system, or you want to use the system fonts in different sizes to the default.

Solution: If you want to use system fonts with special sizing or you want to use other fonts included in the device, you need to first define `TFontSpec`, which defines the name and size wanted for the font. You should then use it to load the font using the screen device's `GetNearestFontInTwips()` function, which locates and loads the nearest match for the font requested.

To know which fonts are installed on the device, you first need to get the count for them by calling the `NumTypefaces()` function defined for the screen device, and then you can get the `TTypefaceSupport` definition for each one by using `TypefaceSupport()` with a zero-based index number. Then, to make the `TFontSpec` variable, use the name defined for the `TTypefaceSupport` and define the size required (100 is the normal size, anything smaller produces a smaller font size and anything bigger a bigger font size).

```
TTypefaceSupport tfs;
CEikonEnv::Static()->ScreenDevice()->TypefaceSupport(tfs, 0);
TFontSpec spec(tfs.iTypeface.iName, 100);
```

```
CFont* useFont;
CEikonEnv::Static()->ScreenDevice()->GetNearestFontInTwips(useFont,
                                                            spec);
if (useFont)
  {
  gc.UseFont(useFont);
  gc.DrawText(....);
  ...
  CEikonEnv::Static()->ScreenDevice()->ReleaseFont(useFont);
  }
```

> **Tip:** Different devices may not have the same sets of fonts installed
> in them. In fact, sometimes even the same device model can have
> different sets of fonts installed (for example, if it is for sale in a different
> region, or for a different language set).
>
> Relying on a device to have a specifically named font installed
> could lead to problems when the code is executed on devices that
> were bought from other regions.

4.5.2.4   Draw Controls Inside Another Control

Amount of time required: 15 minutes
Location of example code: \Graphics_Images
Required library(s): cone.lib
Required header file(s): coecntrl.h
Required platform security capability(s): None

Problem: You want to have multiple controls inside your container.

Solution: In general, controls that are located inside a control are not
constructed in their own window, but are actually using the window of
the container control they are drawn in.

Thus, the main change when constructing controls used inside other
controls is to remove the code that constructs its own window. Don't
call CreateWindowL() in the control's ConstructL() function, but
instead call SetContainerWindowL() with a reference to the container control.

When using system controls defined in the SDK, most often they
don't set the container window by themselves, but you actually need
to call the SetContainerWindowL() function after constructing the
control. You can see this style used with CTextControl in the About-
Container.cpp file:

```
iTextControl = CTextControl::NewL(KtxLongText);
iTextControl->SetContainerWindowL(*this);
iTextControl->SetRect(SmallerRect);
```

When this code has executed, the control is constructed. It has a window to draw in and, after setting the rectangle where it lies inside the container's own window, it also knows where to draw.

To get this control to refresh correctly, you also need to implement the following two functions:

```
TInt CAboutContainer::CountComponentControls() const
  {
  return 1;
  }

CCoeControl* CAboutContainer::ComponentControl( TInt /*aIndex */) const
  {
  return iTextControl;
  }
```

Discussion: When there is a redraw event for a CCoeControl-derived class, the system will first call the Draw() function of that container, and then call CountComponentControls() to determine how many controls inside the container need to be drawn. For each control to be redrawn, it calls ComponentControl() to retrieve a pointer to each of the controls inside the container, in turn. The Draw() function is called on each control, and then CountComponentControls() is called on the control, in case there are controls residing within it.

So the Draw() function is always called, and it is always called first. This means that you could draw the background in it. And it also means that in case your controls are filling the whole screen, then to avoid double drawing (and possible flickering) you probably should avoid doing anything in the Draw() function.

What may go wrong when you do this: In case your control is not showing at all, check that you actually remembered to set the rectangle, since the rectangle area set for controls residing inside another control is relative to the container control, and not relative to the screen. Check that you have specified it correctly (see the example code for this recipe for a demonstration).

In case your container draws once to the screen but then does not update, check that you are implementing CountComponent-Controls() and ComponentControl() correctly.

Tip: Note that only controls that are put into the control stack (that is, those for which you called AddToStackL() in the application user interface class) will receive key events. If, for example, you have an editor inside your own control, then you need to forward all necessary key events in your container control's OfferKeyEventL() function.

4.5.3　Advanced Recipes

4.5.3.1　Use Off-Screen Images for Drawing

Amount of time required: 15 minutes
Location of example code: \Graphics_Images
Required library(s): efsrv.lib, bitgdi.lib, ws32.lib
Required header file(s): f32file.h, bitstd.h, bitdev.h, w32std.h
Required platform security capability(s): None

Problem: You want to implement double-buffering to ensure flicker-free graphics.

Solution: Double-buffering is an established technique for drawing flicker-free graphics. It is an essential idiom used for rendering fluid motion in anything from drag and drop puzzle games to high-speed shoot 'em ups.

Double-buffering makes use of an offscreen bitmap. The first thing to do is construct a bitmap, and then create a graphics context from which we can use the actual drawing functions. To get a graphics context, we need to have a screen device made. The code for this part is as follows:

```
iBitmap = new(ELeave)CFbsBitmap();
iBitmap->Create(ImgSize, EColor16M);

iBitmapDevice = CFbsBitmapDevice::NewL(iBitmap);
User::LeaveIfError(iBitmapDevice->CreateContext(iGraphicsContext));
```

After these four lines are executed, we can use the function provided by iGraphicsContext (which is CFbsBitmapDevice) to draw into the iBitmap (which is CFbsBitmap), and then just call DrawNow(). WSERV will generate a redraw event and the container's Draw() function is called, in which you can use graphics context as usual to draw the iBitmap image onto the screen.

Discussion: The most usual cause of graphics flickering is drawing the same pixels multiple times over one draw event. The easiest way to avoid flickering is to make the draw function code in such a way that all pixels are drawn a minimum time over one draw event – basically what this means is not calling Clear(), DrawRect(), etc. for areas that will be drawn later on in the same draw event.

As can be seen in the example code in AnimationContainer.cpp, off-screen bitmaps can be used to draw GIF animation frames into an image that can be shown on the screen.

> **Tip:** To avoid distortion in the image as well as to make the actual screen drawing code faster, you should construct the off-screen image to be the same size as the actual physical screen size in pixels.

4.5.3.2   Load GIF Animation Images

Amount of time required: 25 minutes
Location of example code: \Graphics_Images
Required library(s): bitgdi.lib, ws32.lib, imageconversion. lib, apgrfx.lib, apmime.lib
Required header file(s): bitstd.h, w32std.h, imagedata.h, imageconversion.h, apgcli.h, apmrec.h
Required platform security capability(s): None

Problem: You want to load and draw all frames from a GIF image.

Solution: You can use the CImageDecoder class also for loading GIF files, and other images that have multiple frames in them. Sometimes it might even be better for the application architecture to load MBM/MIF files with active object loops to enable event receiving while loading multiple frames.

To load GIF images, you first need to construct a CImageDecoder instance, as you did in Recipe 4.5.2.1. You should then check the amount of frames on it:

```
iImageDecoder =
    CImageDecoder::FileNewL(iFsSession,aFileName,KtxTypeImageGif_8);
iCurrCount = iImageDecoder->FrameCount();
```

And then start looping the frame reading:

```
void CAniFrame_Reader::NextImageL(void)
  {
  if(iCurrCount > 0 && !IsActive())
    {
    iCurrImg++;// add 1 to the index, so we can read the next frame
    if(iCurrImg >= iCurrCount || iCurrImg < 0)
      {// in case the index is non-valid, we set it to zero
      // should only happen after reading the last frame
      iCurrImg = 0;
      }

    delete iFrameImg;
    iFrameImg = NULL;

    iFrameImg = new(ELeave) CFbsBitmap();
    iFrameImg->Create(iImageDecoder->
        FrameInfo(iCurrImg).iOverallSizeInPixels,
```

```
        iImageDecoder->FrameInfo(iCurrImg).iFrameDisplayMode);

    delete iFrameMsk;
    iFrameMsk = NULL;
    iFrameMsk = new(ELeave) CFbsBitmap();
    iFrameMsk->Create(iImageDecoder->
            FrameInfo(iCurrImg).iOverallSizeInPixels, EGray2);

    iImageDecoder->Convert(&iStatus, *iFrameImg,*iFrameMsk,iCurrImg);
    SetActive();
    }
}
```

Since the `Convert()` function is asynchronous, `RunL()` will be called when it has finished decoding the current frame. With GIF image frames, some frames are not full frames, but actually only have the pixels that have changed since the previous frame. Also, the frame might need to be drawn in another position than the full image rectangle. To make sure of what is drawn and where, you need to check the information stored in the frame information object for the currently loaded frame:

```
void CAniFrame_Reader::RunL()
  {
  if(iFrameMsk && iFrameImg)
    {
    if(iFrameMsk->Handle() && iFrameImg->Handle())
      {
      TBool reDraw(EFalse);
      TRect drawArea(TPoint(0,0),iFrameImg->SizeInPixels());

      if(TFrameInfo::ERestoreToBackground &
              iImageDecoder->FrameInfo(iCurrImg).iFlags)
        {
        reDraw = ETrue;
        }
      else
        {
        drawArea = iImageDecoder->
                      FrameInfo(iCurrImg).iFrameCoordsInPixels;
        }

      iCallBack.AppendFrameL(*iFrameImg,*iFrameMsk,DrawArea,ReDraw);
      }
    }
  }
```

With this example, the code for the frame and the instructions on where to draw it are directed to another level which, for example, can be implemented with off-screen bitmap drawing:

```
void CAnimationContainer::AppendFrameL(CFbsBitmap& aImage, CFbsBitmap&
                                aMask, TRect aArea, TBool aReDraw)
  {
```

```
if(iGraphicsContext)
  {
  TSize imgSize(aImage.SizeInPixels());

  if(aReDraw)
    {
    iGraphicsContext->
        DrawBitmap(TRect(0,0, imgSize.iWidth,
                   imgSize.iHeight), &aImage);
    }
  else
    {
    iGraphicsContext->DrawBitmapMasked(aArea, &aImage,
        TRect(0, 0, imgSize.iWidth, imgSize.iHeight),
                                  &aMask, EFalse);
    }
  }

DrawNow();
}
```

As you can see from the code samples, if the frame information flags are defining that the background should be restored (with a `ERestoreTo-Background` flag), the mask is not used, but the image is drawn without it. This usually happens at least with the first frame, so the animation can start from fresh.

Tip: The example code uses a defined interval for timing the animation. You could also read the timing information from the frame information and get the frames timed exactly as they were designed to be handled.

What may go wrong when you do this: With this example old frames are not saved, to optimize the speed storage, so you don't need to keep loading them when looping the animation. But you need to remember that the maximum default heap is 1 MB, and if you exceed your application's maximum heap, you will get 'Out of memory error'. For example, 20 frames on 320 × 240 sized images with 24 bits/pixel will take a little over 4.6 MB of memory.

4.5.3.3 Draw Skins as Backgrounds (S60 Only)

Amount of time required: 20 minutes
Location of example code: \Graphics_Images
Libaries: aknskins.lib, aknskinsrv.lib, aknswallpaperutils.lib

Required header file(s): `aknsbasicbackgroundcontrol-context.h`, `aknsskininstance.h`, `aknsdrawutils.h`
Required platform security capability(s): None

Problem: You want to have the background drawn with the currently selected skin.

Solution: The skin is drawn to a container by calling `CAknsBasicBack-groundControlContext`, so first you need to construct one:

```
iBgContext =
    CAknsBasicBackgroundControlContext::NewL(KAknsIIDQsnBgAreaMain,
                                  TRect(0, 0, 1,  1), ETrue);
```

The first argument defines which skin item is used, the second one defines the area to be used and the third defines whether the parent controls (i.e., the control you wish to draw the skin to); the relative position to the screen should also be taken into account.

As you can see, the rectangle for the object is not set here. This is to make sure it is always set correctly and as you can see from the example, the object is constructed before the rectangle area for the container is set. This means that as soon as the rectangle area for the container is set the `SizeChanged()` function will be called, and in this function you should always set the correct position and area:

```
if ( iBgContext )
  {
  iBgContext->SetRect(Rect());
  if ( &Window() )
    {
    iBgContext->SetParentPos( PositionRelativeToScreen() );
    }
  }
```

After this, you are ready to draw the skin into your container's background:

```
void CMySplashContainer::Draw(const TRect& /*aRect*/) const
  {
  CWindowGc& gc = SystemGc();
  MAknsSkinInstance* skin = AknsUtils::SkinInstance();
  AknsDrawUtils::Background(skin, iBgContext, this, gc, Rect());
  }
```

Note that to make the skins actually work, you also need to implement the `MopSupplyObject()` function in your container:

```
TTypeUid::Ptr CMySplashContainer::MopSupplyObject(TTypeUid aId)
  {
```

```
if (iBgContext)
  {
  return MAknsControlContext::SupplyMopObject(aId, iBgContext );
  }

return CCoeControl::MopSupplyObject(aId);
}
```

> **What may go wrong when you do this:** The first argument for the `CAknsBasicBackgroundControlContext` defines which skin item is used. Thus if you select the wrong background, your skin might not look ideal for the situation. In case you have problems with it, check the `AknsConstants.h` header file for different options.

4.5.3.4 Draw Outside the Symbian OS Application Framework

Amount of time required: 40 minutes
Location of example code: \Graphics_NonAFW
Required library(s): ws32.lib, gdi.lib, apgrfx.lib
Required header file(s): w32std.h, gdi.h, apgwgnam.h
Required platform security capability(s): None

Problem: You want to draw without the application framework.

Solution: When constructing GUI applications without using the standard application framework, the first task is to construct the screen device, which presents the device's physical display. The screen device is then used to construct the graphics context within which the actual drawing can be handled:

```
User::LeaveIfError(iWsSession.Connect());
iScreen=new(ELeave) CWsScreenDevice(iWsSession);
User::LeaveIfError(iScreen->Construct());
User::LeaveIfError(iScreen->CreateContext(iGc));
```

Before any drawing can be done, a drawable window has to be constructed and its area in the display needs to be defined:

```
iWg=RWindowGroup(iWsSession);
User::LeaveIfError(iWg.Construct((TUint32)&iWg, EFalse));
iWg.SetOrdinalPosition(0,ECoeWinPriorityNormal);
iWg.EnableReceiptOfFocus(EFalse);

CApaWindowGroupName* wn=CApaWindowGroupName::NewLC(iWsSession);
wn->SetHidden(ETrue);
wn->SetWindowGroupName(iWg);
CleanupStack::PopAndDestroy(wn);
```

```
iMyWindow=RWindow(iWsSession);
User::LeaveIfError(iMyWindow.Construct(iWg, (TUint32)&iMyWindow));

TPixelsTwipsAndRotation SizeAndRotation;
iScreen->GetDefaultScreenSizeAndRotation(SizeAndRotation);
iScreenRect = TRect(TPoint(0,0),SizeAndRotation.iPixelSize);

iMyWindow.Activate();
iMyWindow.SetExtent(iScreenRect.iTl,iScreenRect.Size());
iMyWindow.SetBackgroundColor(KRgbWhite);
iMyWindow.SetOrdinalPosition(0,ECoeWinPriorityNormal);
iMyWindow.SetNonFading(ETrue);
iMyWindow.SetVisible(ETrue);
```

In the `Draw()` function, the graphics context needs to be activated before drawing and deactivated after drawing is finished:

```
void CScreenDrawer::Draw(const TRect& aRect)
  {
  iGc->Activate(iMyWindow);

  iMyWindow.Invalidate(aRect);
  iMyWindow.BeginRedraw();

  // Handle any drawing in here ...

  iMyWindow.EndRedraw();

  iGc->Deactivate();
  iWsSession.Flush();
  }
```

If the application wants to get redraw events it needs to implement the active object for monitoring redraw events generated by WSERV. The redraw event request is handled by the `RWsSession::RedrawReady()` function.

Discussion: The example given is really a minimal application, which could be used as a base for applications that do not need user interaction, but are shown according to some system events (for example, incoming calls).

To make the application more usable you need to also catch focus and key events and to make some kind of menu system to handle menu commands from the user. To catch key events, you could make another small (1 pixel for example) window on top of this one, and construct it like this:

```
iWg=RWindowGroup(iWsSession);
User::LeaveIfError(iWg.Construct((TUint32)&iWg, EFalse));
```

```
iWg.SetOrdinalPosition(1, ECoeWinPriorityNormal+1);
iWg.EnableReceiptOfFocus(ETrue);

CApaWindowGroupName* wn=CApaWindowGroupName::NewLC(iWsSession);
wn->SetHidden(EFalse);
wn->SetWindowGroupName(iWg);
CleanupStack::PopAndDestroy(wn);
```

A call to `RWsSession::EventReady()` will trigger your `RunL()` function, which should look like this:

```
TWsEvent e;
iWsSession.GetEvent(e);
TInt type = e.Type();

switch (type)
  {
  case EEventKey:
  case EEventKeyUp:
  case EEventKeyDown:
    // react to key events here
  break;
  };
```

For focus change monitoring, you could use the same base code, and just add:

```
User::LeaveIfError(iWg.EnableFocusChangeEvents());
```

You could get the application that currently has focus with these lines of code:

```
TInt wgid = iWsSession.GetFocusWindowGroup();

CApaWindowGroupName* gn;
gn = CApaWindowGroupName::NewLC(iWsSession, wgid);

//gn->AppUid(), gives you the Uid of the application that is in focus.

CleanupStack::PopAndDestroy(gn);
```

What may go wrong when you do this: When you are not using the application framework, you will not be able to use the `CEikon-Env::Static()` function, simply because you don't have the CONE environment constructed. This can lead to problems when using some APIs that require an environment variable to be set before they can be used, and for this reason you should be careful in selecting the APIs used.

4.5.3.5 Draw with Direct Screen Access

Amount of time required: 40 minutes
Location of example code: \Graphics_DSA
Required library(s): gdi.lib, ws32.lib
Required header file(s): gdi.h, w32std.h
Required platform security capability(s): None

Problem: You need to improve the performance of your drawing routine by using direct screen access.

Solution: To draw with drect screen access (DSA), you need to construct a CDirectScreenAccess object. CDirectScreenAccess requires a window server session, a drawable window and a screen device to be constructed first. Within the application framework you can get the drawable window by calling the CCoeContainer::Window() function; for a screen device and window session you could use the following code:

```
CWsScreenDevice* screenDev= CEikonEnv::Static()->ScreenDevice();
RWsSession winSession = CEikonEnv::Static()->WsSession();
```

When working outside the application framework, you need to construct these objects as shown in Recipe 4.5.3.4.

Discussion: The example given is a minimal application which could be used as a base for applications using DSA.

A notable issue with the DSA API is that only one application at any given time can use it. Thus to allow another application to use DSA API, you should release it by deleting the CDirectScreenAccess object when your application does not have focus. When using DSA, WSERV allows an application to draw what it wants in a specified region. WSERV only intervenes when an area of the screen being managed by DSA is obscured by another window for which it is responsible.

Another notable issue that you should take into account is the frame rate, which is device-dependent. Thus to optimize your drawing speed you should not exceed the target device's maximum frame rate.

To minimize the drawing time, you should also consider using off-screen bitmaps, as shown in Recipe 4.5.3.1. For more information about DSA and the use of off-screen bitmaps, see the recent Symbian Press book, *Games on Symbian OS* (**developer.symbian.com/gamesbook**) and consult the Symbian Developer Library documentation. For more in-depth information on the workings of WSERV and an introduction to writing GUI applications using the Symbian OS application framework, please see *Symbian OS C++ for Mobile Phones*, Volume 3.

4.6 3D Graphics Using OpenGL ES

OpenGL ES is the embedded software industry's standard of choice for displaying 3D graphics on the screen. It is a subset of the more widely known OpenGL standard, adapted to resource-constrained devices. You can find a link to the OpenGL ES specifications at the end of this set of recipes, in the Resources Section 4.6.6.

There are not that many resources that cover OpenGL ES on Symbian OS, although you will find more information available in the recent Symbian Press book *Games on Symbian OS: A Handbook on Mobile Development* (**developer.symbian.com/gamesbook**). We can't expect you to be particularly familiar with OpenGL ES. However, it is unrealistic to expect this small section to teach you everything there is to know about OpenGL ES, so we are going to teach you the basics of OpenGL ES v1.0 on Symbian OS, and then point you to other resources, so you can expand on the basics to write interesting applications. We will explain how to scale back a full desktop OpenGL application so that it can be ported to a smartphone. (If you do already know OpenGL, you need to realize that a lot of it will not be available in OpenGL ES.) OpenGL ES uses a C-based API and has little to do with Symbian OS C++, so most of the code samples in this section are not really going to look like anything you have seen in this book.

This section is probably the one where domain knowledge is the most important. Creating simple 3D objects is easy, but the amount of calculus required to create complex scenes can seem daunting to the novice.

Open GL ES and Symbian OS
Symbian has provided a software-based implementation of the OpenGL ES 1.0 standard since Symbian OS v8.0a, and both S60 3rd Edition and UIQ 3 SDKs provide plug-ins to upgrade it to OpenGL ES 1.1.[2] In fact, the S60 3rd Edition FP1 SDK includes the OpenGL ES 1.1 plug-in by default.

Currently, Symbian smartphones with support for hardware-accelerated 3D graphics include the N82, N93 and N95 from Nokia, the P990, M600 and W950i from Sony Ericsson and the MOTORIZR Z8 from Motorola. Clearly, this opens the way to a level of quality in game graphics that has not been seen on mobile phones before. The Nokia devices all have the PowerVR MBX graphics processor from Imagination Technologies, which you can read about at **www.imgtec.com/PowerVR/Products/**

---

[2] You can find the plug-in for S60 3rd Edition development at: **www.forum.nokia.com/ info/sw.nokia.com/id/36331d44-414a-4b82-8b20-85f1183e7029/OpenGL_ES_1_1_Plug_ in.html** or by searching for 'OpenGL ES 1.1 Plug-in' from the main page of the Forum Nokia website at **www.forum.nokia.com**.
The OpenGL ES SDK for UIQ 3 is available from **developer.uiq.com/devtools_uiqsdk. html**.

Graphics/MBXLite/index.asp. Sony Ericsson devices contain the 'Lite' version of the same processor.

4.6.1 OpenGL ES Primer

Before we start, you will need a working knowledge of geometry in three-dimensional space. You will also need to understand how to multiply matrices.

In OpenGL ES, a point in space is called a vertex. The most complex shape you can draw is a triangle. Each vertex can belong to several triangles, which facilitates the drawing of contiguous triangles forming more complex geometric shapes. By drawing many triangles, you can approximate pretty complex scenes.

Each separate vertex can have its own color. The color of the area of a triangle depends on the colors of its three vertices.

You can decide how far the coordinate system extends. The axes point toward the right-hand side of the screen, toward the top of the screen and toward you. Beware.

The basic available transformations are translation and rotation. These are executed before you ask the system to draw your vertices.

The OpenGL ES implementation keeps a current state matrix. Each transformation means multiplying the current state matrix by the transformation matrix and storing the result in the current state matrix. When drawing, all coordinates are transformed using the current state matrix. A stack of current state matrices allows for temporary states and you can always revert back to the original identity matrix.

Textures are images that can be applied to a surface, even if it means the OpenGL ES implementation has to bend and warp them to fit your requirements. They give you finer control than colors, but have a much higher footprint.

Since your screen is a 2D plane, the content of the 3D scene you want to draw needs to be flattened. This is called projection. All the examples in this set of recipes will use the orthographic projection, which simplifies the amount of calculus you have to perform but doesn't take perspective into account at all.

4.6.2 OpenGL to OpenGL ES

Each OpenGL ES version maps to an OpenGL version. OpenGL ES v1.0 is a subset of OpenGL v1.3 and OpenGL ES v1.1 is a subset of OpenGL v1.5.

One main difference between the two standards is the availability of integer coordinate systems in OpenGL ES. It was added to reflect the considerable proportion of smartphone CPUs without a Floating Point Unit. This would be a non-trivial change when porting desktop-class code to a mobile platform, but the general performance improvement may be worth the effort.

Because of the APIs that are unavailable in OpenGL ES, you probably won't be able to just use the code generated by your usual modeling tool. You can still display everything you want on the screen, but you may have to invest more effort in getting there.

The later the OpenGL ES version you are targeting, the easier it should get for you, the developer. Unfortunately, this also translates to a lower availability of handsets.

All OpenGL polygons need to be expressed in terms of triangles in order to be drawn using OpenGL ES.

OpenGL ES only supports 2D textures, but you can still apply several textures at once, use reflections, fog, transparency, and so on.

4.6.3 Easy Recipes

4.6.3.1 Full-Screen Setup

Amount of time required: 40 minutes
Location of example code: \3D\Basic
Required libraries: libgles_cm.lib
Required header file(s): GLES\egl.h
Required platform security capability(s): None

Problem: You want to take over the whole screen to display 3D objects.

Solution: Since we are going to display things on the screen, it just makes sense to run all our code inside the standard Symbian OS application framework. The application view is a CCoeControl and you can use the associated RWindow to initialize the OpenGL ES implementation.

Beyond that, the OpenGL implementation needs to know how many bits the colors are encoded on. Assuming you are only interested in displaying 3D graphics on the handset main screen, you can then write code that will work no matter what the configuration of your phone:

```
#include <GLES/egl.h> // and link to libgles_cm.lib
#include <coecntrl.h> // and link to cone.lib
#ifdef __SERIES60_3X__
#include <aknviewappui.h> // and link to avkon.lib, eikcore.lib
                          // and eiksrv.lib
#include <akndef.h>
#else
#include <QikAppUi.h> // and link to qikcore.lib
#endif

class CMyMainControl;

#ifdef __SERIES60_3X__
class C3DAppUi : public CAknAppUi
```

```
#else
class C3DAppUi : public CQikAppUi
#endif
  {
public:
  void ConstructL();
  ~C3DAppUi(); // delete iAppContainer
private:
  CMyMainControl* iAppContainer;
  };

void C3DAppUi::ConstructL()
  {
  BaseConstructL();
  iAppContainer = new (ELeave) CMyMainControl;
  iAppContainer->SetMopParent(this);
  iAppContainer->ConstructL( Rect() );
  }

class CMyMainControl : public CCoeControl
  {
public:
  void ConstructL(const TRect&);
  ~CMyMainControl();
  static void CleanupConfigList(TAny* aList);
private:
  void SizeChanged();
private: // OpenGL ES stuff
  EGLDisplay iEglDisplay;
  EGLSurface iEglSurface;
  EGLContext iEglContext;
  EGLConfig iEglConfig;
  };

void CMyMainControl::CleanupConfigList(TAny* aList)
  {
  EGLConfig* configList = (EGLConfig*)aList;
  User::Free(configList);
  }

void CMyMainControl::ConstructL(const TRect& /*aRect*/)
  {
  CreateWindowL();
  SetExtentToWholeScreen(); // Take the whole screen
  ActivateL();
  iEglDisplay = eglGetDisplay( EGL_DEFAULT_DISPLAY );
  if ( NULL == iEglDisplay )
    {
    User::Leave(KErrGeneral);
    }
  if ( eglInitialize( iEglDisplay, NULL, NULL ) == EGL_FALSE )
    {
    User::Leave(KErrGeneral);
    }

  EGLConfig* configList = NULL;
  EGLint numOfConfigs = 0;
  EGLint configSize   = 0;
```

```
if ( eglGetConfigs( iEglDisplay, configList, configSize,
                            &numOfConfigs ) == EGL_FALSE )
  {
  User::Leave(KErrGeneral);
  }

configSize = numOfConfigs;
configList = (EGLConfig*)
User::Alloc(sizeof(EGLConfig) * configSize);
User::LeaveIfNull(configList);
CleanupStack::PushL(TCleanupItem(
  &CMyMainControl::CleanupConfigList, configList));

TDisplayMode dMode = Window().DisplayMode();
TInt bufferSize = 0;

switch ( dMode )
  {
case(EColor4K):
  bufferSize = 12;
  break;
case(EColor64K):
  bufferSize = 16;
  break;
case(EColor16M):
  bufferSize = 24;
  break;
case(EColor16MU):
case(EColor16MA):
  bufferSize = 32;
  break;
default:
  User::Leave(KErrGeneral);
  break;
  }
  const EGLint attrib_list[] = {EGL_BUFFER_SIZE, bufferSize,
                                               EGL_NONE};

if ( eglChooseConfig( iEglDisplay, attrib_list, configList,
                  configSize, &numOfConfigs ) == EGL_FALSE )
  {
  User::Leave(KErrGeneral);
  }

iEglConfig = configList[0];
CleanupStack::PopAndDestroy();

iEglSurface = eglCreateWindowSurface( iEglDisplay, iEglConfig,
                                          &Window(), NULL );
if ( NULL == iEglSurface )
  {
  User::Leave(KErrGeneral);
  }

  iEglContext = eglCreateContext( iEglDisplay, iEglConfig,
                               EGL_NO_CONTEXT, NULL );
  if ( EGL_NO_CONTEXT == iEglContext )
    {
```

```
      User::Leave(KErrGeneral);
      }

   if ( eglMakeCurrent( iEglDisplay, iEglSurface, iEglSurface,
                                iEglContext ) == EGL_FALSE )
      {
      User::Leave(KErrGeneral);
      }
   const TInt width = Size().iWidth;
   const TInt height = Size().iHeight;
   const GLfloat aspectRatio = (GLfloat)width / (GLfloat)height;
   glMatrixMode( GL_PROJECTION );
   //decide how big our 3D space is.
   //and use orthographic projection.
   glOrthof( PLANE_LEFT*aspectRatio, PLANE_RIGHT*aspectRatio,
           PLANE_BOTTOM, PLANE_TOP, PLANE_NEAR, PLANE_FAR );
   glMatrixMode( GL_MODELVIEW );
   }

CMyMainControl::~CMyMainControl()
  {
  eglMakeCurrent( iEglDisplay, EGL_NO_SURFACE, EGL_NO_SURFACE,
                                EGL_NO_CONTEXT );
  eglDestroySurface( iEglDisplay, iEglSurface );
  eglDestroyContext( iEglDisplay, iEglContext );
  eglTerminate( iEglDisplay );
  }

void CMyMainControl::SizeChanged()
  {
  glViewport( 0, 0, Size().iWidth, Size().iHeight );
  }
```

4.6.3.2 Display a 3D Object

Amount of time required: 40 minutes
Location of example code: \3D\Basic
Required libraries: libgles_cm.lib
Required header file(s): GLES\egl.h
Required platform security capability(s): None

Problem: You want to display a simple 3D object.

Solution: Usually the most basic example in 3D objects is a cube. Let's make one centered on the origin of the integer coordinate system, with each side being a 2 × 2 square.

We can also draw the largest sphere that fits into this cube (except we are going to place it right on top of the cube, so we can see it). Now, this is where math begins and a float coordinate system is useful. What we draw won't be an exact sphere. It will be a model of the sphere built using triangles (a.k.a. polygons). And we have to come up with the coordinates for the three points of each triangle on our own.

We suggest you start by drawing the following on a piece of paper:

- Let's say we want to approximate the quarter of a circle in a 2D plane by drawing 10 points: 1 point per 10 degrees.

- The full circle is 40 points (4 of them are redundant) and all the coordinates can be found by using the sine and cosine mathematical functions.

- Add a dimension: we need 40 circles to simulate a sphere (1 is redundant) and we end up with 1,600 points (266 of them are redundant).

- All that's left is to create all the triangles between adjoining points.

- Looking at our 2D circle and the next one like it in the 3D space (the original circle rotated by 10 degrees on the Y axis), you can see adjoining points forming 36 rectangles, each of them made up of 2 triangles.

- We need to go through the whole 180 degrees (still rotating on the Y axis) worth of rectangles so our sphere model is made up of 1,296 triangles.

Feel free to get up and fetch some kind of mental stimulant to recover. Nothing illegal, though.

Creating a cube made of two triangles per side is easy enough to put all the points into an array in memory. We are going to hardcode the coordinates so you can see them easily. However, the sphere is made up of too many points and triangles. We are going to write a loop to create it dynamically and keep the memory footprint to an acceptable level (it's either that or we reduce the number of points in our sphere but then it stops looking good).

We are also going to give different points different colors, so you can see the triangles when you run the code.

From a Symbian OS perspective, CCoeControl::Draw() tends to interfere with the OpenGL ES API eglSwapBuffers, so the actual code sample introduces a scene rendering callback:

```
class CMyMainControl : public CCoeControl
  {
public:
  void RenderScene();
protected: // sphere building utilities
  static void DrawSlice(TInt aYAngle);
  static void DrawRectangle(TInt aYAngle, TInt aZAngle);
  static void AddVertice(TInt aOffset, TInt aYAngle,
                                       TInt aZAngle);
  static GLfloat FindSine(TInt aAngle);
  static GLfloat FindCosine(TInt aAngle);
```

```
    };

static const GLfloat sinesPer10 =
    {
    0, 0.17365f, 0.34202f, 0.5f, 0.64279f, 0.76604f,
    0.86603f, 0.93969f, 0.98481f, 1.0f
    };

void CMyMainControl::RenderScene()
    {
    // the cube first. 6 sides. 2 triangles per side.
    // 3 vertices per triangles. 3 coordinates per vertex.

    GLubyte triangles [6 * 2 * 3 * 3] =
        {
        /* front */
        1,1,1, /**/ -1,1,1, /**/ -1,-1,1,
        1,1,1, /**/ -1,-1,1, /**/1,-1,1,
        /* right */
        1,-1,1, /**/ 1,-1,-1, /**/1,1,-1,
        1,-1,1, /**/ 1,1,-1, /**/ 1,1,1,
        /* back */
        -1,-1,-1, /**/ -1,1,-1, /**/ 1,1,-1,
        -1,-1,-1, /**/ 1,1,-1, /**/ 1,-1,-1,
        /* left */
        -1,1,1, /**/ -1,1,-1, /**/ -1,-1,-1,
        -1,1,1, /**/ -1,-1,-1, /**/ -1,-1,1,
         /* top */
        1,1,-1, /**/ -1,1,-1, /**/ -1,1,1,
        1,1,-1, /**/ -1,1,1, /**/ 1,1,1,
        /* bottom */
        -1,-1,1, /**/ -1,-1,-1, /**/ 1,-1,-1,
        -1,-1,1, /**/ 1,-1,-1, /**/ 1,-1,1
        };

    glClearColorx( 0, 0, 0, 255 );
    glClear( GL_COLOR_BUFFER_BIT );

    glEnableClientState( GL_VERTEX_ARRAY );
    glVertexPointer( 3, GL_BYTE, 0, triangles );
    glDrawArrays(GL_TRIANGLES, 0, 36);

    // Now, let's make the sphere:
    // We are going to draw one rectangle at a time.
    GLfloat* sphereTriangles = User::Alloc(sizeof(GLfloat) * 12);

    // 4 vertices (see GL_TRIANGLE_STRIP). 3 coordinates each.

    if ( NULL != sphereTriangles )
        {
        glVertexPointer( 3, GL_FLOAT, 0, sphereTriangles);

        for (TInt yRotate = 0 ; yRotate < 180 ; yRotate += 10)
            {
            DrawSlice(yRotate);
            }

        eglSwapBuffers( iEglDisplay, iEglSurface );
```

```
    }
  delete sphereTriangles;
  }

void CMyMainControl::DrawSlice(TInt aYAngle)
  {
  for (TInt zRotate = 0 ; zRotate < 360 ; zRotate += 10)
    {
    DrawRectangle(aYAngle, zRotate);
    }
  }

void CMyMainControl::DrawRectangle(TInt aYAngle, TInt aZAngle)
  {
  AddVertice(0, aYAngle, aZAngle);
  AddVertice(3, aYAngle, aZAngle+10);
  AddVertice(6, aYAngle+10, aZAngle);
  AddVertice(9, aYAngle+10, aZAngle+10);
  glDrawArrays(GL_TRIANGLE_STRIP, 0, 4);
  }

//We are going from our own spherical
//coordinate system to a Cartesian one

void CMyMainControl::AddVertice(TInt aOffset, TInt aYAngle,
                                               TInt aZAngle)
  {
  GLfloat x,y,z;
  GLfloat ySine, yCosine, zSine, zCosine;
  ySine = FindSine(aYAngle);
  yCosine = FindCosine(aYAngle);
  zSine = FindSine(aZAngle);
  zCosine = FindCosine(aZAngle);
  x = zCosine * yCosine;
  y = zSine * yCosine + 2.0f;
  z = ySine;
  iSphereTriangles[aOffset] = x;
  iSphereTriangles[aOffset+1] = y;
  iSphereTriangles[aOffset+2] = z;
  }

GLfloat CMyMainControl::FindCosine(TInt aAngle)
  {
  aAngle += 90;
  if (aAngle>=360)
    aAngle-=360;
  return FindSine(aAngle);
  }

GLfloat CMyMainControl::FindSine(TInt aAngle)
  {
  TInt angle=aAngle;
  if (angle>=180)
    angle-=180; //Sin(X)=-Sin(X-180)
  if (angle>90)
    angle=180-angle; //Sin(X)=Sin(180-X)
  TInt index=angle/10;
  GLfloat result=sinesPer10[index];
```

```
if (aAngle>180)
  result=-result;
return result;
}
```

The sphere vertex coordinate calculus algorithm is far from optimized. Caching some points would help the CPU make fewer floating-point operations. However, it would not be difficult to modify it to display any sphere: position, size and resolution can be made generic.

Once projected to the screen, not all points are equidistant in our example. When you start using lighting to accentuate a three-dimensional environment, you will probably want to keep them equidistant in 3D space rather than trying to make them equidistant when projected.

4.6.3.3   Translate a 3D Object

Amount of time required: 15 minutes
Location of example code: \3D\Basic
Required libraries: libgles_cm.lib
Required header file(s): GLES\egl.h
Required platform security capability(s): None

Problem: You want to move a 3D object along a vector.

Solution: The one thing you need to consider when dealing with the transformation of coordinates is that we are modifying the current state matrix. If you keep the transformation active on the main state matrix, it will be applied to all drawings.

We are going to draw a single, simple triangle in a 3D space and show you how to apply a translation to that object only, using a temporary state matrix. You can reuse the same template to translate more complex objects.

```
void CMyMainControl::RenderScene()
  {
  GLubyte triangle [3 * 3] = {1,1,0, /**/ 0,1,0, /**/ 1,0,0};
  glEnableClientState( GL_VERTEX_ARRAY );
  glVertexPointer( 3, GL_BYTE, 0, triangle );
  glLoadIdentity();
  glPushMatrix();
  // Translate by (-5, -4, -3) bitshifting each
  glTranslatex( -5 << 16 , -4 << 16 , -3 << 16 );
  glDrawArrays(GL_TRIANGLES, 0, 3);
  glPopMatrix();
  glDrawArrays(GL_TRIANGLES, 0, 3);
  eglSwapBuffers(iEglDisplay, iEglSurface);
  }
```

This code will show the same triangle drawn twice on the screen: once in its original position, and once translated.

> **Tip:** Only the first 16 bits of the coordinates you pass to `glTranslatex` are used. This is why there is a bit-shift in the code.

4.6.3.4   Rotate a 3D Object

Amount of time required: 15 minutes
Location of example code: `\3D\Basic`
Required libraries: `libgles_cm.lib`
Required header file(s): `GLES\egl.h`
Required platform security capability(s): None

Problem: You want to rotate a 3D object along the three coordinate axes.

Solution: As we described in Recipe 4.6.3.3, the one thing you need to consider when dealing with the transformation of coordinates is that we are modifying the current state matrix. If you keep the transformation active on the main state matrix, it will be applied to all drawings.

We are going to draw a single simple triangle in 3D space and show how to apply a rotation to that object only by using a temporary state matrix (rotation angles are measured in degrees). You can reuse the same template to rotate more complex objects.

```
void CMyMainControl::RenderScene()
 {
 GLubyte triangle [3 * 3] ={1,1,0, /**/ 0,1,0, /**/ 1,0,0};
 glEnableClientState( GL_VERTEX_ARRAY );
 glVertexPointer( 3, GL_BYTE, 0, triangle );
 glLoadIdentity();
 glPushMatrix();
 // Rotate by 30 degrees on X and Y axes
 glRotatex( 30 << 16 , 1 << 16 , 0 , 0 );
 glRotatex( 30 << 16 , 0 , 1 << 16 , 0 );
 glDrawArrays(GL_TRIANGLES, 0, 3);
 glPopMatrix();
 glDrawArrays(GL_TRIANGLES, 0, 3);
 eglSwapBuffers(iEglDisplay, iEglSurface);
 }
```

This code will show the same triangle drawn twice on the screen: once rotated (by 30 degrees over both the X and Y axes) and once in its original position.

> **Tip:** Only the first 16 bits of the coordinates you pass to `glRotatex` are used. This is why there is a bit-shift in the code.

4.6.4 Intermediate Recipes

4.6.4.1 Apply a Texture to a 3D Object

Amount of time required: 30 minutes
Location of example code: \3D\Basic
Required libraries: libgles_cm.lib
Required header file(s): GLES\egl.h
Required platform security capability(s): None

Problem: You want to apply a bitmap to an area of a 3D object.

Solution: First, you are going to have to make a bitmap available to your code. On a basic level, this is an area in memory containing a set of RGB-coded pixels. The recipes in Section 4.5 cover 2D graphics, and they will teach you how to load and manipulate a CFBsBitmap object.

OpenGL ES v1.1 supports only 2D textures, so we need to tell the system to map a piece of our bitmap to a triangle. Essentially, texture coordinates are used to 'cut' triangles out of bitmaps.

There are a couple of things to keep in mind when using textures:

- Only bitmaps with height and width of a power of 2 are supported (i.e., 256 × 64, 128 × 128, and so on).

- Symmetries in the bitmap are important, since you can rotate your 3D objects and look at the texture on both sides of the triangles it is mapped onto.

We are going to map a texture to a rectangle made up of two triangles. You can repeat this approach with more triangles to form a more complex 3D object.

```
#include <FBS.H> // and link to fbscli.lib

void CMyMainControl::RenderScene(CFbsBitmap& aTexture)
  {
  GLubyte triangles [ 2 * 3 * 3] =
    {
    2,1,1, /**/ -1,1,1, /**/ -1,-1,1,
    2,1,1, /**/ -1,-1,1, /**/ 2,-1,1,
    };

  // (0,0) is bottom-left, (1,1) is top-right
  GLfloat texCoords[2 * 3 * 2] =
    {
    1.0f,1.0f,0.0f,1.0f,0.0f,0.0f,
    1.0f,1.0f,0.0f,0.0f,1.0f,0.0f,
    };

  glEnableClientState(GL_TEXTURE_COORD_ARRAY);
  glEnable(GL_TEXTURE_2D);
```

```
GLuint textureArray[1];
glGenTextures(1, textureArray);
glBindTexture(GL_TEXTURE_2D, textureArray[0]);
glTexParameterf(GL_TEXTURE_2D, GL_TEXTURE_MIN_FILTER,
                                      GL_LINEAR);
aTexture.LockHeap();
glTexImage2D(GL_TEXTURE_2D, 0, GL_RGB,
        aTexture.SizeInPixels().iWidth,
      aTexture.SizeInPixels().iHeight,
          0, GL_RGB, GL_UNSIGNED_BYTE,
              aTexture.DataAddress());
aTexture.UnlockHeap();
glEnableClientState(GL_VERTEX_ARRAY);
glVertexPointer(3, GL_BYTE, 0, triangles);
glTexCoordPointer(2, GL_FLOAT, 0, texCoords);
glDrawArrays(GL_TRIANGLES, 0, 6);
glDisableClientState(GL_TEXTURE_COORD_ARRAY);
eglSwapBuffers(iEglDisplay, iEglSurface);
}
```

What may go wrong when you do this: The pixels in the texture may actually be read as BGR data, instead of RGB. That's not a typo. You may have to modify the heap memory where the bitmap data is stored, rotating colors for each pixel, which means your CFbsBitmap becomes pretty much unusable afterwards. Do not keep your bitmap heap locked when calling eglSwapBuffers or it may block.

Tip: After glTexImage2D returns, the OpenGL ES implementation is meant to have made a copy of all the pixel data so your CFbsBitmap object can be released. Using a JPEG texture instead of a multi-bitmap file will reduce the application footprint but will require an extra asynchronous step with a CImageDecoder. See Recipe 4.5.2.1 for more information.

4.6.4.2   Part-Screen Setup

Amount of time required: 50 minutes
Location of example code: \3D\PartScreen
Required libraries: libgles_cm.lib
Required header file(s): GLES\egl.h
Required platform security capability(s): None

Problem: You want to share the screen between 2D and 3D graphics.

Solution: Instead of an RWindow object we are going to initialize our OpenGL ES surface with a dynamic CWsBitmap (see the 2D graphics recipes in Section 4.5 for more about this class). This approach is a good way to control the size of what OpenGL ES considers to be the screen.

Once the scene has been rendered to the `CWsBitmap`, it can be displayed just like any other 2D object, alongside `CCoeControl` objects.

In this example, we rely on the application view to be a compound control, only allowing our 3D control to use the bottom half of the screen.

```cpp
#include <W32STD.H> // and link to ws32.lib

class CMyMainControl : public CCoeControl
  {
private:
  void MakeSurfaceL(const TRect&, TDisplayMode);
  CWsBitmap* iPixmap;
  };

const EGLint attrib_list[] = {EGL_BUFFER_SIZE, 32,
        EGL_SURFACE_TYPE, EGL_PIXMAP_BIT, EGL_NONE};

void CMyMainControl::MakeSurfaceL(const TRect& aRect,
                                  TDisplayMode aMode)
  {
  iPixmap = new (ELeave) CWsBitmap(iCoeEnv->WsSession());
  TSize halfScreen = Window().Size();
  halfScreen.iHeight /= 2;
  iPixmap->Create(halfScreen, aMode);
  iEglSurface = eglCreatePixmapSurface(iEglDisplay, iEglConfig,
                                          iPixmap, NULL);
  if ( iEglSurface == NULL )
    {
    User::Leave(KErrGeneral);
    }
  }

void CMyMainControl::SizeChanged()
  {
  // Resize the image.
  TInt error = iPixmap->Resize(Window().Size());
  // You may want to display an error warning here.
  glViewport( 0, 0, Size().iWidth, Size().iHeight );
  }

void CMyMainControl::Draw(const TRect& /*aRect*/ ) const
  {
  CWindowGc& gc = SystemGc();
  gc.BitBlt(TPoint(0,0), iPixmap);
  }
```

What may go wrong when you do this: Resizing the bitmap could raise issues with the OpenGL ES implementation so you may have to recreate the EGLSurface. A code sample to illustrate this approach will be included in the downloadable code package.

> **What may (also) go wrong when you do this:** Handsets with hardware-accelerated OpenGL ES implementations (e.g., Nokia N95, Motorola MOTORIZR Z8) may not support bitmap surfaces. The alternative would be to draw only parts of an `RWindow` surface or use a much slower `pBuffer` surface. See the `\3D\PartScreenAlternate` code sample for illustration.

4.6.5   Advanced Recipes

4.6.5.1   Animate a Scene

Amount of time required: 90 minutes
Location of example code: `\3D\animate`
Required libraries: `libgles_cm.lib`
Required header file(s): `GLES\egl.h`
Required platform security capability(s): None

Problem: You want to animate a 3D object (that is, to make it move).

Solution: Animation in OpenGL ES is done by drawing the scene several times per second, modifying it a little bit every time. You can use an active object that regenerates its own request completion to continuously trigger redraw events (Chapter 3 described how to use active objects and active schedulers).

Using a `CPeriodic` object is the most basic way of animating an OpenGL ES scene, but you can also write your own active objects to obtain finer control over the perceived speed of different 3D objects in your scene. We will create an `RTimer` object for this purpose.

The following code sample illustrates both techniques to perform two different transformations at different speeds.

> **Tip:** A little trick is used in this example. Since we want to see a cyclic animation, we use translation along the perimeter of an imaginary circle on the screen. That is why the `iTranslateBy` member variable in the sample below actually contains an angle.

```
// Timer expires at this interval (in microseconds)
const TInt KInterval = 500000;

class CMyMainControl : public CCoeControl
  {
public:
  static TInt DrawCallBack(TAny*);
  TInt TranslateBy() const;
  void SetTranslateBy(TInt);
```

```
  void RenderScene();
private:
  CPeriodic* iRotator;
  CModifier* iModifier;
  TInt iTranslateBy;
  TInt iRotateBy;
  };

class CModifier : public CActive
  {
public:
  static CModifier* NewL(); // Implementation omitted for clarity
  ~CModifier();
  void Start();
private:
  void RunL();
  void DoCancel();
private:
 CModifier(CMyMainControl& aToModify);
private:
  RTimer iTimer;
  CMyMainControl& iToModify;
  };

CModifier::CModifier(CAnimatedControl& aToModify):
  CActive(CActive::EPriorityStandard), iToModify(aToModify)
  {
  iTimer.CreateLocal();
  CActiveScheduler::Add(this);
  }

CModifier::~CModifier()
  {
  iTimer.Cancel();
  iTimer.Close();
  }

void CModifier::Start()
  {
  iTimer.After(iStatus, KInterval);
  SetActive();
  }

void CModifier::DoCancel()
  {
  iTimer.Cancel();
  }

void CModifier::RunL()
  {
  TInt translate = iToModify.TranslateBy();
  if (translate >= 350)
    {
    iToModify.SetTranslateBy(0);
    }
  else
    {
    iToModify.SetTranslateBy(translate + 10);
```

```
    }
  // we will let the CPeriodic update the display
  Start();
  }

const TInt KSecondInterval = 100000;

void CMyMainControl::ConstructL(const TRect& aRect)
  {
  iRotator = CPeriodic::NewL( CActive::EPriorityIdle );
  iRotator->Start(KSecondInterval, KSecondInterval,
      TCallBack(CMyMainControl::DrawCallBack,this));
  iModifier = new (ELeave) CModifier(*this);
  iModifier->Start();
  }

TInt CMyMainControl::DrawCallBack( TAny* aInstance )
  {
  CMyMainControl* instance = (CMyMainControl*) aInstance;
  instance->iRotateBy++;
  instance->RenderScene();
  return KErrNone;
  }

void CMyMainControl::RenderScene()
  {
  GLubyte triangle [3 * 3] = {1,1,0, /**/ 0,1,0, /**/ 1,0,0};
  GLfloat xTranslate, yTranslate;
  xTranslate = 2.0f * FindCosine(iTranslateBy);
  yTranslate = 2.0f * FindSine(iTranslateBy);
  glEnableClientState( GL_VERTEX_ARRAY );
  glVertexPointer( 3, GL_BYTE, 0, triangles );
  glLoadIdentity();
  glPushMatrix();
  glRotatex( (iRotateBy / 2)  << 16 , 1 << 16 , 0 , 0 );
  glRotatex( (iRotateBy / 3) << 16 , 0 , 1 << 16 , 0 );
  glTranslatef(xTranslate, yTranslate, 0.0f );
  glDrawArrays(GL_TRIANGLES, 0, 3);
  glPopMatrix();
  glDrawArrays(GL_TRIANGLES, 0, 36);
  eglSwapBuffers(iEglDisplay, iEglSurface);
  }

TInt CMyMainControl::TranslateBy() const
  {
  return iTranslateBy;
  }

void CMyMainControl::SetTranslateBy(TInt aTranslateBy)
  {
  iTranslateBy = aTranslateBy;
  }
```

What may go wrong when you do this: CPeriodic cannot be used to redraw too frequently to the screen, for risk of triggering a ViewSrv-11 panic.

> **Tip:** On S60 smartphones, you can call `User::ResetInactivity-Time()` periodically to keep the screen backlit.

4.6.5.2 Adapt Performances

Amount of time required: 1 hour to understand – months to execute!

Problem: You want to adapt your animation to your target devices.

Solution: On OpenGL platforms, developers have several techniques that allow for smooth animation of scenes, even when resources are constrained:

- Effects that refine the look of 3D objects can be switched on or off.

- The number of objects displayed on the screen can be adjusted (by screen resolution).

- General code optimization techniques can be used. OpenGL is one level above C-type code, so you cannot rely on the compiler making the right optimizations. A 3D-modeling tool might, though.

- Knowing the inner workings of specific OpenGL implementations is also useful. Constructors' help forums are gold mines of information.

These techniques are still valid in OpenGL ES. However, there are other factors to take into consideration:

- Screen sizes can be diverse, and guaranteeing a suitable user experience across a range of devices requires some experimentation.

- Required configurations need to enumerate specific handset models (or ranges), instead of CPU speed for example.

- The amount and type of memory on smartphones is also more of an issue than on desktop computers, so the speed/size trade-offs will need to be revisited and textures should be used carefully.

- At the time of writing, only a few handsets contain a hardware 3D accelerating chip and their performances are wildly better than those without. Yet, as a developer, you don't want configuration management to become your main nightmare. There are just so many more interesting things to lose sleep over.

- From an engineering standpoint, it makes sense to write an adaptive animation monitor that will decide in real time how complex the 3D scene should be (how deep, how precise, etc.) and how fast 3D objects should move by measuring the time it takes to render a scene.

- Memory consumption can also be monitored in real time to adapt the resolution of the textures in use.

- Mobile users are usually more forgiving about a 3D object not looking as good as it would on their computer than about an error dialog popping up in the middle of a game or a lagging animation.

Since these recipes will probably be used by most to begin the development of games, it is worth mentioning that mobile games are not usually used in the same way as desktop games:

- Users usually have minutes of available time, not hours, so loading time needs to be kept to a minimum and playability is paramount. Porting animation code will not be trivial since you will have to use native Symbian OS APIs.

- The user input controls are also variable between different smartphones and you may have to slow some objects down to make user interaction possible.

- Testing different animation algorithms and detail levels on different handsets will increase your time-to-market (Chapter 6 discusses this further).

- Involuntary interruptions are also common on smartphones. This may lead to the implementation of a relative timer used for animating the 3D scene only when it is in the foreground, as the system time could suddenly jump by several minutes if the game is interrupted by an incoming phone call.

- There is another problem related to interruptions. If you monitor key up and down events (instead of key pressed events) you may only get a key down event when the application is interrupted. The corresponding key up event would be delivered to another application in that case. After an interruption, a game should assume all keys have been released.

4.6.6 Resources

The OpenGL ES specifications:

- ***www.khronos.org/opengles/spec***.

The OpenGL ES v1.1 reference manual:

- ***www.khronos.org/opengles/documentation/opengles1_1/gl_egl_ref_1_1_20041110/index.html***.

The main hub of OpenGL ES resources:

- ***www.khronos.org/developers/resources/opengles/***.

PowerVR also publishes SDKs and code samples:

- ***www.imgtec.com/PowerVR/insider/index.asp***.

The Symbian Developer Library contains information about OpenGL ES in the Graphics section of the Symbian OS Guide. You can find this documentation in your development SDK, or read it online on the Symbian Developer Network:

- ***developer.symbian.com/main/oslibrary/osdocs***.

Both S60 and UIQ SDKs can be upgraded to support OpenGL ES 1.1:

- ***www.developer.sonyericsson.com/getDocument.do?docId=84947***.
- ***www.forum.nokia.com/info/sw.nokia.com/id/36331d44-414a-4b82-8b20-85f1183e7029/OpenGL_ES_1_1_Plug_in.html***.

The Symbian Press book *Games on Symbian OS* discusses OpenGL ES and other Khronos standards. It also includes further discussion of the factors to consider when creating smartphone games:

- ***developer.symbian.com/gamesbook***.

4.7   Multimedia

These recipes discuss aspects of working with multimedia files, such as playing and recording audio or video.

Symbian OS provides a framework called MMF (Multimedia Framework) which supports the following:

- audio playing, recording and conversion
- audio streaming
- tone playing
- video playing and recording.

The MMF is an extensible framework that allows phone manufacturers and third parties to add plug-ins to provide support for audio and video formats. For the application developer, it provides APIs that abstract the underlying hardware, thereby simplifying the code needed to record and play the content. The streaming APIs provided by the framework, which bypass large parts of the MMF, offer a lower-level interface that allows streaming of audio data to and from the audio hardware.

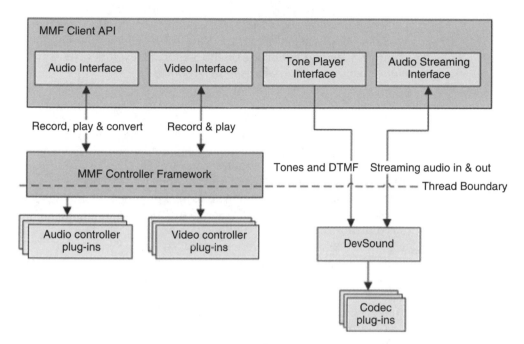

Figure 4.7.1 Architecture of MMF

Figure 4.7.1 shows the architecture of MMF.

The default Symbian OS MMF implementation supports basic audio formats. For example, for audio playback, it supports AU and WAV files and provides codecs for pulse code modulation (PCM) format. Furthermore, in addition to basic formats, most Symbian OS phones provide support for playback of other popular formats. For audio, this includes MP3, advanced audio coding (AAC), and adaptive multi-rate (AMR). Phone manufacturers supply additional controller plug-ins only to selected devices because of dependencies on specific accelerated hardware components, licensing issues, DRM requirements, or other business factors.

In this set of recipes, we will also discuss the Onboard Camera API, which is a generic and extensible API for controlling an onboard digital camera on devices. It supports either still images or videos. Please refer to the recipes in Section 4.5 for a discussion about image processing and general 2D graphics.

As a client of the Symbian OS multimedia APIs, you'll find a lot of the code you write will be implementation of the observer interfaces that are passed to the API and called by the MMF to signal an event or change of state. There is quite a lot to discuss in these recipes and, for clarity, we are going to quote the minimum of source code possible. You can find the full set of example code available for download at ***developer.symbian.com/symbian_press_cookbook***.

Further information about MMF and working with multimedia content on Symbian OS is available from the Symbian Developer Library documentation in your SDK, or online on the Symbian Developer Network (at ***developer.symbian.com/main/oslibrary/osdocs***).

4.7.1   Easy Recipes

4.7.1.1   Play an Audio Clip

Amount of time required: 15 minutes
Location of example code: `\Multimedia\AudioPlaying`
Required libraries: `mediaclientaudio.lib`
Required header file(s): `MdaAudioSamplePlayer.h`
Required platform security capability(s): None

Problem: You want to play an audio clip from a file, such as a WAV, MP3 or AAC file.

Solution: The client API to play an audio clip from a file is the `CMda-AudioPlayerUtility` class. `CMdaAudioPlayerUtility` requires an observer class, which implements `MMdaAudioPlayerCallback`. The observer will be notified when the audio clip has been initialized or played completely.

The following steps explain how to play an audio clip using `CMda-AudioPlayerUtility`:

1. Create an observer class, which implements `MMdaAudioPlayer-Callback`.

2. Create an instance of `CMdaAudioPlayerUtility` and pass it a reference to the observer class.

3. Open the audio clip by calling `CMdaAudioPlayerUtility::OpenFileL()`.

4. Wait until `MMdaAudioPlayerCallback::MapcInitComplete()` is called, with a result indicating either that the file has been opened successfully, or that an error occurred.

5. Call `CMdaAudioPlayerUtility::Play()` to start audio playback.

6. When the audio has been played completely, or if an error occurs, `MMdaAudioPlayerCallback::MapcPlayComplete()` will be called.

7. Call `CMdaAudioPlayerUtility::Close()` to close the file. If you don't close the audio file, there will be a memory leak.

You'll see in the example code for the recipe that the `CSimple-AudioPlayer` class not only creates an instance of `CMdaAudio-PlayerUtility` but also serves as observer, by derivation from `MMda-AudioPlayerCallback`. Figure 4.7.2 shows a sequence diagram for the steps above.

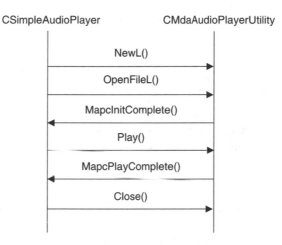

Figure 4.7.2 Sequence Diagram for Playing an Audio Clip from File, Showing the `CMda-AudioPlayerUtility` Class and the Client Class, which Implements the `MMdaAudio-PlayerCallback` Observer

Discussion: If your application has the `MultimediaDD` capability (see Chapter 3 for further discussion of platform security capabilities) you can successfully override the default priority and priority preference parameters of the `CMdaAudioPlayerUtility::NewL()` method. However, none of the examples in this book require this capability.

Besides `NewL()`, class `CMdaAudioPlayerUtility` offers some other factory methods:

- `NewFilePlayerL()`, to construct an audio player to play a file specified by filename.

- `NewDesPlayerL()`, to construct an audio player utility and play data from a descriptor.

- `NewDesPlayerReadOnlyL()`, to construct an audio player utility and play from a read-only descriptor.

Note that the three methods both open and initialize the audio clip. It means `MMdaAudioPlayerCallback::MapcInitComplete()` will be called once the initialization is complete. This is different from the `NewL()` method, because the latter does not initialize the audio player utility, and requires a separate call to `OpenFileL()`. The `OpenFileL()`

method opens an audio clip, which can either be specified by filename or by passing a handle to the file.

Note that we cannot play the file right after `CMdaAudioPlayer-Utility::OpenFileL()` has returned. We have to wait until `MMdaAudioPlayerCallback::MapcInitComplete()` is called on the observer.

There are two other variants of open methods in `CMdaAudioPlayerUtility`:

- `OpenDesL()`, to open an audio clip from a descriptor.

- `OpenUrlL()`, to open an audio clip from a URL.

> **What may go wrong when you do this:** Note that not all devices support all variants of the `OpenXyzL()` methods. For example, S60 devices don't support `OpenUrlL()`.

Once the player utility has been initialized, we are able to start the audio playback. It is done by calling `CMdaAudioPlayerUtility::Play()`. In most cases, you may want to adjust the volume before playing anything by calling `CMdaAudioPlayerUtility::SetVolume()`.

> **Tip:** If you get an extraneous sound at the start of your audio clip, use the `SetVolumeRamp()` function to get rid of it.

> **Tip:** The emulator normally supports only basic formats and codecs, such as AU and WAV. Other advanced formats and codecs, such as MP3, are currently not supported. This means you have to perform testing on the real devices.

> **What may go wrong when you do this:** Some audio clips may be protected using digital rights management (DRM), in formats such as OMA DRM or WMDRM. They cannot be played using `CMdaAudioPlayerUtility`.
>
> You can play DRM-protected files using a specific API for DRM-protected content, such as `CDrmPlayerUtility` in S60, which does not require the DRM capability.
>
> Alternatively, you can use the content access framework (CAF) to read DRM-protected files and pass them to MMF client APIs. Unfortunately, this requires your application to have DRM capability, which is one of the manufacturer-approved capabilities. It requires a

high level of negotiation to win the trust of the phone manufacturer before they will grant it to you. For details of how to apply for the DRM capability, see *www.symbiansigned.com.*

Further discussion of how to play DRM-protected files is outside the scope of this book. However, you can find an example on the Forum Nokia developer wiki, at *wiki.forum.nokia.com/index.php/Playing_ DRM-protected_audio_file_using_CDrmPlayerUtility.*

4.7.1.2 Perform Basic Audio Operations

Amount of time required: 15 minutes
Location of example code: \Multimedia\AudioPlaying
Required libraries: mediaclientaudio.lib
Required header file(s): MdaAudioSamplePlayer.h
Required platform security capability(s): None

Problem: You want to do basic operations on the audio playback, such as stop, play, rewind and fast forward.

Solution: The CMdaAudioPlayerUtility class provides all methods needed to perform basic audio operations, such as:

- Stop(), to stop audio playback.

- Pause(), to pause audio playback.

- SetPosition(), to set the current playback position from the start of the clip.

- GetPosition(), to return the current playback position from the start of the clip.

Discussion: The audio playback can be stopped or paused at any time. To resume the audio playback, simply call CMdaAudioPlayerUtility:: Play().

Performing rewind and fast forward is done by calling CMdaAudio-Player::SetPosition(). It requires a parameter in the type of TTimeIntervalMicroSeconds, which is the interval of the new position in microseconds from the start of the clip (not from the current position).

The following example shows how to rewind the current audio playback by one second:

```
const TInt KOneSecond = 1000000; // 1 second in microseconds
void CSimpleAudioPlayer::Rewind(TInt aIntervalInSeconds)
  {
  iPlayerUtility->Pause();

  // Get the current position of the playback.
  TTimeIntervalMicroSeconds position;
  iPlayerUtility->GetPosition(position);

  // Subtract the interval from the current position
  position = position.Int64() -
                      (aIntervalInSeconds*KOneSecond);

  // Set the new position.
  iPlayerUtility->SetPosition(position);
  iPlayerUtility->Play();
  }
```

What may go wrong when you do this: When you call `Set-Position()`, `CMdaAudioPlayerUtility` does not move the position immediately. It will continue playing for a couple of seconds until its internal buffer is empty. Sometimes, you may notice that the playback continues for a while before it moves to the new position. In order to have immediate rewind/fast forward effect, you must call `Pause()` before setting the new position, and then call `Play()` after that.

4.7.1.3 Play an Audio Tone

Amount of time required: 15 minutes
Location of example code: `\Multimedia\AudioTone`
Required libraries: `mediaclientaudio.lib`
Required header file(s): `MdaAudioTonePlayer.h`
Required platform security capability(s): None

Problem: You want to play an audio tone, such as a beep sound, or a sound from a certain frequency.

Solution: The `CMdaAudioToneUtility` class is used to play an audio tone. It uses an observer class, which implements `MMdaAudioTone-Observer`. This observer will receive events and error notifications, for example when it has been configured, when the tone has been played completely, or when an error occurs.

The following steps explain how to play an audio clip using `CMda-AudioToneUtility`:

- Create an observer class, which implements `MMdaAudioTone-Observer`. In the sample code, we use class `CAudioTonePlayer`.

- Create an instance of `CMdaAudioToneUtility` and pass it a reference to the observer class.

- Open the audio clip by calling one of the variants of the `PrepareToPlay()` method (`CMdaAudioToneUtility::PrepareToPlayXyz()`). See the Discussion section for further details.

- Wait until `MMdaAudioToneObserver::MatoPrepareComplete()` is called.

- Within the callback, call `CMdaAudioToneUtility::Play()` to start audio tone playback.

- When the audio has been played completely, or if an error occurs, `MMdaAudioToneObserver::MatoPlayComplete()` will be called.

Discussion: There are several variants of the `CMdaAudioToneUtility::PrepareToPlayXyz()` methods, for instance:

- `PrepareToPlayTone()` – used to play a single tone.

- `PrepareToPlayDualTone()` – used to play a dual tone, which is a combination of two frequencies.

- `PrepareToPlayDTMFString()` – used to play dual-tone multi frequency (DTMF) tones. These are used in the telephony signalling system.

Tip: You cannot use `PrepareToPlayDTMFString()` to play DTMF tones to the telephony uplink. It only plays DTMF on the local speaker.

Please check the Symbian Developer Library documentation to see the complete list of methods supplied by `CMdaAudioToneUtility`.

4.7.1.4 Play a MIDI File

Amount of time required: 15 minutes
Location of example code: `\Multimedia\MidiPlaying`
Required libraries: `midiclient.lib`
Required header file(s): `midiclientutility.h`
Required platform security capability(s): None

Problem: You want to play a MIDI file on the device.

Solution: The client API to play a MIDI file is `CMidiClientUtility` class. Like the audio player utility, the MIDI client utility class requires an observer, which must implement the `MMidiClientUtilityObserver` interface.

The following steps explain how to play a MIDI file using `CMidiClientUtility`:

- Create an observer class, which implements `MMidiClientUtilityObserver`.

- Create an instance of `CMidiClientUtility` and pass it a reference to the observer class.

- Open the audio clip by calling `CMidiClientUtility::OpenFile()`.

- Wait until `MMidiClientUtilityObserver::MmcuoStateChanged()` is called. The `aNewState` parameter has the value `EOpen` if the file has been opened successfully.

- Call `CMidiClientUtility::Play()` from within the observer to start MIDI playback.

- When the audio has been played completely, wait until `MMidiClientUtilityObserver::MmcuoStateChanged()` is called again. The `aOldState` parameter will be set to `EPlaying` and the `aNewState` parameter will be set to `EOpen`.

In our recipe, the `CMidiPlayer` class implements `MMidiClientUtilityObserver` and is used to play a MIDI file, `\data\sample.mid`, which is located at the same drive as the application. For example, if the sample application is installed on the C: drive, then the file location is `c:\data\sample.mid`.

> **Tip:** The Windows emulator does not support MIDI playback. You can only test this example on the device.

4.7.2 Intermediate Recipes

4.7.2.1 Get the Default Multimedia Storage Location

Amount of time required: 25 minutes
Location of example code: `\Multimedia\AudioRecording` and `\Multimedia\CameraImage`
Header files: `pathinfo.h` (S60), `QikMediaFileFolderUtils.h` (UIQ)
Required libraries: `platformenv.lib` (S60), `qikutils.lib` (UIQ)
Required platform security capability(s): None

Problem: You need to retrieve the default path for storing multimedia files.

S60 and UIQ store multimedia files in different default folder locations. For example, the default path for audio files on S60 on the C: drive is `c:\data\sounds`, while on UIQ it is `c:\Media files\Music`.

The location used to store files on the emulator may also be different from that used on smartphone hardware. For example, the UIQ's emulator uses `c:\Media files\audio` for audio files, compared to `c:\Media files\Music` when storing files on the device.

And that's not all! Even when just considering phone hardware, the location in which files are stored in the phone memory may be different to that used on the memory card. For example, in S60 the default video location in phone memory is `c:\data\videos`, while on the memory card it is `e:\videos`.

How can we write a code that is able to return the media path independent from the platform and media type?

Solution: Unfortunately, there is no single solution to this problem. S60 and UIQ use different ways of getting media paths. You need to create two different implementations for each platform.

Discussion:

S60

The class to handle various media paths on S60 is `PathInfo`. It is declared in the `pathinfo.h` header file, and the library to link against is `platformenv.lib`.

Some of the methods related to media path information are as follows:

- `PathInfo::PhoneMemoryPath()`,
- `PathInfo::MemoryCardPath()`,
- `PathInfo::VideosPath()`,
- `PathInfo::ImagesPath()`,
- `PathInfo::SoundsPath()`.

The `PhoneMemoryPath()` method returns the root path in the phone memory, for example 'c:\data\'. The `MemoryCardPath()` method returns the root path on the memory card, for example 'e:\'. Note that there is a backslash character at the end of the returned path.

The other methods return the path of multimedia files. For example, `VideosPath()` returns 'Videos\'. Again, there is a backslash character at the end of the returned path.

The following code shows how to get an absolute path of the audio folder including the drive letter:

```
void CAudioRecordingAppUi::GetAudioPathL(TChar aDriveLetter,
                                                        TDes& aPath)
 {
 aPath.Zero();
 if ((aDriveLetter == 'c') || (aDriveLetter == 'C'))
   {
   aPath.Append(PathInfo::PhoneMemoryRootPath());
   }
 else if ((aDriveLetter == 'e') || (aDriveLetter == 'E'))
   {
   aPath.Append(PathInfo::MemoryCardRootPath());
   }
 aPath.Append(PathInfo::SoundsPath());
 }
```

The following example shows how to call the method above:

```
TFileName audioPath;
GetAudioPathL('c', audioPath);
```

The audioPath will have the value of 'c:\data\sounds\' after GetAudioPathL() is called.

Similarly, if you call it using the statement:

```
GetAudioPathL('e', audioPath);
```

the audio path will have the value of 'e:\sounds'.

UIQ

Now, let's take a look at UIQ. The class to handle various media paths is CQikMediaFileFolderUtils. It is declared in the QikMediaFile-FolderUtils.h header file. The library name is qikutils.lib.

The methods used to retrieve paths related to multimedia files are GetDefaultPathForMimeType() and GetDefaultPathFor-MimeTypeL().

The only difference between them is that the latter method can leave. The methods require three parameters. The first parameter, aMimeType, is the MIME type to convert to a folder path. It uses only the first part of MIME type. For example, if the MIME type is 'audio/wav', only 'audio' will be used for matching.

The second parameter, aDriveLetter, is the drive to query for the default location. The final parameter, aFolderPath, is a reference parameter which receives the absolute path of the media files excluding drive letter. For example, it returns ':\Media files\audio\' for audio files.

> **Tip:** You can also retrieve the root path of the media folder (i.e., `':\Media files\'`) using the `CQikMediaFileFolderUtils::GetMediaFilesRootL()` method.

The following code shows how to get the audio path in UIQ:

```
void CAudioRecordingAppUi::GetAudioPathL(TChar aDriveLetter,
                                         TDes& aPath)
{
CQikMediaFileFolderUtils* mediaUtils =
                 CQikMediaFileFolderUtils::NewL(*iEikonEnv);
CleanupStack::PushL(mediaUtils);

// Get the path for image
TFileName mediaPath; // To receive the path
mediaUtils->GetDefaultPathForMimeTypeL(KAudioMimeType,
                         aDriveLetter, mediaPath);

// Construct a full path that contains drive letter.
aPath.Zero();
aPath.Append(aDriveLetter);
aPath.Append(mediaPath);

CleanupStack::PopAndDestroy(mediaUtils);
}
```

The following example shows how to call the method above:

```
_LIT(KAudioMimeType, "audio/wav");
TFileName audioPath;
GetAudioPathL('c', audioPath);
```

The `audioPath` will have the value of `'c:\Media files\music\'` on the UIQ device and `'c:\Media files\audio\'` on the emulator.
Similarly, if you call it using the statement below,

```
GetAudioPathL('d', audioPath);
```

the audio path will have the value of `'d:\music\'` on the UIQ device and `'d:\Media files\audio\'` on the emulator.

4.7.2.2 Play a Video Clip

Amount of time required: 30 minutes
Location of example code: `\Multimedia\VideoPlaying`
Required libraries: `mediaclientvideo.lib`
Required header file(s): `VideoPlayer.h`
Required platform security capability(s): None

Problem: You want to play a video clip from a file, such as a 3GP or MP4 file.

Solution: The MMF class that is used to play video is `CVideoPlayerUtility`, which requires you to pass an implementation of the `MVideoPlayerUtilityObserver` observer class.

Using `CVideoPlayerUtility` is similar to `CMdaAudioPlayerUtility`, except there is an additional step; that is, preparing the video clip to be played. It is not possible to play the video clip before `CVideoPlayerUtility` finishes the preparation.

The following steps explain how to play a video clip using `CMdaVideoPlayerUtility`:

- Create an observer class, which implements `MVideoPlayerUtilityObserver`.

- Create an instance of `CVideoPlayerUtility` and pass it a reference to the observer.

- Open the video clip by calling `CVideoPlayerUtility::OpenFileL()`.

- Wait until `MVideoPlayerUtilityObserver::MvpuoOpenComplete()` is called.

- Prepare the video clip to be accessed by calling the `CVideoPlayerUtility::Prepare()` method.

- Wait until `MVideoPlayerUtilityObserver::MvpuoPrepareComplete()` is called.

- Call `CVideoPlayerUtility::Play()` to start video playback.

- When the video has been played completely, `MVideoPlayerUtilityObserver::MvpuoPlayComplete()` will be called.

In the full sample code for this recipe, the `CSimpleVideoPlayer` class implements `MVideoPlayerUtilityObserver`.

Discussion: The factory methods of `CSimpleVideoPlayer` require one parameter to be passed. The type is `CCoeControl&`, and the parameter is the control where the video is to be displayed.

Let's take a look at the constructor of `CVideoPlayerUtility` to see how it is going to be used. The constructor of `CVideoPlayerUtility` is defined as follows:

```
CVideoPlayerUtility* NewL(
    MVideoPlayerUtilityObserver& aObserver,
    TInt aPriority, TMdaPriorityPreference aPref,
    RWsSession& aWs,
```

```
        CWsScreenDevice& aScreenDevice,
        RWindowBase& aWindow,
        const TRect& aScreenRect,
        const TRect& aClipRect);
```

The aObserver parameter is the reference to the observer which will receive notifications.

The aPriority and aPref parameters are the video client's priority and preference, respectively. Like CMdaAudioPlayerUtility, they require MultimediaDD capability. The discussion of MultimediaDD is not in the scope of this book.

The aWs parameter is the reference to the window server session. You can use the shared window server session defined in CCoeEnv::WsSession(). For example:

```
RWsSession& wsSession = aControl.ControlEnv()->WsSession();
```

The aScreenDevice is the reference to the software device screen. You can usually use the default screen device owned by CCoeEnv, which is CCoeEnv::ScreenDevice(). For example:

```
CWsScreenDevice* screenDevice = aControl.ControlEnv()->ScreenDevice();
```

The aWindow parameter is the handle of the window for the video. You can use CCoeControl::DrawableWindow() to get the client-side handle of a control:

```
RWindowBase& windowBase = aControl.DrawableWindow();
```

The aScreenRect parameter is the rectangle where the video is displayed on the screen. The position is relative to the origin of the screen, not to the origin of the control.

The aClipRect parameter is the area of the video clip to be displayed. In most cases, this parameter has the same value as aScreenRect, which means the whole area of the video is displayed. The same as aScreenRect, the position is relative to the origin of the screen, not to the origin of the control.

The supported codecs and formats of CVideoPlayerUtility depend on the installed plug-in on the device. For example, most Symbian OS devices support the H.263 codec, but only some support the H.264 codec.

Note that there are some other methods to open video clips from other sources, such as CVideoPlayerUtility::OpenUrlL().

The CVideoPlayerUtility::SetDisplayWindowL() method changes the display window of the video. It can be used to display the video playback to another control. It can also be used to change the area where the video is played. Its parameters are the same as those used in the constructor of `CVideoPlayerUtility`.

What may go wrong when you do this: There is one additional thing that you need to take care of; that is, the possibility of a screen orientation change. For example, some S60 devices allow orientation change by opening the cover of the device. If you don't respond to the orientation change, your video will not be displayed properly.

What you need to do is override the `CEikAppUi::Handle-ResourceChangeL()` method and then call `CVideoPlayer-Utility::SetDisplayWindowL()` to update the position and size of the video playing area.

4.7.2.3   Audio Streaming

Amount of time required: 30 minutes
Location of example code: `\Multimedia\AudioStreaming`
Required libraries: `mediaclientaudiostream.lib`
Required header file(s): `MdaAudioOutputStream.h`
Required platform security capability(s): None

Problem: You want to play an audio clip in streaming mode. The audio clip is read chunk by chunk incrementally. The audio streaming may be needed; for example, you want to process the audio from the file before you play it or you are getting the audio clip from the network. An Internet radio is an example of an application that needs audio streaming.

Solution: The class to stream audio is `CMdaAudioOutputStream`. The following lists the steps to stream audio:

- Create an instance of `CMdaAudioOutputStream`, which implements `MMdaAudioOutputStreamCallback`.

- Open the audio stream package by calling `CMdaAudioOutput-Stream::Open()`.

- Once the stream has been opened, the callback method, `MMda-AudioOutputStream::MaosOpenComplete()`, is called.

- Start streaming audio by calling `CMdaAudioOutputStream::WriteL()`.

- Once the buffer has been copied to the lower layers of MMF, the callback method, `MMdaAudioOutputStream::MaosBuffer-`

`Copied()`, is called. Now, we can call `WriteL()` to copy the next buffer.

In our recipe, the `CAudioStreamPlayer` class implements `MMda-AudioOutputStream`.

Discussion: The `CMdaAudioOutputStream` class plays the audio using the sound driver. It relies on hardware DSP (Digital Signal Processing) codecs. No MMF controller plug-in is involved. The supported formats depend on the device's DSP. All Symbian OS devices support PCM formats. Some of them support other compressed formats, such as AMR and MP3.

The `CMdaAudioOutputStream::Open()` requires one parameter with the type of `TMdaPackage*`. You can ignore this parameter because it is maintained for historical reasons only.

After `MMdaAudioOutputStreamCallback::MaoscOpenComplete()` is called, you are ready to stream the audio clip. There are several properties that need to be set to match the data you are streaming, such as format, sampling rate and number of channels.

The format is set by calling the `CMdaAudioOutputStream::SetDataTypeL()` method. It requires one parameter in the type of `TFourCC`, which is the FourCC (Four-Character Code) of the audio:

```
TRAP(err, iAudioStream->SetDataTypeL(KMMFFourCCCodePCM16));
```

Note that we use a `TRAP` because we call this method inside a non-leaving method, `MaoscOpenComplete()`.

The list of FourCC constants can be found in `\epoc32\include\mmf\common\MmfFourCC.h`.

Here are some examples of the predefined FourCC constants:

- `KMMFFourCCCodePCM8 = ( ' ', ' ', 'P', '8' )`

- `KMMFFourCCCodePCM16 = (' ', 'P', '1', '6')`

- `KMMFFourCCCodeAMR = (' ','A','M','R')`

- `KMMFFourCCCodeAAC = (' ','A','A','C')`

- `KMMFFourCCCodeMP3 = (' ','M','P','3')`.

You can use `CMMFDevSound::GetSupportedOutputDataTypesL()` to get the list of supported FourCCs on a particular device. Note that some SDKs may not distribute the header file of `CMMFDevSound`.

The sampling rate and number of channels can be set by calling `CMdaAudioOutputStream::SetAudioPropertiesL()`.

The possible values for the sampling rate and number of channels are defined in `TMdaAudioDataSettings`. There are several sampling rates, starting from `ESampleRate8000Hz` to `ESampleRate64000Hz`. There are two supported channels: `EChannelsMono` and `EChannelsStereo` (no surround sound).

After all the properties have been set up, you can start writing the data stream to the audio device. This is done by calling `CMdaAudio-OutputStream::WriteL()`. It requires a parameter with the type of `TDesC8&`:

```
TRAP(err, iAudioStream->WriteL(iBuffer));
```

The optimal size of the buffer depends on your needs and the audio format. Ideally, you want to use the smallest possible amount of memory without risking a buffer underflow situation.

Tip: In order to avoid an out-of-data situation, you may want to use more than one buffer. For example, you may use two buffers. You pass one buffer to the audio stream and use the other buffer to read from the file. When the one buffer is passed to the audio device, you can replace it with the next data. The example in this book uses one buffer for simplicity reasons.

In some applications that have a heavy thread, such as games, a large buffer may not solve the underflow situation. In this case, you may consider running the audio stream in a separate thread with higher priority.

Some audio-intensive applications may need to create proper adaptive buffer management algorithms to deal with different performance situations.

You can stop the streaming by calling `CMdaAudioOutputStream::Stop()`. Note that calling this method will cause the callback method, `MaoscBufferCopied()`, to be called with `KErrAbort` error code, and `MaoscPlayComplete()` with `KErrCancel`. If you are handling the error code in those methods, you have to exclude this situation. Otherwise, you will get an error message when stopping the audio streaming.

What may go wrong when you do this: After you have finished playing the stream, you have to stop the stream or destroy the instance of `CMdaAudioOutputStream`. If you don't do this, the audio device is actually still on. This will drain the battery.

4.7.3   Advanced Recipes

4.7.3.1   Record Audio

Amount of time required: 20 minutes
Location of example code: \Multimedia\AudioRecording
Required libraries: mediaclientaudio.lib
Required header file(s): MdaAudioSampleEditor.h
Required platform security capability(s): UserEnvironment

Problem: You want to record audio from the device microphone or telephone downlink.

Solution: The class to record audio is CMdaAudioRecorderUtility. Here are the steps to record audio:

- Create a new instance of CMdaAudioRecorderUtility, which implements MMdaObjectStateChangeObserver.

- Open the file by calling CMdaAudioRecorderUtility:: OpenFileL().

- Wait until the observer method, MMdaObjectStateChange-Observer::MoscoStateChangeEvent(), is called.

- Start recording by calling CMdaAudioRecorderUtility:: RecordL().

- Stop recording by calling CMdaAudioRecorderUtility::Stop ().

The recording method, CMdaAudioRecorderUtility::Record-L(), requires the UserEnvironment capability.
Like other audio APIs, the supported formats and codecs vary between devices.
In our recipe, the CSimpleAudioRecorder class implements MMda-ObjectStateChangeObserver.

Discussion: CMdaAudioRecorderUtility::OpenFileL() opens the file where the audio sample data will be recorded. It selects the MMF controller automatically based on the file extension. For example, when you specify .amr as the file extension, the controller plug-in for AMR will be loaded.
When the audio file has been opened, the observer method, Mosco-StateChangeEvent(), is called. This callback method has four parameters:

```
void CSimpleAudioRecorder::MoscoStateChangeEvent(CBase* aObject,
    TInt aPreviousState, TInt aCurrentState, TInt aErrorCode)
```

The aObject parameter is the object of the recorder utility. It is useful when you have more than one recorder utility object.

The aPreviousState and aCurrentState parameters are the previous state and the current state of the audio sample, respectively. There are several values defined in CMdaAudioClipUtility that can be assigned to them:

- ENotReady. The audio clip recorder has been constructed but no file has been opened.

- EOpen. The file is opened but no recording or playing is in progress.

- ERecording. New audio sample data is being recorded.

- EPlaying. Audio sample is being played.

aErrorCode is the system-wide error code, as defined in \epoc32\ include\e32err.h.

What may go wrong when you do this: The RecordL() method appends the new recorded audio to an existing file. There is a method, CMdaAudioRecoderUtility::CropL(), that is supposed to discard any existing data before recording. Unfortunately, it does not work with AMR on some S60 devices. In order to support compatibility with as many devices as possible, it is recommended not to use CropL(). If you want to delete existing data, you can use BaflUtils::DeleteFile() before recording audio.

What may go wrong when you do this: If you don't specify the UserEnvironment capability in the MMP file, you will get the KErrAccessDenied (-21) error code in the MoscoState-ChangeEvent() observer.

If your recorded clip is distorted, try a lower gain value by calling CMdaAudioRecoderUtility::SetGain().

There are several recording settings that can be adjusted, such as codec, sampling rate, bit rate and number of channels. The recipe uses the default settings.

Tip: It is possible to set the maximum length of the file that is being recorded by calling CMdaAudioRecoderUtility::SetMax-WriteLength(). It requires one parameter, which is the maximum file size in **bytes** (not kilobytes, as indicated by some SDK documentation).

> **Tip:** The `CMdaAudioRecorderUtility` class can also be used to play an audio file, using the `PlayL()` method. Take a look at `CSimpleAudioRecorder::PlayRecordedL()` in the recipe to see how to use it.

4.7.3.2 Record a Phone Call

The previous recipe, which showed audio recording, can be used to record a phone call. Once you have called `CMdaAudioRecorder-Utility::RecordL()`, audio from the local speaker and telephony downlink will be recorded. Unfortunately, it is not possible to record solely from one source (local speaker or telephony downlink only) because the API, `CMdaAudioRecorderUtility::SetAudio-DeviceMode()`, has been deprecated.

It is also possible to create an answering machine that automatically records a caller's message from the telephony downlink. To create such an application, you need to use `CMdaAudioRecorderUtility` and `CTelephony`. Please see the recipes in Section 4.8 for a discussion about `CTelephony`. The idea is to start recording once an incoming call is detected

The audio recording recipe would have to be modified to monitor telephony events to decide when to start and stop recording.

> **Tip:** Recording a phone conversation is illegal in some countries. Some of them require the person to be notified that the conversation is recorded. That is why some Nokia phones output a beep sound every few seconds when recording is happening. This is to notify the other party on the line that the conversation is being recorded.

4.7.3.3 Display a Camera Viewfinder

Amount of time required: 30 minutes
Location of example code: `\Multimedia\CameraImage`
Required libraries: `ecam.lib`
Required header file(s): `ecam.h`
Required platform security capability(s): `UserEnvironment`

Problem: You want to display the viewfinder of a camera on your application.

Solution: Symbian OS provides the Onboard Camera API, which is an open and extensible generic API for controlling digital camera devices. It can be used to capture still images and record videos.

The `CCamera` class provides the base class for camera devices. It provides virtual methods for controlling a camera, such as acquiring images and videos. Phone manufacturers derive `CCamera` and provide their implementations.

There are two observer classes for `CCamera`: `MCameraObserver` and `MCameraObserver2`. `MCameraObserver2` is the recommended API. Unfortunately, at the time of writing this book, S60 devices do not support `MCameraObserver2` yet. In order to maintain compatibility with S60 devices, this book uses `MCameraObserver` in the examples.

In our recipe, the viewfinder is handled by the `CCameraEngine` class.

Discussion: A number of Symbian smartphones have two camera devices, which is why the `NewL()` factory method of the `CCamera` class allows you to choose a camera index between 0 and (`CCamera::Cameras-Available()` – 1). The camera at index 0 is usually the one with the higher resolution, pointing away from the handset user. A bad camera index will cause a panic.

Getting camera information
The `TCameraInfo` class specifies camera information, such as supported image format, flash support, zoom support and many others. You can get camera information by calling `CCamera::CameraInfo()`.

In the recipe, we use `TCameraInfo::iOptionsSupported`, which has the type of `TOptions`. It is a bit flag that stores the camera's supported options. Here is the list of possible values of the bit flag:

- `EViewFinderDirectSupported`

- `EViewFinderBitmapsSupported`

- `EImageCaptureSupported`

- `EVideoCaptureSupported`

- `EViewFinderMirrorSupported`

- `EContrastSupported`

- `EBrightnessSupported`

- `EViewFinderClippingSupported`

- `EImageClippingSupported`

- `EVideoClippingSupported`.

There are several values that are related to the viewfinder, but for this example we will be using the first two values only. There are basically two viewfinder types:

- Direct viewfinder (`EViewFinderDirectSupported`). The viewfinder can be drawn using direct screen access. It is easier to use and has a better performance. Unfortunately, not all devices support this mode; for example, at the time of writing this book, S60 devices do not support direct viewfinder mode.

- Bitmap viewfinder (`EViewFinderBitmapsSupported`). The viewfinder has to be drawn manually via a bitmap to a device context.

Initializing camera
There are two steps involved in initializing the camera:

- Reserve the camera for exclusive use by calling `CCamera::Reserve()`. This is an asynchronous method. When complete, it will call `MCameraObserver::ReserveComplete()`.
  The camera reservation is based on priority. That means, if there are two applications attempting to reserve a camera, the application with the higher priority will preempt the lower one. As with audio, you need `MultimediaDD` capability to change the priority.

- Switch on the camera power by calling `CCamera::PowerOn()`. This has to be called after `Reserve()` has been called. It is also an asynchronous method. When complete, it will call `MCameraObserver::PowerOnComplete()`.

After you have finished using the camera, you have to turn it off by calling `CCamera::PowerOff()`. Otherwise, your application will drain the battery very fast.

> **What may go wrong when you do this:** The camera consumes a lot of battery power. If you don't use the camera, you have to turn it off. You can react to your application being sent to the background by overriding `CAppUi::HandleForegroundEventL()`.

Displaying the viewfinder
There are two methods to display the viewfinder. These are `CCamera::StartViewFinderDirectL()` and `CCamera::StartViewFinderBitmapsL()`. Each method has some more variants; we will not discuss all of them.

`CCamera::StartViewFinderDirectL()` is used to start the direct viewfinder:

```
virtual void StartViewFinderDirectL(RWsSession& aWs,
    CWsScreenDevice& aScreenDevice, RWindowBase& aWindow,
                           TRect& aScreenRect)=0;
```

You would usually use `CCoeEnv::WsSession()`, `CCoeEnv::ScreenDevice()` and `CCoeControl::DrawableWindow()` to assign the first three parameters.

The last parameter is the area where the viewfinder will be displayed. The position is relative to the origin of the screen.

`CCamera::StartViewFinderBitmapsL()` is used to start the bitmap viewfinder:

```
virtual void StartViewFinderBitmapsL(TSize& aSize);
```

`StartViewFinderBitmapsL()` requires one parameter with type `TSize`, which is the size of the viewfinder to be used. When calling `StartViewFinderBitmapsL()`, you have to initialize `aSize` with the area where you want to display the viewfinder. On return, `aSize` will be assigned to the actual size of the viewfinder. They may be different because the control size and the viewfinder size may have different aspect ratio.

You can only display the viewfinder after the camera's power has been switched on. This means you have to do it after `MCameraObserver::PowerOnComplete()` has been called.

In the case of a direct viewfinder, you don't need to do anything else after calling `StartViewFinderDirectL()`. The viewfinder drawing is done direct to the screen by the API.

When using a bitmap viewfinder, you have to draw the viewfinder manually. `MCameraObserver::ViewFinderFrameReady()` is called periodically when the new viewfinder frame is ready. This callback has one parameter with type `CFbsBitmap&`, which is the viewfinder to be displayed.

There are applications that may require the viewfinder to process the image from the camera without actually capturing it. For example, it can be used in a motion detector application. When the application detects a moving object, it performs a specific action (this is discussed further in the Symbian Press book *Games on Symbian OS* – see ***developer.symbian.com/gamesbook*** for more details). A game may also use a viewfinder as its controller. When the user moves the camera in one direction, a character in the game also moves in the same direction.

4.7.3.4   Capture Still Images from a Camera

Amount of time required: 20 minutes
Location of example code: `\Multimedia\CameraImage`
Required libraries: `ecam.lib`
Required header file(s): `ecam.h`
Required platform security capability(s): `UserEnvironment`

Problem: You want to capture still images from the device's camera. The images are then saved to a file in JPEG format.

Solution: In the recipe, the `CCameraEngine::CaptureImageL()` method is used to capture still images from the camera. This is an asynchronous method. When complete, it calls `CCameraEngine::DoSaveImageL()` to save the image to a file.

Discussion:

Preparing image capture
Capturing a still image using a camera is done by calling `CCamera::CaptureImage()`. This is an asynchronous method. When it completes, it calls `MCameraObserver::ImageReady()`.

Before capturing any image, the `CCamera::PrepareImageCaptureL()` method has to be called to keep the latency of `CaptureImage()` to a minimum. It needs to be called only once for multiple `CaptureImage()` calls.

The `PrepareImageCaptureL()` method requires two parameters. The first parameter is the format of the image. Here is the list of formats for still images:

- `EFormatMonochrome`

- `EFormat16bitRGB444`

- `EFormat16BitRGB565`

- `EFormat32BitRGB888`

- `EFormatJpeg`

- `EFormatExif`

- `EFormatFbsBitmapColor4K`

- `EFormatFbsBitmapColor64K`

- `EFormatFbsBitmapColor16M`

- `EFormatFbsBitmapColor16MU`.

One device may not support all the formats above. You can check which formats are supported by a device from `TCameraInfo::iImageFormatsSupported`. It is a bit flag with type `CCamera::TFormat`.

The second parameter of `PrepareImageCaptureL()` is the index of the image size. It must be in the range of 0 to (`TCameraInfo::iNumImageSizesSupported` – 1). You can get all supported image sizes by calling `CCamera::EnumerateCaptureSizes()`.

For the sake of simplicity, the discussion in this book focuses only on JPEG (Joint Photographic Expert Group) and EXIF (Exchangeable Image File Format) formats. The EXIF format is a specification of an image file format used by digital cameras that contains additional metadata tags, such as date and time information, aperture, shutter speed, ISO speed and many more. It is supported by JPEG and some other formats. It is not supported by JPEG 2000, PNG and GIF though.

> **What may go wrong when you do this:** Before using a format, you have to make sure that it is supported by the device. For example, most S60 devices do not support `EFormatJpeg`. They support `EFormatExif`.

In order to keep the recipe simple, it uses the synchronous overload of `RFile::Write()` to save the captured image. In production code, we recommend that you use the asynchronous method, called using an active object, to keep the GUI responsive.

4.7.3.5   Record Video

Amount of time required: 30 minutes
Location of example code: `\Multimedia\VideoRecording`
Required libraries: `mediaclientvideo.lib`
Required header file(s): `videorecorder.h`
Required platform security capability(s): `UserEnvironment`

Problem: You want to record a video clip from a camera and save it to a file.

Solution: Before you continue reading this recipe, make sure that you already know how to use the `CCamera` class (see Recipe 4.7.3.2).

The class from MMF that is used to record video is `CVideo-RecorderUtility`. As for many other MMF APIs, there is an observer class: `MVideoRecorderUtilityObserver`.

The `CVideoRecorderUtility` class requires `UserEnvironment` capability. There are some methods that require `MultimediaDD`, but they will not be discussed in this book.

> **What may go wrong when you do this:** There is a known issue on some devices, which require that applications that perform video recording possess the `MultimediaDD` capability. A good example of this is the Nokia N93 and on early firmware of the Nokia N93i. Please check the Forum Nokia Technical Library at ***www.forum.nokia.com*** for more information.

Using `CVideoRecorderUtility` is similar to `CMdaAudio-RecorderUtility`, although it is a little more complex. Here are the steps required to record a video:

- Display the viewfinder using `CCamera` class (see Recipe 4.7.3.2).

- Create an observer that implements `MVideoRecorderUtility-Observer`.

- Create a new instance of `CVideoRecorderUtility`.

- Open the file by calling `CVideoRecorderUtility::OpenFile-L()`.

- Wait until the observer method, `MVideoRecorderUtility-Observer::MvruoOpenComplete()`, is called.

- Set some configurations, such as audio type.

- Call `CVideoRecorderUtility::Prepare()` to prepare for video recording.

- Wait until the observer method, `MVideoRecorderUtility-Observer::MvruoPrepareComplete()`, is called.

- Call `CVideoRecorderUtility::Record()` to start recording.

- Stop the recording by calling `CVideoRecorderUtility::Stop()`.

In our recipe, the `CSimpleVideoRecorder` class implements `MVideoRecorderUtilityObserver`.

Discussion: First, let's take a look at the usage of `CVideoRecorder-Utility::OpenFileL()`. This method requires several parameters, as shown below:

```
IMPORT_C void OpenFileL(const TDesC& aFileName, TInt aCameraHandle,
                        TUid aControllerUid, TUid aVideoFormat,
                        const TDesC8& aVideoType=KNullDesC8,
                        TFourCC aAudioType = KMMFFourCCCodeNULL);
```

The first parameter, `aFileName`, is the filename to which the video clip is saved.

The `aCameraHandle` parameter is the handle to the camera to use for recording. You can get the handle of the camera from the `CCamera::Handle()` method.

The `aControllerUid` parameter is the UID of the controller to use for recording. Phone manufacturers provide a controller plug-in to the

MMF, and you must specify the UID of the video controllers in this parameter. This is different from audio recording, where you don't need to specify which controller because the audio recorder utility class selects the controller automatically based on the file extension.

The `aVideoFormat` parameter is the UID of the video format to record to, and it depends on the controller plug-in. If you specify a video format that is not supported by the controller, you will receive an error.

The `aVideoType` parameter is the descriptor containing the video MIME type. There is a difference in how you use this parameter on UIQ and S60 devices. It is required on UIQ devices, but not required on S60 devices. If you forget to specify it on UIQ devices, you will get an error code 103.

The `aAudioType` parameter is the FourCC representing the audio format for recording. The same as for the video type, this parameter is mandatory on UIQ devices but it is not on S60 devices. If you don't specify this parameter on UIQ devices, the audio will not be recorded, and you will record video without audio.

What may go wrong when you do this: Not all methods in `CVideoRecorderUtility` are supported by all Symbian OS devices. For example, `CVideoRecorderUtility::OpenDesL()`, `CVideoRecorderUtility::OpenFileL()` and `CVideoRecorderUtility::OpenUrlL()` are not supported in S60 devices as at the time of writing.

How to select a video controller plug-in

The `CMMFControllerPluginSelectionParameters::ListImplementationsL()` method can be used to retrieve all controller plug-ins that match our search criteria. There are several possible criteria, but we will discuss two of them only: format and media IDs.

The first criterion is the required format support. You can set this by calling `CMMFControllerPluginSelectionParameters::SetRequiredRecordFormatSupportL()`, which takes a `CMMFFormatSelectionParameters` parameter.

Note that you can use a full filename as a parameter for `CMMFFormatSelectionParameters::SetMatchToFileNameL()` as it uses `TParse` (see Recipe 4.1.2.1) for an example of how to use this class.

The next criterion is the media IDs that must be supported by the plug-in, for example audio or video. It is set by calling `CMMFControllerPluginSelectionParameters::SetMediaIdsL()`.

The first parameter is an array of media IDs that the selected plug-ins must support. The second parameter, `aMatchType`, is the type of match to be made. There are three possible values:

- `ENoMediaIdMatch`. This means no media ID match will be performed.

- `EAllowOtherMediaIds`. All plug-ins that support the media ID will be returned. It includes plug-ins that support other media IDs. For example, if you request audio, plug-ins that support video and audio will also be returned.

- `EAllowOnlySuppliedMediaIds`. Only plug-ins that support the exact media IDs will be returned. If you specify audio, then only plug-ins that support audio will be returned.

We can then call `RMMFControllerImplInfoArray::List-ImplementationsL()` to retrieve all the controller plug-ins. This method requires a parameter with the type `RMMFControllerImplInfoArray`, which is an array of `CMMFControllerImplementation-Information`.

At this point, we have an array of controller plug-ins that support our criteria. The recipe simply retrieves the UID of the first plug-in in the list that can record to the specified format.

4.7.4 Resources

- Forum Nokia Multimedia Technology Resources: ***www.forum.nokia.com/main/resources/technologies/multimedia/index.html***.

- Sony Ericsson Developer World's Multimedia and Personalization Docs: ***www.developer.sonyericsson.com/site/global/docstools/multimedia/p_multimedia.jsp***.

- FourCC.org, Video Codec and Pixel Format Definitions: ***www.fourcc.org***.

- Exif.org, unofficial site dedicated to EXIF and related resources: ***www.exif.org***.

4.8 Telephony

On earlier versions of Symbian OS, to access telephony services, it was necessary to use a number of different specialized classes, not all of which were available in the public SDKs. On Symbian OS v9, telephony is accessed using a convenience class called `CTelephony`. Some alternative classes can be used instead of `CTelephony`, such as `RConnectionMonitor` (available in S60), but you will find that they actually require more platform security capabilities and this may prevent you from experimenting with self-signed applications.

Also, when you have learned to use one of the methods provided by `CTelephony`, the other methods become really easy to handle too because, in general, they are used in the same way.

The following sequence is usually required:

1. Check which function to call to get the initial value(s).

2. Check the enumeration value to be passed for monitoring the value when it changes.

3. Check which enumeration value you need to pass to cancel an outstanding request.

All of the methods provided by `CTelephony` use active objects; this is why all the examples that use `CTelephony` are `CActive`-derived classes. For each of the following recipes, to reuse the example code in your own projects, follow these steps:

1. Copy both the `.cpp` source file and the `.h` header file stated at the top of the recipe into your own project directories. This code contains the declaration and definition of the telephony-access active object.

2. Add the `etel3rdparty` library to your project settings and check that you also have the required platform security capabilities set for the project.

3. Derive the C class from which you intend to use the telephony functions from the required callback interface class. Define and implement the required virtual function(s) in that class.

4. Add a pointer member variable to the class to own an instance of the telephony-access active object.

5. Add construction code to instantiate the telephony-access active object, and corresponding code to delete it in the destructor.

For example, if you want to add functionality which dials a phone call to your application, first copy `Call_Dialer.h` and `Call_Dialer.cpp` files into your project. The content of the files is as follows:

```
// Callback interface
class MCallDialerCallBack
  {
public:
  virtual void DialerDone(TInt aError)=0;
  };

// Telephony-access active object
class CMyCallDialer : public CActive
  {
```

```
  enum TMyCallStates
  {
  EMyCallIdle,
  EMyCallDialing,
  EMyCallHangingup,
  EMyCallAnswering
  };
public:// public constructors & destructor
  static CMyCallDialer* NewLC(MCallDialerCallBack& aCallBack);
  static CMyCallDialer* NewL(MCallDialerCallBack& aCallBack);
  ~CMyCallDialer();
  // public functions
  void Dial(const TDesC& aPhoneNumber,
          CTelephony::TCallerIdentityRestrict aRestinction =
                               CTelephony::EIdRestrictDefault);
  void Hangup();
  void AnswerIncomingCall();
protected: // from CActive
  void RunL();
  void DoCancel();
private:
  CMyCallDialer(MCallDialerCallBack& aCallBack);
  void ConstructL();
private:
  MCallDialerCallBack& iCallBack;
  CTelephony* iTelephony;
  CTelephony::TCallId iCallId;
  CTelephony::TCallParamsV1 iCallParams;
  CTelephony::TCallParamsV1Pckg iCallParamsPckg;
  TMyCallStates iState;
  };

// Code for NewL() and NewLC() factory methods is omitted for clarity

CMyCallDialer::CMyCallDialer(MCallDialerCallBack& aCallBack)
 : CActive(EPriorityStandard), iCallBack(aCallBack),
   iCallParamsPckg(iCallParams), iState(EMyCallIdle)
      {}

CMyCallDialer::~CMyCallDialer()
  {
  // always cancel any pending request before deleting the objects
    Cancel();
  delete iTelephony;
  }

void CMyCallDialer::ConstructL()
  {
  // Active objects needs to be added to active scheduler
  CActiveScheduler::Add(this);
  iTelephony = CTelephony::NewL();
  }

void CMyCallDialer::Dial(const TDesC& aPhoneNumber,
  CTelephony::TCallerIdentityRestrict aRestriction)
  {
  if(!IsActive() && iTelephony)
    {
```

```
    CTelephony::TTelNumber telNumber(aPhoneNumber);

    CTelephony::TCallParamsV1 callParams;
    callParams.iIdRestrict = aRestriction;
    CTelephony::TCallParamsV1Pckg callParamsPckg(callParams);

    iState = EMyCallDialing;
    // ask CTelephony to dial new call
    // RunL will be called when the call is connected or it fails
    iTelephony->DialNewCall(iStatus, callParamsPckg,
                                     telNumber, iCallId);
    SetActive();// after starting the request AO needs to be set active
    }
  }

void CMyCallDialer::AnswerIncomingCall()
  {
  if(!IsActive() && iTelephony)
    {
    iState = EMyCallAnswering;
    iTelephony->AnswerIncomingCall(iStatus, iCallId);
    SetActive();// after starting the request AO needs to be set active
    }
  }

void CMyCallDialer::Hangup()
  {
  if(!IsActive() && iTelephony)
    {
    iState = EMyCallHangingup;
    iTelephony->Hangup(iStatus, iCallId);
    SetActive();// after starting the request AO needs to be set active
    }
  }

// Handle completion events
void CMyCallDialer::RunL()
  {
  iState = EMyCallIdle;
  // use callback function to tell owner that we have finished
  iCallBack.DialerDone(iStatus.Int());
  }

void CMyCallDialer::DoCancel()
  {
  // You need to specify what you want to cancel
  // We also need to check first which call is currently active

  if(iState == EMyCallDialing)
    {
    iTelephony->CancelAsync(CTelephony::EDialNewCallCancel);
    }

  if(iState == EMyCallHangingup)
    {
    iTelephony->CancelAsync(CTelephony::EHangupCancel);
    }
```

```
  if(iState == EMyCallAnswering)
    {
    iTelephony->CancelAsync(CTelephony::EAnswerIncomingCallCancel);
    }

  iState = EMyCallIdle;
  }
```

Your class must derive from `MCallDialerCallBack` and override the `DialerDone()` interface. Add an instance of `CMyCallDialer` as a member of the class:

```
#include "Call_Dialer.h"

class CMyClass : public CBase, MCallDialerCallBack
  {
public: // From MCallDialerCallBack
  void DialerDone(TInt aError);
  ...
private:
  ...
  CMyCallDialer* iMyCallDialer;
  ...
  };
```

Your class must implement the `DialerDone()` callback function, which the dialer uses to communicate when it is finished with the task:

```
void CMyClass::DialerDone(TInt aError)
  {
  // do something in here, which must NOT leave...
  }
```

The next step is to pass a reference to this class when instantiating the `CMyCallDialer` active object:

```
iMyCallDialer = CMyCallDialer::NewL(*this);
```

You can then call the `Dial()`, `Hangup()` and `AnswerIncoming-Call()` functions of `CMyCallDialer` to implement the logic of your application.

Finally, do not forget to modify your class destructor to delete the `CMyCallDialer` class instance!

> **Note:** Since the emulator environment does not have telephony hardware included, only very few of the methods of the `CTelephony` class can be tested in the emulator. Construction of classes requiring actual hardware has been disabled for emulator builds with `#ifdef __WINS_` macro.

> Code that uses telephony requires the `NetworkServices` platform security capability to protect against malicious code that could potentially run up a large phone bill. To install code that requires the `NetworkServices` capability on the device you will need to add this capability to the MMP file and sign the SIS file before it can be installed. For more information about this, consult Chapter 3.

4.8.1   Easy Recipes

4.8.1.1   Handle Phone Calls

> **Amount of time required:** 20 minutes
> **Location of example code:** `\Telephony\Telephony_Dialer`
> **Required library(s):** `etel3rdparty.lib`
> **Required header file(s):** `etel3rdparty.h`
> **Required platform security capability(s):** `NetworkServices`

Problem: You want to make a call and hang it up.

Solution: The `CTelephonyAppUi` class shows how to use the `Call_Dialer` code.

In order to dial a call, you need to call `CTelephony::DialNewCall()`. When the call is answered or rejected, `RunL()` will be called and the error code can be retrieved from the `iStatus` variable.

When calling `DialNewCall()`, you could also set restrictions on how your phone number is shown on the receiving handset by setting the `iIdRestrict` variable defined in `CTelephony::TCallParamsV1`. Possible values are:

- `EIdRestrictDefault` (use default phone settings),

- `ESendMyId` (show your number on the receiving end), and

- `EDontSendMyId` (do not show your number on the receiving end).

In order to answer a call, you need to have an incoming call in the ringing state (note that outgoing calls also move to the ringing state right after the dialing state). You can then answer the incoming call by using the `AnswerIncomingCall()` function. When the call is answered, `RunL()` will be called and the error code can be retrieved from the usual `iStatus` variable.

In order to hang up a currently active call (one that has been answered), simply call the `Hangup()` function, which will cause the call to be terminated. Once again, `RunL()` will be called and the error code can be retrieved from the `iStatus` variable.

> **What may go wrong when you do this:** Your phone operator can override the restriction settings, so changing them to anything else than `EIdRestrictDefault` could lead to situations where the call does not get through on certain networks (this behavior has been observed in Thailand with AIS & DTAC networks in August 2007).

4.8.1.2 Send DTMF Tones to the Phone Line

Amount of time required: 15 minutes
Location of example code: `\Telephony\Telephony_Dialer`
Required library(s): `etel3rdparty.lib`
Required header file(s): `etel3rdparty.h`
Required platform security capability(s): `NetworkServices`

Problem: You want to send DTMF tones on a line with an active call.

Solution: The `CTelephonyAppUi` class shows how to use the `Send_DTMF` code.

To be able to send DTMF tones you need to call `CTelephony::SendDTMFTones()`, passing in a string of DTMF tones. The DTMF tones will be transmitted to all currently active voice calls, which means you will also need to check the status of the line before trying to send any tones.

After calling the `SendDTMFTones()` function, all DTMF tones are played in sequence, after which `RunL()` will be called and any possible errors can be checked from the `iStatus` variable.

> **Tip:** Displaying the DTMF tones that are played on the screen makes for a better user interface. For more information about graphics and drawing to the screen, please see the recipes in Section 4.5.

> **Tip:** `CTelephony` does not let you control how long each DTMF tone is played when you send a DTMF string. You may want to send the tones one-by-one and always wait for the callback before sending the next one.

4.8.1.3 Observe the Phone Line State

Amount of time required: 15 minutes
Location of example code: `\Telephony\Telephony_Dialer`
Required library(s): `etel3rdparty.lib`

Required header file(s): `etel3rdparty.h`
Required platform security capability(s): None

Problem: You want to monitor incoming calls and call states.

Solution: The `CTelephonyAppUi` class shows how to use the `Call_Observer` code.

In order to monitor the status of your phone, you need to call `CTelephony::NotifyChange()`. Each status change will then trigger a call to `RunL()` and the error code can be retrieved from its `iStatus` variable. If the error code is `KErrNone`, the line status information will be stored in the `TCallStatusV1` variable given to `NotifyChange()`.

All possible line status values are defined in `TCallStatus` and are as follows:

- `EStatusUnknown` (status is not known).

- `EStatusIdle` (line is idle, i.e., no activity at all).

- `EStatusDialling` (line is dialing an outgoing call).

- `EStatusRinging` (line is ringing, i.e., either incoming call is ringing, or outgoing call is ringing on the other end).

- `EStatusAnswering` (line is currently being answered).

- `EStatusConnecting` (a call is being connected).

- `EStatusConnected` (call is connected, i.e., we have an active phone call).

- `EStatusReconnectPending` (a call is undergoing temporary channel loss and it may or may not be reconnected).

- `EStatusDisconnecting` (a call is being disconnected).

- `EStatusHold` (call is on hold state).

- `EStatusTransferring` (call is being transferred).

- `EStatusTransferAlerting` (a call is alerting the remote party of a transfer).

What may go wrong when you do this: State change events can be lost if you don't exit your `RunL()` method quickly enough, particularly if you trigger a change in your `RunL()` method. We advise using separate active objects to implement the logic of your application and only using the original `NotifyChange()` callback to trigger their execution.

4.8.1.4 Retrieve the Network Signal Strength

Amount of time required: 10 minutes
Location of example code: \Telephony\Telephony_Monitor1
Required library(s): etel3rdparty.lib
Required header file(s): etel3rdparty.h
Required platform security capability(s): None

Problem: You want to know the signal strength for the telephone network.

Solution: The CTelephonyAppUi class shows how to use the Signal_Observer code.

Discussion: You need to call CTelephony::GetSignalStrength(). When the initial signal strength has been retrieved, RunL() will be called.

In order to monitor the signal strength, use the NotifyChange() function with the second parameter set to ESignalStrengthChange.

Since we are using the same active object for two different requests, we keep track of what is currently being done using the iMonitoring variable. The importance of this becomes clear when implementing the DoCancel() function to determine which request needs to be cancelled.

The signal strength values are stored in a TSignalStrengthV1 variable (if iStatus is KErrNone), with which you can get the actual signal strength value (stored as dBm in iSignalStrength) and the bar values (stored in iBar) that should be used when drawing the signal bars on the screen.

4.8.1.5 Retrieve the Battery Status

Amount of time required: 10 minutes
Location of example code: \Telephony\Telephony_monitor1
Required library(s): etel3rdparty.lib
Required header file(s): etel3rdparty.h
Required platform security capability(s): None

Problem: You want to know the battery level (that is, how much charge is left in it).

Solution: The CTelephonyAppUi class shows how to use the Battery_Observer code.

Discussion: You need to call CTelephony::GetBatteryInfo(). When the initial battery status has been retrieved, RunL() will be called.

In order to monitor the battery status, use the `NotifyChange()` function with the second parameter set to `EBatteryInfoChange`.

Since we are using the same active object for two different requests, we keep track of what is currently being done using the `iMonitoring-Battery` variable. The importance of this becomes clear when implementing the `DoCancel()` function to determine which request needs to be cancelled.

The battery status values are stored in a `TBatteryInfoV1` variable, with which you can get the actual battery status value (stored in `iStatus`, which indicates for example whether the charger is connected) and the current charge level of the battery (stored in `iChargeLevel`).

4.8.1.6 Retrieve the IMEI Number of the Device

Amount of time required: 15 minutes
Location of example code: `\Telephony\Telephony_Monitor1`
Required library(s): `etel3rdparty.lib`
Required header file(s): `etel3rdparty.h`
Required platform security capability(s): `None`

Problem: You want to get the device's identifier number (IMEI).

Solution: The `CTelephonyAppUi` class shows how to use the `GetIMEI` code.

Discussion: You need to call `CTelephony::GetPhoneId()`. When the IMEI number of the device has been retrieved, `RunL()` will be called and the error code can be retrieved from the `iStatus` variable.

The IMEI number is stored in a `TPhoneIdV1` variable (if `iStatus` is `KErrNone`), which contains three buffer variables:

- `iManufacturer` (indentifies the manufacturer).

- `iModel` (identifies the model).

- `iSerialNumber` (the actual IMEI number of the device).

> **Tip:** The IMEI number can be used to generate registration keys, and thus to check if the application is correctly registered, you often need the IMEI number before giving the user access to the full application. Basically, in order to make this work well, you could have a splash screen shown first when the application is started and then use a timer to change it to the normal startup screen. When you start the splash screen, you could construct and start `CMyImeiGetter`.

4.8.1.7 Retrieve the Current Network Name

Amount of time required: 10 minutes
Location of example code: \Telephony\Telephony_Monitor1
Required library(s): etel3rdparty.lib
Required header file(s): etel3rdparty.h
Required platform security capability(s): None

Problem: You want to get the current network name.

Solution: The CTelephonyAppUi class shows how to use the Net-WorkName code.

Discussion: You need to call CTelephony::GetCurrentNetwork-Name(). When the current network name has been retrieved, RunL() will be called and the error code can be retrieved from the iStatus variable.
　　The network name is stored in a TNetworkNameV1 variable (if iStatus is KErrNone), which only has one buffer variable iNetwork-Name, where the name for the currently used network is stored.

What may go wrong when you do this: Some networks do not publish their name, and thus you might get an empty string when using this class. See the next recipe for an alternative option. The worst case scenario is to need to use the Cell ID information to identify the network operator.

4.8.1.8 Retrieve the Current Operator Name

Amount of time required: 10 minutes
Location of example code: Telephony_Monitor1
Required library(s): etel3rdparty.lib
Required header file(s): etel3rdparty.h
Required platform security capability(s): None

Problem: You want to get the current operator name.

Solution: The CTelephonyAppUi class shows how to retrieve the operator name.

Discussion: You need to call CTelephony::GetOperatorName(). When the current operator name has been retrieved, RunL() will be called and the error code can be retrieved from the iStatus variable.
　　The operator name is stored in a TOperatorNameV1 variable (if iStatus is KErrNone), which only has one buffer variable iOpera-torName, where the name for the currently used operator is stored.

> **What may go wrong when you do this:** Some network operators do not publish their name with this method, and thus you might get an empty string when using this class. See the previous recipe for an alternative option. The worst case scenario is to need to use the Cell ID information to identify the network operator.

4.8.1.9   Retrieve the Flight Mode Status

Amount of time required: 10 minutes
Location of example code: \Telephony\Telephony_Monitor1
Required library(s): etel3rdparty.lib
Required header file(s): etel3rdparty.h
Required platform security capability(s): None

Problem: You want to find out whether the phone is in flight mode (off-line).

Solution: The CTelephonyAppUi class shows how to use the FlightmodeStatus code.

Discussion: You need to call the CTelephony::GetFlightMode() function. When the initial flight mode status has been retrieved, RunL() will be called.

In order to monitor any flight mode status change, use the NotifyChange() function with the second parameter set to EFlightModeChange.

Since we are using the same active object for two different requests, we keep track of what is currently being done using the iMonitoring variable. The importance of this becomes clear when implementing the DoCancel() function to determine which request needs to be cancelled.

The flight mode status value is stored in a TFlightModeV1 variable (if iStatus is KErrNone), which has one member variable called iFlightModeStatus. The only two possible values for iFlightModeStatus are:

- EFlightModeOff (flight mode is off, e.g., the phone can communicate).

- EFlightModeOn (flight mode is on, e.g., the phone commication is disabled).

> **Note:** If you want to set the flight mode on/off, you need to use a profiles engine. To set the flight mode on, just set the Offline profile on, and to set it off, just set any other profile on.

4.8.1.10 Retrieve the Network Registration Status

Amount of time required: 15 minutes
Location of example code: \Telephony\Telephony_Monitor1
Required library(s): etel3rdparty.lib
Required header file(s): etel3rdparty.h
Required platform security capability(s): None

Problem: You want to know what the network registration status is.

Solution: The CTelephonyAppUi class shows how to use the RegistrationStatus code.

Discussion: You need to call CTelephony::GetNetworkRegistrationStatus(). When the initial network registration status has been retrieved, RunL() will be called.

In order to monitor any network registration status change, use the NotifyChange() function with the second parameter set to ENetworkRegistrationStatusChange.

Since we are using the same active object for two different requests, we keep track of what is currently being done using the iMonitoring variable. The importance of this becomes clear when implementing the DoCancel() function to determine which request needs to be cancelled.

The network registration status values are stored in a TNetworkRegistrationV1 variable, which has one member variable called iRegStatus. The values for the network registration status are as follows:

- ERegistrationUnknown (registration status is not known).

- ENotRegisteredNoService (no network detected, and currently not searching).

- ENotRegisteredEmergencyOnly (network allowing only emergency calls detected).

- ENotRegisteredSearching (not registered, but currently searching for networks).

- ERegisteredBusy (registered, but network is busy).

- ERegisteredOnHomeNetwork (registered on home network).

- ERegistrationDenied (registration attempt was denied by the network).

- ERegisteredRoaming (registered in network that is not home network).

4.8.2   Intermediate Recipes

4.8.2.1   Retrieve the Phone Number from an Incoming/Outgoing Call

Amount of time required: 15 minutes
Location of example code: \Telephony\Telephony_Dialer
Required library(s): etel3rdparty.lib
Required header file(s): etel3rdparty.h
Required platform security capability(s): ReadUserData

Problem: You want to get the phone number of an incoming/outgoing call.

Solution: To retrieve a remote phone number from an incoming call, the call needs to be at least in the ringing state.

To retrieve a remote phone number from an outgoing call, the call needs to be at least in the dialing state.

You will find the source code for this recipe in the same class as the code for Recipe 4.8.1.3 (that's CMyCallObserver), because this allows us to retrieve the remote phone number at the first available opportunity, which is when the call state changes.

The actual function call is GetCallInfo(), for which:

1. The first parameter lets you choose between voice/data/fax lines.

2. The second parameter is a TCallInfoV1 buffer, which will hold information for the call and includes the phone number for outgoing calls.

3. The third parameter is a TRemotePartyInfoV1 buffer, which holds information on the remote party and may include the phone number for incoming calls (if it is available from the Call Line Identification).

What may go wrong when you do this: Some devices have shown 'Out of Memory' errors when using GetCallInfo() directly in a state change event callback, which is why the sample code contains an added User::After() delay before calling the method. This is presumably an internal defect.

A better workaround would be to use a separate active object to handle the delay, but it would need to be cancelled if the call terminated before the timer goes off.

4.8.2.2   Match a Name to a Phone Number

Amount of time required: 15 minutes
Location of example code: Telephony_Dialer

Required library(s): cntmodel.lib
Required header file(s): cntdb.h, cntfield.h, cntfldst.h, cntitem.h
Required platform security capability(s): ReadUserData, WriteUserData

Problem: You want to identify the contact associated with a phone number.

Solution: The CTelephonyAppUi class shows how to use the GetContactsName code.

Discussion: Before using this recipe, you may want to look at the recipes in Section 4.2, which illustrate how to use the Symbian OS contact database.

To retrieve a name from a contacts database, you first need to construct an instance of the CContactDatabase class as shown in the ConstructL() function. Then, because we cannot assume that all numbers are in international or national format (for example, +35840... or just as 040), we need to extract the part of the number which we want to use for processing. In this example, the last eight digits of the number are used (you can change this by changing the value for KTxMaxNumberCut).

The sample sets up an asynchronous search of the entire contact database by using KUidContactFieldMatchAll in a CContactItemFieldDef and calling FindAsyncL().

When the first matching contact is found, IdleFindCallback() is called. Since there might just be one contact matching the search criterion, checking the result of IsComplete() lets us know whether we need to cancel the remainder of the search.

Tip: This example only reports the first hit. If you want to get all of the matching results, you can easily retrieve all the CContactItem from their id and report each one back to the caller through the MContactsNameCallBack interface.

4.8.2.3 Retrieve the IMSI Number of the SIM Card

Amount of time required: 15 minutes
Location of example code: \Telephony\Telephony_Monitor2
Required library(s): etel3rdparty.lib
Required header file(s): etel3rdparty.h
Required platform security capability(s): ReadDeviceData

Problem: You want to get the current SIM card identification number (IMSI).

Solution: The CTelephonyAppUi class shows how to use the Imsi_ Getter code.

Discussion: You need to call the CTelephony::GetSubscriberId() function. When the IMSI number of the SIM card has been retrieved, RunL() will be called and the error code can be retrieved from the iStatus variable.

The IMSI number is stored in a TSubscriberIdV1 variable (if iStatus is KErrNone), which only has one buffer variable iSubscriberId, where the IMSI number of the SIM card is stored. The first three characters of the IMSI number identify the subscriber's home country, the next two or three characters identify the operator used while in the home country. The remaining characters are used to identify the individual subscriber.

> **Tip:** Since each IMSI number is globally unique to a SIM card, you can use this mechanism to generate application registration keys, instead of using the IMEI number.

4.8.2.4 Retrieve the Phone Lock Status

Amount of time required: 20 minutes
Location of example code: \Telephony\Telephony_Monitor2
Required library(s): etel3rdparty.lib
Required header file(s): etel3rdparty.h
Required platform security capability(s): ReadDeviceData

Problem: You want to know the phone's current lock status.

Solution: The CTelephonyAppUi class shows how to use the Lock-Info_Getter code.

Discussion: You need to call CTelephony::GetLockInfo(). The second parameter for this function allows you to choose which lock you are interested in. When the lock status has been retrieved, RunL() will be called and the error code can be retrieved from the iStatus variable.

The requested lock status is stored in a TIccLockInfoV1 variable (if iStatus is KErrNone), which contains two fields:

- iStatus (identifies whether the phone is locked, unlocked or blocked).

- iSetting (identifies whether the specific lock is enabled or not).

It is important to understand the difference between the locking status and the locking setting values. A lock has a status which tells you its current state, for example, whether it is locked, unlocked or blocked. A lock also has a setting, which is more like a policy, which says if the lock should be treated as 'in use'. If the lock is enabled, then the status should be observed. If the lock is disabled, then the status is not important.

> **Note:** Locking and unlocking the device requires usage of non-public APIs, thus if you need more information on the functionality, you would need to contact the manufacturer of the device you are targeting.
>
> This functionality can also be achieved by using AT commands, if the target device supports AT commands for using the phone lock.

4.8.3 Advanced Recipes

4.8.3.1 Retrieve Cell ID and Network Information

Amount of time required: 25 minutes
Location of example code: \Telephony\Telephony_Monitor2
Required library(s): etel3rdparty.lib
Required header file(s): etel3rdparty.h
Required platform security capability(s): ReadDeviceData

Problem: You want to get information about the currently used network cell.

Solution: The CTelephonyAppUi class shows how to use the NWInfo_Observer code.

Discussion: You need to call CTelephony::GetCurrentNetwork-Info(). When the initial network information data has been retrieved, RunL() will be called.

In order to monitor any network information change, use the Notify-Change() function with the second parameter set to ECurrent-NetworkInfoChange.

Since we are using the same active object for two different requests, we keep track of what is currently being done using the iMonitoring variable. The importance of this becomes clear when implementing the DoCancel() function to determine which request needs to be cancelled.

The network information data is stored in a TNetworkInfoV1 variable, which contains a lot more information than just the Cell ID of the currently used Cell. TNetworkInfoV1 contains the following variables:

- `iMode` (network mode, i.e., GSM, cdma2000, etc.).

- `iStatus` (phone network status).

- `iCountryCode` (country code for the Cell's network).

- `iNetworkId` (network ID for the Cell).

- `iDisplayTag` (tag displayed for the Cell, which actually is not the same as the tag shown in the phone).

- `iShortName` (short name for the network).

- `iBandInfo` (network band information, i.e., 800 MHz on Band A, 1900 MHz on Band C, etc.).

- `iCdmaSID` (system identity (SID) of the CDMA or AMPS network).

- `iLongName` (longer name for the network).

- `iAccess` (the access technology that the network is based on).

- `iAreaKnown` (indicates if the area is known).

- `iLocationAreaCode` (location ID for the Cell).

- `iCellId` (the actual Cell ID, which is unique inside the network for a specific operator in a specific country).

4.8.3.2 Retrieve Call Forwarding Status

Amount of time required: 25 minutes
Location of example code: `\Telephony\Telephony_Monitor2`
Required library(s): `etel3rdparty.lib`
Required header file(s): `etel3rdparty.h`
Required platform security capability(s): `ReadDeviceData,Network-`

`Services`

Problem: You want to know whether the phone automatically forwards incoming calls.

Solution: The `CTelephonyAppUi` class shows how to use the `ForwardingStatus_Getter` code.

Discussion: You need to call `CTelephony::GetCallForwarding-Status()`. With this function you also need to specify which call forwarding status is being retrieved. The available options are:

- `ECallForwardingUnconditional` (forwards for all calls).

- `ECallForwardingBusy` (forwards when subscriber is busy).

- `ECallForwardingNoReply` (forwards when subscriber does not reply within timeout).

- `ECallForwardingNotReachable` (forwards when subscriber is unreachable).

When the phone's call forwarding status has been retrieved, `RunL()` will be called and the error code can be retrieved from the `iStatus` variable.

The status for the specified call forwarding condition is stored in a `TCallForwardingSupplServicesV1` variable (if `iStatus` is `KErrNone`), which contains two fields:

- `iCallForwarding` (the status of the forward, i.e., active, not active, etc.).

- `iCallForwardingCondition` (identifies the condition which was requested).

> **Note:** Setting the call forwarding on/off requires usage of a non-public Symbian API but the same functionality can also be achieved by using AT commands, if the target device supports AT commands for changing call forwarding information.

4.8.3.3 Retrieve Call Barring Status

Amount of time required: 20 minutes
Location of example code: `\Telephony\Telephony_Monitor2`
Required library(s): `etel3rdparty.lib`
Required header file(s): `etel3rdparty.h`
Required platform security capability(s): `ReadDeviceData,Network-`

`Services`

Problem: You want to know if the phone is set to prevent some calls.

Solution: The `CTelephonyAppUi` class shows how to use the `BarringStatus_Getter` code.

Discussion: You need to call the `CTelephony::GetCallBarringStatus()` function. With this function you also need to specify which call barring status is being retrieved and the options are:

- `EBarAllIncoming` (barring for all incoming calls).

- `EBarIncomingRoaming` (incoming when roaming).

- `EBarAllOutgoing` (all outgoing calls barred).

- `EBarOutgoingInternational` (international calls barred).

- `EBarOutgoingInternationalExHC` (all international calls except ones to the home network are barred; used when roaming).

When the call barring status has been retrieved, `RunL()` will be called and the error code can be retrieved from the `iStatus` variable.

The call barring status for the specified condition is stored in a `TCall-BarringSupplServicesV1` variable (if `iStatus` is `KErrNone`), which contains two fields:

- `iCallBarring` (the status of the call barring, i.e., active, not active, etc.).

- `iCallBarringCondition` (identifies the condition which was requested).

> **Note:** Setting the call barring requires usage of a non-public Symbian API. If you require this functionality, you need to contact Symbian partnering (see Chapter 5).

4.9   Connectivity

The connectivity features of modern smartphones have grown extensively over the past few years, and you may choose between technologies such as Bluetooth, Infrared and USB for short-range communications. Symbian OS v9.x offers powerful support for each of the above connectivity bearers and provides rich APIs to fulfill any complicated task you may want to implement. Support can be split into two main categories:

- Low-level technologies (e.g., Infrared or Bluetooth) and frameworks (e.g., ESOCK).

- High-level technologies, such as OBEX.

Some of the connectivity methods, for instance, those using USB connections, are generally reserved for use by Symbian's licensees and therefore unavailable to third-party developers. As a result, these recipes illustrate how to use Infrared and Bluetooth connections to address various issue you might need to resolve at both low and high-level protocol layers. As these recipes describe connectivity services, they do not discuss networking and other areas that are based on the low-level components described here. You can find more information about networking in the recipes found in Section 4.3.

As a general rule, communications in Symbian OS are built around a client–server architecture just like many other available services. C32 is the Symbian OS comms server and supplies a client-side API and server-side code, which is run as a thread in the C32 server process. The C32 process contains its main thread, the C32 thread and a number of other threads, namely ESOCK, ETel and Phonebook Synchronizer. The ESOCK framework will be mentioned extensively in these recipes, as it plays an important role in connectivity services provision for applications and high-level technologies in Symbian OS.

The actual implementation of various connectivity components is spread over multiple modules and therefore can be quite confusing in some cases. A good example are the OBEX classes, which are declared in clearly named header files – but you have to link your application against `irobex.lib` even though you intend to use Bluetooth connections.

The usage of different communication techniques may require that appropriate platform security capabilities to be granted to your applications. All such cases are noted explicitly throughout the examples where necessary. High-level protocols, such as OBEX, often rely on the policy declared by low-level ones; hence it is reasonable to assume in most cases that your applications will be expected to have `LocalServices` capability present.

In order to keep them simple the code samples in these recipes are going to use as few active objects as possible. Most asynchronous method calls are simply followed by `User::WaitForRequest()`. This is of course not how production-quality code should behave, and the code samples provided for download to accompany this book will illustrate how to call asynchronous APIs correctly.

4.9.1 Easy Recipes

4.9.1.1 Print over IrDA

Amount of time required: 10 minutes
Location of example code: `\Connectivity\IRPrint`
Required library(s): `c32.lib`
Required header file(s): `c32comm.h`
Required platform security capability(s): None

Problem: You want to print a document to an IR printer.

Solution: This task is quite simple and requires about a dozen lines of code. The solution is to use serial communications over an emulated IrCOMM port:

```
#include <e32base.h>
#include <e32svr.h>
#include <c32comm.h>

_LIT(KIrCOMM,"IrCOMM");
_LIT(KIrCOMM0,"IrCOMM::0");

void PrintDataL(TDes8& aData)
  {
  RCommServ server;
  server.Connect();
  TInt ret=server.LoadCommModule(KIrCOMM);

  User::LeaveIfError(ret);

  RComm commPort;
  ret=commPort.Open(server,KIrCOMM0,ECommExclusive);
  User::LeaveIfError(ret);

  TRequestStatus status;
  commPort.Write(status,KTimeOut,aData);
  User::WaitForRequest(status);

  User::LeaveIfError(status.Int());
  commPort.Close();

  server.Close();
  }
```

It's a simple as that!

Discussion: The snippet above uses the standard Symbian OS client–server mechanism and follows a typical sequence as follows:

1. Open client session to above server.

2. Use this session to communicate data to and from the server.

3. Close the session.

4. Close the server if required.

4.9.1.2   Discover Infrared Devices

Amount of time required: 20 minutes
Location of example code: \Connectivity\IRDevice
Required library(s): esock.lib
Required header file(s): es_sock.h
Required platform security capability(s): LocalServices

Problem: You want to discover the Infrared-enabled devices in range.

Solution: To get the list of available IR-devices in range, you can use the ESOCK classes `RSocketServer` and `RHostResolver` declared in `es_sock.h`. For IrDA protocols the code is quite simple and is presented below. For Bluetooth it is a bit more complicated, as you will see in further recipes.

As a first step, you need to fill in the `TProtocolDesc` structure which defines an address family and a protocol number. `RSocket-Serv::FindProtocol()` takes a protocol name as a parameter and returns the appropriate protocol information. In case of IrDA, only the address family is important. The protocol number is forced to be valid by ESOCK automatically.

The core part of the device discovery process is the `RHostResolver` class. This is where you obtain device names or addresses in either the synchronous or asynchronous method.

```
RSocketServ ss;
TProtocolDesc pInfo;
TInt ret;

If ((ret = ss.Connect()) != KErrNone)
  {
  return ret;
  }

_LIT8(KTinyTP,"IrTinyTP");
ret=ss.FindProtocol(KTinyTP,protoInfo);

// IrTinyTP is the reliable transport layer of IRDA which corresponds
// to sequenced packet service. Irmux corresponds to unreliable
// datagram service.
if (ret!=KErrNone)
  {
  // Error - protocol not loaded - prob. wrong ESOCK.INI
  // or protocol has locked serial port.
  }

RHostResolver hr;
ret=hr.Open(ss,pInfo.iAddrFamily,pInfo.iSockType);

TNameEntry log;
THostName name;

ret=hr.GetByName(name,log);
if (ret!=KErrNone)
  {
  // No devices discovered - may be none present
  }
// Call RHostResolver::Next() on 9.2 here
```

Discussion: The code snippet above demonstrates the synchronous call for host resolution for the sake of simplicity. As with most Symbian OS programming topics, it is preferable to use the asynchronous version of the same method to avoid UI unresponsiveness if it takes a few seconds to actually resolve the available device names.

The first parameter of the `RHostResolver::GetByName()` method defines the device name mask that the caller is interested in. For IrDA connections it is ignored by the protocol. The documentation states that wildcard names are supported in the mask, and you are recommended to specify an asterisk there to ensure that the same code will work with all possible future changes.

On Symbian OS v9.2 and above, `RHostResolver::Next()` returns the next discovered device until no more devices are found. In v9.1 it behaves differently, and always returns the very first device information and no error. Therefore, if your application should work on both OS versions, then the only robust way of detecting the end-of-discovery process is to compare the given device address with already fetched ones.

4.9.1.3 Discover Bluetooth Devices

Amount of time required: 20 minutes
Location of example code: `\Connectivity\BTDeviceSample\DeviceDiscoverer`
Required library(s): `bluetooth.lib`, `btmanclient.lib`, `sdpagent.lib`, `sdpdatabase.lib`, `esock.lib`
Required header file(s): `btdevice.h`, `bt_sock.h`, `btsdp.h`, `bttypes.h`, `es_sock.h`
Required platform security capability(s): `LocalServices`

Problem: You want to discover the Bluetooth-enabled devices in range.

Solution: Whilst it may sound quite complicated at first glance, the discovery process for Bluetooth devices is actually pretty straightforward and practically the same as for IrDA in Symbian OS. You must use the following classes:

- `RSocketServ` – used to establish a session to the ESOCK server and get information about supported communication protocols.

- `RHostResolver` – provides an interface to host name resolution services.

- `TInquirySockAddr` – socket address class which is used for inquiries.

- `TNameEntry`/`TNameRecord` – this class keeps the result of the query.

A typical scenario for device discovery is based on the sequence below.

1. Connect to the socket server (RSocketServ), and then select the protocol to be used using RSocketServ::FindProtocol(). Address and name queries are supplied by the stack's BTLink-Manager protocol layer, so this should be selected:

```
RSocketServ sockServ;
sockServ.Connect();
TProtocolDesc pd;
_LIT(KL2Cap, "BTLinkManager");
User::LeaveIfError(sockServ.FindProtocol(KL2Cap, pd));
```

2. Create and initialize RHostResolver:

```
RHostResolver hr;
User::LeaveIfError(hr.Open(sockServ, pd.iAddrFamily, pd.iProtocol));
```

3. Set up the TInquirySockAddr variable so that its Inquiry Access Code (IAC) equals KGIAC ('General Unlimited') and an action is KHostResInquiry. The actual query is started by an RHost-Resolver::GetByAddress() call.

```
TInquirySockAddr addr;
TNameEntry entry;
addr.SetIAC(KGIAC);
addr.SetAction(KHostResInquiry);
TRequestStatus status;
hr.GetByAddress(addr, entry, status);
User::WaitForRequest(status);
```

4. On completion, the TNameEntry variable contains the address and the class of the first found device. Subsequent calls to RHost-Resolver::Next() provide the data about other discovered devices until KErrHostResNoMoreResults is returned.

5. In order to retrieve the name of the BT device instead of its address, use the KHostResName flag in the TInquirySockAddr:: SetAction() function. Both flags may be combined with OR operation if you want to know the device name and address simultaneously.

Discussion: Device discovery is usually an asynchronous process, as are many other communication APIs, and therefore it is often suitable to encapsulate it in an active object. Discovery process completion may take a long time, especially if there are many Bluetooth-enabled devices in the surrounding area – hence an active object model provides a convenient way of processing the data for every found device 'just in time'.

Inquiry results are cached, so it may result in 'ghost' devices in the discovered list while the device is no longer in range. This fact does not lead to additional problems, as a particular device may be in- and out-of-range between its discovery and the actual communication session.

You may find more information about protocol-related constants in the `bt_sock.h` header file.

4.9.1.4   Discover Bluetooth Services for a Given Device

Amount of time required: 20 minutes
Location of example code: `\Connectivity\BTDeviceSample\`
`ServiceDiscoverer`
Required library(s): `bluetooth.lib`, `btmanclient.lib`,
`sdpagent.lib`, `sdpdatabase.lib`, `esock.lib`
Required header file(s): `btdevice.h`, `btmanclient.h`, `bt_sock.h`,
`btsdp.h`, `bttypes.h`, `es_sock.h`
Required platform security capability(s): `LocalServices`

Problem: You want to discover the services available for a particular Bluetooth-enabled device.

Solution: After remote Bluetooth devices have been discovered using the Bluetooth Sockets API, the next step is to retrieve the services those devices advertise along with the remote port or channel number which your application will connect to at later stages. The following classes allow you to perform this task:

- `CSdpAgent` – service discovery agent.

- `CSdpSearchPattern` – service discovery search pattern.

- `CSdpAttrIdMatchList` – attribute ID match list.

- `MSdpAgentNotifier` – observer interface to provide callbacks for various queries.

A service search returns the record handles of services that are of a specified class or classes (UUID numbers). You can find exact values in `btsdp.h`. If the search is for more than one UUID, then all the UUID numbers must exist in a service record for it to be considered a match. Service search results are returned through asynchronous callbacks to an `MSdpAgentNotifier` interface, which the caller (that is, your code) must implement in order to be notified about the query completion.

The steps to perform a service search are as follows:

1. Create a `CSdpAgent` object, supplying it with an `MSdpAgent-Notifier` object and the device address of the remote Bluetooth device obtained from the device discovery procedure:

```
CSdpAgent* agent = CSdpAgent::NewLC(aObserver, aDevAddr);
```

2. Create a `CSdpSearchPattern` object to specify the service classes to search for. Classes can be added through `CSdpSearch-Pattern::AddL()` calls:

```
CSdpSearchPattern* list = CSdpSearchPattern::NewL();
list->AddL(KL2CAPUUID);
```

3. Set the search pattern on the agent object:

```
agent->SetRecordFilterL(*list);
```

4. Call `CSdpAgent::NextRecordRequestL()` to get search results until results are exhausted, or sufficient results have been obtained:

```
agent->NextRecordRequestL();
```

The result is returned by a `MSdpAgentNotifier::NextRecord-RequestComplete()` method call.

In addition to the available services list, you usually need to fetch more information about a particular service. This data is contained in service attributes and can be gathered via a similar mechanism as for the services:

```
CSdpAttrIdMatchList* matchList = CSdpAttrIdMatchList::NewL();
CleanupStack::PushL(matchList);
matchList->AddL(KSdpAttrIdProtocolDescriptorList);
agent->AttributeRequestL(serviceHandle, *matchList);
CleanupStack::PopAndDestroy();
```

The result is returned by the `MSdpAgentNotifier::Attribute-RequestResult()` method implemented by the observer.

Discussion: Clients that make service and attribute queries through `CSdp-Agent` must implement the `MSdpAgentNotifier` interface to handle the responses.

All queries are asynchronous, so the interface functions that receive responses are only called when the thread's active scheduler can schedule the handling of the completion of the query.

When a service search request completes, it calls NextRecord-
RequestComplete(). When an attribute request completes, each sin-
gle attribute is returned with its attribute ID using AttributeRequest-
Result(). A schematic example is shown below:

```
void CServiceDiscoverer::AttributeRequestResult(
                        TSdpServRecordHandle /*aHandle*/,
                            TSdpAttributeID /*aAttrID*/,
                                CSdpAttrValue* aAttrValue)
 {
 // process it here
 }
```

The ID of the attribute is given in aAttrID, and the attribute value itself
in aAttrValue parameters. You can find the type of the attribute through
aAttrValue->Type() and cast aAttrValue on this basis to the
correct subclass of CSdpAttrValue; for instance, for ETypeBoolean
you get CSdpAttrValueBoolean.

When there are no more attributes to be returned, the Attribute-
RequestComplete() method is called:

```
void CServiceDiscoverer::AttributeRequestComplete(
                        TSdpServRecordHandle /*aHandle*/,
                                        TInt aError)
 {
 if (aError==KErrNone)
   {
   // done with attributes for this record, request next
   // service record
   TRAPD(err, iAgent->NextRecordRequestL());
   if(err != KErrNone)
     {
     // handle an error here
     }
   }
 else
   {
   // error, should terminate discoverer?
   }
 }
```

4.9.2   Intermediate Recipes

4.9.2.1   Use the Sockets API

Amount of time required: 20 minutes
Location of example code: \Connectivity\IRSocket
Required library(s): bluetooth.lib, btmanclient.lib,
sdpagent.lib, sdpdatabase.lib, esock.lib
Required header file(s):
Required platform security capability(s): LocalServices

Problem: You want to use the Sockets API to transfer data over Bluetooth or IrDA.

Solution: The ESOCK framework can be helpful in many programming tasks which deal with connectivity on Symbian OS – for instance, to discover devices for a number of communication protocols such as IrDA or Bluetooth. In this recipe we will use the Sockets API for data transfers with regard to Infrared and Bluetooth. The whole scenario is pretty much the same as the one you might follow for regular networking, but with a few additional steps for selected protocols.

The first step for both Infrared and Bluetooth transports at client-side is to discover the available devices to communicate with, just as described in previous recipes in this section. The rest is exactly the same as for regular sockets; that is, you should open the socket, define a remote port, connect the client socket to the remote host or bind the server socket to a local address and listen for an incoming connection. If you are developing both client and server applications then you do not need to worry about remote port querying because it will be well known for both parts. In all other cases you will be required to perform service discovery to detect the remote port number. Thus, on the client side, you might write something like the following snippet:

```
TNameEntry log;
TProtocolInfo pInfo;
...
// log and pInfo variables get their values during device resolution
// process, as well as portNo

RSocket sender;
sender.Open(ss,pInfo.iAddrFamily,pInfo.iSockType,pInfo.iProtocol);
log.iAddr.SetPort(portNo);

TRequestStatus stat;
sender.Connect(log.iAddr,stat);
User::WaitForRequest(stat);

TBuf<100> b;
b.FillZ();

sender.Write(b,stat);
User::WaitForRequest(stat);

sender.Read(b,stat);
User::WaitForRequest(stat)
```

At the same time, on the server side you have to code it as:

```
// Open a listener socket for given protocol
RSocket listener;
sock.Open(ss,pInfo.iAddrFamily,pInfo.iSockType,pInfo.iProtocol);
// Set a port number and bind the socket to the local address
```

```
TSockAddr a;
a.SetPort(portNo);
listener.Bind(a);
// Start listening
listener.Listen(1);
// Create data socket
RSocket acceptor;
acceptor.Open(ss); // Create a null socket to hold the connection
// Accept the incoming connection when the request arrives
TRequestStatus stat;
listener.Accept(acceptor,stat);
User::WaitForRequest (stat); // con now holds the connected socket
// Read from connected socket
TBuf<100> b;
b.FillZ();
acceptor.Read(b,stat); // Reading from accepted socket.
User::WaitForRequest (stat);
// Write data back
acceptor.Write(b,stat);
User::WaitForRequest (stat);
```

Discussion: IrDA sockets usually connect to known ports on the remote device. The SDK documentation contains samples for a simple beaming application to illustrate straightforward ways of making IR connections. In more complicated situations your code may employ an IAS query to gather all required information about the remote IR device. You will not do this often unless you have to interface to devices that require it. The code below is just one possible example of an IAS query implementation:

```
void IASQuery(RNetDatabase &aIAS,const TDesC8 &aClassName,
           const TDesC8 &aAttributeName,TUint aRemDevAddr)
//
// Synchronous IAS query. RTimer timeout of 5 seconds on the query.
//
  {
  TBuf<64> res;
  TIASQuery querybuf(aClassName,aAttributeName,aRemDevAddr);
  TRequestStatus stat1,stat2;
  TIASResponse results;

  aIAS.Query(querybuf,results,stat2);
  RTimer tim;
  tim.CreateLocal();
  tim.After(stat1,5000000L);
  User::WaitForRequest(stat1,stat2);

  if (stat1.Int()==KErrNone) // TIMER COMPLETED - IAS QUERY
  {
  // REQUEST HAS TIMED OUT.
  aIAS.Cancel();
  return;
  }

  else if (stat2.Int()==KErrNone) // IAS QUERY COMPLETED OK.
  {
  switch(results.Type())
```

```
      {
   case EIASDataMissing: // Missing
    break;

  case EIASDataInteger: // Integer
   TInt num;
   if (results.GetInteger(num)==KErrNone)
       {
       TinyTPPort=TUint8(num);
       }
   else
       {
       // Bad type
       }
   break;

  case EIASDataOctetSequence: // Byte sequence
   results.GetOctetSeq(res);
   DumpBuf(res);
   break;

  case EIASDataUserString: // String
    res.Copy(results.GetCharString8());
    break;

  default: // Bad type
   break;
   }
  tim.Cancel();
  }

else if (stat2.Int()!=KErrNone) // IAS QUERY COMPLETED UNSUCCESSFULLY.
  {
  switch (stat2.Int())
     {
   case KErrUnknown: // No such attribute
    break;

   case KErrBadName: // No such class
    break;

   default: // Unknown error
    break;
     }
  tim.Cancel();
   }
  else
   {
   tim.Cancel(); // Unknown error on IAS query
   }
};
```

> **What may go wrong when you do this:** If the client application uses the Bluetooth PAN profile for data transfer, the application will need the `NetworkServices` platform security capability in addition to `LocalServices`.

4.9.2.2   Create a Simple OBEX Client

Amount of time required: 20 minutes
Location of example code: \Connectivity\ObexClientApp
Required library(s): irobex.lib, obex.lib
Required header file(s): obex.h, btsdp.h
Required platform security capability(s): LocalServices

Problem: You want to create an OBEX client connection over IrDA or Bluetooth and send an object.

Solution: The CObexClient class handles all that you need to instantiate and set up a simple OBEX client. It allows you to pass the TObexProtocolInfo-derived parameter to the CObexClient::NewL() method, which describes the transport layer you want to use. In this particular case we will use IrDA, so we need to supply TObexIr-ProtocolInfo as described below:

```
_LIT8(KIrdaClassName, "OBEX");
_LIT8(KIrdaTransportAttrName, "IrDA:TinyTP:LsapSel");

// Create transport info
TObexIrProtocolInfo transportInfo;
//assigning the unique name for the irda transport
transportInfo.iTransport = KObexIrTTPProtocol;
//assigning IrDA specific attributes
transportInfo.iClassName = KIrdaClassName;
transportInfo.iAttributeName = KIrdaTransportAttrName;

//create the OBEX client
iClient = CObexClient::NewL(transportInfo);
```

The next step is to establish a connection to the OBEX server, which is as simple as this:

```
_LIT8(KSampleLocalInfo," IrOBEXFile ");

TObexConnectInfo localInfo = iClient->LocalInfo();
localInfo.iWho = KNullDesC8;
iLocalInfo.iWho.Append(KSampleLocalInfo);
// Connect to Obex client
iClient->Connect(iStatus);
```

Once the connection to the OBEX server is established, we can use various OBEX commands. You may also need to set up OBEX objects, which can be done in a few different ways. Please refer to the documentation for more details. In this simple case we just PUT the file to the server (please note that the iFileObject member variable is of CObexFileObject type):

```
TRAPD (err, iFileObject->InitFromFileL (aFilename));
iClient->Put(*iFileObject,iStatus);
```

Finally, the client has to disconnect from the server after all transfers are completed:

```
iClient->Disconnect(iStatus);
```

You can use a Bluetooth connection for OBEX communication pretty much in the same manner as over IrDA. Again, CObexClient handles all you need to instantiate and set up a simple OBEX client. The obvious difference is that you should launch a device and service discovery prior to any connection attempts, and supply appropriate protocol information to the CObexClient::NewL() method. For Bluetooth it will be a TObexBluetoothProtocolInfo structure. The sample code below assumes that we have already performed the device and service discovery, as in a Recipe 4.9.1.4 and have obtained a Bluetooth address for a given remote device:

```
// Create transport info
TObexBluetoothProtocolInfo transportInfo;
// Set Bluetooth address
transportInfo.iAddr.SetBTAddr(devAddr);
// Set the port
transportInfo.iAddr.SetPort(devPort);
// Set transport as RFComm
transportInfo.iTransport = KObexRfcommProtocol;

//create the OBEX client
iClient = CObexClient::NewL(transportInfo);
```

After the OBEX client is created successfully, the rest is just the same as with the IrDA client described earlier in this recipe.

Discussion: IrDA OBEX servers use IAS to publish their service information. To access the default OBEX server, the IAS class value should be OBEX and the IAS attribute name IrDA:TinyTP:LsapSel. If there are other OBEX services available, they have to be registered and the standard IAS discovery procedure should be used by clients to detect them.

Bluetooth OBEX servers also publish their services in the service discovery database, which can be queried using the service discovery protocol (SDP) as you will see later in this set of Recipe 4.9.3.1. You will usually use RFCOMM or L2CAP as Bluetooth transport protocols.

4.9.2.3   Create a Simple OBEX Server over Bluetooth

Amount of time required: 30 minutes
Location of example code: \Connectivity\ObexSrvApp

Required library(s): `bluetooth.lib`, `btmanclient.lib`, `sdpagent.lib`, `sdpdatabase.lib`, `esock.lib`
Required header file(s): `obex.h`, `btsdp.h`, `es_sock.h`
Required platform security capability(s): `LocalServices`

Problem: You want to create a simple OBEX server communicating over Bluetooth.

Solution: In order to implement a basic OBEX Bluetooth server, you have to perform a few steps even before you get to the actual OBEX code. This involves setting up a Bluetooth subsystem ready to listen to incoming connections. This is described below.

1. Create a socket and open it:

```
RSocketServ socketServ;
socketServ.Connect();
RSocket listen;
listen.Open(socketServ, KRFCOMMDesC);
```

2. Set up RFCOMM port number and Bluetooth security settings:

```
TBTSockAddr addr;
addr.SetPort(KRfcommPassiveAutoBind);

TBTServiceSecurity serviceSecurity;
serviceSecurity.SetUid(KUidServiceSDP);
serviceSecurity.SetAuthentication(EFalse);
serviceSecurity.SetEncryption(EFalse);
serviceSecurity.SetAuthorisation(EFalse);
serviceSecurity.SetDenied(EFalse);

addr.SetSecurity(serviceSecurity);
```

3. Set up, create and start OBEX server:

```
TObexBluetoothProtocolInfo info;
info.iAddr.SetPort(listen.LocalPort());
info.iTransport = KObexRfcommProtocol;

CObexServer *server = CObexServer::NewL(info)
User::LeaveIfError(server->Start (this));
```

Discussion: The parameter passed to the server's `Start()` method is a pointer to an implementation of `MObexServerNotify` or `MObex-ServerNotifyAsync` (available only in Symbian OS v9.2 onwards). Typically, you will have an observer class which will be notified at an appropriate stage. Here is the stripped down declaration of this mixin class:

```
class MObexServerNotify
  {
public:
  virtual void ErrorIndication(TInt aError) =0;
  virtual void TransportUpIndication() =0;
  virtual void TransportDownIndication() =0;
  virtual void ObexConnectIndication(
                       const TObexConnectInfo& aRemoteInfo,
                                    const TDesC8& aInfo) =0;
  virtual void ObexDisconnectIndication(const TDesC8& aInfo) =0;
  virtual void PutRequestIndication() =0;
  virtual TInt PutPacketIndication() =0;
  virtual void PutCompleteIndication() =0;
  virtual void GetRequestIndication(
                       CObexBaseObject* aRequiredObject) =0;
  virtual TInt GetPacketIndication() =0;
  virtual void GetCompleteIndication() =0;
  virtual void SetPathIndication(
                       const CObex::TSetPathInfo& aPathInfo,
                                    const TDesC8& aInfo) =0;
  virtual void AbortIndication() =0;
  virtual void CancelIndicationCallback() =0;
  };
```

As you can see, it has dedicated methods for the status of OBEX transport, PUT or GET operation arrivals, and so forth. This is a place where you can handle all these events in terms of UI or other means.

4.9.3 Advanced Recipes

4.9.3.1 Advertise Bluetooth Services

Amount of time required: 30 minutes
Location of example code: \Connectivity\BTDeviceSample\ServiceAdvertiser
Required library(s): bluetooth.lib, btmanclient.lib, sdpagent.lib, sdpdatabase.lib, esock.lib
Required header file(s): btmanclient.h, btdevice.h, bt_sock.h, btsdp.h, bttypes.h, es_sock.h
Required platform security capability(s): LocalServices

Problem: You want to advertise Bluetooth server services.

Solution: After another Bluetooth device has found the listening Bluetooth server, it is necessary to check whether this server actually provides the required services. It would be useless if we connect to a device and then discover that it doesn't even supply the service that we require. The code listed below shows how to add FTP to the service discovery protocol database (refer to the comments within the code for a more detailed explanation).

```
// Assuming  RSdp and RSdpDatabase object have been declared.
// To make use of sdp the developer will need to include btsdp.h
// as a header and sdpdatabase.lib as a library in the MMP file
// Connect to the sdp object
User::LeaveIfError(sdp.Connect());
// Open database passing RSdp object
User::LeaveIfError(sdpdb.Open(sdp));
// Create a record handle
TSdpServRecordHandle ftphandle;
// Create new service, in this case we wish to create a new FTP record,
// the UUIID for FTP is 0x1106, if the developer wish to use another
// they should refer to the Bluetooth specification.
sdpdb.CreateServiceRecordL(TUUID(0x1106), ftphandle);
// Update the attribute of the FTP handle to add a textual description.
// The 0x100 parameter in this function call is of type TSdpAttributeID,
// 0x100 is the attribute ID for the service description
// if the reader wishes to update any other attributes their
// corresponding ID can be found at www.bluetooth.org
sdpdb.UpdateAttributeL(ftphandle, 0x100, _L8("File transfer server"));
// New CSdpAttrValueDES object
protDescList = CSdpAttrValueDES::NewDESL(0);
// Add L2CAP, RFCOMM and OBEX to CSdpAttrValueDES object to be able to
// use those protocols with FTP
protDescList
    ->StartListL()
        ->BuildDESL()
        ->StartListL()
            ->BuildUUIDL(TUUID(TUint16(KL2CAPUUID)))
        ->EndListL()
        ->BuildDESL()
        ->StartListL()
            ->BuildUUIDL(TUUID(TUint16(KRFCommUUID)))
        //set the port to port that RSocket (listen) was bound to
            ->BuildUintL(TSdpIntBuf<TInt8>(listen.LocalPort()))
        ->EndListL()
        ->BuildDESL()
        ->StartListL()
            ->BuildUUIDL(TUUID(TUint16(KObexProtocolUUID)))
        ->EndListL()
    ->EndListL();
// Attribute value of Protocol list
const TInt KProtocolDescList = 4;
// Update database with CSdpAttrValueDES
sdpdb.UpdateAttributeL(ftphandle, KProtocolDescList, *iProtDescList);
delete protDescList;
```

Discussion: The code listed in the solution may look a bit cryptic at first glance, especially the part where an addition of services to the service discovery protocol database is taking place. You can consider this technique in the same manner as stream classes in the Standard Template Library. Every method in a sequence of calls such as StartListL(), BuildDESL() and so forth returns a pointer to the MSdpElement-Builder interface. This process can be conveniently structured as you might see above, so it is easy to follow and maintain at later stages.

4.10 Location-Based Services

Location-based services (LBS) offer the opportunity to extend applications, including, for example:

- location-stamping artefacts such as photographs and notes,

- finding nearby services and facilities,

- navigation,

- route recording.

Location-based services are enabled by the use of global positioning. The global positioning system (GPS) is a global network of at least 24 satellites orbiting Earth 24 hours a day. It provides positioning, navigation and timing (PNT) services for military and civil needs and is available all over the world.

GPS consists of three segments:

- Satellite constellation – the group of satellites that send one-way data signals, containing the satellite location and time.

- Ground control and monitoring network – a number of control stations that provide path correction and other control.

- Consumer GPS receiving equipment – devices that process the information received from the satellites.

GPS relies on retrieving information from at least three satellites, and affords an accuracy of location of approximately 2–10 meters. GPS provides 3D coordinates if there are more than three satellites available, so you can also learn the user's current height. The distance to the satellite is calculated by measuring the signal delivery time delay. A number of Earth stations sending additional data (Differential GPS) can also support GPS.

The accuracy of location can depend on the weather, surrounding buildings and a number of other factors. GPS has some major restrictions, such as limited coverage in urban environments and inside buildings due to the requirement that mobile users be in 'view' of the satellites, and a slow location acquisition time (in the region of 10 to 60 seconds).

On Symbian smartphones, the prime location technology is expected to be integrated assisted GPS (A-GPS). A-GPS systems overcome some of the limitations of GPS position acquisition by using the fixed mobile network infrastructure to reduce acquisition time to less than 5 seconds, and may provide indoor accuracy to within 50 meters. However, as with infrastructure time of arrival (TOA) schemes, multipath interference and the lack of a line of sight measurement can degrade performance, so A-GPS can be less accurate than GPS under certain conditions. For network operators, the main benefit from integration of A-GPS is the ability to charge users for positioning information, because it uses the network infrastructure.

The Symbian OS LBS subsystem allows local and network-based applications to determine the current location of the handset. The subsystem support integrated A-GPS hardware, but there is no specific support for other possible positioning modules (like external Bluetooth GPS devices, for example). The same universal API is used with any available modules such as A-GPS, Bluetooth GPS or network-based A-GPS.

As the primary purpose of having GPS integrated on the phone is to allow the user to be located during an emergency, the architecture supports the handling of network requests in low-memory conditions. This helps to ensure that these requests always succeed.

LBS API available for third-party applications splits into the following main groups:

- location information API

- positioning technology module information API

- positioning technology module selection criteria API.

Let's briefly outline the common terminology and these three API groups. Further information is available in the Symbian Developer Library documentation, found in the SDK or online on the Symbian Developer Network.

The location information API allows you to obtain various positioning information (for instance, latitude and longitude values). Its use is demonstrated in Recipe 4.10.2.1. The API requires a positioning technology module, which refers to the technique used to get the location information. You can retrieve the characteristics of that module using the positioning technology module information API. The LBS subsystem has the default positioning module, which is used to perform location requests. You can either explicitly specify the required module or use the module selection criteria API to specify the criteria the positioning module has to satisfy to be selected during the location request. The LBS subsystem will try to identify all such modules and select the most suitable one.

The following recipes discuss the LBS API and demonstrate how to use it to fulfill different programming tasks. The recipes mention and describe in more detail a number of the various classes you would use during the development. Let us briefly overview them here in order to make the recipes easier to follow.

Client applications use the `RPositionServer` and `RPositioner` classes as part of the location information API to get position updates. `RPositionServer` provides the means to manage a session with the location server and to get positioning technology module information. `RPositioner` manages a subsession with the location server and allows getting position updates. The position information is returned in the set of T classes, like `TPositionInfo`, `TPosition`, and so on. Depending on the positioning module capabilities, extended location information may be returned. This could include information about the course and the satellite, and is provided using an extended set of classes: `TPositionCourseInfo/TCourse` and `TPositionSatelliteInfo/TSatelliteData`. Extended location information is discussed further in Recipe 4.10.2.2.

The positioning technology module information API and the positioning technology module selection criteria API are represented by the set of T classes that describe different aspects of the LBS subsystem. Some of them are listed below:

- `TPositionModuleInfo`

- `TPositionModuleStatus`

- `TPositionModuleStatusEvent`

- `TPositionCriteria`

- `TPositionQuality`

- `TPositionSelectionOrder`.

As you go through the recipes, you will see them in action, to make it clearer how to use them. For detailed information, please refer to the class reference in the Symbian Developer Library documentation (the 'Location Acquisition API' section).

There are various privacy and potential legal issues in being able to determine where someone is. On a mobile device, it is a concern that a user will unwittingly enable other people to discover their whereabouts. It is also an anxiety that a malicious application will transmit its location to a remote party. Appropriate security and privacy mechanisms should be implemented to give the user confidence that their location is secure. The `Location` platform security capability is required by the examples given with these recipes. The user can authorize individual requests to determine the location of the smartphone as they arrive from the network.

Testing
You can test the LBS recipes and your own LBS-related code on either the emulator or on a device. The S60 emulator usually has built-in GPS support, so you can run and debug your code directly in IDE.

For the simple cases, you do not need to do any further configuration. The device manufacturer may provide some GPS simulation tools to allow the developers to test their code in more complicated scenarios. For instance, Nokia has introduced a Positioning Simulation Tool available in the S60 3rd Edition SDK that you can use on the emulator and on the phones without GPS hardware or GPS accessories available. You can find more details about using and configuring this tool on the emulator and the phone under 'Tools Collection for Location-Based Application Development' section of the S60 3rd Edition SDK documentation. A description of the usage of these simulation tools with Nokia's free Remote Device Access service can be found at ***wiki.forum.nokia.com/index.php/Using_positioning_simulation_tool_with_RDA*** and a set of documentation provided by Forum Nokia is available at ***www.forum.nokia.com/main/resources/technologies/location_based_services.html***.

At the time of going to press, UIQ does not provide such support for GPS simulations, but you can reuse any generic Symbian OS LBS code, tested on S60, on the UIQ platform.

4.10.1 Easy Recipes

4.10.1.1 Get the List of Available Positioning Technology Modules

Amount of time required: 20 minutes
Location of example code: \Location
Required library(s): lbs.lib (S60), lbsselflocate.lib (UIQ)
Required header file(s): lbs.h
Required platform security capability(s): Location

Problem: You want to list positioning technology modules available on the handset.

Solution: A positioning technology module is a low-level software component that allows the location server to communicate with the mobile device hardware that obtains position data. When a client application or remote party makes a request for new location information, a module must be used to service the request. The LBS API allows applications to discover the positioning technology modules available to it. Applications can make a choice of the specific positioning technology module to use to get the device's location. This module choice can be made in three ways:

- The client application chooses a particular module to use for location information requests and specifies this choice to the location server passing module ID in the RPositioner::Open() call. This method returns KErrNotFound if the specified module ID does not exist.

This recipe illustrates how to obtain the list of available technology modules.

- The application specifies a set of position quality criteria to the location server passing the appropriate parameter to `RPositioner::Open()`. When the application makes a location information request, the server chooses the module that best satisfies the quality criteria. Position quality criteria are discussed in the next recipe.

- The application does not specify a particular module or any location quality criteria, so the location server uses the default module to obtain the location information, as specified by `RPositionServer::GetDefaultModuleId()`.

The code snippet below demonstrates how to request the list of available modules and filter them according to desired type and capabilities:

```cpp
#include <lbs.h>

TInt GetModuleIdsL(RArray<TPositionModuleId>& aModuleIds,
             TPositionModuleInfo::TTechnologyType aType,
             TPositionModuleInfo::TCapabilities aCaps)
  {
  RPositionServer server;

  TUint numModules;
  TPositionModuleId modId;
  TPositionModuleInfo modInfo;
  TPositionModuleStatus modStatus;

  aModuleIds.Reset();

  // 1. Create a session with the location server
  User::LeaveIfError(server.Connect());
  CleanupClosePushL(server);

  // 2. Get the number of modules installed
  User::LeaveIfError(server.GetNumModules(numModules));

  // 3. Iterate over the modules to get information about
  //    each module
  // 4. Get the availability of a module
  // 5. Get information about the module technology, quality etc.

  for (TUint i=0; i<numModules; i++)
    {
    User::LeaveIfError(
        server.GetModuleInfoByIndex(i, modInfo));

    // Check module technology type and availability
    if ( modInfo.IsAvailable() &&
        (modInfo.TechnologyType() == aType) )
      {// Check module capabilities
      TPositionModuleInfo::TCapabilities caps =
                          modInfo.Capabilities();
```

```
   if (caps & aCaps == aCaps)
     {// Check module position quality
     TPositionQuality quality;
     modInfo.GetPositionQuality(quality);

     // In this example, check for horizontal
     // accuracy better than 10 metres
     if (!Math::IsNaN(quality.HorizontalAccuracy()) &&
                  quality.HorizontalAccuracy() < 10 )
       {// This module has all the required characteristics!
       modId = modInfo.ModuleId();
       aModuleIds.AppendL(modId);
       }
     }
   }
 }

// 6. Close the location server session
CleanupStack::PopAndDestroy(&server);
return aModuleIds.Count();
}
```

4.10.1.2   Retrieve the Current Module Status Information

Amount of time required: 15 minutes
Location of example code: \Location
Required library(s): lbs.lib (S60), lbsselflocate.lib (UIQ)
Required header file(s): lbs.h
Required platform security capability(s): Location

Problem: You want to retrieve the current positioning module status information.

Solution: A positioning module has a status defined in TPositionModuleStatus object. The status describes the low-level state of a module, such as whether it is disabled, initializing or ready to retrieve location data, as well as its data quality status. You can also receive notification when the status changes, as the next recipe demonstrates.

The module status can be obtained by calling TPositionModuleStatusEvent::GetModuleStatus() and providing a TPositionModuleStatus reference as parameter. The latter class has the methods to return device and data quality information, respectively.

The following sample describes how to obtain the current module state information:

```
#include <lbs.h>

TPositionModuleStatus modStatus;

// Assume that the app has established the session with
// the location server and gathered the module Id for which it
```

```
// wants status. Get the module status.
User::LeaveIfError(server.GetModuleStatus(modStatus, modId));

// Use the status
TPositionModuleStatus::TDeviceStatus deviceStatus =
                        modStatus.DeviceStatus();
TPositionModuleStatus::TDataQualityStatus qualityStatus =
                        modStatus.DataQualityStatus();

// Can check the status of the module device - for example
// check for device error
if (deviceStatus == TPositionModuleStatus::EDeviceError)
  {// Device error for this module
  }

// Can check the data quality for the module - for example check for
// loss of data quality
if (qualityStatus == TPositionModuleStatus::EDataQualityLoss)
  {// Loss of quality for this module
  }

// Don't forget to close the location server session!
```

4.10.1.3   Receive Module Status Change Notifications

Amount of time required: 20 minutes
Location of example code: \Location
Required library(s): lbs.lib (S60), lbsselflocate.lib(UIQ)
Required header file(s): lbs.h
Required platform security capability(s): Location

Problem: You want to receive notifications about positioning module status changes.

Solution: A change in module status is indicated by a status event. Details of the event are held in a TPositionModuleStatusEvent object. Client applications can receive notification of status events from the location server.

There are three types of module status events:

• Data quality status events.

• Device status events.

• System-level events, which indicate that a module has been added or removed in the system.

Quality status events are useful for applications that need to modify their behavior based on the quality of location information that can be received. For example, an application may need to show a message when a user moves into an area where the accuracy of location information is degraded to a lower quality than is required because of distance from a base station or inability to receive satellite signals.

Device status events and system module events are most useful to software components that perform administrative operations, such as taking a positioning module online or offline. The events can be used to notify when such an administrative operation is complete.

Device status events can also be used to keep a user informed as to the status of a particular positioning technology module. For example, a phone status bar could be updated to show that GPS is active when location information is being received.

An application calls `RPositionServer::NotifyModule-StatusEvent()` to receive notification of module status changes, passing a reference to a `TPositionModuleStatusEvent` object on which it has set the requested events. An application also supplies a `TRequest-Status` object and optionally a `TPositionModuleId` object if status changes from only one module are required.

When the status of a module changes, the client application is notified. The `TPositionModuleStatusEvent` object that was supplied to the location server now also contains details of the events that have occurred and these are obtained by calling `TPositionModuleStatus-Event::OccurredEvents()`.

The following sections describe the steps to get module status change notifications, as shown in the code example below.

1. Define the types of module status events for which notification is required.
    The client application creates a `TPositionModuleStatusEv-ent` object with a `TPositionModuleStatusEventBase::TMo-duleEvent` variable which defines the status events in which it is interested.

2. Request module status change notifications.
    The client application calls the method `RPositionServer::NotifyModuleStatusEvent()` to make a request for module status change notifications.
    Depending on whether the `TPositionModuleId` parameter is passed to the function, the application is notified of status changes for that given module only or for all modules.
    On completion, the `TPositionModuleStatusEvent` object holds details of the types of events that have occurred.

3. Check the types of status changes that have occurred.
    The `TModuleStatusEvent` object contains both the requested event types and the event types that occurred.

    • The requested event types are accessed by calling `TPosition-ModuleStatusEvent::RequestedEvents()`.

- The event types that have occurred are accessed by calling `TModuleStatusEvent::OccurredEvents()`.

- Both of these methods return bit mask values of type `TPosition-ModuleStatusEventBase::TModuleEvent`.

Partial updates can occur. For example, an application can request notification of both device status and quality status changes and it will receive notification when either one of these occurs. It may be necessary for an application to check the types of events that have occurred.

A client application can only have one outstanding request for module status updates per server session. An attempt to make a second request for location information while one is still outstanding causes a panic. An application must cancel an outstanding request before it makes another request.

The sample code below demonstrates the discussed technique in its simplest form. Production-quality applications do not use `User::Wait()` but use an active object class to receive events, as the sample code to accompany this recipe will illustrate.

```
#include <lbs.h>

// Assume that the app has established the session with
// the location server ('server' variable)

TPositionModuleStatus modStatus;
TPositionModuleStatusEvent modEvents;

// 1. Define the types of status events for which notification is
//    required
TPositionModuleStatusEventBase::TModuleEvent requestedEvents =
         TPositionModuleStatusEventBase::EEventDeviceStatus |
         TPositionModuleStatusEventBase::EEventDataQualityStatus;

modEvents.SetRequestedEvents(requestedEvents);

// 2. Request module status change notifications for all modules
TRequestStatus status;
server.NotifyModuleStatusEvent(modEvents, status);

// Wait for an event to occur.
// Normally, the application should use an active object in
// production code -  this is for simplicity only
User::WaitForRequest(status);

// 3. Check the types of status changes that have occurred
TPositionModuleStatusEventBase::TModuleEvent occurredEvents =
                                 modEvents.OccurredEvents();

// Check the type of event that occurred...
modEvents.GetModuleStatus(modStatus);

TPositionModuleStatus::TDeviceStatus deviceStatus =
```

```
                                modStatus.DeviceStatus();
TPositionModuleStatus::TDataQualityStatus qualityStatus =
                                modStatus.DataQualityStatus();

if (deviceStatus == TPositionModuleStatus::EDeviceError)
  {// Device error for this module
  }

// Can check the data quality for the module
if (qualityStatus == TPositionModuleStatus::EDataQualityLoss)
  {// Loss of quality for this module
  }

// Don't forget to close the location server session!
```

4.10.1.4   Set the Module Selection Criteria

Amount of time required: 20 minutes
Location of example code: \Location
Required library(s): lbs.lib (S60), lbsselflocate.lib(UIQ)
Required header file(s): lbs.h
Required platform security capability(s): Location

Problem: You want to set positioning technology module selection criteria.

Solution: Applications use the TPositionCriteria class to define module selection criteria. Module selection criteria consist of:

• The capabilities required of a module, for example, the ability to provide speed or altitude data. The TPositionModuleInfo class defines all those capabilities.

• The quality of position required from a module, for example, a required horizontal accuracy to within 100 meters and a time to obtain a position of not greater than 30 seconds. The TPositionQuality class defines the quality of the position.

• A relative ranking or ordering of the different quality of position parameters, for example, cost may be more important than accuracy. Class TPositionSelectionOrder defines the relative importance of the different quality values specified in TPositionQuality. The location framework uses ordering to choose between candidate modules that could satisfy a client application's module selection criteria.

An application uses the method RPositioner::Open() to open a subsession with the location server. There are several overloaded Open() methods that an application can use to open the subsession, one of which allows a TPositionCriteria object to be passed to the location server. If the application passes a `TPositionCriteria` object in `RPositioner::Open()`, the LBS framework:

- chooses the positioning module with the capabilities that best match those specified in `TPositionCriteriaBase::Required-Capabilities()`. The chosen module is used to obtain location updates for location requests made on the open client–server subsession.

- uses the position accuracy and timeout values specified in `TPositionCriteriaBase::TPositionQuality()` when the client makes `RPositioner::NotifyPositionUpdate()` location requests.

A client application does not have to supply module selection criteria when it calls `RPositioner::Open()`. If no criteria are specified then a set of default criteria are used in which horizontal position (latitude and longitude) is the only required module capability. The handset manufacturer or Symbian OS licensee may provide its own quality profile to be taken by default.

If no criteria are given, the LBS APIs use default criteria that specify a horizontal accuracy of 50 meters, a vertical accuracy of 1,000 meters and a timeout of 30 seconds. The priority ranks accuracy first followed by least cost.

The following sample demonstrates how to deal with various criteria classes in order to define certain requirements for positioning module. It is quite simple and can be used in conjunction with the recipe, which describes how to get position information:

```
#include <lbs.h>

RPositionServer server;
RPositioner positioner;

// Create a session with the location server
User::LeaveIfError(server.Connect());
CleanupClosePushL(server);

// Define module selection criteria
TPositionCriteria criteria;
TPositionQuality quality;
TPositionSelectionOrder order;

// Set required capabilities - want altitude information...
criteria.AddRequiredCapabilities(
        TPositionModuleInfo::ECapabilityVertical);

// Set quality - want vertical position within 100m
quality.SetVerticalAccuracy(100);

// Set ordering - make vertical accuracy a high priority
```

```
User::LeaveIfError(
order.SetOrderVerticalAccuracy(TPositionSelectionOrder::EOrderHigh));

criteria.SetRequiredQuality(quality);
criteria.SetSelectionOrder(order);

// Pass it to the Open() method
User::LeaveIfError(positioner.Open(server, criteria));
CleanupClosePushL(positioner);
...
// Close the subsession and session
CleanupStack::PopAndDestroy(2, &server); // positioner, server
```

4.10.2 Intermediate Recipes

4.10.2.1 Request Location Information

Amount of time required: 40 minutes
Location of example code: \Location
Required library(s): lbs.lib (S60), lbsselflocate.lib(UIQ)
Required header file(s): lbs.h
Required platform security capability(s): Location

Problem: You want to obtain location information.

Solution: Client applications use the RPositionServer and RPositioner classes to get position updates. RPositionServer is used by client applications to manage a session with the location server and to get positioning technology module information. RPositioner is used by client applications to manage a subsession with the location server and to get position updates.

For each location request from a client, the LBS subsystem can operate in one of several different positioning modes. The Location Acquisition API hides most of the details of which positioning mode is in use from client applications. A client makes the same sequence of calls to the API to get a position update whichever positioning mode is used. Each mode is a different way of getting a position fix:

- *Autonomous*
  LBS uses a GPS positioning module to calculate position fixes without assistance data from the network. This mode typically takes the longest time to obtain a location fix compared with the other modes.

- *Terminal-Based Positioning*
  LBS uses an A-GPS positioning module to calculate position fixes using assistance data from the network. Assistance data specifies the GPS satellites that are above the horizon as seen from the mobile device's

current location. Assistance data is used by an A-GPS positioning module to reduce the time necessary to obtain a position fix.

The network can also supply a reference position to the LBS subsystem as part of the sequence of events. This position is calculated in the network using cell-based techniques and may be less accurate than that obtained from GPS. A reference position may be returned to the client before a GPS position. See Location Acquisition API runtime behavior for more information about the position updates that can be returned by LBS.

- *Terminal-Assisted Positioning*

  LBS uses an A-GPS positioning module to obtain GPS measurements (using assistance data from the network). GPS measurements are the raw data used to calculate a GPS fix. Measurements are sent to the network and a position fix is calculated by a remote server. The remotely calculated position fix is returned to the mobile device and is known as the final network position. The LBS subsystem returns this position to the client.

- *Hybrid Positioning*

  This mode is a combination of Terminal-Based Positioning and Terminal-Assisted Positioning.

  LBS passes GPS measurements to the network (as in Terminal-Assisted Mode), but also attempts to use those measurements to calculate a GPS position fix (as in Terminal-Based Mode). The position returned to the client may be either a GPS position (calculated in the mobile device) or a final network position (calculated using the measurements by a remote server in the network). The position that is calculated first (the GPS position or the final network position) is generally returned to the client. The final network position may also be returned to the client after the return of the GPS position.

- *Cell-Based Positioning*

  LBS obtains a position fix from the network without using GPS. This position fix is sometimes less accurate than that obtained using GPS.

A client application cannot directly choose the positioning mode that is used for its location request. A handset manufacturer may provide an LBS 'control panel' type of application where the GPS mode can be selected by an end user. However, for modes that involve the network (Terminal-Based Positioning, Terminal-Assisted Positioning, Hybrid and Cell-Based Positioning), it is possible for a network operator to override the GPS mode as part of the location request. If a client wants to know precisely how a position fix was calculated, this information is available in the returned position information object.

A typical scenario might be as follows:

- Create a session with the location server (LS).

- Create a subsession with the LS using default positioning module.

- Set required update options.

- Issue a location information request.

- Get requested data in TPositionInfo variable or handle possible errors.

- Close the subsession and the session.

The code sample below implements this scenario for the simplest case. A production-quality application will not use User::Wait() to receive an asynchronous notification, but uses an active object to handle events.

```
#include <lbs.h>

TInt GetPositionInfoL(TPosition& aPos)
  {
  RPositionServer server;
  RPositioner positioner;

  // 1. Create a session with the location server
  User::LeaveIfError(server.Connect());
  CleanupClosePushL(server);

  // 2. Create a subsession using the default positioning module
  User::LeaveIfError(positioner.Open(server));
  CleanupClosePushL(positioner);

  // 3. Set update options
  TPositionUpdateOptions puo;
  // Update the position every 30 sec
  puo.SetUpdateInterval(30000000);
  // Set update request timeout to 15 seconds
  puo.SetUpdateTimeOut(15000000);
  // Set the options
  positioner.SetUpdateOptions(puo);

  // 4. Request location information
  // Could also call positioner.GetLastKnownPosition(posInfo, status)
  // to get cached location information

  // Set position requestor
  _LIT(KRequestor,"Location Sample Application");
  TInt err =
        positionerEx.SetRequestor( CRequestor::ERequestorService,
        CRequestor::EFormatApplication, KRequestor );

  TPositionInfo posInfo;
  TRequestStatus status;
  positioner.NotifyPositionUpdate(posInfo, status);
```

```
// Wait on an event (in production code, you should
// use an active object)
User::WaitForRequest(status);

// 5. Receive location information
if (status.Int() != KErrNone)
    {
    // Handle possible client-server errors
    CleanupStack::PopAndDestroy(2, &server); // positioner, server
    return status.Int();
    }

// Get the position data object from the wrapper info object
posInfo.GetPosition(aPos);

// Later on, use the obtained position information, e.g. calling
// aPos.Latitude() etc. methods

// 6. Close the subsession and session
CleanupStack::PopAndDestroy(2, &server);
}
```

Various LBS classes hold position information as 32- and 64-bit real numbers for most of the cases unless stated otherwise. The standard measurement units are as follows:

- Latitude and longitude are held in 64-bit real numbers. Altitude is held in a 32-bit real number. By default, the WGS-84 datum is used to reference coordinates. All positions returned by the location server use this coordinate reference system. Latitude values are in the range $[-90, +90]$ ($-90 <=$ latitude $<= +90$), whereas longitude values are in the range $[-180, +180)$ ($-180 <=$ longitude $< +180$).

- Both horizontal and vertical accuracy are held in 32-bit real numbers that represent the error offset in meters. In practice, the actual position lies within the respective accuracy circle with 68 % probability.

- Bearings and headings are held in 32-bit real numbers and represent the direction in degrees from the true north. Their corresponding accuracies are also held in 32-bit real numbers and represented in degrees.

If you need to convert those values to the regular string representation, for instance, in the ±DDD'MM?SS.SSS form, the following long (but simple) function gives you some idea of how to do it:

```
void GetDegreesString(const TReal64& aDegrees,
                      TBuf<16>& aDegreesString)
  {
  const TReal KSecondsInMinute = 60.0;
  const TInt KNumWidth = 3;
```

```
// Degrees sign delimeter used in formatting methods
_LIT(KDelimDegree,"\xb0"); // "°" symbol
// Dot delimeter used in formatting methods
_LIT(KDelimDot,"\x2e"); // "." symbol
// Plus sign delimeter used in formatting methods
_LIT(KDelimPlus,"\x2b"); // "+" symbol
// Minus sign delimeter used in formatting methods
_LIT(KDelimMinus,"\x2d"); // "-" symbol
// Quotation sign delimeter used in formatting methods
_LIT(KDelimQuot,"\x22"); // "" symbol
// Apostrophe sign delimeter used in formatting methods
_LIT(KApostrophe,"\x27"); // "'" symbol
// Not-a-number string
_LIT(KNan,"NaN");


TReal64 realTmp = 0;


// Check if aDegree is a proper number and exit otherwise
if ( Math::IsNaN(aDegrees) )
  {
  aDegreesString = KNan;
  return;
  }


// Integer part of the degrees
TInt intDegrees = 0;
if ( Math::Int(realTmp,aDegrees) == KErrNone )
   {intDegrees = (TInt)realTmp;}
// Positive float of the degrees
TReal64 realDegrees = aDegrees;


// Convert to positive values
if ( intDegrees < 0 )
  {
  intDegrees = -intDegrees;
  realDegrees = -realDegrees;
  }


// Minutes
TReal64 realMinutes = 0;
if ( Math::Frac(realMinutes,realDegrees) == KErrNone )
{
realMinutes *= KSecondsInMinute;
}
else
{
realMinutes = (realDegrees - intDegrees) * KSecondsInMinute;
}


// Integer part of the minutes
TInt intMinutes = 0;
if ( Math::Int(realTmp,realMinutes) == KErrNone )
{intMinutes = (TInt)realTmp;}
// Seconds
TReal64 realSeconds = 0;
if ( Math::Frac(realSeconds,realMinutes) == KErrNone )
{
realSeconds *= KSecondsInMinute;
```

```
}
  else
{
realSeconds = (realMinutes - intMinutes) * KSecondsInMinute;
}

TInt intSeconds = 0;
if ( Math::Int(realTmp,realSeconds) == KErrNone )
{intSeconds = (TInt)realTmp;}
// Check the sign of the result
if ( aDegrees >= 0 )
{
aDegreesString.Append(KDelimPlus);
}
else
{
aDegreesString.Append(KDelimMinus);
}

// Add the degrees
TInt64 value = intDegrees;
aDegreesString.AppendNum(value);

// Add the separator
aDegreesString.Append(KDelimDegree);

// Add the minutes
value = intMinutes;
aDegreesString.AppendNum(value);

// Add the separator
aDegreesString.Append(KApostrophe);

// Add the seconds
value = intSeconds;
aDegreesString.AppendNum(value);

// Add the separator
aDegreesString.Append(KDelimQuot);

// Add the separator
aDegreesString.Append(KDelimDot);

// Get six last digits
realSeconds -= intSeconds;
realSeconds *= 1000;

// Add the seconds
aDegreesString.AppendNumFixedWidth(static_cast<TInt>(realSeconds),
                                   EDecimal, KNumWidth);
}
```

4.10.2.2 Request Extended Location Information

Amount of time required: 30 minutes
Location of example code: \Location
Required library(s): lbs.lib (S60), lbsselflocate.lib(UIQ)

Required header file(s): `lbs.h`
Required platform security capability(s): `Location`

Problem: You want to obtain extended location information.

Solution: In addition to the general position classes, there are two other position classes: `TPositionCourseInfo` and `TPositionSatelliteInfo`. The latter class inherits from the former.

`TPositionCourseInfo` incorporates a `TCourse` object, which provides information about the current speed at which the device is moving, the device's direction in terms of bearing, and also the accuracy of these parameters.

In turn, `TPositionSatelliteInfo` contains information about the satellites used in locating: how many satellites are available, which of those were used to produce the current estimate, and a list of the satellites with their data. The `TSatelliteData` class represents a satellite.

A client gets the information by sending the appropriate `TPositionInfo` object to the location server via `NotifyPositionUpdate()`. If the currently used positioning module supports the requested data, it fills the object with the data and returns it to the client. Since all such classes should inherit from `TPositionInfo`, the client gets the extended information simultaneously with the general data in one request. However, you have to be careful and verify that the current module supports the particular position information class before issuing a request, otherwise it will fail.

As the code snippet is much the same as for the previous recipe, let us just mention here how to ensure that the given positioning module supports the required capabilities. You can verify the data from the positioning module information or apply appropriate selection criteria when you open the subsession to `RPositioner`. The latter case is illustrated below:

```
#include <lbs.h>

void SetCriteriaL(TPositionCriteria& aCriteria)
  {
  // Set required capabilities for satellite and course info...
  aCriteria.AddRequiredCapabilities(
              TPositionModuleInfo:: ECapabilitySatellite |
              TPositionModuleInfo:: ECapabilitySpeed |
              TPositionModuleInfo:: ECapabilityDirection);

  // Later on you can use RPositioner::Open(server, criteria)
  // to allow selecting suitable module
  }
```

When the `NotifyPositionUpdate()` request is completed successfully, the position information structure is filled in by requested information. For example, if the `TPositionSatelliteInfo` object was passed to the request, you can enumerate available satellites and request the `TSatelliteData` object by calling the `GetSatellite-Data()` method:

```
void SatelliteInfoL()
  {
  TPositionSatelliteInfo satInfo;
  . . .
  // Assume that the location info request was issued
  // and completed successfully
  . . .
  // Now we can iterate through all detected satellites and
  // get some additional info
  TInt numSatellites = satInfo.NumSatellitesInView();
  TInt err = KErrNone;
  for (int i = 0; i < numSatellites; i++)
    {// Get the satellite data
    TSatelliteData satData;
    err = satInfo.GetSatelliteData(i,satData);
    if ( err != KErrNone )
      {
      continue;
      }

    // Get some info
    TReal32 azimuth = satData.Azimuth();
    TInt satSignalStrength = satData.SignalStrength();
    }

  // Now get the course info
  TCourse course;
  satInfo.GetCourse(course);
  TReal32 heading = course.Heading();
  TReal32 speed = course.Speed();
  }
```

The location acquisition API can be extended by defining new positioning data classes by deriving new classes from `TPositionInfoBase` or any of its descendants, such as the `HPositionGenericInfo` class found in S60. This has to be supported by an appropriate positioning module.

5

Next Level Development

This chapter gives you a glimpse of some advanced features of Symbian OS. If you want to take full advantage of these features, you will probably need to use some additional resources, such as the Symbian Developer Library, Symbian Press books or technical papers available on Symbian C++ developer community websites.

5.1 Advanced Technologies

5.1.1 Publish and Subscribe: System-wide Properties

You can find a full introduction to the Publish and Subscribe API at **developer.symbian.com/main/downloads/papers/publishandsubscribe/ PublishAndSubscribe_v1.0.pdf.**

The Publish and Subscribe API in Symbian OS is basically a kernel-side hashtable that can only contain one value per key. The key of the hashtable should be a UID that you allocated. The value of the hashtable is a `TInt` or a `TDesC` (binary data or text, limited to 512 bytes).

Your code accesses the hashtable through the `RProperty` class. The API is fairly basic: add/remove key, get/set value. You can also receive notification if a value changes using `RProperty::Subscribe()`, which is an asynchronous request. Only one such request is allowed per `RProperty` instance at any given time.

Each property belongs to a category, identified by yet another UID. The category UID defaults to the secure identifier of the current process. It can be useful to you as a developer to have a look at all the properties in the `KUidSystemCategoryValue` category.

The main issue with the system category is to find all the property keys that belong to it. They are scattered across many technologies, like Bluetooth, Backup and Restore and the Software Installer. Looking for `KUidXyzPropertyKey` or `KPropertyKeyXyz` in `...\epoc32\ include\` is a good first step. When looking into the documentation for a specific technology, be on the lookout for public property keys, and search the developer forums.

Read and write access to properties is controlled through security policies based on the secure ID for the process, the application's Vendor ID and platform security capabilities, using the `TSecurityPolicy` class. For other data-sharing mechanisms used on Symbian OS, such as message queues, the central repository or DBMS, you should also consult the Data Sharing Tips booklet published at *developer.symbian.com/booklets*.

5.1.2 Creating a Server Process: File Sharing

Most developers know that not all executables need a graphical user interface (GUI). In Symbian OS, you can develop a program designed to run in the background, with no GUI and accessible by other applications via Inter Process Communication (IPC). You have had occasion to use several such server processes already: the window server, the font and bitmap server and the file server, to name a few.

If all you want to do is monitor the state of another process, you can use the `RProcess` class. It allows you to launch a new process, react to a process terminating or rendezvous with another process. What is more useful is to be able to create your own server process so that several other applications can use it at the same time.

The example we have chosen to demonstrate is very important because of the data caging feature of platform security in Symbian OS. You will find that you may want some files that are private to your server process to be shared only with the applications using this server process. Developing your own simple file server is a common solution to this problem.

The source code for this example is in `\Advanced\FileSharing Server` and `\Advanced\FileSharingClient`.

The following `RFile` member methods support file handle sharing between processes:

- `RFile::TransferToClient()`
- `RFile::AdoptFromClient()`
- `RFile::TransferToServer()`
- `RFile::AdoptFromServer()`
- `RFile::TransferToProcess()`
- `RFile::AdoptFromCreator()`.

The `TranferToXyz()` methods are used to transfer the file handle to another process, which includes another server or client. The `Adopt`

`FromXyz()` methods are used to read the file handle that is shared by another process.

The example shows how to transfer a handle that allow access to a text file, from the data cage of the process that owns it, `FileSharingServer.exe`, to another process, `FileSharingClient.exe`.

The main classes that are always used when implementing a server are `CServer2`, `CSession2`, `RMessage2`, `TSecurityPolicy` and `CPolicyServer` on the server side and `RSessionBase` and `TIpcArgs` on the client side. In most cases, it is useful to define a subclass of `RSubSessionBase`.

You should definitely have a look at the IPC examples in your SDK and consult the transient server example template code available from the Symbian Developer Network (***developer.symbian.com/main/oslibrary/cpp_papers/advanced.jsp***).

Since we are talking about starting an active scheduler from scratch in your own process, you cannot use the Symbian OS application framework and you will instead need to start with an `E32Main()` method. Create a `CActiveScheduler`, install it, create your `CServer2` object, add it to the active scheduler, start it, then start the active scheduler. The example code illustrates how to do this.

`RMessage2` encapsulates a single IPC request. IPC requests can be synchronous, but the asynchronous version is usually preferred. `TIpcArgs` is used to create and populate the IPC request. An IPC request is triggered from the client side by a call to `RSessionBase::SendReceive()`.

Since `TIpcArgs` can only contain integers, you will need to use pointers when sending buffers across processes. The `RMessage2::ReadL()` methods allow you to make a server-side copy of client-side descriptors. The `RMessage2::WriteL()` methods allow you to send data back to the client process.

The important thing to realize about `CServer2` is that it is actually an active object. The main particularity is that you should not overwrite its `RunL()`, `DoCancel()` or `RunError()` methods, but instead define your own `CSession2::ServiceL()` method where the IPC request will be processed.

When the server-side processing is complete, the server needs to notify the client side with `RMessage2::Complete()`, which has a similar effect as `User::RequestComplete()` but over IPC.

Error handling and multi-threading inside your own process can help you restart the server, but you need to realize that a system panic will be fatal.

5.1.3 Advanced Platform-Specific User Interface

Both the S60 and UIQ platforms have their own set of publicly available controls that can be used in the GUI of your application.

S60 3rd Edition

- On S60 3rd Edition, you can access full-featured GUI controls and dialogs for the contact application using all the CPbkXyz, TPbkXyz and MPbkXyz classes. We recommend particularly CPbkContactE-ditorDlg and the subclasses of CPbkAddressSelect, as those are the ones you are most likely to want to use.

- You can make the handset vibrate using the CHWRMVibra class.

- You can give the user access to the handset time and date using CClkDateTimeView.

- You can embed the view of a remote web page using CBrCtl Interface.

- You can modify the way predictive input works in your text fields by using the Predictive Input Engine API: CPtiEngine.

- You can lock the phone's keypad with RAknKeyLock.

- You can let the user manipulate files using AknCommonDialogs.

We recommend that you read all the S60 Platform Avkon UI Resources documents that you will find on the Forum Nokia website at ***www.forum.nokia.com***.

UIQ 3

The application management in UIQ 3 is fairly unusual and that has an impact on user interface development.

If the 'back' command is going to work properly, the system has to not only consider applications but also each of these applications' single view separately. The framework that allows view-based GUI switches is called Dynamic Navigation Links (DNL).

There is a very nice side-effect to this. When a third-party application implements a self-contained functionality in a single view and makes that view available to DNL (like most applications preloaded on your handset), you can use it from your own code – very much like a simple method call – and benefit from the functionality, including its full-fledged GUI. CCoeAppUi::ActivateViewL() is the main method used for DNL.

With DNL, letting the user look at his scheduled meetings is simplicity itself thanks to the TAgnDnlXyz classes, manipulating contacts can easily be achieved thanks to the TCntDnlXyz classes and messaging functionality comes from the TQMappDnlXyz classes.

The UIQ platform also provides you with simple controls and dialogs that you can reuse: CQBTUISelectDialog lets the user select Bluetooth devices, `CQikCameraCaptureDlg` allows the user to take a picture and `CContactUiFindDialog` is pretty self-explanatory by now.

You can let the user select a date with `CEikCalendar` but you will probably prefer `CQikDateEditor`. You can refine this with `CQik DurationEditor` or `CQikTimeEditor`.

`CQikBuildingBlock` will help you with the layout of the screen.

`CQikColorSelector` will be most useful when the user has to draw something or to allow visual customization.

File manipulation is usually helped by `CQikSelectFileDlg`, `CQik SelectForlderDlg`, `CQikCopyFilesAndFoldersDlg`, `CQikMove FilesAndFoldersDlg` and `CQikRenameFileorfolderDlg`.

Some advanced drawing primitives are defined in the `QikDrawUtils` class.

Some even more advanced and animated GUI components can even be used, like `RQikdigitalClock`.

We recommend that you read the 'Programmer's guide to new features in UIQ 3' that you will find in the UIQ documentation, and that you take a look at *UIQ 3: The Complete Guide* at ***books.uiq.com***.

5.1.4   Advanced Messaging: A New Protocol

Symbian OS defines the concept of Message Type Module (MTM). An MTM plug-in is a set of binaries that extend the messaging features of a handset, with the help of the Messaging Store and the Messaging Server. An MTM can be used for several purposes: bypassing the handset messaging application (and writing your own), synching your corporate messages with your handset, creating your own messaging protocol (i.e., to send messages to a social networking system), and so on.

An MTM is composed of a minimum of four libraries:

- a client DLL

- a client UI DLL

- a client UI data DLL

- a server DLL.

Each DLL has a specific UID that indicates which part of an MTM it is. In addition, you will need to allocate another UID for each DLL and an extra UID for the new MTM as a whole.

The server DLL, as its name indicates, is only loaded by the messaging server.

The three client-side DLLs should be available to all messaging-related applications, not just any applications you would write.

The MTM server DLL that you will develop needs to be able to listen for incoming messages via the networking or telephony APIs. A new message event can also simply be triggered by a message being moved to the Inbox folder.

The MTM client DLL needs to translate basic messaging operations into the correct binary format for the messaging protocol. For example, a recipient address would have a different format for email than for SMS.

The MTM client UI DLL mirrors the MTM server DLL a lot. This is where the messaging application forwards user requests like moving messages between folders.

The MTM client UI data DLL is the interface with the messaging browser on your handset. This means checking how messages can be transferred from one MTM to another and customizing the look of the messaging browser with your own icons.

What you cannot change right now, on any platform, is the way the message index browser (the application that shows you the different messaging services and folders) handles folders and messaging account entries. The messaging browser will display the icons you want it to and it will launch your messaging application, but you may not be able to force it to display your MTM's Inbox as a special item, for example.

The message browser could be the same actual binary as the default messaging application on your handset. However, this won't prevent you from developing your own messaging application. The handset just needs something to act as a messaging browser, capable of handling messaging database entries regardless of the MTM to which they 'belong'.

Similarly, the default messaging application on your handset could be able to handle SMS, MMS and email messages even though these services would typically be implemented as three different MTMs since the binary formats and networking protocols are so wildly different.

When writing a new messaging application, you should make full use of the GUI controls, views and dialogs already available in your platform, including the ones discussed in Section 5.1.3 as they allow you to simplify the logic behind adding recipients to a message or scheduling meetings.

Developing a new messaging application is anticipated to get easier from Symbian OS v9.3 on S60 as the main messaging application becomes more customizable.

You should also expect any messaging application you develop to need engine-level (as opposed to GUI) changes when running on different platforms. The basic structure of folders and accounts under a service entry is different in S60 and UIQ. You will need to experiment for a little while.

Finally, simply installing DLLs from a SIS file is not enough for a new MTM to become available to the entire operating system. You also need to use the `CMtmRegistryControl` API. See Section 5.3.2 for how to do this at install-time.

It is technically possible to develop an MTM without becoming a Symbian partner and procuring a DevKit, but we don't recommend it. In fact, some experts regard MTMs as the single most difficult Symbian OS C++ development endeavor, but the select few who have seen it through to completion don't regret it. (That last part was an outright lie.)

If you plan on attempting to develop a new MTM with extended functionality, we recommend that you read chapters 8 and 9 of Iain Campbell's *Symbian OS Communications Programming*, 2nd Edition from Symbian Press (***developer.symbian.com/commsbook***).

5.2 Symbian Partners Only

Several advanced features cannot be properly implemented without becoming a Symbian Partner, which will cost you money but gives access to more development resources (plus some additional benefits, which are described in Chapter 6, Section 6.3.2). The technical paper *What Symbian development kit do I need* is also a useful place to find more information, and is available at ***www.symbian.com/symbianos/whitepapers/whitepaperscasestudies.html***.

5.2.1 File Server Plug-in: Separate File System

By now, you already know that file access operations are centralized in the system's File Server process. Symbian OS allows you to create plug-ins for this file server to overwrite default behaviors. This feature is commonly used to protect parts of the file system through encryption, in case the handset is lost or stolen, but could also be useful for RAID data duplication or networked storage, and so on.

As you can easily imagine, you will require a high level of platform security capability to distribute something that is potentially dangerous. Chapter 6 can help you with that.

The first class to look at if you want to develop a file server plug-in is `CBaseExtProxyDrive`.

5.2.2 Advanced Multimedia: Additional Format Streaming

As you have seen from the recipes in Section 4.7, your handset has a fairly wide range of multimedia functionality. You can probably play and record both audio and video. Just as importantly, the media data you want to access doesn't need to be on your phone, since the media framework is able to use a simple URL as input and play what it points to pretty much just as if it were on your phone – as long as you have the right to access it.

Symbian OS contains a modular Multimedia Framework system that allows you to develop controller plug-ins that can extend those multimedia capabilities. Controller plug-ins can be used to support more media file formats and/or more networking protocols, although the emphasis in the system is that one controller plug-in should, if at all possible, support all the networking protocols that allow access to a particular set of media types.

By default, remote access to media data should be streamed (as opposed to downloaded) by a controller plug-in.

The first classes to look at if you want to develop a Multimedia Framework controller plug-in are `CMMFController`, `CMMFAudio Output`, `CMMFUrlSource`, `CMMFFormatDecode`, `MDataSink` and `MDataSource`.

The most well-known and advanced set of source code for a Multimedia Framework controller plug-in can be found at ***www.helixcommunity. org***.

5.3   Advanced Application Deployment

5.3.1   Automatic Installation

This is an interesting trick that can greatly benefit a commercial-grade application.

Normally, when you select a SIS file and choose to install the application it deploys, the installation process leaves a small stub file in the private data-caged folder of the application, saving it on the memory card. You can exploit this knowledge to enable automatic installation.

If you save the SIS file for your application in its private data-caged folder on a clean memory card, application installation will be automatically initiated when the card is put into a device which has not had the application previously installed. The installation is not silent, but it does not require the user to navigate to the SIS file and start it manually. The original SIS file is left on the memory card, no stub SIS file is created, which is a potential waste of disk space, depending on the size of the file.

This approach only works if the application was never previously installed on the handset. From a commercial standpoint, it allows you to distribute your application on a memory card, facilitating an extra distribution channel.

5.3.2   Custom Install

As we've seen from the examples that accompany this book, applications are deployed to the device through SIS files, which are generated by packaging application binaries according to the instructions in a human-readable PKG file. The PKG file can be modified to include binaries that will be executed at install-time. In the case of a set of binaries that require some additional setup, you can structure your PKG file in the following order:

- A cleanup executable, run at uninstall-time only and blocking (options `",FR,RR,RW"`).

- Your binaries.

- A setup executable, run at install only and non-blocking (options `",FR,RI"`).

The options would be added at the end of the line for the binary in the PKG file.

There are many useful features to the PKG file format, like conditional selection of binaries, language selection (so you can deploy the same SIS to several countries without wasting memory on the handsets), displaying information dialogs to the user at install-time, and so on.

The Symbian Developer Library supplies documentation and examples of how to use PKG files. Take a look at the Software Installation Toolkit in the Symbian OS Tools and Utilities section for more information.

5.3.3 Embedded Binaries

You can package a SIS file within another SIS file, just like any other binary. What this does is effectively embed the SIS file within the enclosing SIS file. At installation time, when the instruction to install the embedded SIS file is reached, the installation of other files within the enclosing SIS file is automatically interrupted in order to install the embedded SIS.

At first sight, this doesn't really seem like a particularly important feature. One could ask, why not copy-and-paste the content of the smaller PKG file into the bigger one? Use cases become more obvious when considering inter-company development, allowing one company to redistribute another company's binaries. The approach can also be used to sign reusable libraries, for example, to give them additional platform security capabilities.

6

Releasing Your Application

This chapter describes some of the common issues that you may face when you come to release your application. Regardless of whether you intend to charge for your application, release it as freeware or start an open source project, there are some issues that you may wish to consider in order to ensure that it is of the best possible quality. Having discussed those issues, we then move on to describe some of the ways to distribute your application, and finish by directing you to some further resources that may be helpful throughout the software development lifecycle.

6.1 What To Do Before You Release Your Application

As with all platforms, there are good C++ applications for Symbian smartphones, and there are others that are not so good. It is not just about how the application looks, but also about how the code performs under the hood. There's a lot you can do to make sure your application is not just 'good enough', but is of great quality. This section discusses some things to consider.

6.1.1 Look At It!

When you create an application, you have two choices:

- You can use the controls provided by the platform UI, and integrate with the standard look and feel.

- You can create your own UI code, perhaps because you want to retain the look and feel of the application as it runs on another platform (this is a standard technique used by games). The size of this task can be significant if you need a number of controls for different kinds of user interaction, such as list boxes, dialogs and progress bars. Creating a custom UI may require the use of direct screen access to write to the screen, which is discussed in Recipe 4.5.3.5.

Most application developers take the first option, which is to use the UI controls provided by Avkon (for S60) or Qikon (for UIQ), so it is this approach that we examine in this section.

If you are planning to use the standard platform look and feel, we recommend that you familiarize yourself with documentation about how to use the UI classes provided by the platform, which is available on the developer community websites listed in Section 1.2. For UIQ development, the book *UIQ 3: The Complete Guide* is another useful resource, and is available in printed form and online in the form of a wiki at ***books.uiq.com***.

Both S60 and UIQ publish style guides that describe the best practice for designing an intuitive UI using the standard platform controls. Links to these guides can be found on this book's wiki page at ***developer. symbian.com/quickrecipesbook***.

Studying these is an excellent way to familiarize yourself with what is in the 'control toolbox' for each UI platform and learn how they are expected to be used, since they have been created and considered by the designers of each UI platform. Following the guidelines will give your application a degree of consistency with others running on the smartphone and make it intuitive, which will give the user confidence that they are able to use it easily.

It is also worthwhile studying the layout of the applications supplied on the phone, and the behavior of other popular products. The user experience is, to some extent, subjective, so it is also important to gather empirical evidence by performing usability testing on your application. Get user feedback on the design – from users who are new to the application, and those who have used it for some time, those who have never used that type of application previously and those who are experienced with a competing product, or a similar style of application. Your testers will be able to give you the best feedback on what 'feels right' and what doesn't.

The user interface of a mobile device is significantly different to that of a desktop machine and, if you're new to S60 or UIQ, it's worth taking some time to research what works, according to the platform and the input style of the target devices (for example, whether it has a touchscreen or uses softkey input, whether it has a keypad or a QWERTY keyboard, the style of input controller, if it has one, and the screen's orientation, size and resolution).

If you are targeting a range of devices, or working on both UI platforms, your design is constrained further, and testing becomes more complex. The Windows emulator is useful for preliminary testing, and can be set up with different screen resolutions, orientations and input modes, so you can 'smoke test' layouts and determine how the application works when deployed on different form factors. For UIQ 3 applications, make sure that you try out all the different screen layouts and input types. For example, you should not assume that the phone will have a 4-way controller (for up, down, left and right) because some phones, such as the Sony Ericsson M600i, do not. To assist you in this, you may find it useful to download some of the emulator skins from **developer.uiq.com/devtools_other.html#skins** and use those to simulate each of the UIQ smartphones you wish to test with. Each download contains the image file, configuration file and an installation guide for the skin.

A useful tool for S60 is the remote device access (RDA) service from Forum Nokia, which allows you to test on different Nokia devices remotely over the Internet, without the need to buy every Nokia S60 smartphone in the range. The service is free, and allows you to control a device remotely, to install and run applications, transfer files and analyze log files in real-time, almost as if you had the device in your hand. You can find out more about RDA from **www.forum.nokia.com/main/technical_services/ testing/rda_introduction.html**.

The usability section on the Forum Nokia website (found at **www. forum.nokia.com/main/resources/documentation/usability**) maintains a number of documents, guides and examples to illustrate how to create a positive user experience on S60. You may also be interested in a book about the design of the original S60 interface, written by its designers in 2003, which is called *Mobile Usability: How Nokia Changed the Face of the Mobile Phone* (please see **www.mhprofessional.com/product.php? isbn=0071385142** on the publisher's website for more information).

6.1.2 Test It!

This book has reinforced the message that, on mobile platforms, you need to aim for code which is well-behaved – it shouldn't leak or unduly consume memory, disk space or other resources such as battery power. For example, running tight loops, writing code which continuously polls for a result, keeping the backlight on the phone constantly enabled or overusing the vibra motor are all likely to degrade the battery life of the device. It's important to consider where code can go wrong, and guard against the potential problems by testing, testing and more testing.

Code reviews are a good way to share coding tips and learn from your colleagues. Inspections can range from formal reviews when code reaches a particular milestone to informal checks whenever a defect fix is submitted into the code base. Find a way that works for your team and review regularly, so everyone is familiar with the issues encountered in the code, the solutions and any items still on the to-do list. We have published the set of coding standards used by developers within Symbian on the Symbian Developer Network at ***developer.symbian.com/coding_ standards_wikipage***.

Having discovered the fundamentals of good Symbian C++, you will want to test that your code meets your quality expectations as you write it and as you prepare to deploy it. Testing can be performed at all stages of development, and you and your team will have your own preferences and procedures. These could include writing a test case for every bug you fix to build up a regression test suite, developing a test framework for automated unit testing on your nightly builds, and designing out-of-memory loop tests, out-of-disk-space tests, and those that deliberately try to break the code by submitting illegal or invalid inputs to APIs or by rapidly firing random key presses at the UI. The more you hit your code with tests, the more confident you can be that it will be you that finds a problem – which is preferable to it being found by your ultimate user, the customer.

But you know all this; it's why you are still reading this book, to get the most out of developing C++ applications for Symbian OS. You're here because you want to get it right. So how does Symbian help you? What tools are available?

There are a number of commercial tools available for S60 and UIQ platforms:

- **AppTestPro** from SysOpenDigia (***www.sysopendigia.com***) allows automated functional, integration and user interface testing.

- **SymbianOSUnit** from Penrillian (***www.penrillian.com***) is a port of the popular C++ unit testing framework CxxUnit and allows fully automated building and testing of the project source.

- **TestQuest Pro** from TestQuest (***www.testquest.com***) is another automated test tool to verify the system under by becoming a 'virtual user' and replacing the need for manual testing.

If you don't have access to these tools, or they don't meet your requirements, you can always roll your own test cases. For example, Symbian OS provides a range of debug macros for checking the heap to ensure that it is balanced before and after code executes. The `__UHEAP_MARK` and `__UHEAP_MARKEND` macros can be used to check for memory leaks, while the `__UHEAP_FAILNEXT` and `__UHEAP_SETFAIL` macros can be used to simulate out-of-memory conditions, to check that code behaves correctly.

One of the fundamental rules of mobile application development is that you must test your code thoroughly on hardware. The Windows emulator gives you a good idea of the application's behavior while you are developing it, and it is invaluable when you are debugging. But it's generally the case that subtle bugs, such as those associated with performance, only manifest when you test the application on a smartphone. You will also find usability much easier to determine, and some code will only work on hardware anyway, such as that using the accelerometer or camera APIs. Make sure you test on a range of devices from each UI platform you are targeting. For example, if you create an S60 application, be sure to test it on both Nokia and Samsung devices.

Static Analysis

The Professional and OEM Editions of Carbide.c++ v1.3 ship with a tool call CodeScanner, which is a static code analysis tool. While you cannot automate a code review entirely, you can use static code analysis to run through code to detect areas where potential problems may lurk, for example:

- Methods that may leave but are not named with a trailing 'L'.

- Descriptor parameters passed by value rather than passed by reference.

- 'Worrying comments' such as the words 'hack' or 'to do'.

The automated source code analysis company Coverity announced in late 2007 that it will also be adding support for Symbian C++ to its Prevent SQS static code analysis tool. The Symbian C++ checker is expected to be available soon, and more information about Prevent is available at *www.coverity.com/html/prod_prevent.html*.

6.1.3 Optimize It!

Before releasing your code, it is worth taking some time to consider whether it is as efficient as it could possibly be. For example, Carbide.c++ Professional and OEM Editions ship with Performance Investigator, which is a profiling tool for analyzing the performance of applications running on S60 3rd Edition devices. The tool runs as the application executes and it can be used to determine which sections of code should be optimized to improve performance, memory, CPU usage or power consumption. You can find out more about Performance Investigator, and the other tools that Carbide.c++ ships with, from the product page on Forum Nokia, at *www.forum.nokia.com/main/resources/tools_and_sdks/carbide_cpp*.

Sometimes there are a few simple adjustments that can make a difference to its performance. A number of these are summarized in the free *Performance Tips* booklet published by Symbian Press at *developer.symbian.com/main/learning/press/books/pdf/Performance_Tips.pdf*, which examines a few performance killers (such as inefficient heap usage, repeated code within loops and over-enthusiastic 'future proofing' of code) in detail, and summarizes a number of other quick tips.

It is important to understand the basics of the compiler you are using. Modern compilers contain a number of optimization phases which produce smaller or faster code, depending on the chosen settings. It is important to understand the consequences of some of the settings and how they affect the code produced. If you understand how the code is generated by your chosen compiler, you can avoid working against it. For example, you can avoid writing code that is too prescriptive and forces the compiler to generate code in a particular way, rather than allowing it to optimize it.

When writing application code for Symbian v9 platforms, you can use the free GCC-E compiler, supplied with your chosen SDK, to build code that runs on a phone. More information about the compiler is available at *gcc.gnu.org/onlinedocs/gcc*.

The RVCT Compiler

While the free GCC-E compiler produces EABI-compatible binaries that can be used for Symbian OS v9 application development, it cannot be used when developing code that runs kernel-side (such as device drivers). Developers working within Symbian, and in Symbian's licensee or partner companies, opt instead to use the Real View Compilation Tools (RVCT), available, at a charge, from ARM.

In fact, if you want optimal code, when compared to GCC-E, the RVCT compiler binaries give better performance and smaller binaries. See *www.arm.com/products/DevTools/RealViewDevSuite.html* for more information about RVCT, the versions used to build Symbian projects and how to acquire a license. RVCT is available to Symbian's Partners at a special discount – partnering with Symbian is discussed in more detail later in this chapter.

6.1.4   Protect It!

Protecting your IP, to prevent your application from being resold, is a complex problem and there is no single or instant solution to it. Different approaches are appropriate for different applications and business models. Sometimes the effort required to fully protect your software may not be worth it, and it is better to just release your software and rely on people's honesty. However, if you really do feel the need to prevent your software from being freely copied, then there are a few ways of going about it. In all of them, the important thing is to make purchasing an application as simple as possible for the user.

SMS Activation

One popular way to protect smartphone software is to use an activation SMS. The user sends a one-off SMS to a particular SMS number, and an

SMS is sent in reply to activate the software. This can also be a handy way of letting the user pay for the use of the software, by setting up a premium SMS number.

It has the advantage that if the user changes phones, then they can resend the activation SMS to the server, which can detect that the phone's number is already in its database and reactivate the application without recharging the user.

However, although this is a useful approach, it does have some disadvantages:

- You need to pay to set up an SMS gateway.

- By setting up an SMS gateway, you may be restricting the number of countries from which a user can register.

- If the user changes phones and phone numbers, the reactivation will not work and the user will have to purchase a new copy of the application.

Using an Authorization Server

Another way of protecting a smartphone application is to require it to connect to a server, either from code within the application, or by launching the phone's web browser with a URI, on the first use. You can then download a token associated with the phone's IMEI that authorizes the application for use.

The problem with this is that you need to set up a server with a database that can store a list of IMEIs and record the fact that they are registered. It also depends on the user's phone having Internet access, which cannot be guaranteed. In addition, if the user gets a new phone, then he or she won't be able to download the application from the server again, since it will consider the new phone (with its different IMEI) to belong to a new customer.

Selling the Application Over the Internet

Another approach is to require users to use a PC to log on to a website to purchase the application. This poses a difficulty in that you need to find a way of associating an application bought on a PC with a particular phone. A good way of doing this is by using the IMEI of the phone. However, users don't necessarily know about IMEIs and it is not very user friendly to expect them to type in this long, arcane number, ascertained by first typing in the *#06# code as they would a phone number. Furthermore, it cannot be guaranteed that the user will know how to download and install a SIS installation file from their PC once they have it, and it also restricts how you distribute, and how the user purchases, your application.

Unfortunately, each of the methods described has drawbacks, and it is up to you to choose the method that best fits your software.

6.1.5 Sign It!

Signing is the process of encoding a tamper-proof digital certificate into an application. The certificate identifies the application's origin, and grants access to those APIs that are protected by Symbian OS platform security capabilities. Protected APIs are those that allow sensitive operations, such as those that may potentially:

- access the end users' private data, thus breaching their privacy;

- create billable events, thus costing the end user money;

- access the mobile phone network, which may affect its operation;

- access handset functions that can affect the normal behavior of the phone;

- impact the performance of other applications running on the phone.

If you don't use any protected APIs, you may find it possible to avoid the signing process altogether. Approximately 60 % of Symbian OS APIs require no capability to use them, so it may be possible to take this approach if you are creating a fairly simple application.

Alternatively, where certain capabilities are required, you may be able to rely on the user to grant permission to the application at install-time (called 'blanket' permission), or at runtime ('single-shot' permission). For example, the user can accept a request to send a message when the application needs to do so. However, this is somewhat dependent on the security policy applied to the smartphone by the device manufacturer. There is no guarantee that manufacturers or network operators will always allow applications to install on their devices or use APIs protected by user capabilities if they are not certified by Symbian Signed.

If you need, or choose, to get your application Symbian Signed, there are several options available. The costs of the different options vary depending on whether a Publisher ID is required, and whether independent testing is required. More information is available on the Symbian Signed portal at ***www.symbiansigned.com***.

Publisher IDs

Publisher ID digital certificates form part of the public key infrastructure, and are issued by Certificate Authorities (CAs). The CA for Symbian Signed is TC TrustCenter.

You can purchase Publisher IDs directly from TC TrustCenter at ***www.trustcenter.de/order/publisherid/dev***. The cost of acquiring a Publisher ID is relatively low, and there are several benefits associated with holding one, which include the following:

- More flexible developer certificates can be requested, enabling much wider deployment during development, for example, when performing beta testing.

- Owning a Publisher ID opens more signing options and gives you control over publisher identity and branding.

- Trust is important to end users of your application. Owning a Publisher ID allows you to enhance your reputation for delivering trusted applications.

Symbian Signed Testing

As we've already discussed, testing is an essential part of all software development, and Symbian Signed defines specific tests to ensure a minimum level of robustness and stability for applications running on Symbian smartphones.

The Symbian Signed tests are defined in the Symbian Signed Test Criteria, and are divided into two main groups.

Universal tests (prefixed UNI) focus on installation, uninstallation, reliability, robustness and normal operational behavior in accordance with mobile phone end user expectations. For example:

- Applications must install, uninstall and reinstall correctly, leaving no installation files behind after uninstall, and must install correctly from external mass memory storage (for example, memory cards).

- Applications must back up and restore successfully, and use appropriate file creation locations.

- Applications must survive stress tests including low memory at start-up, handling exceptional events like out-of-memory and power down or rebooting while running, and must handle service interruptions, as well as rapid and repeated switching.

- Applications must handle system events correctly and comply with Task List behavior guidelines.

Capability-related tests (prefixed CAP) are additional tests that need to be passed by applications using certain specific capabilities only. For example:

- Applications with `MultimediaDD` capability must not interfere with voice calls.

- Phone applications must present a UI to enable the user to control the application.

- VoIP applications must present a Device Manufacturer disclaimer, and must not interfere with GSM-based telephony functions, including the ability to make emergency calls.

All applications are expected to comply with the universal tests, and applications that use certain capabilities are required to comply with the capability-related tests

The Symbian Signed test criteria document is constantly assessed and updated, and the latest version is available from ***www.symbiansigned.com***, where you can also find additional information about Symbian Signed. In addition, there is a comprehensive manual about Symbian Signed at ***developer.symbian.com/main/signed***.

Freeware and Open Source

Freeware and open source applications can be submitted for Symbian Signing free of charge, without the need for a Publisher ID. For more information, visit the 'Open Signed' page at ***www.symbiansigned.com/app/page***.

6.1.6   Internationalize It!

If you intend your application to run in more than one language, you will need to consider how you will 'internationalize' it (sometimes this task is also known as 'localization'). Internationalization generates software variants in multiple languages from a single set of source files. Typically, you should aim to have a core of code which contains all the functionality of your application and doesn't change regardless of the language it is presented in. A second part contains the changing content, such as text strings displayed in the UI.

Not only do you need to consider the differences in language when you internationalize, but you must also consider variations in writing systems, regional differences (such as layout of numbers, time or measurements) and specific customizations. Although this may seem unduly complex, by making your application accessible in different regions, you can reap additional benefits in the form of wider market appeal and the ability to enter markets that would otherwise have been unavailable to you. Symbian OS was designed as an international OS from the ground up, and this makes it relatively easy to design applications for multiple languages and regions. That said, internationalization needs to be designed into your product from the start. Rewriting code at late stages of development introduces complexity and the risk of regression.

For example, when creating an application, it is easy to place all the text displayed in the UI directly, such as dialog titles or menu options, within the application's RSS resource file. While this works perfectly for a single-language application, when you come to create additional, different language versions, it makes it harder because you have to search the files to locate and translate each of the text elements. Symbian recommends splitting the text out into a separate file, known as an RLS file. RLS files contain token-value pairs which can then be used in the RSS file.

For example, for an S60 MENU_PANE resource, specified in the RSS file:

```
// example.rss
#include "example.rls"
...
// Define the menu items that comprise a menu pane
RESOURCE MENU_PANE r_filebrowse_menu
  {
  items=
    {
    MENU_ITEM { command=ECmdFileBrowseOpen;
        txt - STRING_r_filebrowse_loc_Open; },
    MENU_ITEM { command=EAknCmdExit;
        txt = STRING_r_filebrowse_loc_Exit; }
    };
  }

In the associated RLS file, for the English version:

// example.rls
rls_string STRING_r_filebrowse_loc_Open   "Open"
rls_string STRING_r_filebrowse_loc_Exit   "Exit"
```

The RLS file can then be sent to translators to create a separate version, for example, in French or Japanese. A translator will not necessarily be a programmer and, for this reason, the structure of the RLS file is restricted to straightforward token-value pairs. However, you can also include C- or C++-style comments in the text localization file to inform the translator of the context in which each text item appears, and to give information about any constraints, such as the maximum length permitted for a string.

To build an application in multiple languages, the LANG specifier is used in an application's MMP file. The keyword must be followed by a list of two-character codes, one for each language, for example:

```
LANG 01 02
```

The codes can be anything you like, but are normally taken from the two-digit values specified in the TLanguage enum in e32const.h.

The Symbian OS build tools use the LANG statement to build the application's resource files once for each code in the list. For each build:

- A LANGUAGE_XX symbol is defined.
- The resulting binary is given a .rXX extension where XX represents the language code for that build.

These codes are listed in the Software Installation Toolkit, included in the Symbian Developer Library, which can be found in the documentation set of your S60 3rd Edition or UIQ 3 SDK.

You should include the appropriate RLS files in each of the application's localizable resource scripts, for example:

```
// example.rss

#ifdef LANGUAGE_01
#include "exampleenglish.rls"
#elif defined LANGUAGE_02
#include "examplefrench.rls"
#endif

...
// Define the menu items that comprise a menu pane
RESOURCE MENU_PANE r_filebrowse_menu
  {
 items=
    {
   MENU_ITEM { command=ECmdFileBrowseOpen;
       txt = STRING_r_filebrowse_loc_Open; },
   MENU_ITEM { command=EAknCmdExit;
       txt = STRING_r_filebrowse_loc_Exit; }
    };
  }
```

In this case, the result of the build is to generate two resource files, named example_loc.r01 and example_loc.r02, containing English and French text, respectively. These replace the example.rsc file, which is created if no LANG keyword is used in the MMP file, and need to be included in the PKG package file, for installation to the phone.

The PKG package file, used to build the software installation package, can be used to specify the language options available for the application. At install-time, only those language files specific to the language selected by the user will be installed. The PKG file can also be used to specify the text for the application's name as it is displayed in the phone's main display.

You can find a lot more information about how to create an installation file for a multilingual application in the Symbian Developer Library. Information is available in the Software Installation Toolkit, which can be found in the Tools and Utilities section, and in the Locale Settings guide in the Base section of the Symbian OS Guide section.

6.2 How To Distribute Your Application

Recent data suggests that smartphone buyers show particular enthusiasm for purchasing and installing software for their phones. Part of the reason for buying a smartphone, after all, is that powerful aftermarket software can be installed onto it. To meet this demand, over 8,000 third-party installable applications are commercially available for Symbian smartphones at the time of writing.[1] Furthermore, according to data from m:metrics, Symbian smartphone users perform at least 20 % more tasks that raise the average revenue per user (ARPU) for network operators than other 3G users. For example, data from October 2007 suggests that, in the UK, 45 % of Symbian smartphone users spend more than £35 (US$70) per month on 3G network services (such as sending photos, videos, accessing maps and news).[2] Feature phone owners spend less; only 20 % spend that amount or more.

This section covers how to get your application to its potential consumers. Having considered the topics discussed in the previous section, you're sure you have a great product, but how best to deliver it? Who can help you market it?

6.2.1 Network Operators

Network operators, or carriers as they are sometimes known, make the largest number of sales of mobile applications because most purchases are from users who buy content directly from their portals. The operators can be subdivided into: international carriers, such as Vodafone, T-Mobile and Orange; national network operators, such as Cingular and Verizon in the USA and DoCoMo in Japan; and other smaller carriers, such as mobile virtual network operators (MVNOs).[3]

To work with a network operator, you must build a good relationship in order to get selected for a sales slot on their portal. Many of the large operators have so many developers wanting to work with them, that they do not engage with new contacts, but only use their established relationships to provide content. However, there are developer programs which are worth investigating. Some examples include 3neXt from Hutchinson (*next.three.com/suggest/developer.aspx*), Orange Partner (*www.orangepartner.com*) or AT&T devCentral (*developer.att.com*).

Network operators look for applications that meet their own propositions, and one key goal is to promote data consumption. If your

---

[1] *www.symbian.com/about/fastfacts/fastfacts.html*.

[2] *www.mmetrics.com*.

[3] MVNOs are companies that build on top of the traditional network operators, because they do not have their own allocation of the radio frequency spectrum nor the infrastructure required to provide a mobile telephone service.

application requires the user to download even small amounts of data on a regular basis, the network operators will find it far more interesting than one that never requires the user to make a data connection. (You can find out more about the other 'hot' areas that operators are keen to promote by listening for key messages whenever the operators speak at developer events or when they issue press releases or other material to help analysts 'sync up'). In turn, network operators research the market and, if your applications are receiving good feedback from users, or the operators have access to download statistics and see that you have a popular product, you may be invited into a tendering process in order to be selected to supply applications to them.

It is worth noting that network operators have individual processes for testing and certifying new applications before they allow them to be published for sale. The certification process can take a significant amount of time and, once an application is complete, it can take up to six months of negotiation over the results before the application is released onto a portal.

6.2.2   Independent Software Channels

Some mobile application sales channels are not owned by network operators but are independent. These channels inevitably have less traffic than the operator channels, but application developers still find they offer potential for application distribution.

There are a number of channels that provide mobile applications; some do so as part of their offering, while others specialize in them. Examples include Handango,[4] Motricity and MobiHand. The channels offer a web or WAP site for buyers to browse using their mobile phone, allowing the purchase of applications by direct download over the air (OTA), with payment made by means of sending a premium-rate SMS.

Some purchases, such as those from Handango, can also be made over the Internet (OTI). The user visits the website on his PC, buys and downloads an application to it, and then transfers it to his phone, for example, using Bluetooth wireless technology. OTI purchasing offers the benefit of allowing the user to browse for applications using a familiar medium of the PC, and find information about them, such as screenshots and reviews. The user can also download larger applications more quickly and without needing the phone to be set up with a data connection, which is an advantage, particularly in regions where it is expensive, or slow, to download large amounts of data to a phone. OTI download also avoids being charged twice – once to purchase the application (by the channel)

---

[4] In 2006, more than 250 new content providers and 3,500 new content titles were available on Handango for Symbian smartphones. Handango is a key channel for the distribution of aftermarket software for smartphones (based on Symbian OS, BlackBerry, Palm OS and Windows Mobile) and regularly releases sales trend data, which it calls 'Yardstick Data', on **www.corp.handango.com**.

and then to download it (by the network operator). However, a number of network operators lock down their phones against what they call 'side loading', which means that applications cannot be installed except by direct download to the phone. The lock down ensures that the operator retains some profit from application installation, even when it is not purchased from one of their portals. (Some network operators go further still and prevent the phones they distribute from making purchases *except* from their portals.)

The downside of OTI purchasing, if it is allowed by a network operator, is that the user must own, or have access to, a PC, and must know how to connect the phone to the PC to transfer the downloaded application and install it.

Purchasing from the web also requires electronic payment, for example using a credit card, rather than direct billing from the network operator. Not everyone has this option, especially when the target market for some applications, such as games, may be under the age of credit card ownership. The channels work around this through the use of gift certificates or vouchers.

Of course, you can always consider setting up your own independent sales channel; that is, selling your application through your own website. This has the advantage that you don't have to give away any royalties, and can decide how to market your application, and what testing and certification it requires. However, you will need to work hard to achieve visibility in the marketplace, and you will need to determine how to manage the incoming payments – and any support requests that come in when they fail, or the user claims dissatisfaction with the application and wants a refund. Selling through a channel or operator shields you from these issues, to some extent.

Some phone manufacturers also provide sales channels, such as the Nokia Software Market. These channels are a way for manufacturers to make software available and encourage the uptake of their handsets. Rather than decide themselves what these sites provide, the channels often use the services of a content aggregator, such as Jamba (also known as Jamster in English-speaking regions) or Handango (which is a content aggregator in its own right, as well as an independent channel), to put together the content offered. We will discuss content aggregators in more detail in Section 6.2.3.

The Nokia Software Market is available for users to buy applications (and other applications) OTI (***www.softwaremarket.nokia.com***) or directly on the phone using an application called Nokia Catalogs. The Catalogs application is a client on the Nokia Content Discoverer system and is available for S60 smartphones. The application allows delivery of graphics, themes and ring tones, Java ME applications, native Symbian OS C++ applications, videos, music and content developed using Flash technology.

Independent channels are usually the preferred route to market for application developers working alone or in small companies, because it is easier to place an application for sale with the channel than to forge a relationship with a network operator or content aggregator. The channel will take a percentage of each sale of the application, but this is typically less than a network operator or aggregator, and the channel will allow developers to set the price of the application themselves. For example, the Nokia Software Market takes 40 % of the sales price set by the developer, with revenue paid every quarter. For more information about working with the Nokia Software Market and Catalogs application, please see ***www.forum.nokia.com/main/software_market/index.html*** or consult the Nokia Sales Channels section on the main Forum Nokia developer site at ***www.forum.nokia.com***.

6.2.3   Content Aggregators

Content aggregators are specialists at gathering content, such as mobile applications, video, and ring tones. The content is acquired from suppliers such as games publishers or independent channels, and distributed by the aggregators to sales channels. Content aggregators provide an easy way for businesses to source downloadable material without having to seek it out and build a relationship with each supplier. An example of a content aggregator is Jamba, which is one of the largest channels for mobile content and applications. Jamba also distributes content and applications via the Nokia Catalogs client on Nokia devices, as described in the previous section. Forum Nokia publishes a comprehensive list of mobile content aggregators at ***www.forum.nokia.com/main/go_to_market/aggregators.html***.

6.2.4   Pre-Installed Applications

One way to distribute your application to users while avoiding the complicated relationship between publishers, content aggregators and network operators is to get the application built onto a phone handset by the manufacturer (or provided on a CD ROM in the box that contains the handset). Naturally, there are far fewer opportunities for built-in applications than there are developers who wish to get their application pre-installed onto a phone! The market exposure of an embedded application is an excellent opportunity; however, it is not without its problems. Trying to ship an application on a handset that is not released means the developer is often working with pre-commercial firmware and hardware. Final versions of the hardware may become available just days before the deadline for embedded software on the handset, resulting in uncomfortable 'crunch' periods.

6.2.5 Open Source

If you are interested in setting up an open source project, a good place to start is the open source page on Symbian Developer Network at ***developer.symbian.com/main/tools/opensrc***. You will also find a thriving open source community at ***opensource.nokia.com*** and, of course, at ***www.sourceforge.net***.

6.3 Where To Go Next

A range of technical papers, which can be found at ***developer.symbian. com/oslibrary***, are published weekly on Symbian Developer Network. The papers cover all aspects of Symbian OS C++ programming, as well as programming in other languages and runtimes, and range from the basic through to the most advanced levels. The technical papers cover topics such as the best techniques for debugging and error handling, how to use Symbian's C++ idioms, how to solve particular problems and introductions to using the new technologies available on Symbian OS.

You can also find the Symbian OS System Model, as shown in Figure 6.1, at ***www.developer.symbian.com/main/oslibrary/sys_models***.

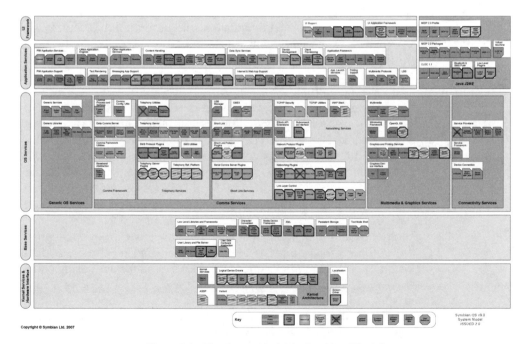

Figure 6.1 The System Model for Symbian OS v9.2

A collection of FAQs is provided at ***developer.symbian.com/main/learning/faq***.

The Symbian Developer Network also has a wiki site, where you can post contributions to content of relevance and of use to Symbian developers. The wiki is found at ***developer.symbian.com/wiki*** and is regularly updated by both Symbian staff and external developers – for example, to record errata lists for the Symbian Press books, publish presentations given at public developer events, and post useful links to developer blogs and websites, information about tools, open source projects and example code. The wiki page for this book is ***developer.symbian.com/quickrecipesbook***.

6.3.1 Symbian Press Books

Symbian Press has published a range of books for beginners and advanced developers, and project managers. The following titles are a few examples that may be of interest if you are, respectively, new to Symbian OS, looking for a definitive Symbian C++ reference book, working on UIQ 3, a games developer or a project manager.

Developing Software for Symbian OS, 2nd edition, by Steve Babin, is an excellent place to start if you have not used Symbian C++ before. It guides you through the basics, starting with an explanation of common terms and building your first application, discussing the build tools and environment to work with Symbian OS v9. The main part of the book covers the fundamentals needed when writing for Symbian OS, including sections about the architecture of Symbian OS, platform security and GUI application programming.

If you already have some Symbian OS development experience, *Symbian OS C++ for Mobile Phones*, volume 3 is a recommended reference guide. The book starts with an overview of build tools and the emulator, and then devotes over 700 pages to the essentials of Symbian OS with deeper coverage, particularly in the area of graphics and user interfaces.

A recent publication supported by Symbian Press is *UIQ 3: The Complete Guide*, which is partially available in wiki form on ***books.uiq.com*** and will be published by John Wiley & Sons Ltd in mid-2008.

Another recent book in the Symbian Press range is *Games on Symbian OS: A Handbook for Mobile Development*. Published in February 2008, it shows how to create mobile games for Symbian smartphones using native C++, Java ME, DoJa, Flash Lite, as well as the support for porting games using standard C/C++. The book also describes the support available for standards such as OpenGL ES, examines the N-Gage platform and discusses the use of middleware solutions such as Ideawork3D's Airplay.

If you are a project manager, then David Wood's *Symbian Software for Leaders* is an essential guide, explaining how to manage projects involving Symbian OS, from the creation of smartphones to the development of applications. There are unique components to Symbian OS projects; this book helps you to avoid costly mistakes.

You can find more information at **developer.symbian.com/books**, where you can also download the example code for each book and find free sample chapters, provided for download as PDF files.

Symbian Press also offers a range of booklets which can be downloaded for free from the website (**developer.symbian.com/booklets**). The paper copies are available at Symbian developer events. There are several series of booklets, designed to provide useful reference on core Symbian OS subjects, and to keep you informed of the latest smartphone technology. A recent booklet publication, based on this chapter, covers how to get your application market in detail, and can be found at **developer.symbian.com/main/learning/press/books/pdf/Getting%20to%20 market_booklet%20-%20FINAL.pdf**. There is a link to the booklet on the wiki page for this book.

Furthermore, many of our books and booklets have now been translated into a range of languages, including Chinese, Japanese, Korean, Spanish and Russian.

6.3.2 Partnering with Symbian

Symbian partners with those companies with a technology or a strategic position that is key to the success of Symbian OS phones in the market, with product or service offerings based around Symbian OS technology.

Symbian Partners benefit from early and exclusive access to the Symbian OS Development Kit ('DevKit'), which includes some of the source code that makes up Symbian OS, as it is delivered to mobile phone manufacturers licensing Symbian OS (some of the more sensitive code has restricted distribution and is not available). The DevKit supplied includes test code, internal documentation, kernel and device driver programming interfaces and ROM building tools.

Other benefits of partnership include:

- Priority access to key market channels and pre-market showcases.

- Access to Symbian 1:1 support, which provides higrtnerh-quality technical services to Symbian's partners.

- A discount on Symbian OS training courses, which range from Symbian OS development to the advanced operating systems internals course. The courses are hands-on, covering the whole development cycle, and may be customized according to the partner's requirements.

More information about the Symbian Partner Network is available at **www.symbian.com**.

6.3.3   Partnering Within the Symbian Ecosystem

Forum Nokia Launchpad and Forum Nokia PRO

Forum Nokia Launchpad is Nokia's mobile development resource for those working on Nokia platforms. Through the Launchpad program, Forum Nokia also evaluates member companies for further engagement and additional business channel opportunities.

More information about Forum Nokia Launchpad is available at ***pro.forum.nokia.com/site/global/home/program_details/p_launchpad. jsp***.

Forum Nokia PRO is an invitation-only program for companies operating in the mobile world. In addition to early access to development resources and information, a dedicated business development manager (BDM) from Forum Nokia is assigned to each Forum Nokia PRO member company. The BDM makes sure that the company receives appropriate attention within Nokia and provides additional channel opportunities to accelerate revenue growth. Forum Nokia PRO also connects its members to exclusive, early access technical resources.

More information about Forum Nokia PRO is available at ***pro.forum. nokia.com***.

UIQ Alliance

UIQ Alliance is a network of key companies in the mobile handset industry. Membership of the UIQ Alliance is by invitation, and more details are available at ***partner.uiq.com/portal/partner.nsf/external/howto***.

Index

Note: Page numbers in italics refer to figures and tables.